SURVIVING SCHIZOPHRENIA

A Family Manual

A "landmark book," Sandy Rovner in the *Washington Post* (July 20, 1984, p. D-5)

An "excellent book . . . a well-written book . . . a valuable resource for the families of schizophrenics. . . . It is a much-needed compendium of information about schizophrenia for families, who increasingly are being asked to bear the major responsibility for aftercare." Jeri A. Doane, *Contemporary Psychology* (June 1984)

"Clearly the most complete book yet written for families of people suffering from schizophrenia. . . ." Dr. Agnes Hatfield, "Newsletter," National Alliance for the Mentally Ill

"To put it bluntly, every family in America that has a relative suffering from schizophrenia should buy *Surviving Schizophrenia.*" Harriet Shetles, "Newsletter," Alliance for the Mentally Ill of Wisconsin (Aug. 1983)

"This book is both refreshing and important. . . . If schizophrenia has touched you, your family, or friends, the book should be in your home." Bertram S. Brown, M.D., former director, NIMH; president Hahnemann University

"*Surviving Schizophrenia* is a much needed, clarifying account of a widely misunderstood problem. . . . It is an informative labor of love by a knowledgeable clinician and dedicated researcher in the field of biological psychiatry. A highly readable book." Robert L. Taylor, M.D., consulting psychiatrist, California Department of Mental Health

"*Surviving Schizophrenia* is an invaluable asset for the millions of families and friends of people with this disease and will better equip them to be helpful. It should be required reading." Sidney M. Wolfe, M.D., director, Public Citizen Health Research Group

Surviving
SCHIZOPHRENIA

A Family Manual

E. Fuller Torrey, M.D.

HARPER COLOPHON BOOKS
Harper & Row, Publishers
New York, Cambridge, Philadelphia, San Francisco
London, Mexico City, São Paulo, Singapore, Sydney

Permissions acknowledgments appear on pages xiii–xiv.

Designer: C. Linda Dingler

Library of Congress Cataloging in Publication Data

Torrey, E. Fuller (Edwin Fuller), date
    Surviving schizophrenia

    Bibliography: p.
    Includes index.
        1. Schizophrenia. 2. Schizophrenia—United States.
I. Title.
RC514.T633 1983   616.89′82   82-48138
ISBN 0-06-015112-9
ISBN 0-06-091217-0 (pbk.)

85 86 87 88 89 10 9 8 7 6 5 4 3

In memory of
Rebecca Torrey McCarthy

About the Author

A clinical and research psychiatrist in Washington, D.C., Dr. E. Fuller Torrey specializes in schizophrenia. Dr. Torrey's work in psychiatry has included four years as a Special Assistant to the Director of the National Institute of Mental Health. From 1976 to 1984, Dr. Torrey was affiliated with St. Elisabeths Hospital in Washington, D.C. He has also done field research on schizophrenia in Papua New Guinea and in Ireland. Author of nine books and over one hundred lay and professional papers, Dr. Torrey is a contributing editor to *Psychology Today*.

CONTENTS

ACKNOWLEDGMENTS

I am indebted for many kindnesses in the gathering of information for this book. Leslie J. Scallet and Joseph F. Vargyas of the Mental Health Law Project, Roy E. Praschil and Harry Schnibbe of the National Association of State Mental Health Program Directors, and H. Bernard Smith and Lynne Saunders of the National Alliance for the Mentally Ill all contributed generously. The library staff at St. Elizabeths Hospital has been unfailingly helpful. Lou AvRutick, Ann Harris, and Carol Cohen of Harper & Row believed in the book and have been very supportive throughout. Jane Beemer provided technical support, and the typing was capably supplied by Gloria Davis, Karen Thomas, and Bernadette O'Brien.

I am also grateful to the following:

Richard Abrams for permission to reprint excerpts from his book review in the *American Journal of Psychiatry*.

Joseph H. Berke for permission to reprint excerpts from *Mary Barnes: Two Accounts of a Journey Through Madness*.

Malcolm B. Bowers and Science Press for permission to reprint excerpts from *Retreat from Sanity: The Structure of Emerging Psychosis*.

Donald F. Klein for permission to reprint excerpts from his article in the *Schizophrenia Bulletin*.

Eliot T. O. Slater for permission to reprint excerpts from *Clinical Psychiatry*.

John A. Talbott and Grune & Stratton, Inc., for permission to reprint excerpts from *The Death of the Asylum*.

Andrew McGhie and The British Psychological Society for permission to reprint excerpts from an article in the *British Journal of Medical Psychology*.

British Journal of Psychiatry for permission to reprint excerpts from an article by James Chapman.

Journal of Abnormal and Social Psychology for permission to reprint excerpts from an article by Anonymous.

Anchor Press and Doubleday for permission to reprint excerpts from *These Are My Sisters,* by Lara Jefferson.

National Schizophrenic Fellowship for permission to reprint excerpts from *Autobiography of a Schizophrenic Girl,* by Marguerite Sechehaye.

W. W. Norton and Company for permission to reprint excerpts from *In a Darkness,* by James A. Wechsler.

Presses Universitaires de France for permission to reprint excerpts from *Coping with Schizophrenia,* by H. R. Rollin.

G. P. Putnam and Sons for permission to reprint excerpts from *This Stranger, My Son,* by Louise Wilson.

University Books for permission to reprint excerpts from *The Witnesses,* by Thomas Hennell.

PREFACE

"Your daughter has schizophrenia," I told the woman.

"Oh, my god, anything but that," she replied. "Why couldn't she have leukemia or some other disease instead?"

"But if she had leukemia she might die," I pointed out. "Schizophrenia is a much more treatable disease."

The woman looked sadly at me, then down at the floor. She spoke softly. "I would still prefer that my daughter had leukemia."

This book is a product of a thousand such conversations. Conceived in the darkness of despair, it was fathered by education and mothered by hope. It is written for the two million American families whose lives are currently touched by schizophrenia. My sister is afflicted; perhaps your brother, aunt, or son is also. The book provides a scientific framework for understanding its symptoms, causes, and treatment and suggests how families can come to terms with the disease. Above all the book tries to dispel the multitude of myths and alleviate the millstone of guilt which families have been condemned to carry by mental health professionals; surely this has been Original Psychiatric Sin.

Schizophrenia is a cruel disease. The lives of those affected are often chronicles of constricted experiences, muted emotions, missed opportunities, unfulfilled expectations. It leads to a twilight existence, a twentieth-century underground man. The fate of these patients has been worsened by our propensity to misunderstand, our failure to provide adequate treatment and rehabilitation, our meager research efforts. A disease which should be found, in the phrase of T. S. Eliot, in the "frigid purgatorial fires" has become through our ignorance and neglect a living hell.

Perhaps it is a disease whose time has come. There are rays of hope—research, treatment, the organizations of families and friends. If this book contributes just a little toward bringing schizophrenia out of the Slough of Despond and into the mainstream of American medicine then it will have accomplished its purpose.

The purpose of this book is to make you aware of the progress of schizophrenia and the possible ways in which it may develop. The assessment of symptoms requires an expert. Proper diagnosis and therapy of all symptoms, real or apparent, connected with schizophrenia call for careful attention to your concerns by your doctor.

1

OUT OF THE CLOSET

There are as many schizophrenics in America as there are peo-
ple in Oregon, Mississippi and Kansas, or in Wyoming, Vermont,
Delaware and Hawaii combined.
President's Commission on Mental Health, 1978

Schizophrenia, I said. The word itself is ominous. It has been called "one of
the most sinister words in the language." It has a bite to it, a harsh grating
sound that evokes visions of madness and asylums. It is not fluid like *démence,*
the word from which "dementia" comes. Nor is it a visual word like *écrassé,*
the origin of "cracked" and meaning that the person was like a cracked pot.
Nor is it romantic like "lunatic," meaning fallen under the influence of the
moon (which in Latin is *luna*). "Schizophrenia" is a discordant and cruel term,
just like the disease it signifies.

And it is common, much more common than most people realize. It
strikes approximately 1 out of every 100 Americans sometime during their
lifetime. In Scandinavia it is at least twice as common, and in western Ireland
as many as 1 out of every 25 people is affected. There are over 2 million people
in the United States who have or will have schizophrenia; this is as many
people as live in Oregon, Mississippi, and Kansas, or in Wyoming, Vermont,
Delaware, and Hawaii combined. On any given day there are 600,000 people
with schizophrenia under active treatment and each year another 100,000
Americans are diagnosed with it for the first time. According to one prominent
psychiatrist, "The care and treatment of the severely and chronically mentally
ill is the largest problem, numerically, that psychiatry faces, despite the fact
that to date the care of the severely and chronically mentally ill has probably
had the lowest priority in the entire areas of human services."

But these are just numbers. They have little meaning for most people, like
the numbers of people killed in a flood in India or in an earthquake in Turkey.
The numbers fail to evoke the human suffering and personal tragedy which
accompany the disease. It is a tragedy which goes on, year after year, for those
who recover only partially or not at all. And each year one hundred thousand
new patients and their families hear the devastating pronouncement for the
first time—schizophrenia.

Despite its widespread prevalence, the disease is remote to most people because we have become experts in hiding it. It lurks behind the curtain in many families, but nobody bothers to mention it. It is the aunt who used to live with them but then moved; what they don't add is that she moved to the state hospital. It is the son who got in trouble in late adolescence and is now said to be living in Pennsylvania; what they don't add is that he is committed to the state hospital there. It is the sister who tragically committed suicide over, it is rumored, a love affair; what they don't add is that she committed suicide because she was plagued by voices and chose to not live with her disease. We hide it in the family closet, hoping nobody will tell, hoping nobody will find out. It is a stigma.

The stigma of schizophrenia makes it all the more tragic. Not only must persons affected and their families bear the disease itself, but they must bear the stigma of it as well. Schizophrenics are the lepers of the twentieth century. The aunt, son, or sister being hidden in the closet may be discovered at any minute, and then the word will be out. Disaster, Dishonor, Disgrace. The magnitude of schizophrenia as a national calamity is exceeded only by the magnitude of our ignorance in dealing with it.

For it is only our ignorance which continues to keep schizophrenics in the closet. It is only our lingering mystical mentality, our heritage of examining entrails to predict the future, our aversion to the evil eye, which keeps us from putting schizophrenia into its proper 1980s perspective. Schizophrenia is a brain disease, now definitely known to be such. It is a real scientific and biological entity as clearly as diabetes, multiple sclerosis, and cancer are scientific and biological entities. It exhibits symptoms of a brain disease, symptoms which include impairment in thinking, delusions, hallucinations, changes in emotions, and changes in behavior. And, like cancer, it probably has more than one cause. Thus, though we speak of schizophrenia and cancer in the singular, we really understand them as being in the plural; there are probably several different kinds of schizophrenia of the brain just as there are several different kinds of cancer of the brain.

We use the term "schizophrenia" loosely and broadly in American culture. A Secretary of the Treasury says that "schizophrenia crippled our economic policy." Other officials speak of "a schizophrenia in the Atlantic Alliance" and "our schizophrenic foreign policy process." What they mean is a pursuit of two simultaneous policies, often mutually exclusive, with consequent indecision and confusion. Thus this metaphorical use of the term incorporates the idea of impaired thinking common in schizophrenia but otherwise fails to convey the breadth of the disease.

Even greater confusion arises from the widespread but erroneous belief that schizophrenia is the same as a split personality. The type of split personality most people think of is Dr. Jekyll and Mr. Hyde, Sybil, or the Three Faces of Eve. Such individuals do not in fact have schizophrenia but rather have another psychiatric condition called a dissociative disorder or hysterical neurosis; it is a rare condition compared with schizophrenia. The "splitting" in schizophrenia is not into separate personalities but rather is a splitting within a single personality of the person's thought content and his or her accompanying emotion. The important point to stress is that schizophrenia is *not* the same as a split personality, and the continued propagation of this erroneous stereotype impedes clear thinking about the disease. Such clear thinking is needed for accurate diagnosis and proper treatment.

Schizophrenia is sometimes also used interchangeably with the term "psychosis." Psychosis means not in touch with reality. Most, but not all, persons with psychosis do in fact have schizophrenia. However, the category "psychosis" also includes manic-depressive illness (now often called bipolar disorder), so for the sake of precision it is preferable to say schizophrenia if that is what you mean. This distinction will become clearer in chapter 3, where manic-depressive illness is discussed. In common usage, when the term "psychotic" is used it implies the loss-of-reality symptoms found in both schizophrenia and manic-depressive illness.

Much confusion about schizophrenia has also been engendered by the popular theories propagated by Thomas Szasz, R. D. Laing, and other members of the antipsychiatry movement. Szasz and Laing both maintain that schizophrenia is not really a disease, rather it is just an idiosyncratic way of thinking and behaving. Schizophrenia is presented as a reasonable reaction to an unreasonable society and as a label for scapegoating those among us who are different. These theories are poetic nonsense and there is much evidence to prove it. They betray a woeful lack of exposure to people with schizophrenia and an even more appalling lack of exposure to current research findings. But they are popular theories, and they will die slowly. Perhaps the most effective rebuttal to these theories is a whimsical article by Mark Vonnegut, who had himself undergone a schizophreniclike illness, in which he detailed the social circumstances under which he intended to bite R. D. Laing.

The most remarkable thing about schizophrenia as a disease is how little attention has been paid to it, given its prevalence and severity. Its cost in the United States alone has been estimated at between ten and twenty billion dollars annually, including the costs of hospitalization, Social Security benefits for the disabled, welfare payments, lost wages. Demographically it is the most expensive of any chronic disease, since the individual remains well throughout the years of rearing and education, then becomes ill and often dependent on society just at the point where he/she would become a contributing wage earner. One would think that we would be interested in it for economic reasons alone, to say nothing of the personal tragedies which accompany it. But no, schizophrenia is the nondisease, the condition not talked of, the disease of two million people which we try to forget.

We pay it lip service periodically, of course. Most recently this occurred when President Jimmy Carter set up a President's Commission on Mental Health. Because of the genuine concern of the President's wife, the Commission addressed the problem of chronic schizophrenia in some detail. The proceedings of the Commission are voluminous and offer many good suggestions for what *should* occur. Not much has come of this, nor is it likely to. Not even a President's wife can change things if there is no concern or interest at a more public level. Indeed, it may be said that the best service offered to persons with schizophrenia in contemporary America is lip service.

But this is the twentieth century, not the twelfth century. Isn't it time to face schizophrenia directly and look it in the eye? Isn't it time to see what it really is? Must we remain in the Dark Ages of psychiatry forever? It is time to put down our amulets and maturely face schizophrenia for what it is—the most tragic chronic disease remaining in twentieth-century western civilization.

2

THE INNER WORLD OF MADNESS

What then does schizophrenia mean to me? It means fatigue
and confusion, it means trying to separate every experience into
the real and the unreal and not sometimes being aware of where
the edges overlap. It means trying to think straight when there
is a maze of experiences getting in the way, and when thoughts
are continually being sucked out of your head so that you become embarrassed to speak at meetings. It means feeling
sometimes that you are inside your head and visualising yourself
walking over your brain, or watching another girl wearing your
clothes and carrying out actions as you think them. It means
knowing that you are continually "watched," that you can never
succeed in life because the laws are all against you and knowing
that your ultimate destruction is never far away.

Schizophrenic patient, quoted in Henry R. Rollin,
Coping with Schizophrenia

When tragedy strikes, one of the things which make life bearable for people
is the sympathy of friends and relatives. This can be seen, for example, in a
natural disaster like a flood and with a chronic disease like cancer. Those
closest to the person afflicted offer help, extend their sympathy, and generally
provide important solace and support in the person's time of need. "Sympathy," said Emerson, "is a supporting atmosphere, and in it we unfold easily
and well." A prerequisite for sympathy is an ability to put oneself in the place
of the person afflicted. One must be able to imagine oneself in a flood or getting
cancer. Without this ability to put oneself in the place of the person afflicted,
there can be abstract pity but not true sympathy.

Sympathy for those afflicted with schizophrenia is sparse because it is
difficult to put oneself in the place of the sufferer. The whole disease process
is mysterious, foreign, and frightening to most people. It is not like a flood,
where one can imagine all one's possessions being washed away. Nor like a
cancer, where one can imagine a slowly growing tumor, relentlessly spread-
ing from organ to organ and squeezing life from the body. No, schizophrenia
is madness. Those who are afflicted act bizarrely, say strange things, withdraw from us, and may even try to hurt us. They are no longer the same

person—they are *mad!* We don't understand why they say and do what they do. We don't understand the disease process. Rather than a steadily growing mass, which we can understand, it is as if another person has taken over their brain. How can we sympathize with a person who is possessed by unknown and unseen forces? How can we sympathize with a madman or a madwoman?

The paucity of sympathy in schizophrenia makes it that much more of a disaster. Being afflicted with the disease is bad enough by itself. Those of us who have not had this disease should ask ourselves, for example, how we would feel if our brain began playing tricks on us, if unseen voices shouted at us, if we lost the capacity to feel emotions, and if we lost the ability to reason logically. This would certainly be burden enough for any human being to have to bear. But what if, in addition to this, those closest to us began to avoid us or ignore us, to pretend that they didn't hear our comments, to pretend that they didn't notice what we did? How would we feel if those we most cared about were embarrassed by our behavior each day?

Because there is little understanding of schizophrenia, so there is little sympathy. For this reason it is the obligation of everyone with a relative or close friend with schizophrenia to learn as much as possible about what the disease is and what the afflicted person is experiencing. This is not merely an intellectual exercise or a way to satisfy one's curiosity but rather to make it possible to sympathize with the person. For friends and relatives who want to be helpful, probably the most important thing to do is to learn about the inner workings of the schizophrenic brain. With sympathy schizophrenia is a personal tragedy. Without sympathy it becomes a family calamity, for there is nothing to knit people together, no balm for the wounds. Understanding schizophrenia also helps demystify the disease and brings it from the realm of the occult to the daylight of reason. As we come to understand it, the face of madness slowly changes before us from one of terror to one of sadness. For the sufferer, this is a significant change.

The best way to learn what a schizophrenic is experiencing is to listen to a person with the disease. For this reason I have relied heavily upon patients' own accounts in describing the signs and symptoms. There are some excellent descriptions scattered throughout English literature; the best of these are listed in appendix D, Recommended Further Reading. By contrast one of the most widely read books about a "schizophrenic," Hannah Green's *I Never Promised You a Rose Garden,* is not at all helpful. It describes a patient who, according to a recent analysis, should not even be diagnosed with schizophrenia but rather with hysteria (now often referred to as somatization disorder).

When one listens to persons with schizophrenia describe what they are experiencing and observes their behavior, certain abnormalities can be noted:

1. Alterations of the senses
2. Inability to sort and synthesize incoming sensations, and an inability therefore to respond appropriately
3. Delusions and hallucinations
4. Altered sense of self
5. Changes in emotions
6. Changes in behavior

No one symptom or sign is found in all schizophrenic patients; rather the final diagnosis rests upon the total symptom picture. Some patients have much more of one kind of symptom, other patients another. Conversely, there is no single symptom or sign of schizophrenia which is found exclusively in that disease. All symptoms and signs can be found at least occasionally in other diseases of the brain, such as brain tumors and temporal lobe epilepsy.

ALTERATIONS OF THE SENSES

In Edgar Allan Poe's "The Tell-Tale Heart," the main character, clearly lapsing into a schizophreniclike state, exclaims to the reader, "Have I not told you that what you mistake for madness is but overacuteness of the senses?" An expert on the dark recesses of the human mind, Poe put his finger directly on a central theme of madness. Alterations of the senses are especially prominent in the early stages of schizophrenic breakdown and can probably be found in at least half of all patients.

The alterations may be either enhancement (more common) or blunting; all sensory modalities may be affected. For example, Poe's protagonist was experiencing predominantly an increased acuteness of hearing:

> True!—nervous—very, very dreadfully nervous I had been and am! but why will you say that I am mad? The disease had sharpened my senses—not destroyed—not dulled them. Above all was the sense of hearing acute. I heard all things in the heaven and in the earth. I heard many things in hell. How, then, am I mad? Harken! and observe how healthily—how calmly— I can tell you the whole story.

Another described it this way:

> During the last while back I have noticed that noises all seem to be louder to me than they were before. It's as if someone had turned up the volume. . . . I notice it most with background noises—you know what I mean, noises that are always around but you don't notice them. Now they seem to be just as loud and sometimes louder than the main noises that are going on.

> . . . It's a bit alarming at times because it makes it difficult to keep your mind
> on something when there's so much going on that you can't help listening
> to.

Visual sensations may also be heightened, as they are for these two patients:

> Colours seem to be brighter now, almost as if they are luminous painting.
> I'm not sure if things are solid until I touch them.

> I seem to be noticing colours more than before, although I am not artistically
> minded. The colours of things seem much clearer and yet at the same time
> there is something missing. The things I look at seem to be flatter as if you
> were looking just at a surface. Maybe it's because I notice so much more
> about things and find myself looking at them for a longer time. Not only the
> colour of things fascinates me but all sorts of little things, like markings in
> the surface, pick up my attention too.

More often, however, both hearing *and* visual sensations are increased, as
happened to this young woman:

> These crises, far from abating, seemed rather to increase. One day, while I
> was in the principal's office, suddenly the room became enormous, il-
> luminated by a dreadful electric light that cast false shadows. Everything
> was exact, smooth, artificial, extremely tense; the chairs and tables seemed
> models placed here and there. Pupils and teachers were puppets revolving
> without cause, without objective. I recognized nothing, nobody. It was as
> though reality, attenuated, had slipped away from all these things and
> these people. Profound dread overwhelmed me, and as though lost, I
> looked around desperately for help. I heard people talking, but I did not
> grasp the meaning of the words. The voices were metallic, without warmth
> or color. From time to time, a word detached itself from the rest. It re-
> peated itself over and over in my head, absurd, as though cut off by a
> knife.

Closely related to the overacuteness of the senses is the flooding of the
senses with stimuli. It is not only that the senses become more sharply attuned
but that they see and hear everything. Normally our brain screens out most
incoming sights and sounds, allowing us to concentrate on whatever we
choose. This screening mechanism appears to become impaired in many persons with schizophrenia, releasing a veritable flood of sensory stimuli into the
brain simultaneously.

This is one person's description of flooding of the senses with auditory
stimuli:

> Everything seems to grip my attention although I am not particularly inter-
> ested in anything. I am speaking to you just now, but I can hear noises going
> on next door and in the corridor. I find it difficult to shut these out, and it
> makes it more difficult for me to concentrate on what I am saying to you.

Often the silliest little things that are going on seem to interest me. That's not even true: they don't interest me, but I find myself attending to them and wasting a lot of time this way.

And with visual stimuli:

Occasionally during subsequent periods of disturbance there was some distortion of vision and some degree of hallucination. On several occasions my eyes became markedly oversensitive to light. Ordinary colors appeared to be much too bright, and sunlight seemed dazzling in intensity. When this happened, ordinary reading was impossible, and print seemed excessively black.

Frequently these two things happen together.

I can probably tell you as much or more about what really went on those days than lots of people who were sane: the comings and goings of people, the weather, what was on the news, what we ate, what records were played, what was said. My focus was a bit bizarre. I could do portraits of people who were walking down the street. I remembered license numbers of cars we were following into Vancouver. We paid $3.57 for gas. The air machine made eighteen dings while we were there.

In these disturbing circumstances I sensed again the atmosphere of unreality. During class, in the quiet of the work period, I heard the street noises—a trolley passing, people talking, a horse neighing, a horn sounding, each detached, immovable, separated from its source, without meaning. Around me, the other children, heads bent over their work, were robots or puppets, moved by an invisible mechanism. On the platform, the teacher, too, talking, gesticulating, rising to write on the blackboard, was a grotesque jack-in-the-box. And always this ghastly quiet, broken by outside sounds coming from far away, the implacable sun heating the lifeless immobility. An awful terror bound me; I wanted to scream.

As the last example makes clear, it becomes very difficult to concentrate or think clearly when so much sensory data is coming in. Mark Vonnegut expressed this well:

Had someone asked me about what was going on, I would have had quite a bit of trouble taking the questions seriously and even more trouble getting my voice and words to work right. I would have been much more interested in their clothes or face than the questions and would have thought they were really asking something much deeper. I was on my way to Vancouver, and knew it most of the time, but if asked where I was, that would have been a long way down the line of answers that came to mind.

As did this patient:

Sometimes when people speak to me my head is overloaded. It's too much to hold at once. It goes out as quick as it goes in. It makes you forget what you just heard because you can't get hearing it long enough. It's just words in the air unless you can figure it out from their faces.

Sensory modalities other than hearing and vision may also be affected in schizophrenia. Mary Barnes in her autobiographical account of "a journey through madness" recalled how "it was terrible to be touched. . . . Once a nurse tried to cut my nails. The touch was such that I tried to bite her." Another patient described the horror of feeling a rat in his throat and tasting the "decay in my mouth as its body disintegrated inside me." Increased sensitivity of the genitalia is occasionally found, explained by one patient as "a genital sexual irritation from which there was no peace and no relief." I recently took care of a young man with such a sensation who became convinced that his penis was turning black. He countered this delusional fear by insisting that doctors —or anyone within sight—examine him every five minutes to reassure him. His hospitalization was precipitated by his having gone into the local post office where a girlfriend worked and asking her to examine him in front of the customers.

Another aspect of the overacuteness of the senses is a flooding of the mind with thoughts. It is as if the brain is being bombarded both with external stimuli (e.g., sounds and sights) and with internal stimuli as well (thoughts, memories). One psychiatrist who has studied this area extensively claims that we have not been as aware of the internal stimuli in persons with schizophrenia as we should be.

> My trouble is that I've got too many thoughts. You might think about something, let's say that ashtray, and just think, oh! yes, that's for putting my cigarette in, but I would think of it and then I would think of a dozen different things connected with it at the same time.

> My concentration is very poor. I jump from one thing to another. If I am talking to someone they only need to cross their legs or scratch their heads and I am distracted and forget what I was saying. I think I could concentrate better with my eyes shut.

And this person describes the flooding of memories from the past:

> Childhood feelings began to come back as symbols, and bits from past conversations went through my head. . . . I began to think I was hypnotized so that I would remember what had happened in the first four and a half years of my life. . . . I thought that my parents had supplied information about the nursery school teacher and pediatrician to someone—perhaps my husband—with the hope that I would be able to straighten myself out by remembering the early years.

Perhaps it is this increased ability of some schizophrenic patients to recall childhood events which has mistakenly led psychoanalysts to assume that the recalled events were somehow causally related to the schizophrenia (as will be discussed in chapter 5). There is no evidence to support such theories, however, and much evidence to support contrary theories.

A variation of flooding with thoughts occurs when the person feels that someone is inserting the flood of thoughts into his/her head. This is commonly referred to as thought insertion and when present is considered by many psychiatrists to be an almost certain symptom of schizophrenia.

> All sorts of "thoughts" seem to come to me, as if someone is "speaking" them inside my head. When in any company it appears to be worse (probably some form of self-consciousness), I don't want the "thoughts" to come but I keep on "hearing" them (as it were) and it requires lots of will power sometimes to stop myself from "thinking" (in the form of "words") the most absurd and embarrassing things. These "thoughts" do not mean anything to me and cause "lack of concentration" in whatever I am doing at work, etc. When listening to music I find that the words of the song come to me involuntarily, or if I don't know the particular song that is being played, I seem to "make up words" to the song against my will. Another thing similar to the above is the fact that if there is any banging or suchlike noise going on, I do the same thing, which is to "think-up" words to "rhyme"—as you might say—with whatever noise I can hear.

With this kind of activity going on in a person's head, it is not surprising that it would be difficult to concentrate.

> I was invited to play checkers and started to do so, but I could not go on. I was too much absorbed in my own thoughts, particularly those regarding the approaching end of the world and those responsible for the use of force and for the charge of homicidal intent. By nightfall my head was all in a whirl. It seemed to be the Day of Judgment and all humanity came streaming in from four different directions.

Concentrating on even as simple a task as walking from one building to another may become impossible.

> Fear made me ill; just the same I ran out to visit a friend who was staying at a nearby sanatorium. To get there, a way led through the woods, short and well marked. Becoming lost in the thick fog, I circled round and round the sanatorium without seeing it, my fear augmenting all the while. By and by I realized that the wind inspired this fear; the trees, too, large and black in the mist, but particularly the wind. At length I grasped the meaning of its message: the frozen wind from the North Pole wanted to crush the earth, to destroy it. Or perhaps it was an omen, a sign that the earth was about to be laid waste. This idea tormented me with growing intensity.

> When all aspects of overacuteness of the senses are taken together, the consequent cacophony in the brain must be frightening, and it is so described

by most patients. In the very earliest stage of the disease, however, before this overacuteness becomes too severe, it may be a pleasant experience. Many descriptions of the initial days of becoming schizophrenic are descriptions of heightened awareness, commonly called "peak experiences"; such experiences are also common in manic-depressive illness and in getting high on drugs. Here is one patient's description:

> Suddenly my whole being was filled with light and loveliness and with an upsurge of deeply moving feeling from within myself to meet and reciprocate the influence that flowed into me. I was in a state of the most vivid awareness and illumination. What can I say of it? A cloudless, cerulean blue sky of the mind, shot through with shafts of exquisite, warm, dazzling sunlight.

Many patients interpret such experiences within a religious framework and believe they are being touched by God.

> Before last week, I was quite closed about my emotions; then finally I owned up to them with another person. I began to speak without thinking beforehand and what came out showed an awareness of human beings and God. I could feel deeply about other people. We felt connected. The side which had been suppressing emotions did not seem to be the real one. I was in a higher and higher state of exhilaration and awareness. Things people said had hidden meaning. They said things that applied to life. Everything that was real seemed to make sense. I had a great awareness of life, truth, and God. I went to church and suddenly all parts of the service made sense. My senses were sharpened. I became fascinated by the little insignificant things around me. There was an additional awareness of the world that would do artists, architects, and painters good. I ended up being too emotional, but I felt very much at home with myself, very much at ease. It gave me a great feeling of power. It was not a case of seeing more broadly but deeper. I was losing touch with the outside world and lost my sense of time. There was a fog around me in some sense, and I felt asleep. I could see more deeply into problems that other people had and would go directly into a deeper subject with a person. I had the feeling I loved everybody in the world.

> A few weeks before my illness I began to regress into success daydreams somewhat similar to, though not quite as naive and grandiose as, those I had had during the early adolescence. I was puzzled by this tendency, though not greatly alarmed because it hardly seemed that my daydreaming self was a part of my adult ethical self. At the onset of panic, I was suddenly confronted with an overwhelming conviction that I had discovered the secrets of the universe, which were being rapidly made plain with incredible lucidity. The truths discovered seemed to be known immediately and directly, with absolute certainty. I had no sense of doubt or awareness of the possibility of doubt. In spite of former atheism and strong antireligious sentiments, I was suddenly convinced that it was possible to prove rationally the existence of God.

In view of such experiences it is hardly surprising to find excessive religious preoccupation listed as a common early sign of schizophrenia.

Sensations can be blunted, as well as enhanced, in schizophrenia. Such blunting is more commonly found late in the course of the disease whereas enhancement is often one of the earliest symptoms. The blunting is described "as if a heavy curtain were drawn over his mind; it resembled a thick deadening cloud that prevented the free use of his senses." One's own voice may sound muted or faraway, and vision may be wavy or blurred: "However hard I looked it was as if I was looking through a daydream and the mass of detail, such as the pattern on a carpet, became lost."

One sensation which may be blunted in schizophrenia is that of pain. Although it does not happen frequently, when such blunting does occur it may be dramatic and have practical consequences for those who are caring for the person. It is now in vogue to attribute such blunting to medication, but in fact it was clearly described twenty and thirty years before drugs for schizophrenia became widely available. There are many accounts in the older textbooks of surgeons, for example, being able to do appendectomies and similar procedures on some schizophrenic patients with little or no anesthesia. One of my patients had a massive breast abscess which was unknown until the fluid from it seeped through her dress; although this is normally an exceedingly painful condition, she insisted she felt no pain whatsoever. Nurses who have cared for schizophrenic patients over many years can recite stories of fractured bones, perforated ulcers, or ruptured appendixes which the patient said nothing about. Practically, it is important to be aware of this possibility so that medical help can be sought for persons if they look sick, even if they are not complaining of pain. It is also the reason that some schizophrenics burn their fingers when they smoke cigarettes too close to the end.

It may well be that there is a common denominator for all aspects of the alterations of the senses discussed thus far. All sensory input into the brain passes through the limbic area in the lower portion of the brain. It is this area that is most suspect as being involved in schizophrenia, as will be discussed in chapter 5. The limbic system filters this sensory input, and it is likely that disease of this system accounts for many or most schizophrenic symptoms. Norma MacDonald, a woman who published an account of her schizophrenic illness in 1960, foresaw this possibility in a particularly clear manner several years before psychiatrists and neurologists understood it, and she wrote about her conception of the breakdown in the filter system.

> At first it was as if parts of my brain "awoke" which had been dormant, and I became interested in a wide assortment of people, events, places, and ideas which normally would make no impression on me. Not knowing that I was ill, I made no attempt to understand what was happening, but felt that there

was some overwhelming significance in all this, produced either by God or Satan, and I felt that I was duty-bound to ponder on each of these new interests, and the more I pondered the worse it became. The walk of a stranger on the street could be a sign to me which I must interpret. Every face in the windows of a passing streetcar would be engraved on my mind, all of them concentrating on me and trying to pass me some sort of message. Now, many years later, I can appreciate what had happened. Each of us is capable of coping with a large number of stimuli, invading our being through any one of the senses. We could hear every sound within earshot and see every object, hue, and colour within the field of vision, and so on. It's obvious that we would be incapable of carrying on any of our daily activities if even one-hundredth of all these available stimuli invaded us at once. So the mind must have a filter which functions without our conscious thought, sorting stimuli and allowing only those which are relevant to the situation in hand to disturb consciousness. And this filter must be working at maximum efficiency at all times, particularly when we require a degree of concentration. What had happened to me in Toronto was a breakdown in the filter, and a hodge-podge of unrelated stimuli were distracting me from things which should have had my undivided attention.

INABILITY TO SYNTHESIZE AND RESPOND

In normal people the brain functions in such a way that incoming stimuli are sorted and synthesized; then a correct response is selected and sent out. Most of the responses are learned, such as saying "thank you" when a gift is given to us. These responses also include logic, such as being able to predict what will happen to us if we do not arrive for work at the time we are supposed to. Our brains sort and synthesize incoming stimuli and send out responses hundreds of thousands of times each day. The site of this function is also thought to be the limbic system, and it is intimately connected with the screening function referred to above.

A fundamental defect of schizophrenics' brains is their frequent inability to sort, synthesize, and respond like normal brains. Textbooks of psychiatry describe this as a thought disorder, but it is more than just thoughts which are involved. Visual and auditory stimuli, emotions, and some actions are misarranged in exactly the same way as thoughts; the brain defect is probably similar for all.

We do not understand the human brain well enough to know precisely how the system works; but imagine a telephone operator sitting at an old plug-in type of switchboard in the middle of your limbic system. He or she receives all the sensory input, thoughts, ideas, memories and emotions coming in, sorts them, and synthesizes those which go together. For example, normally our brain takes the words of a sentence and synthesizes them automatically into a pattern of thought. We don't have to concentrate on the individual words but rather can focus on the meaning of the whole message.

Now what would happen if the switchboard operator decided not to do the job of sorting and synthesizing? In terms of understanding auditory stimuli, two schizophrenic patients describe this kind of defect:

> When people are talking I have to think what the words mean. You see, there is an interval instead of a spontaneous response. I have to think about it and it takes time. I have to pay all my attention to people when they are speaking or I get all mixed up and don't understand them.

> I can concentrate quite well on what people are saying if they talk simply. It's when they go on into long sentences that I lose the meanings. It just becomes a lot of words that I would need to string together to make sense.

Difficulties in synthesizing visual stimuli are similar to those described for auditory stimuli.

> I have to put things together in my head. If I look at my watch I see the watchstrap, watch, face, hands and so on, then I have got to put them together to get it into one piece.

> Everything is in bits. You put the picture up bit by bit into your head. It's like a photograph that's torn in bits and put together again. If you move it's frightening. The picture you had in your head is still there but broken up. If I move there's a new picture that I have to put together again.

One patient had similar problems when she looked at her psychiatrist, seeing "the teeth, then the nose, then the cheeks, then one eye and the other. Perhaps it was this independence of each part that inspired such fear and prevented my recognizing her even though I knew who she was."

In addition to difficulties in synthesizing individual auditory and visual stimuli into coherent patterns, many persons with schizophrenia have difficulty putting the two kinds of stimuli together.

> I can't concentrate on television because I can't watch the screen and listen to what is being said at the same time. I can't seem to take in two things like this at the same time especially when one of them means watching and the other means listening. On the other hand I seem to be always taking in too much at the one time and then I can't handle it and can't make sense of it.

> I tried sitting in my apartment and reading; the words looked perfectly familiar, like old friends whose faces I remembered perfectly well but whose names I couldn't recall; I read one paragraph ten times, could make no sense of it whatever, and shut the book. I tried listening to the radio, but the sounds went through my head like a buzz saw. I walked carefully through traffic

to a movie theater and sat through a movie which seemed to consist of a lot
of people wandering around slowly and talking a great deal about something
or other. I decided, finally, to spend my days sitting in the park watching
the birds on the lake.

These persons' difficulties in watching television or movies are very typical. In
fact it is striking how few schizophrenic patients on hospital wards watch
television, contrary to what is popularly believed. Some may sit in front of it
and watch the visual motion, as if it were a test pattern, but few of them can
tell you what is going on. This includes patients of all levels of intelligence and
education, among them college-educated persons who, given little else to do,
might be expected to take advantage of the TV for much of the day. On the
contrary, you are more likely to find them sitting quietly in another corner of
the room, ignoring the TV; if you ask them why, they may tell you that they
cannot follow what is going on, or they may try to cover up their defect by
saying they are tired. One of my patients was an avid New York Yankees
baseball fan prior to his illness, but he refuses to watch the game now even
when the Yankees are on and he is in the room at the time, because he cannot
understand what is happening. As a practical aside, the favorite TV programs
and movies of many persons with schizophrenia are cartoons and travelogues;
both are simple and can be followed visually without the necessity of integrat-
ing auditory input at the same time.

But the job of the switchboard operator in our brain does not end with
sorting and synthesizing the incoming stimuli. The job also includes hooking
up the stimuli with proper responses to be sent back outside. For example, if
somebody asks me, "Would you like to have lunch with me today?" my brain
focuses immediately on the overall content of the question and starts calculat-
ing: Do I have time? Do I want to? What excuses do I have? What will other
people think who see me with this person? What will be the effect on this
person if I say no? Out of these calculations emerges a response which, in a
normal brain, is appropriate to the situation. Similarly, news of a friend's death
gets hooked up with grief, visual and auditory stimuli from a Woody Allen
movie are hooked up with mirth, and a new idea regarding the creation of the
universe is hooked up with logic and with previous knowledge in this area. It
is an orderly, ongoing process, and the switchboard operator goes on, day after
day, making relatively few mistakes.

The inability of schizophrenic patients not only to sort and synthesize
stimuli but to select out appropriate responses is one of the hallmarks of the
disease. It led Swiss psychiatrist Eugen Bleuler in 1911 to introduce the term
"schizophrenia," meaning in German a splitting of the various parts of the
thought process. Bleuler was impressed by the inappropriate responses frequently given by persons with this disease; for example, when told that a close

friend has died, a schizophrenic may giggle. It is as if the switchboard operator not only gets bored and stops sorting and synthesizing but becomes actively malicious and begins hooking the incoming stimuli up to random, usually inappropriate, responses.

The inability to synthesize and respond appropriately is also at the core of schizophrenics' difficulties in relating to other people. Not being able to put the auditory and visual stimuli together makes it difficult to understand others; if in addition you cannot respond appropriately, then interpersonal relations become impossible. One patient described such difficulties:

> During the visit I tried to establish contact with her, to feel that she was actually there, alive and sensitive. But it was futile. Though I certainly recognized her, she became part of the unreal world. I knew her name and everything about her, yet she appeared strange, unreal, like a statue. I saw her eyes, her nose, her lips moving, heard her voice and understood what she said perfectly, yet I was in the presence of a stranger. To restore contact between us I made desperate efforts to break through the invisible dividing wall but the harder I tried, the less successful I was, and the uneasiness grew apace.

It is for this reason that many persons with schizophrenia prefer to spend time by themselves, withdrawn, communicating with others as little as possible. The process is too difficult and too painful to undertake except when absolutely necessary.

Just as auditory and visual stimuli may not be sorted or synthesized by the schizophrenic brain and may elicit inappropriate responses, so too may actions be fragmented and lead to inappropriate responses. This will be discussed in greater detail in a subsequent section (see pages 38–44), but it is worth noting that the same kind of brain deficit is probably involved. For example, compare the difficulties this patient has in the simple action of getting a drink of water with the difficulties in synthesizing auditory and visual stimuli described above:

> If I do something like going for a drink of water, I've got to go over each detail—find cup, walk over, turn tap, fill cup, turn tap off, drink it. I keep building up a picture. I have to change the picture each time. I've got to make the old picture move. I can't concentrate. I can't hold things. Something else comes in, various things. It's easier if I stay still.

It suggests that there may be relatively few underlying brain deficits leading to the broad range of symptoms which comprise the schizophrenic disease.

When schizophrenic thought patterns are looked at from outside, as when they are being described by a psychiatrist, such terms as "disconnectedness," "loosening of associations," "concreteness," "impairment of logic," "thought blocking" and "ambivalence" are used. To begin with disconnectedness: one of my patients comes into the office each morning and asks my secretary to write a sentence on paper for him. A recent request was "Write all kinds of black snakes looking like raw onion, high strung, deep down, long winded, all kinds of sizes." This patient had put together several apparently disconnected ideas which a normally functioning brain would not join. Another patient wrote:

> My thoughts get all jumbled up, I start thinking or talking about something but I never get there. Instead I wander off in the wrong direction and get caught up with all sorts of different things that may be connected with the things I want to say but in a way I can't explain. People listening to me get more lost than I do.

Sometimes there may be a vague connection between the jumbled thoughts in schizophrenic thinking; such instances are referred to as loose associations. For example, in the sentence about black snakes above, it may be that the patient juxtaposed onions to black snakes because of the onionlike pattern on the skin of some snakes. On another occasion I was drawing blood from a patient's arm and she said, "Look at my blue veins. I asked the Russian women to make them red," loosely connecting the color of blood with the "Reds" of the Soviet Union. Other examples of loose associations are:

> "Sun," I intoned. "From the Sun to Son to Son of God to Jesus Christ. From Christ to Christmas, Christmas to Mass. Mass to solid mass. Solid mass to earth. Earth to element. Element to four elements to earth, air, fire, water, the four elements. Four elements to Universe. Universe to everything."

And the great Russian dancer Nijinsky wrote the following as he was becoming schizophrenic, jumping from the round shape of a stage to his eye to people's criticism of him:

> I am not artificial. I am life. The theatre is not life. I know the customs of the theatre. The theatre becomes a habit. Life does not. I do not like the theatre with a square stage. I like a round stage. I will build a theatre which will have a round shape, like an eye. I like to look closely in the mirror and I see only one eye in my forehead. Often I make drawings of one eye. I dislike polemics and therefore people can say what they like about my book; I will be silent. I have come to the conclusion that it is better to be silent than to speak.

Occasionally the loose association will rest not upon some tenuous logical connection between the words but merely upon their similar sound. For example, one young man presented me with a written poem one morning.

> I believe we will soon
> achieve world peace. But
> I'm still on the lamb.

He confused the lamb associated with peace with the expression "on the lam," the correct spelling of which he apparently did not know. There is no logical association between "lamb" and "lam" except for their similar sound; such associations are referred to as clang associations.

Another characteristic of schizophrenic thinking is concreteness. This can be tested by asking the person to give the meaning of proverbs, which require an ability to abstract in order to be able to move from the specific to the general. When most people are asked what "People who live in glass houses shouldn't throw stones" means, they will answer something like: "If you're not perfect yourself, don't criticize others." They move from the specific glass house and stones to the general concept without difficulty.

But the schizophrenic frequently loses this ability to abstract. I asked one hundred consecutive schizophrenic patients to explain the above proverb; less than one-third were able to think abstractly about it. The majority answered simply something like "It might break the windows." In many instances the concrete answer also demonstrated some disconnected thinking.

Well, it could mean exactly like it says 'cause the windows may well be broken. They do grow flowers in glass houses.

Because if they did they'd break the environment.

Because they might be put out for the winter.

A few patients personalized it:

People should always keep their decency about their living arrangements. I remember living in a glass house but all I did was wave.

Because it might bust the wall and people could see you.

Others responded with totally irrelevant answers that illustrated many facets of the schizophrenic thinking disorder.

Don't hit until you go—coming or going.

Some people are up in the air and some in society and some up in the air.

A few patients were able to think abstractly about the proverb, but in formulating their reply incorporated other aspects of schizophrenic thinking.

People who live in glass houses shouldn't forget people who live in stone houses and shouldn't throw glass.

If you suffer from complexities, don't talk about people. Don't be agile.

The most succinct answer came from a quiet, chronically schizophrenic young man who pondered it solemnly, looked up and said, "Caution."

Concrete thinking can also occur during the everyday life of some schizophrenic persons. For example, one day I was taking a picture of my schizophrenic sister. When I said, "Look at the birdie," she immediately looked up to the sky. Another patient, passing a newspaper stand, noticed a headline announcing that a star had fallen from a window. "How could a big thing like a star get into a window?" he wondered, until he realized it referred to a movie star. *Death of a Salesman*, read the movie marquee, and a patient "speculated vaguely that a salesman might be a native of some country named Sales, probably in Asia."

An impairment of the ability to think logically is another facet of schizophrenic thinking, as illustrated in several of the previous examples. Another example was a patient under my care who, in psychological testing, was asked, "What would you do if you were lost in a forest?" He replied, "Go to the back of the forest, not the front." Similarly, many schizophrenic patients lose the ability to reason causally about events. One, for example, set his home on fire with his wheelchair-confined mother in it; when questioned carefully he did not seem to understand the fact that he was endangering her life.

In this kind of impaired thinking, opposites can coexist.

> I was extremely unhappy, I felt myself getting younger; the system wanted to reduce me to nothing. Even as I diminished in body and in age, I discovered that I was nine centuries old. For to be nine centuries old actually meant being not yet born. That is why the nine centuries did not make me feel at all old; quite the contrary.

> I had no time to go to sleep. Instantly the board of judges appeared. I could not see them clearly and was unable to identify any of them since there were no features on any of the faces . . . hardly faces at all, just blank oval spaces, poised on shoulders. They were seated behind a raised wooden platform, peering over at me. How could they peer without eyes? Perhaps they had eyes but I could not see them? Of course, I didn't have my glasses. In any case, they were definitely peering.

In the first instance no attempt is made to resolve the disparity between being very old and not yet born; in the second the person realizes that a face cannot peer yet have no eyes, but is unable to resolve the discrepancy. Given this impairment of causal and logical thinking in many persons with this disease, it is not surprising that they frequently have difficulty with daily activities, such as taking a bus, following directions, or planning meals.

In addition to disconnectedness, loosening of associations, concreteness, and impairment of logic, there are other features of schizophrenic thinking. Neologisms—made-up words—are occasionally heard. They may sound like gibberish to the listener, but to those saying them they are a response to their inability to find the words they want.

The worst thing has been my face and my speech. The words wouldn't come out right. I know how to explain myself but the way it comes out of my mouth isn't right. My thoughts run too fast and I can't stop the train at the right point to make them go the right way. Big magnified thoughts come into my head when I am speaking and put away words I wanted to say and make me stray away from what was in my mind. Things I am speaking just fade away and my head gets very heavy and I can't place what I wanted to say. I've got a lot to say but I can't focus the words to come out so they come out jumbled up. A barrier inside my head stops me from speaking properly and the mind goes blank. I try to concentrate but nothing comes out. Sometimes I find a word to replace what I wanted to say.

Another uncommon but dramatic form of schizophrenic thinking is called a word salad; the person just strings together a series of totally unrelated words and pronounces them as a sentence. One of my patients once turned to me solemnly and asked, "Bloodworm Baltimore frenchfry?" It's difficult to answer a question like that!

Generally it is not necessary to analyze a schizophrenic's thought pattern in detail to know that something is wrong with it. The overall effect on the listener is both predictable and indicative. In its most common forms, it makes the listener feel that something is fuzzy about the thinking, as if the words have been slightly mixed up. John Bartlow Martin wrote a book about mental illness called *A Pane of Glass*, and Ingmar Bergman portrayed a schizophrenic onset in his *Through a Glass Darkly*. Both were referring to this opaque quality in schizophrenic speech and thinking. The listener hears all the words, which may be almost correct, but at the end of the sentence or paragraph realizes that it doesn't "make sense." It is the feeling evoked when, puzzled by something, we squint our eyes, wrinkle our forehead, and smile slightly. Usually we exclaim, "What?" as we do this. It is a reaction evoked often when we listen to people with a schizophrenic thinking disorder.

I am glad as well as sorry not to have heard from you for a long time. I begin to confirm my suspicions along a totally different aspect of the nature of religions, nationalism or imperialism. I admit I never even dreamt that it centered around the laziness, imperfection, or improper understanding of the tendencies in the nature of human fight and struggle against this religious approach which was partially forced on me.

I feel that everything is sort of related to everybody and that some people are far more susceptible to this theory of relativity than others because of either having previous ancestors connected in some way or other with places or things, or because of believing, or by leaving a trail behind when you walk through a room you know. Some people might leave a different trail and all sorts of things go like that.

There can, of course, be all degrees of these thinking disorders in schizophrenic patients. Especially in the early stages of illness there may only be a vagueness or evasiveness that defies precise labeling, but in the full-blown illness the impairment usually is quite clear. It is an unusual patient who does not have some form of thinking disorder. Some psychiatrists even question whether schizophrenia is the correct diagnosis if the person's thinking pattern is completely normal: they would say that schizophrenia, by definition, must include some disordered thinking. Others claim that it is possible, though unusual, to have genuine schizophrenia with other symptoms but without a thinking disorder.

A totally different type of thinking disorder is also commonly found in persons with schizophrenia: blocking of thoughts. To return to the metaphor of the telephone operator at the switchboard, it is as if she suddenly dozes off for a few moments and the system goes dead. The person is thinking or starting to respond and then stops, often in midsentence, and looks blank for a brief period. John Perceval described this as long ago as 1840:

> For instance, I have been often desired to open my mouth, and to address persons in different manners, and I have begun without premeditation a very rational and consecutive speech . . . but in the midst of my sentence, the power has either left me, or words have been suggested contradictory of those that went before: and I have been deserted, gaping, speechless, or stuttering in great confusion.

Other people have given these accounts:

> I may be thinking quite clearly and telling someone something and suddenly I get stuck. You have seen me do this and you may think I am just lost for words or that I have gone into a trance, but that is not what happens. What happens is that I suddenly stick on a word or an idea in my head and I just can't move past it. It seems to fill my mind and there's no room for anything else. This might go on for a while and suddenly it's over. Afterwards I get a feeling that I have been thinking very deeply about whatever it was but often I can't remember what it was that has filled my mind so completely.

> If I am reading I may suddenly get bogged down at a word. It may be any word, even a simple word that I know well. When this happens I can't get past it. It's as if I am being hypnotized by it. It's as if I am seeing the word for the first time and in a different way from anyone else. It's not so much that I absorb it, it's more like it is absorbing me.

Everyone who has spent time with persons with schizophrenia has observed this phenomenon. James Chapman claims it occurs in 95 percent of all patients. Some of the patients explain it by saying the thoughts are being taken out of their head. This symptom—called thought withdrawal—is considered by many psychiatrists to be strongly suggestive of a diagnosis of schizophrenia when it is present.

Ambivalence is another common symptom of schizophrenic thinking. Although now a fashionable term used very broadly, it was originally used in a narrower sense to describe schizophrenic patients who were unable to make up their minds. For example, one of my patients frequently leaves the front door of the building, turns right, then stops, takes three steps back to the left and stops, turns back and starts right, and may continue in this way for a full five minutes. It is not found as dramatically in most patients, but is of sufficient frequency and severity for Bleuler to have named it as one of the cardinal symptoms of schizophrenia. It is as if the ability to make a decision has been impaired. Normally our brain assesses the incoming thoughts and stimuli, makes a decision and then initiates a response. The brains of some schizophrenic persons are apparently impaired in this respect, initiating a response but then immediately countermanding it with its opposite, then repeating the process. It is a truly painful spectacle to observe.

DELUSIONS AND HALLUCINATIONS

Delusions and hallucinations are probably the best-known symptoms of schizophrenia. They are dramatic and are therefore the behaviors usually focused on when schizophrenia is being represented in popular literature or movies. The person observed talking to himself or to inanimate objects is almost a *sine qua non* for schizophrenia; it is the image evoked in our minds when the term "crazy" or "mad" is used.

And certainly delusions and hallucinations are very important and common symptoms of this disease. However, it should be remembered that they are not essential to it; indeed no *single* symptom is essential for the diagnosis of schizophrenia. There are many true schizophrenics who have a combination of other symptoms, such as a thought disorder, disturbances of affect, and disturbances of behavior, who have never had delusions or hallucinations. It should also be remembered that delusions and hallucinations are found in brain diseases other than schizophrenia, so their presence does not automatically mean that schizophrenia is present. Finally, it is important to realize that most delusions and hallucinations, as well as distortions of the body boundaries, are a direct outgrowth of overacuteness of the senses and the brain's inability to synthesize and respond appropriately to stimuli. In other words, most delusions and hallucinations are logical outgrowths of what the brain is experiencing. They are "crazy" only to the outsider; to the person experiencing them they form part of a logical and coherent pattern.

Delusions are simply false ideas believed by the patient but not by other people in his/her culture and which cannot be corrected by reason. One simple form of a delusion is the conviction that random events going on around the person all relate in a direct way to him or her. If you are walking down the street and a man on the opposite sidewalk coughs, you don't think anything of it and may not even consciously hear the cough. The schizophrenic person, however, not only hears the cough but immediately decides it must be a signal of some kind, perhaps directed to someone else down the street to warn him that the schizophrenic person is coming. The schizophrenic *knows* this is true with a certainty that few people experience. If you are walking with the schizophrenic and try to reason him/her out of his delusions your efforts will probably be futile. Even if you cross the street, and in the presence of the schizophrenic, question the man about his cough, the schizophrenic will probably just decide that you are part of the plot. Reasoning with schizophrenics about their delusions is like trying to bail out the ocean with a bucket. If, shortly after the cough incident, a helicopter flies overhead, the delusion may enlarge. Obviously the helicopter is watching the person, which further confirms suspicions about the cough. And if in addition to these happenings, the person arrives at the bus stop just too late to catch the bus, the delusional system is confirmed yet again; obviously the person who coughed or the helicopter pilot radioed the bus driver to leave. It all fits together into a logical, coherent whole.

Normal persons would experience these events and simply curse their bad luck at missing the bus. The person with schizophrenia, however, is experiencing different things so the events take on a different meaning. The cough and the helicopter noise may be very loud to him/her and even the sound of the bus may be perceived to be strange. While the normal person responds correctly to these as separate and unrelated events, similar to the stimuli and events of everyday life, the schizophrenic puts them together into a pattern. Thus both overacuteness of the senses and impaired ability to logically synthesize incoming stimuli and thoughts may lie behind many of the delusions experienced by many schizophrenics. To a schizophrenic the person who *cannot* put these special events together must be crazy, not the other way around.

There are many excellent examples of delusional thinking in literature. From Rilke's *The Notebooks of Malte Laurids Brigge* there is this example:

Why did she keep walking beside me and watching me? As if she were trying to recognize me with her bleared eyes, that looked as though some diseased person had spat slime into the bloody lids? And how came that little grey woman to stand that time for a whole quarter of an hour by my side before a shopwindow, showing me an old, long pencil, that came pushing infinitely

slowly out of her miserable, clenched hands? I pretended to look at the
display in the window and not notice anything. But she knew I had seen her,
she knew I stood there wondering what she was really doing. For I understood quite well that the pencil in itself was of no consequence; I felt it was
a sign, a sign for the initiated, a sign the outcast knew; I guessed she was
indicating to me that I should go somewhere or do something.

Chekhov, in his well-known "Ward No. 6," described it as follows:

In the morning Ivan Dmitritch got up from his bed in a state of horror, with
cold perspiration on his forehead, completely convinced that he might be
arrested any minute. Since his gloomy thoughts of yesterday had haunted
him so long, he thought, it must be that there was some truth in them. They
could not, indeed, have come into his mind without any grounds whatever.

A policeman walking slowly passed by the windows: that was not for
nothing. Here were two men standing still and silent near the house. Why?
Why were they silent? And agonizing days and nights followed for Ivan
Dmitritch. Everyone who passed by the windows or came into the yard
seemed to him a spy or a detective.

Another good example was written by a patient:

I got up at seven A.M., dressed and drove to the hospital. I felt my breathing
trouble might be due to an old heart lesion. I had been told when I was young
that I had a small ventricular septal defect. I decided that I was in heart
failure and that people felt I wasn't strong enough to accept this, so they
weren't telling me. I thought about all the things that had happened recently
that could be interpreted in that light. I looked up heart failure in a textbook
and found that the section had been removed, so I concluded someone had
removed it to protect me. I remembered other comments. A friend had
talked about a "walkie-talkie," and the thought occurred to me that I might
be getting medicine without my knowledge, perhaps by radio. I remembered
someone talking about a one-way plane ticket; to me that meant a trip to
Houston and a heart operation. I remembered an unusual smell in the lab
and thought that might be due to the medicine they were giving me in secret.
I began to think I might have a machine inside me which secreted medicine
into my bloodstream. Again I reasoned that I had a disease no one could
tell me about and was getting medicine for it secretly. At this point, I
panicked and tried to run away, but the attendant in the parking lot seemed
to be making a sign to motion me back. I thought I caught brief glimpses
of a friend and my wife so I decided to go back into the hospital. A custo-
dian's eyes attracted my attention; they were especially large and piercing.
He looked very powerful. He had to be "in on it," maybe he was giving
medicine in some way. Then I began to have the feeling that other people
were watching me. And, as periodically happened throughout the early
stages, I said to myself that the whole thing was absurd, but when I looked
again the people really were watching me.

Even as innocuous an incoming stimulus as the sound of the wind can trigger off delusional thinking in some persons.

> I should emphasize that the unreality had grown greater and the wind had taken on a specific meaning. On windy days in bad weather I was horribly upset. At night I could not sleep, listening to the wind, sharing its howls, its complaints and despairing cries, and my soul wept and groaned with it. More and more I imagined the wind bore a message for me to divine.

In many cases the delusions of a schizophrenic become more complex and integrated. Rather than simply being watched, the schizophrenic person becomes convinced that he/she is being controlled by other persons, manipulated, or even hypnotized. Such persons are constantly on the alert for confirmatory evidence to support their beliefs; needless to say, they always find it from among the myriad visual and auditory stimuli perceived by all of us each day. A good example of this was a kind, elderly Irish lady who was a patient on my ward. She believed that she had been wired by some mysterious foreign agents in her sleep and that through the wires her thoughts and actions could be controlled. In particular she pointed to the ceiling as the place from which the control took place. One morning I was dismayed to come onto the ward and discover workmen installing a new fire alarm system; wires were hanging down in all colors and in all directions. The lady looked at me, pointed to the ceiling, and just smiled; her delusions had been confirmed forever!

Delusions of being wired or radio controlled are relatively common. Often it is the FBI or the CIA which is the suspected perpetrator of the scheme. One patient was convinced that a radio had been sewn into his skull when he had had a minor scalp wound sutured and had tried to bring legal suit against the FBI innumerable times. Another man, at one time a highly successful superintendent of schools, became convinced that a radio had been implanted in his nose. He went to dozens of major medical centers, even to Europe, seeking a surgeon who would remove it. He even had an X ray of his nose showing a tiny white speck which he was convinced was the radio.

Friends of the unfortunate people often try to reason them out of their delusions. Rarely is this successful. Questions about why the FBI would want to control them are deftly brushed aside as irrelevant; the important point is that they do, and the person is experiencing sensations (such as strange noises) which confirm the fact. Reasoning a schizophrenic out of a delusion is hampered by the distorted stimuli he/she is perceiving and also by the fact that the thinking processes may not be logical or connected. A further impediment is the fact that delusions frequently become self-fulfilling. Thus someone who believes others are spying on him/her finds it logical to act furtively, perhaps running from shelter to shelter and peering anxiously into the faces of passersby. Such behavior inevitably invites attention and leads to the delusional person actually being watched by other people. As the saying goes, "I used to be paranoid but now people really *are* watching me."

Delusions in which the person is being watched, persecuted, or attacked are commonly called paranoid delusions. Paranoia is a relative concept; everybody experiences bits and pieces of it from time to time. In some places a little paranoia even has survival value; the fellow who works across the hall may really be stealing your memos, because he wants your job. Paranoid thinking by itself is not schizophrenia; it is only when it becomes a frank delusion (unaffected by reason) that it *may* be. Even then, however, it must be remembered that paranoid delusions can occur in brain diseases other than schizophrenia.

Paranoid delusions may on occasion be dangerous. "During the paranoid period I thought I was being persecuted for my beliefs, that my enemies were actively trying to interfere with my activities, were trying to harm me, and at times even to kill me." The paranoid person may try to strike first when the threat is perceived as too close. Facilities for the criminally insane in every state include among their inmates a large number of schizophrenic persons who have committed a crime in what they believed to be self-defense. It is this subgroup of schizophrenics who have produced the general belief that schizophrenics as a whole are dangerous. In fact, when we take into consideration all schizophrenics, this subgroup is very small. Most persons with schizophrenia are not dangerous at all, and I would far rather walk the halls of any mental hospital than walk the streets of any inner city.

Delusions may be of many types other than paranoid; grandiose delusions are quite common: "I felt that I had power to determine the weather, which responded to my inner moods, and even to control the movement of the sun in relation to other astronomical bodies." This often leads to a belief by the person that he/she is Jesus Christ, the Virgin Mary, the President, or some other exalted or important person. One recent admission to our hospital believed himself to be Mao Zedong. We began him on medication and, by the next day, knew he was getting better because he had become only the brother of Mao Zedong. Grandiose delusions can be dangerous, however. Persons who believe they can fly or can stop bullets often place themselves in a position to test out their beliefs with predictably tragic consequences.

Another common delusion is that the person can control other people's minds. One young woman I saw had spent five years at home because each time she went into the street she believed that her mind compelled other people to turn and look at her. She described the effect of her mind as "like a magnet —they have no choice but to turn and look." Another patient believed he could change people's moods by "telepathic force": "I eventually felt I could go into a crowded restaurant and while just sitting there quietly, I could change everyone's mood to happiness and laughter." Here is a variant on this delusion:

> I like talking to a person but not in audible words. I try to force my thoughts into someone. I concentrate on how they move. I think of a message and concentrate in my head. It's thought you're passing over. I send the messages by visual indication. Sometimes the shoulder, sometimes my whole body.

Another variant is the delusional belief that one's thoughts are radiating out of one's head and being broadcast over radio or television; this is called thought broadcasting and is considered to be an almost certain indication of schizophrenia.

In evaluating delusions it is very important to keep in mind that their content is culture-bound. It is not the belief *per se* that is delusory, but how far the belief differs from the beliefs shared by others in the same culture or subculture. A man who believes he is being influenced by others who have "worked roots" (put a hex) on him may be completely normal if he grew up in lowland South Carolina where "working roots" is a widespread cultural belief. If he grew up in Scarsdale, on the other hand, his belief in being influenced by "worked roots" is more likely to suggest schizophrenia. Minority groups in particular may have a culturally induced high level of paranoid belief, and this belief may be based upon real discrimination and real persecution. Thus beliefs of persons suspected of having schizophrenia must *always* be placed within a cultural context and regarded as only one facet of the disease.

Occasionally individuals come to attention who have odd thoughts, but it may be very difficult to decide whether these thoughts constitute true delusions. Such an individual, apparently, is John Hinckley, who in 1981 attempted to assassinate President Ronald Reagan. According to court testimony, Hinckley had a fantasy relationship with Jodi Foster, a young movie actress, and spent much of his time and energy trying to engage her attention; the assassination attempt was said to be Hinckley's ultimate effort to prove his love for Jodi Foster. At his trial, psychiatrists for the defense and the prosecution differed sharply on whether such thinking constituted a true delusion.

Hallucinations are very common in schizophrenia and are the end of that spectrum which begins with overacuteness of the senses. To take vision as an example: the spectrum has overacuteness of vision at one end of it, that is, lights are too bright, colors take on a more brilliant hue. In the middle of the spectrum are gross distortions of visual stimuli (also called illusions), such as a dog which takes on the appearance of a tiger. And on the far end of the spectrum are things which are seen by the schizophrenic person when there is nothing there; this is a true hallucination. The experiences described by schizophrenics are usually a mixture of different points on the spectrum.

Gross distortions of visual or auditory stimuli are not uncommon experiences in schizophrenia.

I was sitting listening to another person and suddenly the other person became smaller and then larger and then he seemed to get smaller again. He did not become a complete miniature. Then today with another person, I felt he was getting taller and taller. There is brightness and clarity of outline of things around me. Last week I was with a girl and suddenly she seemed to get bigger and bigger, like a monster coming nearer and nearer. The situation becomes threatening and I shrink back and back.

One day we were jumping rope at recess. Two little girls were turning a long rope while two others jumped in from either side to meet and cross over. When it came my turn and I saw my partner jump toward me where we were to meet and cross over, I was seized with panic; I did not recognize her. Though I saw her as she was, still it was not she. Standing at the other end of the rope she seemed smaller, but the nearer we approached each other, the taller she grew, the more she swelled in size.

I cried out, "Stop, Alice, you look like a lion; you frighten me!" At the sound of the fear in my voice which I tried to dissemble under the guise of fooling, the game came to an abrupt halt. The girls looked at me, amazed, and said, "You're silly—Alice, a lion? You don't know what you are talking about."

This phenomenon can perhaps best be depicted by a description of the first time I experienced it. I was one of four men at a bridge table. On one of the deals, my partner bid three clubs. I looked at my hand: I had only one small club. Though my hand was weak, I had to bid to take him out. My bid won. When my partner laid down his cards, he showed only two small clubs in his hand. I immediately questioned why he had bid three clubs. He denied having made such a bid. The other two men at the table supported him. There was no opportunity and no reason for the three clubs despite the fact that I had distinctly heard him do so. Not only had the hallucination included a spatial component synchronized with the man's position, but it had also duplicated exactly the vocal tones of the man. Furthermore, the man had actually declared a different bid at the time I had heard him bidding three clubs. This bid I had not heard. Somewhere along the line of my nervous system the words which he had actually spoken were blocked and the hallucinatory words substituted.

In all three instances there was a stimulus of some kind, but the person saw or heard it in a grossly distorted way. It is as if the schizophrenic's brain is playing tricks.

Even worse tricks are played in forming true hallucinations, in which there is no initial stimulus at all. The brain makes up what it hears, sees, feels, smells, or tastes. Such experiences may be very real for the person. A person who hallucinates voices talking to him may hear the voices just as clearly as, or even more clearly than, the voices of real people talking to him. There is a tendency for people close to schizophrenics to scoff at the "imaginary" voices, to minimize them and not believe the persons really hear them. But they do, and in the sense that the brain hears them, they are real. The voices are but an extreme example of the malfunctioning of the schizophrenic's sensory apparatus.

Auditory hallucinations are by far the most common form of hallucination in schizophrenia. They are so characteristic of the disease that a person with true auditory hallucinations should be assumed to have schizophrenia until proven otherwise. They may take a variety of forms. They may be a simple swishing or thumping sound, such as the beating of the heart in Poe's famous short story:

> No doubt I now grew very pale;—but I talked fluently, and with a heightened voice. Yet the sound increased and what could I do? It was a low, dull, quick sound—much such a sound as a watch makes when enveloped in cotton. I gasped for breath—and yet the officers heard it not. I talked more quickly—more vehemently; but the noise steadily increased. Why would they not be gone? I paced the floor to and fro with heavy strides, as if excited to fury by the observation of the men—but the noise steadily increased. Oh, God; what could I do? I foamed—I raved—I swore! I swung the chair upon which I had been sitting, and grated it upon the boards, but the noise arose over all and continually increased. It grew louder—louder—louder! And still the men chatted pleasantly, and smiled. Was it possible they heard not? Almighty God!—no, no! They heard!—they suspected—they knew!—they were making a mockery of my horror!

They may be a single voice: "Thus for years I have heard daily in hundredfold repetition incoherent words spoken into my nerves without any context, such as 'Why not?' 'Why, if,' 'Why, because I,' 'Be it,' 'With respect to him.' "

Or they may be multiple voices:

> The voices . . . were mostly heard in my head, though I often heard them in the air, or in different parts of the room. Every voice was different, and each beautiful, and generally, speaking or singing in a different tone and measure, and resembling those of relations or friends. There appeared to be many in my head, I should say upwards of fourteen. I divide them, as they styled themselves, or one another, into voices of contrition and voices of joy and honour.

Or they may even be choirs:

> There was music everywhere and rhythm and beauty. But the plans were always thwarted. I heard what seemed to be a choir of angels. I thought it the most beautiful music I had ever heard. Two of the airs I kept repeating over and over until the delirium ended. One of them I can remember imperfectly even now. This choir of angels kept hovering around the hospital and

shortly afterward I heard something about a little lamb being born upstairs in the room just above mine.

The hallucinations may be heard only occasionally or they may be continuous. When occasional, the most common time for them, in my clinical experience, is at night when going to sleep.

> For about almost seven years—except during sleep—I have never had a single moment in which I did not hear voices. They accompany me to every place and at all times; they continue to sound even when I am in conversation with other people, they persist undeterred even when I concentrate on other things, for instance read a book or a newspaper, play the piano, etc.; only when I am talking aloud to other people or to myself are they of course drowned by the stronger sound of the spoken word and therefore inaudible to me. But the well-known phrases recommence at once, sometimes in the middle of a sentence, which tells me that the conversation had continued during the interval, that is to say that those nervous stimuli or vibrations responsible for the weaker sounds of the voices continue even while I talk aloud.

I have taken care of people with similar manifestations. One unfortunate woman had heard voices continuously for twenty years. They became especially loud whenever she tried to watch television, so she couldn't watch it at all.

In the vast majority of cases, the voices are unpleasant. They are often accusatory, reviling the victims for past misdeeds, either real or imagined. Often they curse them, and I have had many people refuse to tell me what the voices say to them because they were embarrassed by it. In a minority of cases the voices may be pleasant, as in the example with lovely music cited above. Occasionally they are even helpful, as with a woman who announced to me one day that she was getting well: "I know I am, because my voices told me so."

The precise mechanism of auditory hallucinations is not well understood and has received remarkably little attention from researchers. The most plausible explanation is that the schizophrenic disease process selectively affects the auditory tracts or centers in the brain, thereby activating them. Many nerve tracts having to do with hearing are located close to the limbic system, the part of the brain most likely affected in schizophrenia. Another possible explanation was put forth by Julian Jaynes, who suggested that auditory hallucinations are simply historical holdovers from the function of the right side of the brain in ancient man. His theories, although interesting, are inconsistent with other data, including the fact that schizophrenia is probably a disease primarily of the left side of the brain (see chapter 5).

Visual hallucinations also occur but much less frequently. One schizophrenic patient described the variety of these hallucinations:

> At an early stage the appearance of colored flashes of light was common. These took the form either of distant streaks or of near-by round glowing patches about a foot in diameter. Another type, which took place five or six times, was the appearance of words or symbols on blank surfaces. Closely connected with this was the occasional substitution of hallucinatory matter for the actual printed matter in books which I have been reading. On these occasions, the passage which I have been seeing has dissolved while I have been looking at it and another and sometimes wholly different passage has appeared in its place. . . . A further form of visual hallucinations that happened on two occasions was the appearance on a wall of the pictures of the heads of young women as though projected from a projection machine. These pictures were of women whom to the best of my knowledge I had never met.

Visual hallucinations usually appear in conjunction with auditory hallucinations. When only visual hallucinations appear, it is unlikely that schizophrenia is the cause. Many other brain diseases, notably drug intoxications and alcohol withdrawal, cause purely visual hallucinations and are the more likely diagnosis in such cases.

Hallucinations of smell or taste are very unusual but do occur. One patient gave this description of hallucinations of smell:

> On a few occasions, I have experienced olfactory hallucinations. These have consisted of the seeming smelling of an odor as though originating from a source just outside the nose. Sometimes this odor has had a symbolical relationship with the thoughts-out-loud, as for instance, the appearance of an odor of sulphur in connection with a threat of damnation to hell by the thoughts-out-loud.

Another patient illustrated the same phenomenon of associating a smell with a thought:

> During the time I was getting sick again, I began to think about the abortions I had before I was married. I was feeling guilty about them again. In those days you always tried to abort yourself first by taking quinine. When I was taking a shower and thinking about the past, I suddenly noticed the unmistakable smell of quinine. Soon after that, my mother and I were talking and she said something about oranges. I immediately began to smell oranges.

Hallucinations of taste usually consist of familiar food tasting differently. I have had two patients with paranoid schizophrenia, for example, who decided that they were being poisoned when their food began tasting "funny." Certainly if one's food suddenly starts changing in taste, it is logical to suspect that somebody is adding something to it.

Hallucinations of touch are also found among schizophrenic patients, although not commonly. I have provided care for one woman who feels small insects crawling under the skin on her face; it is an understatement to say that this is very upsetting to her. Another patient experienced hallucinatory pain.

To the person who experiences hallucinatory pains, the pains feel identical with actual pains. There is no difference between the sensation of hallucinatory and the sensation of actual pain. The person who experiences it can distinguish it only by its lack of normal cause and its interrelations with other hallucinatory phenomena. The person who feels it undergoes real suffering. The fact that the cause of the pain is obscure and abnormal does not reduce the actuality of the suffering. Rather, insofar as it makes more difficult the correction of the causative factor and the removal of the pain, it tends to add depressive factors which increase the suffering caused by the sensation itself.

To give some specific data concerning hallucinatory pains that I have experienced, it may be stated that they have varied considerably in intensity, in duration, and in locus. In intensity, they have ranged from a fraction of a second up to ten minutes or so. In locus, they have ranged over all parts of the body. In type, they have included smarting, burning, aching.

ALTERED SENSE OF SELF

Closely allied with delusions and hallucinations is another complex of symptoms which is characteristic of many schizophrenic patients. Normal individuals have a clear sense of self; they know where their bodies stop and where inanimate objects begin. They know that their hand, when they look at it, belongs to them. Even to make a statement like this strikes most normal persons as absurd because they cannot imagine its being otherwise.

But many persons with schizophrenia can imagine it, for alterations in their sense of self are not uncommon in this condition. Renée, in Marguerite Sechehaye's poignant biography, describes how she began to confuse herself with a doll:

I was present when Mamma first held a doll in her arms, a baby doll whom I named Ezekiel. She covered him, kissed him affectionately, put him to bed in his cradle. In the beginning it was enough for me to watch him avidly. All at once I experienced profound amazement that Ezekiel should receive Mamma's love and affection without the occurrence of anything untoward. At any moment I expected Mamma to cast Ezekiel off because I did not deserve to live. In my mind reigned utter confusion concerning Ezekiel and me. When Mamma held him in her arms, I trembled lest she drop him precipitously in his cradle, and if she did, I had the uncanny impression that it was I who had been so treated.

At another time she was unable to clearly distinguish herself from Mamma.

> Sometimes I did not know clearly whether it was she or I who needed something. For instance if I asked for another cup of tea and Mamma answered teasingly, "But why do you want more tea; don't you see that I have just finished my cup and so you don't need any?" Then I replied, "Yes, that's true, I don't need any more," confusing her with myself. But at bottom I did desire a second cup of tea, and I said, "But I still want some more tea," and suddenly, in a flash, I realized the fact that Mamma's satiety did not make me sated too. And I was ashamed to let myself be thus trapped and to watch her laugh at my discomfiture.

Renée also describes how much more comfortable she felt when she was referred to in the third person ("Renée do this") rather than in the second person as "you."

Another patient described a similar experience in which

> I saw myself in different bodies. . . . The night nurse came in and sat under the shaded lamp in the quiet ward. I recognized her as me, and I watched for some time quite fascinated; I had never had an outside view of myself before. In the morning several of the patients having breakfast were me. I recognized them by the way they held their knives and forks.

Parts of a schizophrenic's body may develop lives of their own, as if they have become disassociated and detached. One patient described this feeling:

> I get shaky in the knees and my chest is like a mountain in front of me, and my body actions are different. The arms and legs are apart and away from me and they go on their own. That's when I feel I am the other person and copy their movements, or else stop and stand like a statue. I have to stop to find out whether my hand is in my pocket or not. I'm frightened to move or turn my head. Sometimes I let my arms roll to see where they will land. After I sit down my head clears again but I don't remember what happened when I was in the daze.

Renée describes confusion regarding where her body stopped and the rest of the world began: "This was equally true in body functions. When I urinated and it was raining torrents outside, I was not at all certain whether it was not my own urine bedewing the world, and I was gripped by fear."

Confusion about one's sexual characteristics is also not uncommonly found among schizophrenics, as in this man who believed his body was acquiring a feminine appearance:

> My breast gives the impression of a pretty well-developed female bosom; this phenomenon can be *seen* by anybody who wants to observe me *with his own eyes*. . . . A brief glance would not suffice. The observer would have to go to the trouble of spending ten or fifteen minutes near me. In that way anybody would notice the periodic swelling and diminution of my bosom.

The altered sense of self may be further aggravated if hallucinations of touch or delusions about the body are also present. Rilke described the horror of such feelings very graphically:

> Now it was there. Now it grew out of me like a tumor, like a second head, and was a part of me, though it could not belong to me at all, because it was so big. It was there like a huge, dead beast, that had once, when it was still alive, been my hand or my arm. And my blood flowed both through me and through it, as if through one and the same body. And my heart had to make a great effort to drive the blood into the Big Thing; there was hardly enough blood. And the blood entered the Big Thing unwillingly and came back sick and tainted. But the Big Thing swelled and grew over my face like a warm bluish boil and grew over my mouth, and already the shadow of its edge lay upon my remaining eye.

Another possible example of this is Kafka's famous story "The Metamorphosis," in which Gregor awakens in the morning and slowly realizes that he has been transformed into a huge beetle. Such passages in Kafka have led some scholars to speculate that Kafka himself may have been schizophrenic at times.

The origin of this altered sense of self in schizophrenic persons is unknown. Normally our sense of self is formed by a complex set of tactile and visual stimuli through which we can feel and see the limits of our body and by which we differentiate it from the objects around us. It is likely that the same disease process which alters the senses and the thinking process is also responsible for the altered sense of self.

CHANGES IN EMOTIONS

Changes in emotions—or affect, as it is often called by professionals—are one of the most common and characteristic changes in schizophrenia. These changes are especially prominent in the later stages of the disease. They are probably the most tragic of its symptoms, for they often result in individuals who appear to be unable to feel emotion at all. This in turn makes it difficult for us to relate to them, so we tend to shun them more and more.

Very early in the course of illness the schizophrenic patient may feel widely varying and rapidly fluctuating emotions. Exaggerated feelings of all kinds are not unusual, especially in connection with the peak experiences described previously.

> During the first two weeks of my psychosis, religious experience provided that dominant factor of the psychotic phenomena. The most important form of religious experience in that period was religious ecstasy. The attempts of the thoughts-out-loud to persuade myself to adopt a messianic fixation

formed the hallucinary background. In affective aspects, a pervasive feeling of well-being dominated the complex. I felt as though all my worries were gone and all my problems solved. I had the assurance that all my needs would be satisfied. Connected with this euphoric state, I experienced a gentle sensation of warmth over my whole body, particularly on my back, and a sensation of my body having lost its weight and gently floating.

Guilt is another commonly felt emotion in these early stages:

> Later, considering them appropriate, I no longer felt guilty about these fantasies, nor did the guilt have an actual object. It was too pervasive, too enormous, to be founded on anything definite, and it demanded punishment. The punishment was indeed horrible, sadistic—it consisted, fittingly enough, of being guilty. For to feel oneself guilty is the worst that can happen, it is the punishment of punishments. Consequently, I could never be relieved of it as though I had been truly punished. Quite the reverse, I felt more and more guilty, immeasurably guilty. Constantly, I sought to discover what was punishing me so dreadfully, what was making me so guilty.

And fear is frequently described by patients, often a pervasive and nameless fear that exists without any specific object. Rilke captured this feeling skillfully:

> I am lying in my bed, five flights up, and my day, which nothing interrupts, is like a dial without hands. As a thing long lost lies one morning in its old place, safe and well, fresher almost than at the time of its loss, quite as though someone had cared for it—so here and there on my coverlet lie lost things out of my childhood and are as new. All forgotten fears are there again. The fear that a small, woollen thread that sticks out of the hem of my blanket may be hard, hard and sharp like a steel needle; the fear that this little button on my night shirt may be bigger than my head, big and heavy; the fear that this crumb of bread now falling from my bed may arrive glassy and shattered on the floor, and the burdensome worry lest at that really everything will be broken, everything for ever; the fear that the torn border of an opened letter may be something forbidden that no one ought to see, something indescribably precious for which no place in the room is secure enough; the fear that if I fell asleep I might swallow the piece of coal lying in front of the stove; the fear that some number may begin to grow in my brain until there is no more room for it inside me; the fear that it may be granite I am lying on, grey granite; the fear that I may shout, and that people may come running to my door and finally break it open; the fear that I may betray myself and tell all that I dread; and the fear that I might not be able to say anything, because everything is beyond utterance—and the other fears . . . the fears.

Exaggerated feelings usually are not found in schizophrenic patients beyond the early stages of the disease. If they are, they should raise questions as to whether schizophrenia is the correct diagnosis. It is the *retention* of such feelings and emotions which is the single sharpest dividing line between schizophrenia and manic-depressive illness (see chapter 3). If the person retains exaggerated feelings to a prominent degree beyond the early stages of the disease, it is much more likely that the correct diagnosis will turn out to be manic-depressive illness.

The most characteristic changes in emotions in schizophrenia are inappropriate emotions or flattened emotions. It is an unusual patient who does not have one or the other—and sometimes both—by the time the disease is full blown.

Inappropriate emotions are to be expected in light of the previous analogy of the telephone operator at the switchboard. Just as he/she hooks up the wrong thoughts with incoming stimuli, so she also hooks up wrong emotions. The incoming call may carry sad news but she hooks it up with mirth and the patient laughs. In other instances a patient responds with an inappropriate emotion because of the other things going on in his/her head which cause laughter.

> Half the time I am talking about one thing and thinking about half a dozen other things at the same time. It must look queer to people when I laugh about something that has got nothing to do with what I am talking about, but they don't know what's going on inside and how much of it is running round in my head. You see I might be talking about something quite serious to you and other things come into my head at the same time that are funny and this makes me laugh. If I could only concentrate on the one thing at the one time I wouldn't look half so silly.

These inappropriate emotions produce one of the most dramatic aspects of the disease—the victim suddenly breaking out in cackling laughter for no apparent reason. It is a common sight in mental hospitals, and one familiar to those who have worked or lived with people with this disease.

The flattening of emotions may be subtle in the earlier stages of the disease. Chapman claims that "one of the earliest changes in schizophrenic experience involves impairment in the process of empathy with other people." The schizophrenic person loses the ability to put him/herself in the other person's place or to feel what the other person is feeling. As the disease progresses this flattening or blunting of the emotions may become more prominent: "During my first illness I did not feel the emotions of anger, rage, or indignation to nearly as great an extent as I would have normally. Attitudes of dislike, estrangement, and fear predominated."

Emotions may become detached altogether from specific objects, leaving the victim with a void, as poignantly described by this patient:

> Instead of wishing to do things, they are done by something that seems mechanical and frightening, because it is able to do things and yet unable to want to or not to want to. All the constructive healing parts that could

be used healthily and slowly to mend an aching torment have left, and the feeling that should dwell within a person is outside, longing to come back and yet having taken with it the power to return. Out and in are probably not good terms, though, for they are too black and white and it is more like gray. It is like a constant sliding and shifting that slips away in a jelly-like fashion, leaving nothing substantial and yet enough to be tasted.

And Michael Wechsler summarized it neatly in a statement to his father: "I wish I could wake up feeling really bad—it would be better than feeling nothing."

In the advanced stage of flattening of the emotions there appear to be none left at all. This does not happen frequently, but when it does it is an unforgettable experience for those who interact with the victims. I have two such patients in whom I am unable to elicit *any* emotion whatsoever under any circumstances. They are polite, at times stubborn, but never happy or sad. It is uncannily like interacting with a robot. One of these patients set fire to his house, then sat down placidly to watch TV. When it was called to his attention that the house was on fire he got up calmly and went outside. Clearly the brain damage in these cases has seriously affected the centers mediating emotional response. Fortunately most persons with schizophrenia do not have such complete damage to this area of the brain.

Often associated with a flattening of emotions are apathy, slowness of movement, underactivity, lack of drive, and a paucity (usually called poverty) of thought and speech. The composite picture is frequently seen in schizophrenic patients who have been sick for many years. They appear to be desireless, apathetic, seeking nothing, wanting nothing. It is as if their will had eroded: and indeed something like that probably does happen as part of the disease process.

It is fashionable nowadays to believe that much of the flattening of emotions and apathy common in patients with schizophrenia are side effects of the drugs used to treat the disease. In fact there is only a little truth to this. Many of the drugs used to treat schizophrenia do have a calming or sedative effect (see chapter 6). Most of the flattening of emotions and weakening of the will, however, are products of the disease itself and not of the drug effects. This can easily be proved by reviewing descriptions of schizophrenic patients in the literature prior to the introduction of these drugs. Emotional flattening and apathy are just as prominent in those early descriptions as they are today.

CHANGES IN BEHAVIOR

Changes in behavior are usually secondary rather than primary symptoms of schizophrenia; that is, the behaviors shown by persons with this illness are most often a response to other things occurring in their brains. For example, if the person with schizophrenia is beset by overacuteness of the senses and an inability to synthesize incoming stimuli, it makes perfect sense for him/her to withdraw into a corner. Many of the other behaviors seen in this disease can be similarly and logically explained.

Withdrawing, remaining quietly in one place for long periods, and immobility are all common behaviors in this illness. The extreme versions of such behaviors are catatonia, where the person remains rigidly fixed in one position for long periods of time, and mutism, where the person does not speak at all. Catatonia and mutism are part of a continuum that includes the less blatant forms of withdrawal and immobility so commonly seen in schizophrenic persons.

A schizophrenic may withdraw and remain silent for any one of a number of reasons. Sometimes this occurs when the person becomes lost in deep thought:

> When I am walking along the street it comes on me. I start to think deeply and I start to go into a sort of trance. I think so deeply that I almost get out of this world. Then you get frightened that you are going to get into a jam and lose yourself. That's when I get worried and excited.

Or it may be adopted in order to slow down the incoming sensory stimuli so the brain can sort them out:

> I don't like moving fast. I feel there would be a breakup if I went too quick. I can only stand that a short time and then I have to stop. If I carried on I wouldn't be aware of things as they really are. I would just be aware of the sound and noise and the movements. Everything would be a jumbled mass. I have found that I can stop this happening by going completely still and motionless. When I do that, things are easier to take in.

> Everything is all right when I stop. If I move, everything I see keeps changing, everything I'm looking at gets broken up and I stop to put it together again.

Unexpected sensory stimuli can also result in a slowing.

> I get stuck, almost as if I am paralysed at times. It may only last for a minute or two but it's a bit frightening. It seems to happen even when something unexpected takes place, especially if there's a lot of noise that comes on suddenly. Say I am walking across the floor and someone suddenly switches on the wireless: the music seems to stop me in my tracks, and sometimes I freeze like that for a minute or two.

> My responses are too slow. Things happen too quickly. There's too much to take in and I try to take in everything. Things happen but I don't respond. When something happens quickly or unexpectedly it stuns me like a shock.

> I just get stuck. I've got to be prepared and ready for such things. Nothing must come upon me too quickly.

The movements may also be slowed so as to allow them to be integrated into a whole in exactly the same way that visual and auditory stimuli may need to be integrated.

> I am not sure of my own movements any more. It's very hard to describe this but at times I am not sure about even simple actions like sitting down. It's not so much thinking out what to do, it's the doing of it that sticks me. . . . I found recently that I was thinking of myself doing things before I would do them. If I am going to sit down, for example, I have got to think of myself and almost see myself sitting down before I do it. It's the same with other things like washing, eating, and even dressing—things that I have done at one time without even bothering or thinking about at all. . . . All this makes me move much slower now. I take more time to do things because I am always conscious of what I am doing. If I could just stop noticing what I am doing, I would get things done a lot faster.

Withdrawal and mutism may also be a defense the individual assumes to get away from the horrors of other symptoms, as is illustrated by Renée:

> As a matter of fact, these "things" weren't doing anything special; they didn't speak, nor attack me directly. It was their very presence that made me complain. I saw things, smooth as metal, so cut off, so detached from each other, so illuminated and tense that they filled me with terror. When, for example, I looked at a chair or a jug, I thought not of their use or function —a jug not as something to hold water and milk, a chair not as something to sit in—but as having lost their names, their functions and meanings; they became "things" and began to take on life, to exist. . . . When I protested, "Things are tricking me; I am afraid," and people asked specifically, "Do you see the jug and the chair as alive?" I answered, "Yes, they are alive." And they, the doctors too, thought I saw these things as humans whom I heard speak. But it was not that. Their life consisted uniquely in the fact that they were there, in their existence itself. To flee from them I hid my head in my hands or stood in a corner. I lived through a period of intense suffering. Everything was alive, defied me. Outside in the street people were struck mad, moved around without reason, encountered each other and things which had become more real than they.

Other unusual behaviors are also found in persons with schizophrenia. Ritualistic behaviors are not uncommon. Some patients repeatedly walk in circles, and I have one who walks through all doors backwards. There are reasons why they do such things, as explained by this woman who felt compelled to beat eggs a certain way when making a cake:

> As the work progressed, a change came. The ingredients of the cake began to have a special meaning. The process became a ritual. At certain stages the

stirring must be counter-clockwise; at another time it was necessary to stand up and beat the batter toward the east; the egg whites must be folded in from the left to the right; for each thing that had to be done there were complicated reasons. I recognized that these were new, unfamiliar, and unexpected, but did not question them. They carried a finality that was effective. Each compelling impulse was accompanied by an equally compelling explanation.

Another example of ritualistic behavior is the following:

The state of indifference reigning until now was abruptly replaced by inner and outer agitation. At first I felt obliged to get up and walk; it was impossible to stay in bed. Singing a requiem without pause, I marched three steps forward and three steps back, an automatism that wearied me exceedingly and which I wished someone would help me break. I could not do it alone, for I felt forced to make these steps and if I stopped from exhaustion, even for a moment, I felt guilty again. Moreover, when any behavior became automatic, I felt guilty in interrupting it. But no one could believe that I wanted to stop, for as soon as they made me give up some stereotyped procedure, I began anew.

Certain gestures may be repeated often, for reasons which are quite logical to the person doing them but appear bizarre to the onlooker. One patient shook his head rhythmically from side to side to try and shake the excess thoughts out of his mind. Another massaged his head "to help to clear it" of unwanted thoughts.

Specific postures may also be adopted by persons with schizophrenia. One of my patients marches endlessly up and down the sidewalk with his left hand placed awkwardly on his left shoulder. It appears to be uncomfortable but he invariably returns to it for reasons I have not been able to ascertain. Another posture was described by Perceval:

There were two or three other delusions I laboured under of which I hardly recollect how I was cured—one in particular, that I was to lean on the back of my head and on my feet in bed, and twist my neck by throwing my body with a jerk from side to side. I fancy that I never attempted this with sincerity, because I feared to break my neck.

Occasionally a person with schizophrenia will repeat like a parrot whatever is said to him/her. In psychiatric language this is called echolalia. Chapman believes that repeating the words probably is useful to the patient because it allows time to absorb and synthesize what was said. Much rarer is the occurrence of behavior which is parroted, called echopraxia. When it occurs it may be the consequence of a dissolution of boundaries of the self so that the schizophrenic person does not know where his/her body leaves off and where the body of the other person begins.

Another form of behavioral abnormality found very commonly in schizophrenia is the occurrence of clumsiness and awkwardness in voluntary movements. One study found such movements "in virtually all cases of conservatively defined schizophrenia" and concluded that they were consequences of the disease process and not of the medication being taken by the patients. Repetitious movements are also found, as are tics, tremors, tongue movements, and sucking movements. It is the vogue to attribute all such behavioral abnormalities in schizophrenia to the side effects of medication. In fact similar abnormalities were clearly described in patients in the years prior to the use of medication and so are, at least in some cases, another manifestation of the disease process (this will be discussed in greater detail in chapter 6). Even subtle body movements like eye blinking may be affected in schizophrenia. Some patients with the disease blink much less often than normal people. Drugs can account for some of this decrease but not for all of it. Balzac noted it in a patient in the early years of the nineteenth century: "[He] stood, just as I now saw him, day and night, with fixed eyes, never raising or lowering the lids, as others do."

Most worrisome to friends and relatives of schizophrenic patients, for obvious reasons, are socially inappropriate behaviors. Fortunately most schizophrenic patients who act inappropriately on hospital wards usually act quite appropriately when taken out of the hospital on trips. It is always impressive to see patients from even the most regressed hospital wards go to public places; they are usually more distinguishable by their dress (characteristically poorly fitting) than by their behavior. A small number of schizophrenic patients are so ill that they continue inappropriate behaviors (such as random urination, open masturbation, spitting on others) even in public, but such patients are comparatively rare. Some—but not all—of them can be improved by proper medication or conditioning techniques.

Self-mutilation is an extreme form of inappropriate behavior that occurs rarely, though dramatically. It may take a variety of forms. One of my patients tried twice to cut off his penis with a piece of glass when he was very ill. Voices had told him to do it to atone for his sins. Another patient went to Sears, purchased a chain saw, then calmly took it to the women's room and cut off her leg; she too had been told to do it by voices. Such cases are very uncommon, but they become notorious (and often are highly publicized) because of their obvious drama. Patients like these usually give advance warning of their actions, and if they are being regularly followed and properly medicated the occurrence of such episodes should be reduced to almost zero. Other forms of undesirable behavior, including suicide and homicide, will be discussed in chapter 8.

It should always be remembered that the behavior of schizophrenic persons is internally logical and rational; they do things for reasons which, given their disordered senses and thinking, make sense *to them*. To the outside observer the behavior may appear irrational, "crazy," "mad," the very hallmark of the disease. To the schizophrenic person, however, there is nothing "crazy" or "mad" about it at all. Here, for example, is an account of a schizophrenic woman who broke two pairs of glasses worn by her nurses, an action which must have seemed inexplicable ("crazy") to those who observed it.

> My feelings about excessive light and truth were shown in ideas I had about glasses. I was afraid of people who wore glasses, and thought that I was being deliberately persecuted by doctors and nurses who refracted an excessive amount of light into my eyes by wearing glasses. At the same time glasses symbolized false or literary vision, a barrier between the individual and the direct apprehension of life. I myself normally wear glasses (slightly tinted, as my eyes are normally somewhat oversensitive to light). I grabbed and broke two pairs of glasses worn by nurses.

Similarly Daniel P. Schreber, in the autobiographical account of his illness, describes sleeping with his feet out the window and clinging to icy trees with his hands until they were almost frozen in order to accomplish an important goal—such exposure to cold was the only way he could successfully divert the "rays" that afflicted him away from his head.

This same point can be made about everything a schizophrenic person says and does. It is "crazy" only to the outsider who sits on the sidelines and observes from afar. To someone who will take the time to listen, a schizophrenic is not "crazy" at all if by "crazy" one means irrational. The "craziness" has its roots in the disordered brain function that produces erroneous sensory data and disordered thinking. Given the disordered brain function as a starting point, many schizophrenic persons are heroic in their attempts to keep a mental equilibrium. And the proper response of those who care about the unfortunate persons with this disease is patience and understanding. Perhaps nowhere is this better illustrated than by Balzac's heroine in *Louis Lambert*, a young woman who married a man who developed schizophrenia. She then dedicates her life to caring for him:

> "No doubt Louis appears to be 'insane,'" she said, "but he is not so, if the word insanity is applied only to those whose brain, from unknown causes, becomes vitiated, and who are, therefore, unable to give a reason for their acts. The equilibrium of my husband's mind is perfect. If he does not recognize you corporeally, do not think that he has not seen you. He is able to disengage his body and to see us under another form, I know not of what nature. When he speaks, he says marvellous things. Only, in fact often, he completes in speech an idea begun in the silence of his mind, or else he begins a proposition in words and finishes it mentally. To other men he must appear insane; to me, who lives in his thought, all his ideas are lucid. I follow the path of his mind; and though I cannot understand many of its turnings and digressions, I nevertheless reach the end with him. Does it not often happen

that while thinking of some trifling matter, we are drawn into serious
thought by the gradual unfolding of ideas and recollections? Often, after
speaking of some frivolous thing, the accidental point of departure for rapid
meditation, a thinker forgets, or neglects to mention the abstract links which
have led him to his conclusions, and takes up in speech only the last rings
in the chain of reflections. Common minds to whom this quickness of mental
vision is unknown, and who are ignorant of the inward travail of the soul,
laugh at dreamers and call them madmen if they are given to such forgetful-
ness of connecting thoughts. Louis is always so; he wings his way through
the spaces of thought with the agility of a swallow; yet I can follow him in
all his circlings. That is the history of his so-called madness."

Such dedication and understanding, unachievable except in fiction, is a worthy
ideal. It exists to some degree in many families with schizophrenic members
and among some nursing staff who must care for such individuals on the wards
of mental hospitals. As Louis Lambert's wife illustrates, compassion follows
understanding. It is therefore incumbent on us to understand as best we can;
the burden of disease will become lighter for all.

3

WHAT SCHIZOPHRENIA IS
AND WHAT IT IS NOT

For me, madness was definitely not a condition of illness; I did
not believe that I was ill. It was rather a country, opposed to
Reality, where reigned an implacable light, blinding, leaving no
place for shadow. . . . And I—I am lost in it, isolated, cold,
stripped, purposeless under the light. A wall of brass separates
me from everybody and everything. In the midst of desolation,
in indescribable distress, in absolute solitude, I am terrifyingly
alone; no one comes to help me. This was it; *this was madness.*
Marguerite Sechehaye, *Autobiography of a*
Schizophrenic Girl.

The definition of most diseases of mankind has been accomplished. We can
define typhoid fever by the presence of the bacteria which cause it, kidney
failure by a rise in certain chemicals in the blood, and cancers by the appearance of the cells under the microscope. In almost all diseases there is something
which can be seen or measured, and this can be used to define the disease and
separate it from nondisease states.

Not so with schizophrenia! To date we have no single thing which can be
measured and from which we can then say: Yes, that is schizophrenia. Because
of this, the definition of the disease is a source of great confusion and debate.
This confusion is exacerbated because of the likelihood that schizophrenia is
more than one disease entity.

Since we do not yet have anything which can be reliably measured to help
define schizophrenia, we are left only with its symptoms. These may be misleading, however, for different diseases may cause the same symptoms. For
example, a pain in the abdomen is a symptom, but the diseases which may
cause this symptom number well over one hundred. Thus to use symptoms to
define diseases is risky. Such is the state of the art with schizophrenia; yet
precise diagnosis is of utmost importance. It will both determine the appropriate treatment for the patient and provide the patient and family with an
informed prognosis. It also makes research on the disease easier because it will
allow researchers to be certain that they are talking about the same thing.

DEFINING SCHIZOPHRENIA

Although there is no single symptom that is found only in schizophrenia, there are several that are found very uncommonly in diseases other than schizophrenia. When these are present they should elevate the index of suspicion considerably. Bleuler, for example, believed that loosening of associations in the thinking process was central to the disease. More recently, Kurt Schneider, a German psychiatrist, proposed a list of symptoms which he called "first rank" symptoms, meaning that when one or more of them are present they point strongly toward schizophrenia as the diagnosis. This is his list:

1. Auditory hallucinations in which the voices speak one's thoughts aloud
2. Auditory hallucinations with two voices arguing
3. Auditory hallucinations with the voices commenting on one's actions
4. Hallucinations of touch when the bodily sensation is imposed by some external agency
5. Withdrawal of thoughts from one's mind
6. Insertion of thoughts into one's mind by others
7. Believing one's thoughts are being broadcast to others, as by radio or television
8. Insertion by others of feelings into one's mind
9. Insertion by others of irresistible impulses into one's mind
10. Feeling that all one's actions are under the control of others, like an automaton
11. Delusions of perception, as when one is certain that a normal remark has a secret meaning for oneself

These symptoms are commonly used in European countries as grounds for the diagnosis of schizophrenia, although less so in the United States. Studies have shown that at least three-quarters of schizophrenic patients have one or more of these symptoms. However, they cannot be considered as definitive for the disease because they are also found in at least one-quarter of patients with manic-depressive illness.

Until recently, the term "schizophrenia" was used much more loosely and broadly in the United States than in most European countries. In fact the only other country in the world where schizophrenia was diagnosed just as loosely was in the Soviet Union, where it has been abused as a label to discredit and stigmatize opponents of the government.

American psychiatry took a major step forward in 1980 when it adopted a revised system of diagnosis and nomenclature and issued it in the third edition of the *Diagnostic and Statistical Manual of Mental Disorders,* usually simply referred to as *DSM-III.* Under this system a diagnosis of schizophrenia should only be made when the following criteria have been fulfilled:

1. Symptoms of illness have been present for at least six months
2. There has been some deterioration of functioning from previous levels in such areas as work skills, social relations, and self-care
3. The disease began before age 45
4. The disease symptoms do not suggest organic mental disorders or mental retardation
5. The disease symptoms do not suggest manic-depressive illness (see page 52)
6. At least one of the following symptoms is present:
   a. Bizarre delusions where the content is patently absurd and has no possible basis in fact, such as delusions of being controlled, thought insertion, thought withdrawal, and thought broadcasting
   b. Delusions of a grandiose, religious, nihilistic, or somatic nature if ideas of persecution or jealousy are absent
   c. Delusions of persecution or jealous content if accompanied by hallucinations of any type
   d. Auditory hallucinations in which a voice comments on the person's behavior or thoughts or two or more voices converse with each other
   e. Auditory hallucinations heard on several occasions with more than one or two words and having no apparent relation to depression or elation
   f. Marked loosening of associations, markedly illogical thinking, incoherence, or marked poverty of speech if associated with either blunted or inappropriate affect, delusions, hallucinations, catatonia, or grossly disorganized behavior

These criteria for diagnosing schizophrenia are achieving wide acceptance in the United States and may be utilized by families who are seeking a definition of the disease. If these criteria are not met, the diagnosis of schizophrenia should not be made.

Requiring that symptoms be present for at least six months before schizophrenia can be diagnosed is a sharp departure from traditional American practice. It is a useful advance, however, for schizophrenia is a serious diagnosis and should not be applied indiscriminately to anyone who has any schizophreniclike symptom, however brief, as happened frequently in the past. For persons with schizophreniclike symptoms of less than six months duration, the *DSM-III* recommends the use of schizophreniform disorder as a diagnosis. If the duration is less than two weeks the diagnosis of brief reactive psychosis (see page 000) should be used.

Although the new *DSM-III* criteria will be valuable in clarifying the diagnosis of schizophrenia, it will not solve all the problems. Diagnosis remains based on the psychiatrist's subjective evaluation of patients' behavior and what patients say they are experiencing. What is clearly needed, and may be available before many years, are objective measures for diagnosis, such as laboratory tests of blood and cerebrospinal fluid. Until that time the diagnosis of schizophrenia will remain a complicated matter requiring skilled clinical judgment.

A highly publicized experiment carried out by Dr. David L. Rosenhan, a psychologist at Stanford University, in 1973 illustrates some of the ongoing diagnostic problems. Rosenhan had volunteers go to psychiatric hospitals seeking admission and claiming to be hearing voices which had lasted for three weeks. Auditory hallucinations of any kind are unquestionably important and common symptoms of schizophrenia, with the majority of patients experiencing them at some point in the course of their illness. They are so important as symptoms that most psychiatrists take their presence as an indication of schizophrenia until proven otherwise. Thus it should not have been surprising that all the volunteers were admitted as genuine patients. Rosenhan used this study to mock psychiatrists and their ability to diagnose patients, but this is erroneous. It would have been much *more* disturbing if these volunteers, who said they were being greatly troubled by the voices, had *not* been admitted for further investigation. Auditory hallucinations are to schizophrenia what abdominal pain is to appendicitis or vomiting blood is to a peptic ulcer. They are all danger signs suggesting that more definitive studies need to be done. Dr. Seymour Kety illustrates the fallacy of the Rosenhan study nicely:

> If I were to drink a quart of blood and, concealing what I had done, come to the emergency room of any hospital vomiting blood, the behavior of the staff would be quite predictable. If they labeled and treated me as having a bleeding ulcer, I doubt that I could argue convincingly that medical science does not know how to diagnose that condition.

SCHIZOPHRENIC SUBTYPES AND PARANOID DISORDERS

During the last half of the nineteenth century different subtypes of what we now call schizophrenia were described as separate diseases. Thus paranoid psychosis was characterized in 1868, hebephrenia in 1871, and catatonia in 1874. These three were grouped together in 1896 by Emil Kraepelin and called dementia praecox (dementia of early life). Bleuler changed the name to schizophrenia in 1911 and added the simple schizophrenia subtype as well.

Since that time these subtypes of schizophrenia have continued to be widely used. Their differentiation is based exclusively on the symptoms of the illness. Thus paranoid schizophrenia is characterized by delusions and/or hallucinations with a predominantly persecutory or, less commonly, a grandiose content. Hebephrenic schizophrenia, called the "disorganized type" in the *DSM-III* nomenclature, has as its predominant symptoms inappropriate emotions, extreme social impairment, and frequently disorganized thinking; well-developed delusions are usually absent. Catatonic schizophrenia is diagnosed when the outstanding features of the disease are behavioral disturbances, such as posturing, rigidity, stupor, and often mutism. And simple schizophrenia, no longer included as a separate entity under *DSM-III,* is characterized by an insidious loss of interest and initiative, withdrawal, blunting of emotions, and the absence of delusions or hallucinations.

The validity and utility of these subtypes is very questionable despite their widespread usage. Few patients fall cleanly into one subtype or another, with most having some mix of symptoms. Of greater concern is the fact that persons with schizophrenia often show a shift in their symptoms over time, so that initially the person may appear to be a catatonic subtype but a few years later may have symptoms of a hebephrenic nature. Even the old psychiatric axiom, "once a paranoid always a paranoid," has been found not to hold up; I have seen many patients who present initially classic paranoid schizophrenia symptoms and five years later may have a quite different constellation of symptoms. For these reasons there has been an increasing tendency among psychiatrists in recent years to diagnose most patients as having the "undifferentiated type," which simply means that their symptoms are mixed, and to rely less on the traditional four-part division.

Paranoid schizophrenia presents special diagnostic problems because it is one end of the spectrum of a common personality type. Paranoid personalities are found in all walks of life and are known for being suspicious, mistrusting, guarded, quick to take offense, and emotionally distant. The other end of the spectrum is the full-blown paranoid schizophrenic with delusions and hallucinations of persecution. Between these two poles, however, can be found a continuum of individuals with more or less disabling paranoid personality traits. The architects of *DSM-III* chose to restrict the diagnosis of paranoid schizophrenia only to those individuals who had the fully developed disease and to classify less severely disabled paranoid individuals as a paranoid disorder, paranoia, or a paranoid personality disorder. Thus a patient with fixed delusions of persecution or jealousy without other symptoms of schizophrenia should not technically be classified as schizophrenic under the new criteria.

There is also a belief among some researchers that paranoid schizophrenia and its related disorders are a separate disease entity altogether and probably have causes different from the larger group of schizophrenias. Such researchers point to genetic studies suggesting that paranoid schizophrenics are more likely to occur within the same family than are other types of schizophrenics and to biochemical studies which found an increase in some brain chemicals in paranoid schizophrenics but not in other types. This research area remains completely unresolved, and for the time being paranoid schizophrenia should continue to be viewed as a legitimate variant of schizophrenia.

Another method of classifying schizophrenia is that which is in use in the Soviet Union. Rather than utilizing the symptoms of the disease, this classification focuses on its course. Thus Soviet psychiatrists divide schizophrenia into a periodic type in which the person has attacks of the disease but recovers from each one; a "shiftlike" type in which the person recovers some but not complete function; and a continuous type in which the person has a steady downhill course. Each of these types is in turn divided into subtypes. Because this method of classification can only be utilized retrospectively with any accuracy, it has not proven any more useful than the traditional classification based on symptoms and its use has not become widespread elsewhere.

GOOD OUTCOME AND POOR OUTCOME GROUPS

There is one method of subtyping schizophrenia which *has* proven useful. It has been known for years that many persons diagnosed with schizophrenia recover much, or even all, of their mental function and lead relatively normal lives. This fact is contrary to the widespread stereotype of schizophrenia as a hopeless disease from which nobody recovers. This stereotype is wrong. Even if only those cases of schizophrenia that require initial hospitalization are followed over time, it will be found that many of them recover most of their mental function. This will be discussed more fully in chapter 4.

The knowledge that many patients with schizophrenia recover led psychiatrists to look at their data to see if this would enable them to predict, at the time of the original illness, which patients would recover. The result of these efforts has been a series of predictive factors each of which, taken by itself, has limited usefulness, but which taken together may be very useful. From this a subtyping of schizophrenia into good outcome (good prognosis) and poor outcome (poor prognosis) has emerged and is becoming widely used. It is probably the most valid way to classify the disease which has been found to date.

The factors which are included in determining whether the person fits the good outcome or the poor outcome group are:

1. *History of adjustment prior to onset of illness:* Schizophrenic patients who are more likely to have a good outcome are those who were considered to be relatively normal prior to getting sick. Thus, if as children they were able to make friends with others, did not have major problems with delinquency and achieved success levels in school reasonable for their intelligence level, their outcome is likely to be good. Conversely, if they are described by relatives as "always a strange child," had major problems in school or with their peers,

were considered delinquent, or were very withdrawn, they are more likely to fall into the poor outcome group.

2. *Family history:* Patients with the best outcome are those with no history of schizophrenic relatives. The more close relatives who have schizophrenia, the poorer the outcome becomes. If there is a history of depression or manic-depressive psychosis in the family, the person is likely to have a good outcome. Thus a good outcome is suggested by a family history with no mental disease or only depression and/or manic-depressive illness. A poor outcome is suggested by a family history of schizophrenia.

3. *Age of onset:* In general, the younger the age at which schizophrenia develops, the poorer the outcome. A person who first is diagnosed with schizophrenia at age 15 is more likely to have a poorer outcome than a person with the onset at age 25. Persons who are first diagnosed with schizophrenia in older age groups, especially over age 30, are likely to fall into the good outcome group.

4. *Suddenness of onset:* This is an important predictor of recovery, with the best outcomes occurring in those patients whose onset is most sudden. A relative who describes the gradual onset of the person's symptoms over a period of many months is painting a bleak picture, for it is much more likely that the person will fall into the poor outcome group. Conversely, as a practicing psychiatrist I am very happy when a relative tells me that "John was completely normal up until about a month ago," for I know that such a history bodes well for the future.

5. *Precipitating events:* These are very difficult to evaluate and therefore less reliable as predictors. The reason is that during the time of life when most schizophrenic persons become ill for the first time (ages 15 to 25), there is a great deal—much of it stressful—happening in their lives. Changing girl-friends and boyfriends, separations and divorces, school failures and new jobs, vocational plans, the death of parents, and existential crises, all flow naturally through these years. Ask anyone in the 15 to 25 age range on any given day what is going on in his/her life that is important and you will probably get a long list in answer. If, however, there have been major life events immediately preceding the schizophrenic breakdown, this points toward a good outcome. The absence of such precipitating factors signals the greater likelihood of a poor outcome.

6. *Clinical symptoms:* The symptoms of the person during his/her initial breakdown are often suggestive of the eventual outcome of the disease and can be used as predictive factors. Some of the more important of these are:

    a. Catatonic symptoms are a good sign.

    b. Paranoid symptoms are a good sign.

    c. The presence of depression or other emotions is a good sign. If the person is diagnosed as "schizoaffective" (see page 53), that too is a good sign. Conversely, emotions which are flattened or absent are signs of a poor outcome.

d. The presence of confusion (e.g., "I don't understand what is happening to me") is a good sign.

e. The presence of a marked thinking disorder, withdrawal, apathy, or indifference is in each instance a sign of a poor outcome.

It should be emphasized again that each of these factors *by itself* has limited predictive value. It is only when they are all put together that an overall prognosis can be assigned. Many patients will, of course, have a mixture of good and poor outcome signs, whereas others will fall quite clearly into one category or the other.

It should also be remembered that all predictions are only statistical assertions of likelihood. There is nothing in the least binding about them. All of us who regularly care for patients with schizophrenia have seen enough exceptions to these guidelines to make us humble about any predictions. Thus I have seen a schizophrenic patient with a normal childhood, no family history for the disease, a rapid onset at age 22, clear precipitating events, and initial catatonic symptoms who never recovered from even his initial illness and whose outcome is poor. More optimistically, I have seen patients with virtually every poor prognostic sign go on to almost complete recovery.

The ultimate subtyping of schizophrenia, of course, will come about when its precise causes are known. Presumably there will be different treatments for the different causes so the ability to diagnose and classify correctly will be important. It is possible, for example, that there are different causative agents for good outcome and poor outcome schizophrenia. Until these problems are clarified, both mental health professionals and families should retain open minds on the best way to subtype this disease.

MANIC-DEPRESSIVE ILLNESS AND SCHIZOAFFECTIVE DISORDER

Manic-depressive illness, referred to as bipolar disorder under *DSM-III*, is a disease which is easily recognizable in its fully developed form. In the manic phase the mood of the victims is euphoric or irritable and they exhibit some combination of decreased need for sleep, increased activity, talkativeness, rapid thoughts (which when exaggerated is called a flight of ideas), a short attention span, and inflated self-esteem. They may have delusions (e.g., a belief that they are President) or hallucinations, but these are congruent with the mood of inflated self-worth. In the depressed phase their mood is sad or irritable, they may have difficulty sleeping or sleep too much, have a poor appetite and weight loss, fatigue, feelings of worthlessness or guilt, and lose interest in their usual activities; delusions or hallucinations when present are congruent with the depressed mood (e.g., the person believes he/she will be punished for sins).

Persons with manic-depressive illness usually have periodic episodes of either mania or depression. It is the rare individual who cycles from mania to depression and back to mania, as is the popular stereotype of the disease; rather, most may have several episodes of either mania or depression. The attacks may occur only every few years, and between attacks the person returns to normality. Many highly responsible and successful people have suffered from manic-depressive illness but have been able to pursue their careers, between episodes of illness and by taking maintenance medication (usually lithium) to control the episodes.

In its fully developed form, then, manic-depressive illness is relatively easy to differentiate from schizophrenia. The clinical picture is dominated by the patient's mood (either elevated or depressed), and when delusions or hallucinations are present they coincide with the mood. Bizarre delusions, hallucinations unrelated to mood, blunted or inappropriate affect, and thinking disorders are usually absent. Manic-depressive illness is a disorder of *mood* whereas schizophrenia is a disorder of *thought,* to oversimplify the difference.

Manic-depressive illness also differs from schizophrenia in several other respects. Returning to normality between episodes of illness is the rule in manic-depressive illness, whereas in schizophrenia it is the exception (see chapter 4). Manic-depressive illness is only one-half to one-third as common as schizophrenia in most population groups; and it tends to occur more frequently in higher socioeconomic groups, in contrast to schizophrenia which occurs more frequently in lower socioeconomic groups (see chapter 10). Moreover, both genetic studies and biochemical research on manic-depressive illness suggest that it is a separate disease entity from schizophrenia.

Unfortunately, many patients have symptoms which place them somewhere on a spectrum between schizophrenia and manic-depressive illness. Most psychiatrists have seen individual patients who fit only one of these disease entities perfectly, but most have also seen patients with a confusing mélange of symptoms of both diseases. Textbooks of psychiatry are written as if patients had one disease or the other and imply that all patients can be placed under one of the two disease categories. It has been facetiously suggested that we need either to insist that patients read the books and choose which disease they wish to have or we need to become more flexible in our psychiatric thinking. I personally have seen patients with virtually every possible combination of schizophrenic and manic-depressive symptoms.

The resolution of this problem to date has been the creation of an intermediate disease category called schizoaffective disorder. Prior to *DSM-III* it was officially included as a subtype of schizophrenia. *DSM-III* classifies it independently and notes that "at the present time there is no consensus on how this category should be defined." Many clinicians and researchers suspect that the problems of most patients in this category are more closely related to manic-depressive illness than they are to schizophrenia, but this issue is far from resolved.

From the point of view of families and relatives of schizophrenic patients all of this would have been thought irrelevant, merely a tempest in a teapot, until recent years. Now, however, such distinctions have important implications both for the projected outcome and for the treatment of such patients. Those who are carefully diagnosed as schizoaffective are more likely to have a good outcome to their illness, especially if they are properly treated. And proper treatment means a trial of lithium, the drug which has been used so successfully to treat manic-depressive illness. Any person with a schizoaffective disorder who has not responded to other treatment deserves a trial of lithium, and relatives of such a patient should continue shopping for a psychiatrist until they find one who uses lithium in such cases. This will be discussed further in chapter 6.

BRIEF REACTIVE PSYCHOSIS

Brief episodes of schizophreniclike symptoms occur occasionally among individuals who are otherwise normal. Characteristically the illness begins suddenly, lasts a few days, and then remits suddenly. The causes of these illnesses are unknown but probably include brief viral infections of the brain (encephalitis), as well as other brain diseases which may mimic schizophrenia. Such illnesses may apparently also be precipitated by overwhelming stress and are seen in some soldiers undergoing enemy fire, inmates in prisons or concentration camps, and in individuals in extreme sensory deprivation situations (e.g., alone in a lifeboat for several days at sea).

The symptoms displayed by such patients may mimic schizophrenia closely, with delusions and hallucinations being prominent; disorders of thinking are much less common. Here is an example of such a patient:

Frank, a 21-year-old Peace Corps volunteer, had only been in Ethiopia for a month. Assigned to a small village with two coworkers, he was having difficulty mastering the language and complained of feeling isolated. One evening he began complaining that the Ethiopians were spying on him. Within twenty-four hours his illness had developed into a full-blown psychosis with delusions of persecution and hallucinations. When seen by a physician, he was hiding under the bed saying that he could hear the Ethiopian army marching down the road to take him and hang him.

At this stage of his illness, based on symptoms alone, Frank looked very much like a schizophrenic. He was removed from his village and hospitalized, treated with drugs, and within one week he was completely well again. Such patients will usually recover whether they are treated with drugs or not and usually do not get sick again.

These patients should not be diagnosed with schizophrenia but rather with brief reactive psychosis. If the illness persists for longer than two weeks but less than six months, it should then be called a schizophreniform disorder. One-third of such cases will recover completely and not become ill again (see chapter 4). The more rapid the onset and the shorter the duration of illness, the more likely the person is to return to full normality and not experience recurrence.

INFANTILE AUTISM AND CHILDHOOD SCHIZOPHRENIA

Infantile autism, first described by Leo Kanner in 1943, is a profound disturbance of early childhood beginning within the first two-and-one-half years. The infant or toddler is noted to have abnormal responses to stimuli, either overreacting or underreacting to sounds and touch. Repetitive movements, such as hand-flapping, rocking, twirling, head-banging, and lip-chewing, are marked, and the child prefers inanimate objects to people. Speech development is very slow and often includes unconnected words and bizarre sounds. The classical picture, then, is of a two-year-old child playing with a water faucet and rocking for hours at a time, avoiding all contact with people and periodically screaming unintelligible phrases when touched or approached. It is a dramatic and unforgettable picture.

Fortunately, infantile autism is uncommon as compared to adult schizophrenia, occurring only one-twentieth as frequently. It differs from adult schizophrenia not only in its age of onset but also in that hallucinations and delusions are unusual in infantile autism and mental retardation frequently accompanies it. It also differs in being four times more common in boys than in girls (in schizophrenia the sexes are afflicted approximately evenly), and occurring much more commonly in higher socioeconomic groups (whereas schizophrenia occurs more commonly in lower socioeconomic groups). The reasons for these differences in occurrence are unknown.

The cause or causes of infantile autism are also unknown, although there is a general consensus that it is a disease of the brain and that it probably begins during pregnancy. One study of the disease found that mothers who give birth to children who become autistic have more bleeding during the middle three months of pregnancy. It is generally believed that the causes of infantile autism and schizophrenia are different and that the two conditions are separate disease entities. Genetic studies showing that cases of infantile autism and schizophrenia do not tend to occur in the same families support this belief.

Childhood schizophrenia is an imprecise term which has been used to encompass all children who develop psychotic symptoms during the period between the autistic group (up to age two-and-one-half) and the adult schizophrenic group (beginning after puberty). Many of these children have other signs of brain dysfunction, such as retardation, seizures, and neurological dysfunction, and so may be diagnosed by one clinician as "childhood schizophrenia with seizures" and by the next clinician as "generalized seizures of childhood with psychosis." The precise incidence of childhood schizophrenia differs according to the diagnostic criteria used, but most researchers estimate its occurrence to be less frequent than infantile autism. Like autism, childhood schizophrenia occurs more commonly in male children, in a ratio of approximately three to one.

In terms of symptoms, childhood schizophrenia looks almost exactly like its adult counterpart, except that paranoid symptoms are rarely seen. Some researchers have claimed that childhood schizophrenia and adult schizophrenia are found in the same families, although others have disputed this. A small number of these children will recover from their psychosis, but the majority continue into adulthood and in later years are indistinguishable from their adult counterparts. A good description of a childhood schizophrenic is provided by Louise Wilson in *This Stranger, My Son.*

SCHIZOPHRENICLIKE SYMPTOMS DUE TO OTHER DISEASES

There are several diseases of the body which can produce symptoms similar to schizophrenia. In most cases there is no ambiguity because the disease is clearly diagnosable; in a few cases, however, there may be some confusion, especially in the early stages of the disease.

Examples of diseases which may produce schizophreniclike symptoms are temporal lobe epilepsy, brain tumors, viral infections of the brain (encephalitis), hypothyroidism, porphyria, syphilis of the brain, trypanosomiasis (in tropical countries), and nutritional deficiencies, such as pellagra. This is an example of schizophreniclike symptoms due to another disease:

> Ruth was an 18-year-old navy nursing aide. Following a flulike illness she developed headaches, began hearing voices talking to her, had feelings of unreality and loss of body boundaries, and became depressed. She slashed her wrists on instruction from the voices and was hospitalized. Her emotions were then noted to be inappropriate, and she had mild

disorders in her thinking. She was alternately treated as a depressive reaction and as a schizophrenic, although neurologists were also asked to see her because of the continuing headaches. She improved slowly over a three-month period and was discharged to be followed as an outpatient. Three months after discharge she died suddenly and without warning during an all-night prayer service. Autopsy revealed a viral infection of the brain which appeared to have been present for several months.

Such cases are unusual in that a correct diagnosis of the underlying disease is usually made prior to death. They happen just often enough, however, to make it mandatory that all patients diagnosed with schizophrenia for the first time have a thorough history taken, a physical examination including neurological examination, and standard laboratory tests. An alert clinician can often spot other diseases masquerading as schizophrenia on the basis of the history alone. A very useful aide for such a task is a recent book by Dr. Robert L. Taylor aimed at nonphysicians, *Mind or Body: Distinguishing Psychological from Organic Disorders.*

SCHIZOPHRENICLIKE SYMPTOMS FOLLOWING CHILDBIRTH

Some degree of depression in mothers following childbirth is relatively common and on occasion may be severe. Much less common, occurring approximately once in every thousand births, are schizophreniclike symptoms which develop in the mother. These usually begin between three and seven days postpartum and may include delusions (e.g., believing her baby is defective or has been kidnapped) or hallucinations (voices telling her to kill the baby). Depression may occur as well, and a schizoaffective diagnosis is frequent. Because of the unpredictability of such patients, the baby is usually separated from the mother until she improves. Treatment with medication usually produces rapid improvement, with resolution of the symptoms in most cases within two weeks. A small percentage of such cases persist and proceed to become a full-blown schizophrenic disorder.

The cause of this disorder is not known. Formerly it was believed that psychological factors, such as the mother's ambivalent feelings toward the baby, were primary. In recent years more attention has been focused on possible biochemical factors, especially the massive hormonal changes which take place following childbirth. Such theories receive added impetus from the observation that some female schizophrenic patients regularly become more symptomatic just prior to or at the time of their menstrual period. Those cases which go on to true schizophrenia may be women who would have become schizophrenic even if they had not become pregnant. Since the onset of schizophrenia occurs most often during the same years in which most childbearing takes place, such a coincidence is occasionally inevitable.

> Mary had just returned from the hospital after delivering her first child, a girl. Within the next three days her husband noted that she was talking strangely and appeared confused. She acknowledged that voices were telling her to kill the baby. Mary was hospitalized, treated with drugs, and completely returned to normal within ten days.

The use of the term "schizophrenia" is not appropriate for illnesses such as this.

CULTURALLY INDUCED OR HYSTERICAL PSYCHOSIS

Occasionally confusion will arise between schizophrenia and culturally induced or hysterical psychosis. This is an altered state of consciousness usually entered into voluntarily by an individual; while in this altered state of consciousness the person may exhibit symptoms which look superficially like schizophrenia. For example, the person may complain of altered bodily sensations and hallucinations and may behave in an excited and irrational manner. In the United States these conditions are seen most commonly in connection with fundamentalistic religious services. In other cultural groups and in other countries these conditions are known by such names as moth craziness (Navajo Indians), windigo (Cree and Ojibwa Indians), zar (Middle East), koro (China), susto (Latin America), latah (Southeast Asia), and amok (worldwide).

> Cecelia led a perfectly normal life except for the monthly all-night worship service at her fundamentalist church. During the service she claimed to hear voices talking to her, often spoke in tongues, and occasionally behaved in a wild and irrational way so that others had to restrain her. Other members of the congregation regarded her with both fear and awe, suspecting that she was possessed by spirits.

People like Cecelia should not be labeled as schizophrenic unless there have been other symptoms of the disease. Occasionally persons who have schizophrenia will be attracted to fundamentalist religious groups or religious cults, however, since such groups often value hearing voices or "speaking in tongues." This will be discussed at greater length in chapter 8.

DRUG ABUSE AND SCHIZOPHRENIA

It is a well-recognized fact that many drugs which are abused for their psychic effects may produce symptoms similar to schizophrenia. Even after ingesting a comparatively mild drug like marijuana the user may experience strange bodily sensations, loss of body boundaries, and paranoid delusions. There is even a subgroup of people who give up using marijuana because it leads to an unpleasant paranoid state after each usage. Stronger drugs, such as LSD and PCP, regularly produce hallucinations (although these are more likely to be visual than auditory), delusions, and disorders of thinking. Occasionally these symptoms become so severe that the person must be hospitalized and, if the history of drug abuse is not known, the person may be diagnosed as schizophrenic by mistake. Amphetamines (speed) in particular are well known for producing symptoms which may look identical to those of schizophrenia.

The question naturally arises whether drug abuse can *cause* schizophrenia. It is a question asked frequently by families and relatives of schizophrenic patients. There is now abundant evidence that chronic and repeated usage of many of the mind-altering drugs can damage the brain, impairing intellectual functions and memory. However, there is no evidence that they cause schizophrenia *per se*.

Why, then, is it so common to see schizophrenia begin after a person has used mind-altering drugs? The answer is probably twofold. First, both drug abuse and the onset of schizophrenia occur in the same age range of the late teens and early twenties. The percentage of people in this age range who have at least smoked a few "joints" is very high. Assuming there is no connection whatsoever between drug abuse and schizophrenia, it would still be expected that a considerable number of people developing schizophrenia would also have tried mind-altering drugs.

Second, and more important, is the common sequence of people developing the early symptoms of schizophrenia and then turning to mind-altering drugs to provide a rationalization for what they are experiencing. Hearing voices for the first time in your life, for example, is a very frightening experience; if you then begin using hashish, PCP, or some similar drug, it provides you with a persuasive reason for hearing the voices. Drug use can put off the uncomfortable confrontation with yourself that tells you something is going wrong—very wrong—with your mind. You are, quite literally, losing it. Drugs, and alcohol as well, may also partially relieve the symptoms. In these cases persons can be said to be medicating themselves.

The families of schizophrenic persons are usually not aware of the earliest symptoms of the disease. Not knowing what their relative is experiencing, all they see is him/her turning to increasingly heavy drug abuse. Three or six months later the person is diagnosed with schizophrenia and the family immediately concludes that it was caused by the drug abuse. Such reasoning also relieves any burden of guilt on their part by making it clear that they had nothing to do with causing it. This may be especially attractive to relatives if they are faced with a psychiatrist who implies that problems of child rearing or problems of family communication contributed to the genesis of the disease.

In these cases relatives will often seize on drug-abuse-causes-schizophrenia as a defense against the psychiatrist.

> Ted was a promising college student who had his life well planned. Midway through his sophomore year he began having episodes of euphoria, strange bodily sensations, and ideas that he had been sent to save the world. His grades dropped sharply, he began going to church every day, and then began using LSD. Prior to that time he had only used marijuana occasionally at parties. His roommate, college authorities, and finally his parents became alarmed about his turn to drugs. Within one month he was admitted to the local hospital with overt schizophrenic symptomatology. His parents believe it was caused by his drug use and have never been persuaded otherwise.

In most such instances, a careful questioning of the schizophrenic patient will establish the existence of early symptoms of the disease prior to his or her turning to significant drug abuse.

MILD SCHIZOPHRENIA AND SCHIZOID PERSONALITY

One of the great unknowns with schizophrenia is whether there are people who have mild cases of the disease. With many other diseases mild cases exist. In diabetes, for example, a person may have a moderately elevated blood sugar causing minor symptoms. Some people had tuberculosis which remained stable for years, causing occasional fever or coughing of blood but little else, and the concept of mild hypertension is well established.

Whether there is or is not such a thing as having mild schizophrenia is completely unknown at this time. Many people have thought that there may be, but there is no evidence to support such a theory. Criminologists in particular have suspected that among the criminal population are many who have experienced some schizophrenic symptoms. Violent juvenile offenders have been said to have more paranoid delusions and hallucinations than would be expected. And Hans Eysenck, a well-known English psychologist, claims:

> Primary psychopathy has often been seen by psychiatrists as a half-way stage to psychosis; could it be that there is a dimension of personality which leads from outright psychosis through psychopathy to normality? In short, the answer seems to be yes.

Some criminal personality characteristics which Eysenck believes may be related to mild schizophrenia are lack of feelings for other people, trouble fitting in, a liking for odd and unusual things, solitariness, and liking to make fools of other people.

Related to such theories are those which claim that certain personality types are really manifestations of cases of mild schizophrenia. The personality types most often cited are the schizoid personality and the schizotypal personality (using *DSM-III* terms). Schizoid individuals are unable to form close personal relationships, are seen as emotionally cold and aloof, and are indifferent to praise, criticism, or the feelings of others. They are usually loners and often work at jobs requiring little or no contact with other people (e.g., forest ranger, night security guard).

Schizotypal personalities usually share the social characteristics of the schizoid personality but in addition have a propensity for odd speech (e.g., vague and unusual use of words), magical thinking (clairvoyance, telepathy), suspiciousness and paranoid ideas, and feelings of unreality. Some such individuals will go on to become frankly schizophrenic months or even years after these personality characteristics have been noted. A link between schizotypal personalities and schizophrenia is also suggested by genetic studies showing more schizophrenia among family members of schizotypal personalities and by the finding that such individuals often improve in functioning when treated with medication.

The problem, of course, is that these personality characteristics are vague and nonspecific. Concepts like "odd speech" and "social isolation" are relative and difficult enough to quantify in cases of full-blown schizophrenia. When they are used to try to define a theoretical group of mildly sick people, only chaos can follow. It also opens the door to potentially great abuse by authorities who would gladly label everybody as schizophrenic who did not agree with prevailing attitudes or government. This has actually occurred in the Soviet Union and is made possible there by the vague and extended use of schizophrenia as a disease concept.

Probably this issue will not be fully settled until we have found some quantitative method of diagnosing schizophrenia more precisely than we can do at present. Until this happens schizophrenia should not be used as a label for people who do not have the full-blown disease. Terms like "borderline schizophrenia," "latent schizophrenia" and "schizotypal schizophrenia" should be explicitly avoided; instead we should continue using the terms which have served for hundreds of years—odd, queer, shy, and eccentric. To do otherwise is pseudoscience, not science.

CREATIVITY AND SCHIZOPHRENIA

An oft-debated question around firesides and pubs is whether there is a relationship between creativity and schizophrenia. John Dryden reflected the views of many people when he wrote three hundred years ago, "Great wits are sure to madmen near allied." Since then we have moved a little closer to a definitive answer to this question.

It is known that creative persons and schizophrenics share many cognitive traits. Both use words and language in unusual ways (the hallmark of a great poet or novelist), both have unusual views of reality (as great artists do), both often utilize unusual thought processes in their deliberations, and both tend to prefer solitude to the company of others. When creative persons are given traditional psychological tests, they manifest more psychopathology than noncreative persons, and creative persons are often viewed as eccentric by their friends. Conversely, when nonparanoid schizophrenics are given traditional tests of creativity they score very high (paranoid schizophrenics do not).

Several surveys have shown that highly creative persons are not themselves more susceptible to schizophrenia. The few who have developed the disease, for example Nijinsky and perhaps Van Gogh, are well known and may simply represent chance occurrence. However, one study has suggested that the immediate relatives of creative persons may be more susceptible to schizophrenia. As a case in point one thinks of Robert Frost, whose aunt, son, and perhaps daughter, all developed schizophrenia. Looking at the problem from the other side, the same study found that the immediate relatives of schizophrenic patients scored higher on tests of creativity than would be expected by chance. Such studies need to be replicated before one can seriously suggest a link between schizophrenia and creativity. If such a link exists, it would most likely be a genetic predisposition to both conditions.

There is one fundamental difference between the creative person and the schizophrenic, of course. The creative person has his/her unusual thought processes under control and can harness them in the creation of a product. The schizophrenic, on the other hand, is at the mercy of disconnected thinking and loose associations which tumble about in cacophonic disarray. The creative person has choices whereas the schizophrenic does not. Until further studies have been done on this question, the definitive relationship between creativity and schizophrenia must remain in the realm of speculation.

4

THE THREE COURSES OF SCHIZOPHRENIA

Being crazy is like one of those nightmares where you try to call
for help and no sound comes out. Or if you call, no one hears
or understands.

Thomas Hennell, *The Witnesses*

When diagnosed with schizophrenia for the first time, a person is faced with
inevitable questions about what will happen next. What are the chances for
complete recovery? Partial recovery? For spending many years in a mental
hospital? Because there was no effective treatment for schizophrenia prior to
the introduction of drugs for it in the 1950s, we had many decades to observe
and record the natural course of the disease. How much that natural course
is being changed by the use of these drugs is currently being debated within
psychiatry.

ONSET

One of the most remarkable things about schizophrenia as a disease is the
predictability of its age of onset. Three-quarters of all cases begin in the
16-to-25 age group, a fact observed by Kraepelin in 1899 which still holds true.
After the age of 30 the onset of the disease becomes uncommon, and after 40
it becomes rare. Many psychiatrists even suspect that schizophrenia which
begins in older age groups is a different disease altogether from that which
begins younger, but there is no evidence to prove this either way.

It has also been observed for over one hundred years that the age of onset
for men who develop schizophrenia is younger than that for women. The age
difference varies in different studies but appears to average five years. Thus in
the 16-to-20 age group there will be more men with the disease, whereas first
admissions in the 25-to-30 age group will be predominantly women. The only
exception to this rule is paranoid schizophrenics, who have an older age of
onset regardless of gender. These are merely statistical assertions, of course,
and any given family may be faced with a 17-year-old young woman with
schizophrenia or a 29-year-old man being diagnosed with it for the first time.

The reasons for the age of onset are not known. Psychoanalytic and psychosocial theoreticians have speculated that the stresses of adolescence and early adulthood are responsible, whereas biologically oriented researchers point to hormonal changes of puberty as triggering the disease process. Several chronic neurological diseases, such as multiple sclerosis and Alzheimer's disease, have onsets in specific age groups and are thought to be caused by viruses with long incubation periods; perhaps schizophrenia will be found to fit this model. The predisposition toward an earlier onset in men can be viewed as yet another manifestation of the known greater vulnerability of men to diseases in general (men *are* the weaker sex biologically) or perhaps as a consequence of female hormones partially protecting women from the disease process.

In this regard it is also of interest that men who develop schizophrenia have a poorer outlook, as a group, than do women. The men are more likely to have typical schizophrenic symptoms, whereas women are more likely to receive a schizoaffective label; men are also more likely to be hospitalized for longer periods of time. Whether this is due to the earlier age of onset in men (the earlier the age of onset, the worse the prognosis) and/or due to a more malignant disease process in men is not known. It too is merely a statistical observation; there are, of course, many men who have recovered from the disease fully and many women who have been severely affected and hospitalized with schizophrenia for most of their lives.

As we have noted before, the earliest stages of schizophrenia are difficult to identify, since many of the feelings and symptoms are merely exaggerations of normal teenage and early adult feelings. Overacuteness of the senses is one of the earliest and commonest symptoms, yet what teenager has not had some such experiences? Moodiness, withdrawal, apathy, loss of interest in personal appearance, perplexity, the belief that people are watching one, preoccupation with one's body, and vagueness in thoughts may all be harbingers of impending schizophrenia, but they may also be just normal manifestations of early adulthood and its accompanying problems. For this reason families should *not* worry about every quirk in their children, but rather should assume they are normal until proven otherwise. This can be particularly difficult for a parent who has already had one child diagnosed with schizophrenia and who is expecting the worst for the younger children, but it is important. A 15-year-old has enough to worry about without being told things like "Don't daydream. That's what your brother did and it got him sick and into the hospital."

When *should* parents begin to worry that something may be wrong? When do the normal psychological vicissitudes of early adulthood cross the line and enter the realm of early symptoms of schizophrenia? The following is a list of some early warning signs (see pages 14–38 for fuller explanations of these signs):

1. Changes in the thought pattern from being coherent and logical to being vague and illogical. The appearance of loose associations is often part of this.
2. The loss of a sense of bodily boundaries in the person.
3. Auditory hallucinations in which another voice is heard definitely and regularly. Families may hear the person talking to the voices when he/she is alone in a room. This should not be confused with the occasional religious peak experience (in which a god talks to them) of highly religious young adults, nor with the harmless habit some people have of talking to themselves for company.
4. Changes in emotions, either marked flattening or grossly inappropriate emotions, in a person who was previously able to express emotions normally.
5. Feelings that other people are inserting thoughts, controlling a person's actions, or trying to persecute him/her in a systematic way.

The appearance of such early warning signs should mobilize the family to seek a professional consultant. Drug abuse as a cause of these symptoms must be ruled out, for, as we have noted, many street drugs commonly used by teenagers and young adults can cause symptoms and feelings identical to those of early schizophrenia. If no drugs are being used in the presence of such symptoms, the family has genuine cause for concern.

POSSIBLE COURSES

Given one hundred persons hospitalized for schizophrenia for the first time, how many of them are likely to be well ten or fifteen years later? How many partially well? How many still sick and in the hospital? This question is of crucial concern to both schizophrenics and their families, for it is on the basis of such odds that plans and life decisions are made. Will they be self-supporting? Able to live on their own? Able to hold a job? Or will they need to live at home? Remain dependent? If so, what will happen after the parents die? The statistical probabilities of outcome will be addressed in this chapter, and suggestions for possible living arrangements for the poor-outcome cases will be given in chapter 7.

The best summary of possible courses of schizophrenia was published by J. H. Stephens. He analyzed twenty-five studies in which schizophrenic patients had all been followed for an average of at least ten years and then assessed as to whether they were "recovered" (completely recovered with no remaining symptoms), "improved" (fewer symptoms but not completely recovered; may require occasional hospitalization) or "unimproved" (symptoms not improved, hospitalized most of the time). Over 4,400 patients were followed up in these studies.

The number of patients rated as "recovered" in these studies averaged 29 percent. In one study it was 66 percent and in another study 70 percent. The differences in percentage recovered were due to differences in the kinds of patients selected for follow-up. If the only patients included in a study were those with indications of poor outcome, then not surprisingly the number recovered was small. On the other hand, if the patients selected were mostly those with acute schizophrenic episodes or brief reactive psychosis, then the percentage recovered achieved a figure of 60 to 70 percent. Based on the patients followed in the twenty-five studies, it seems reasonable to conclude that *one-third* of all patients hospitalized and diagnosed with schizophrenia will be found to be completely recovered when followed up ten years later.

On the other end of the spectrum, the number of patients rated as "unimproved" at the end of ten years averaged 44 percent. However, many of these studies included only the poor outcome patients, and the unimproved rate is strongly influenced by this. When those studies using current American criteria for schizophrenia are examined (for example, Stephens's own study at Johns Hopkins University), then approximately *one-third* of the patients were unimproved.

This leaves the remaining *one-third* in the middle category of improved but not completely recovered. And it supports an axiom commonly voiced among psychiatrists in the United States called the rule of thirds. This rule says that of all people diagnosed and hospitalized with schizophrenia, one-third will get completely well, one-third will get partially well, and one-third will not get well. Such data should be encouraging to families who are devastated when told a family member has schizophrenia and who have accepted the myth that nobody recovers from it. The data should also be sobering to those of us who have the responsibility to find the causes and cures for the unfortunate two-thirds who do not recover completely.

It is also a well-known fact that the more breakdowns or relapses a person with schizophrenia has, the poorer become the chances for complete recovery. Therefore a schizophrenic who has only been hospitalized once or twice and who has been sick for less than two years still has a one-third chance of full recovery. If the patient has been hospitalized more than three times, or if he/she has been sick even intermittently for longer than five years, the chances for full recovery become negligible. It is as if each attack of the disease causes further damage to the brain and leaves more residual scars; and in fact this may well be the case.

Medications have certainly influenced the course of schizophrenia, but it is too early to say exactly how much. At a minimum the drugs have decreased the number of relapses and rehospitalizations; whether this prevents some of the brain damage from occurring is not known. It is most likely that the drugs have improved the functioning of the "improved" middle one-third, allowing more of them to live independently and to hold jobs. This is no small accomplishment. It is less clear whether the drugs have altered the course of the recovered one-third, who would probably have recovered with or without drugs although drugs may well have speeded the process. Nor is it certain yet whether drugs decrease the size of the group who are unimproved on follow-up, although it is likely that they do so, at least modestly. And in addition to probably moving some patients from the unimproved to the improved category, the drugs significantly improve functioning in some remaining unimproved patients. For example, many chronically ill schizophrenic patients, when properly medicated, can be given ground privileges and weekend passes, and taken on trips outside the hospital; whereas without medication they are too acutely disturbed to do any of these things.

Changes in social attitudes and the availability of aftercare facilities also undoubtedly influence the course of schizophrenia. Twenty years ago, when there was no expectation that schizophrenic patients would leave the hospital once they entered, most of them obliged and did not leave. Now there is an expectation that most can leave, and most do, at least for periods of time. The United States is comparatively backward in providing aftercare and rehabilitative facilities for schizophrenic patients (see chapter 7). Scandinavian countries have been more progressive in this regard, but unfortunately to date no study has been done to ascertain whether better aftercare and rehabilitation facilities alter the course and outcome of the disease.

Another factor which may influence the course of schizophrenia and which is tied to social attitudes is institutionalism. Patients who have been hospitalized for a few years become dependent on the institution and are much less likely to leave it. Currently, patients are expected to leave the hospital within a matter of weeks after an episode of schizophrenia, whereas in the past it was often a matter of years. This change should sharply reduce the number of institutionally dependent patients and increase the number who can live in the community. Whether it will actually decrease that one-third who are unimproved, or simply move them from the hospital to a boardinghouse with the same degree of continuing illness, remains to be ascertained.

LATE STAGES OF ILLNESS

For the two-thirds of schizophrenic patients who do not completely recover, the later stages of the disease are quite characteristic. That one-third of patients who are improved have symptoms of their illness intermittently or more subtly, while the third who are unimproved have clearly visible symptoms.

The major changes which occur are a gradual shift over the years from delusions, hallucinations, and overt thinking disorders to increased symptoms of apathy, flattening of emotions, poverty of thought, withdrawal, and loss of interest in things. This chronic state is well described in a standard textbook of psychiatry:

> The patient, living in an institution or outside, has come to an *arrangement with his illness.* He has adapted himself to the world of his morbid ideas with more or less success, from his own point of view and from that of his environment. Compared with the experiences during the acute psychosis, his positive symptoms, such as delusions or hallucinations, have become colorless, repetitive and formalized. They still have power over him but nothing is added and nothing new or unexpected happens. Negative symptoms, thought disorder, passivity, catatonic mannerisms and flattening of affect rule the picture, but even they grow habitual with the patient and appear always in the same inveterate pattern in the individual case. There is a robotlike fixity and petrification of attitude and reactions which are not only due to poverty of ideas but also to a very small choice of modes of behavior. The patient has lost all flexibility, he has no future and his interest in present and past are narrowed and restricted [italics in original].

Behaviorally such patients will often sit all day simply staring into space. Their interest may be engaged briefly in projects or new events, but it soon flags and they return to their bland and vacant staring. The flattening of emotions is often striking, and one has the impression of interacting with an automaton when trying to engage such patients. They are capable of enjoyment but are unable to express it; this becomes clear when we take such patients on trips to new places and then find them referring to the trip weeks later. It takes unusually gifted and dedicated hospital staff and family members to work with such patients over a long period of time without becoming discouraged.

Kraepelin believed that this late stage of schizophrenia was inevitable and so named the disease dementia praecox. By dementia he meant chronically brain-damaged, like the late stages of other neurological conditions. Even Kraepelin, however, acknowledged that the "dementia" of chronic unimproved schizophrenia was different from the dementia of diseases like brain syphilis, Alzheimer's disease, or senile dementia. In schizophrenia intellectual functions, such as intelligence, memory, and orientation, are better retained, and the dementia is more an erosion of emotion and will. Fortunately, Kraepelin was wrong in his assessment of inevitability, as this end state occurs only in one-third of the patients who get schizophrenia.

As with all rules, there are exceptions, so this final course can vary. Occasional patients retain their more florid symptoms all their lives. For example, I had under my care a 75-year-old man who hallucinated all day every day and had been doing so for fifty years. His illness was virtually unaffected by medications. These kinds of patients are certainly exceptional, but they do exist.

It is currently popular to attribute the late symptoms of schizophrenia to drug effects. The truth is that exactly the same picture was described for fifty years before the drugs were introduced. Drugs used in schizophrenia may certainly produce some sedation, especially in older patients, but such effects account for a minuscule portion of the total picture on a properly run hospital ward. Similarly these late schizophrenic symptoms are often blamed on the effects of chronic institutionalization; this also accounts for only a small portion of the picture. The late symptoms may be attributed to depression and hopelessness in a patient who is chronically ill and sees no possibility of leaving the hospital; this too may account for a small portion. The vast majority of the late clinical symptoms seen in schizophrenic patients, however, has been shown to be a direct consequence of the disease and its probable effects on the brain.

THE COURSES OF SCHIZOPHRENIA IN CROSS-CULTURAL PERSPECTIVE

Since schizophrenia occurs in all parts of the world (although with varying prevalence), it is of interest to learn whether the three courses of the disease are similar in other countries. Does the rule of thirds hold up elsewhere?

There is unfortunately little hard information with which to answer this question. The major impediment to cross-cultural inquiries of this kind is the different diagnostic practices and various meanings of the term "schizophrenia." Since the term is used more strictly in European countries than in the United States, the patients who are used for follow-up studies are usually sicker. Thus their recovered rate appears to be lower. Allowing for these differences, however, it appears that the courses of schizophrenia in western European countries are quite similar to those in the United States, and the rule of thirds probably does hold.

When we turn to developing countries the answer is different. In several preliminary studies it appears that the courses of schizophrenia in these countries are more likely to be favorable: that is, more than one-third will completely recover and less than one-third will be unimproved. Why this should be so is not known; it may be related to different causes of the disease in developing countries, to easier reabsorption of schizophrenic patients back into village life, or to more cultural support from the extended family. In work done more than thirty years ago among the aborigines on Taiwan, it was noted that "the prognosis in the aboriginal patients was also fairly good. They do not seem to deteriorate into the chronic schizophrenic state that we see in many Chinese and Western communities." And on Mauritius a twelve-year follow-up study found more schizophrenics who had fully recovered (59 percent) than in Britain (34 percent). Finally, data from the World Health Organization nine-nation schizophrenia study showed that patients in developing countries (especially Colombia and Nigeria) had considerably better courses than patients in developed countries (Denmark, England, United States, Czechoslovakia, and USSR).

There is also some international discussion on the question of whether the courses of schizophrenia are becoming more benign in western countries. Manfred Bleuler in Switzerland believes that they are and that this is related to the introduction of medications. E. H. Hare in England claims that the improvement began before the drugs were introduced. K. A. Achte has also noted an improvement in the courses of schizophrenic patients in Scandinavia. Whatever the cause, they appear to be going in the right direction.

THREE SCHIZOPHRENIC PATIENTS

To conclude this chapter three patients will be described to illustrate the three courses of recovered, improved, and unimproved. Identifying data have been changed to preserve anonymity.

Recovered

Alex was admitted to the hospital on two separate occasions for schizophrenia. He was a divorced father of three who had finished high school and held a steady job as a bus driver. He had an older brother who had been hospitalized for schizophrenia for many years. Alex was 29 at the time of his first admission, which came shortly after he had struck a pedestrian in a bus accident; he blamed himself for the accident.

On his first admission Alex showed catatonic symptoms. He had been mute for almost two weeks, sat immobile in one position for hours at a time, and appeared to respond to auditory hallucinations. He recovered completely over a month's time on medication and was discharged. Two years later he was readmitted with paranoid symptoms. He was certain that people were following him, acknowledged hearing voices giving him instructions, took off his clothes in the street in an effort to defend himself, and was eventually arrested and brought to the hospital for throwing stones at a telephone repairman who he believed was bugging his house. He again recovered over a month's time and returned to his job as a bus driver. In the ensuing six years he has had no further illness, and there are no residual symptoms of the disease. Alex denies that he ever was sick and has never taken any medicine after leaving the hospital.

Improved

Peter had a normal childhood and successful high school career. He then married and joined the army to get training and travel. There was no family history of mental illness. At age 21, while assigned to Germany, he began to have strange feelings in his body and later to hear voices. He started drinking heavily, which seemed to relieve the voices, then turned to the use of hashish and cocaine. His condition deteriorated rapidly, and he was arrested for hitting an officer who he believed was trying to poison him. He was hospitalized and eventually discharged from the army with a full service-connected disability. Over the next three years he was hospitalized three more times with schizophrenic symptoms. On the final admission he was extremely hostile and paranoid, sitting suspiciously in the corner wearing sunglasses and threatening staff members with a pool cue. He believed he had the body of a woman, and also had bizarre delusions about being the king of a group of people who were half-human and half-fish. He acknowledged continuous auditory hallucinations, occasional visual hallucinations (e.g., presidential portraits), and occasional hallucinations of smell.

Peter responded slowly to very high doses of medication and was released from the hospital two months later almost completely well. He returned faithfully for an injection of medicine every week, lived in his own apartment, and visited his family (including his divorced wife and children) and friends during the day. He clearly was capable of holding a job, but declined to do so for fear that it would jeopardize his monthly army disability check. His only remaining symptoms were voices which he heard late in the day but which he was able to ignore. After two years he insisted on trying to continue without medicine, and stopped it under close psychiatric supervision. His schizophrenic symptoms returned almost immediately and he resumed his medication. He continues to get an injection every week.

Unimproved

Dorothy was known as a quiet child who attained straight A's in school. Her mother was hospitalized for schizophrenia for two years during Dorothy's childhood, and a brother was in an institution for the mentally retarded. She was first hospitalized at age 15 for one month; information on this hospitalization was not obtainable except for a diagnosis of "transient situational reaction of adolescence." Following this, Dorothy dropped out of school, went to work as a domestic, married, and had three children. She remained apparently well until age 22, at which time she believed people were trying to kill her, believed people were talking about her, and heard airplanes flying overhead all day. She neglected her children and housework and simply sat in a corner with a fearful expression on her face. On examination she had a marked thinking disorder and catatonic rigidity and was noted to be very shy and withdrawn.

Over the ensuing fifteen years Dorothy has been hospitalized most of the time and has responded minimally to medication. During the earlier years she was returned to her home for brief periods, with homemaker services; and in more recent years she lived for several months in a halfway house. There she was invariably victimized by men and was judged not to be capable of defending herself. She remains in the hospital, sitting quietly in a chair day after day. She answers politely but with absolutely no emotion and shows marked poverty of thought and of speech.

5

THE CAUSES OF SCHIZOPHRENIA

Something has happened to me—I do not know what. All that was my former self has crumbled and fallen together and a creature has emerged of whom I know nothing. She is a stranger to me—and has an egotism that makes the egotism that I had look like skimmed milk; and she thinks thoughts that are—heresies. Her name is insanity. She is the daughter of madness—and according to the doctor, they each had their genesis in my own brain.

Lara Jefferson, *These Are My Sisters*

We are in the midst of an explosion of knowledge about the causes of schizophrenia. In the past, we have had only theories. We still have the theories, but in addition we have knowledge, based on facts. As the knowledge accumulates the theories will become fewer and fewer, as it becomes clear that some of them do not fit the emerging facts.

The knowledge we are accumulating about schizophrenia's causes is almost entirely a product of the last ten years. It is related to the new technology which has been developed to study the brain. We can now visualize the brain, using computerized tomography (CT); follow radioactive elements as they go through the brain's arteries; and measure its electrical impulses and chemicals in ways much more sophisticated than in the past. The next ten years promise to increase our knowledge of schizophrenia's causes dramatically. It is an exciting time.

Because our understanding of schizophrenia is changing so quickly, it should not be surprising to find significant lags in awareness of this knowledge. Physicians trained in decades past, for example, may be completely unaware of the new information. They may still be thinking in terms of what they were taught at the time they were trained, such as psychoanalytic theories and family interaction theories. These theories have been largely discredited as the new knowledge has accumulated.

What we now *know* about schizophrenia includes the following:

1. It is a brain disease or diseases, probably the latter. The brains of people with schizophrenia are different from the brains of people who do not have schizophrenia.

2. The area of the brain which is responsible for schizophrenia appears to be the limbic system and its connections.
3. Schizophrenia tends to run in families.
4. Some cases of schizophrenia begin with brain damage very early in life, perhaps even before the child is born, even though the symptoms of the disease do not become manifest until many years later.

The above list is based upon facts and qualifies as true knowledge. Beyond this we move into the realm of theories. There are many theories about schizophrenia's causation. Some of them, such as genetic, biochemical, viral, and nutritional theories, fit the known facts quite well. Others, such as psychoanalytic and family interaction theories, do not fit the facts very well and should be discarded. These facts and theories are explored here one by one.

SCHIZOPHRENIA IS A BRAIN DISEASE

There is no longer any doubt that the brains of people with schizophrenia are different from the brains of people who do not have the disease. The precise causes of these differences remain a subject of lively debate, but their existence is now an accepted fact. There are both structural differences and functional differences.

In order to understand these differences, it is necessary to understand something about the human brain. It is a mushroomlike organ with a stem narrowing into the spinal cord, which runs down the back. The bulk of the brain consists of four lobes (frontal, parietal, temporal, and occipital), which are divided in two by a deep vertical cleft. At the bottom of the cleft is the corpus callosum, a thick band carrying nerve fibers back and forth between the two halves of the brain. The four major lobes perform functions such as muscle coordination, thinking, memory, language, hearing, and vision. It is now clear, however, that the two halves of the brain are not identical; in most persons the left half controls language skills and conceptual thinking whereas the right half is in charge of spatial skills and intuitive thinking.

The four lobes come together at the base of the brain beneath the corpus callosum. There lie the thalamus, hypothalamus, pituitary gland, limbic system, basal ganglia, midbrain, and brain stem tapering into the spinal cord. It is this area which controls all vital functions (e.g., heart, respiration, eating and the body's endocrine [hormone] system); and which acts as a gatekeeper for all incoming and outgoing stimuli for the major lobes. Attached to the back of this area, as if by afterthought, is the cerebellum, which until recently was thought to function exclusively to coordinate muscle function; it is now thought to interact with the brain stem on other functions as well.

The entire brain is housed in the vaultlike bony skull and surrounded by a layer of cerebrospinal fluid for further protection. The fluid circulates around the brain and goes through the center of the major lobes by a series of canals which widen into ventricles. It is because the brain is so well protected that we understand comparatively little about it or its diseases. It has been facetiously suggested that if we could persuade the brain to change places with the liver we might then understand its functioning and what causes schizophrenia.

The actual work of the brain is performed by approximately fifty billion nerve cells. Each has branches with which it can transmit and receive messages from other cells; one cell can receive messages from as many as ten thousand other cells. The branches do not physically touch each other but rather release chemical messengers, called neurotransmitters, which carry the messages from the end of one nerve branch to the end of an adjacent branch. We already know of over thirty different kinds of neurotransmitters, and it is likely that there are many more. Some of these neurotransmitters, such as dopamine, norepinephrine, serotonin, GABA, and the endorphins, are of great interest to schizophrenia researchers.

Claims that the brains of schizophrenics are different in structure from the brains of nonschizophrenics date back to the early years of the twentieth century. Over the years these claims gradually fell into disrepute because the differences could be found in some schizophrenic brains but not in others. Since it was widely believed, until recently, that schizophrenia was a single disease, the structural differences were assumed not to be important because they could not be found in all cases.

However, if one begins with the assumption that schizophrenia is not a single disease but rather consists of several different diseases, then the structural differences look much more impressive. Many studies (such as Drs. Cecile and Oskar Vogt's description of "dwarf cells" and Dr. Karin Von Buttlar-Brentano's finding of cellular changes in schizophrenic brains) were done twenty and thirty years ago, when methodological problems in this research area were greater. Therefore we will confine ourselves to research done in the last ten years.

In 1972, three interesting studies were published. E. J. Colon in the Netherlands autopsied three schizophrenia patients immediately after death and found a decrease in neurons in several parts of their brains as compared with normal brains. Dionisio Nieto and Alfonso Escobar in Mexico described diffuse cellular changes in ten schizophrenic patients, as compared with controls; since the brains had been collected from patients who died before the advent of drugs for schizophrenia, these changes cannot be ascribed to drugs. At the same time Randall Rosenthal and Llewellyn Bigelow in the United

States found in schizophrenic brains differences in the measurement of the corpus callosum, the structure which carries information from one half of the brain to the other.

Anatomical peculiarities of schizophrenic brains continue to be described. In 1975 M. Fisman in South Africa found lesions in the upper brain stem of eight patients with schizophrenia. In 1981 P. Averback in England reported finding swollen and degenerated brain cells in eleven young schizophrenic patients, and most recently Janice R. Stevens in the United States described impressive abnormalities in brain cells in thirty-eight schizophrenic patients.

An important advance in schizophrenia research took place in the 1970s when computerized tomography (CT) scans became available, allowing brain structures in living subjects to be visualized more clearly than was ever before possible. Initial studies were done by research groups led by Eve C. Johnstone in London and Daniel R. Weinberger in Washington, D.C., who found that approximately one-third of schizophrenic patients have abnormalities in brain structure (e.g., enlargement of the fluid-carrying ventricles, loss of brain substance, called atrophy, and/or abnormalities of the cerebellum). Three other research groups (under Drs. Nancy C. Andreasen and Charles J. Golden at the University of Nebraska and Dr. Henry A. Nasrallah at the University of Iowa) have replicated these findings, while a fourth group (Dr. Terry L. Jernigan and associates at Stanford University) was unable to, but was studying a less severely affected group of patients. Schizophrenics with CT scan abnormalities are more likely to have symptoms such as withdrawal and flattening of their emotions, impairment of their intellectual functioning and evidence of neurological dysfunctions, and are less likely to respond to medication. CT scan studies have clearly established, then, that the brains of some schizophrenics are structurally different from the brains of nonschizophrenics.

Even more impressive than the structural changes found in schizophrenic brains are the functional differences. Brains of people with schizophrenia simply do not function in the same way as do brains of normal people. For example, electrical impulses, another method used by the brain to send messages, have been shown to be abnormal in many schizophrenic patients. This is true when the electrical impulses are measured as evoked potentials, a special electrical impulse elicited by auditory, visual, or sensory input. It is also true when electrical activity is recorded on electroencephalograms (EEGs); approximately one-third of persons with schizophrenia have abnormal EEGs. Abnormal EEGs among schizophrenics are found twice as commonly as among persons with mania, and four times more commonly than among persons with depression. The EEG differences between normal persons and schizophrenic persons become even clearer when computers are used in the analysis; as one researcher summarized it: "Chronic schizophrenics have sig-

nificantly different EEG profiles than matched groups of normal volunteers."
The abnormal EEGs appear to be found most frequently among schizophrenics who do not have a family history of the disease.

Abnormal brain function is also suggested by the multiple abnormal eye
movements which occur commonly in schizophrenia. Increased or decreased
blink rates, poor eye contact (many schizophrenics will not look you directly
in the eye), abnormal eye reflexes, inequality in pupil size, and abnormal eye
movements have all been well documented by Janice R. Stevens at the University of Oregon and Philip S. Holzman in Boston. Abnormalities in the inner
ear and its connections to the brain are suggested by the finding of difficulties
in balance among some schizophrenics. And brain function generally appears
to be abnormal when psychological tests to measure it are given to schizophrenic patients; in 1981, for example, Richard Abrams and his associates at the
Chicago Medical School reported that "schizophrenic patients . . . were no
different from those with organic brain disease" on such tests.

Testing schizophrenics neurologically also reveals more abnormal brain
function than is found in normal persons. This is most true for such neurological tests as identifying numbers drawn on the palm of the hand, the ability to
appreciate two separate simultaneous sensory inputs (e.g., being touched in
two different places at the same time), and certainty or confusion about the
right and left sides of the body. In six different studies of neurological function
using tests such as these, a significant number of schizophrenic patients showed
abnormalities.

A newly devised test of brain function is the measure of its use of oxygen
and glucose. Using radioactive elements and serial X rays, it is possible to trace
the flow of blood through the different regions of the brain and to assess the
rate at which oxygen and glucose are used. In 1974 David H. Ingvar and his
associates in Sweden reported that schizophrenic patients showed decreased
blood flow to their frontal lobes compared with normal subjects, and other
research teams have extended these findings. In 1982 Monte S. Buchsbaum
and colleagues at the National Institute of Mental Health in Bethesda, using
the positron-emission tomography (PET) scanner, showed decreased glucose
utilization in the frontal lobes of schizophrenics. The technology to measure
such brain functions is developing rapidly and promises to enhance our knowledge of brain diseases further in coming years.

Another area of exciting research activity in the 1980s will be the study
of chemicals in the brains of persons with schizophrenia. Techniques for such
measurements are still being perfected but already suggest that schizophrenics
have definite chemical abnormalities and that these do not seem to be related
to having been treated with drugs. Abnormalities of both neurotransmitters
and proteins have also been reported in studies of the cerebrospinal fluid of

such patients. We are on the threshold of a knowledge explosion about brain chemistry.

Thus, both the structure and the function of schizophrenic brains have been shown to be different. In the past psychiatrists frequently made a distinction between "organic" causes of psychosis, in which underlying brain disease was known to be present, and "functional" psychosis (schizophrenia and manic-depressive illness), in which there was said to be no known underlying brain disease. This dichotomy is now known to be invalid and the term "functional" psychosis should be discarded. It was succinctly put by Seymour Kety, one of the most respected American researchers on schizophrenia: "I find it difficult to avoid the conclusion that in a substantial fraction of typical chronic schizophrenics there is an underlying neurological disturbance. . . . It is not unlikely that the actual fraction so affected is considerably larger than has thus far been demonstrated."

THE LIMBIC SYSTEM: THE SITE OF THE PROBLEM

In the early part of this century, when scientists began looking at autopsies for abnormalities in the brains of schizophrenics, they looked mostly in the outer layer of the brain. At that time it was believed that most of the important functions of the brain were closest to the surface. The limbic system, which lies deep below the surface in the center of the brain, was thought to be merely an ancestral remnant of the primitive system for smelling.

All this has changed radically. The limbic system is now known to be the gate through which most incoming stimuli must pass. It has "selective, integrative, and unifying functions by which raw experience is harmonized into reality and coherent activity is organized." According to Dr. Paul MacLean, the modern father of the limbic system, it is "able to correlate every form of internal and external perception."

All of this takes place in an area which is anatomically very small. It is composed of contiguous portions of the frontal and temporal lobes, and its main structures include the amygdala and the hippocampus. However, its size is deceptive, for the limbic system has direct connections to all the areas of the brain, including the upper brain stem and the cerebellum. Increasingly it has been realized that the brain works as a functionally interdependent and intricate system and an abnormality anywhere within it can throw the whole system off. It is analogous to an electrical system with a short circuit in it; the short circuit may occur at any one of several places, but the result will be the same.

Evidence that the limbic system is the site of pathology for some, if not most, cases of schizophrenia is strong. Abnormalities in this system in animals may produce profound changes in emotion, inappropriate behavior, and an impairment in the animal's ability to screen out multiple visual stimuli. Abnormalities in the limbic system in human beings may produce, in addition to the above effects, distortions of perception, illusions, hallucinations, feelings of depersonalization, paranoia, and catatoniclike behavior. In short, the symptoms of schizophrenia described in chapter 2 are a logical consequence of impaired limbic system dysfunction, given what we know about it.

Diseases of the brain which affect the limbic system are also more likely to produce schizophreniclike symptoms. This is seen, for example, with brain tumors located in the limbic system. Cases of encephalitis which produce schizophreniclike symptoms have been found in several studies to involve the limbic system, and epilepsy, when it originates in the limbic area, is more likely to be accompanied by schizophreniclike symptoms.

The strongest evidence linking the limbic system to schizophrenia has come from studies of electrical activity in this area. Robert Heath and his coworker in New Orleans found abnormal limbic electrical activity in schizophrenic patients; these findings have been replicated by at least three other groups of researchers. One group found abnormal electrical impulses in the limbic area of sixty-one out of sixty-two schizophrenic patients tested, and as the electrodes were moved away from the limbic area, the abnormalities became less frequent. Another group was able to correlate the occurrence of abnormal electrical activity and bizarre behavior in a patient.

Also significant in this regard is the discovery that many of the structural changes described in the brains of schizophrenic persons have been found in the limbic area, or in nearby areas with which it is closely connected. The widening of the corpus callosum, the abnormalities in the upper brain stem, and the dopamine and norepinephrine neurochemical changes are all specifically linked to the limbic system. It seems incontrovertible that the limbic system is the part of the brain which is primarily affected in many, if not most, cases of schizophrenia.

There is one other curious fact about the anatomical location of schizophrenia, which should be mentioned. In recent years there have been several studies suggesting that the left side of the brain is primarily affected in schizophrenia much more often than the right side of the brain. Patients with temporal lobe epilepsy, for example, will be more likely to have schizophreniclike symptoms if the epilepsy is in the left temporal lobe. Similarly, studies of visual evoked potentials, abnormal EEGs, lateral eye movements, auditory discrimination, galvanic skin response, information processing, and neurological signs, all suggest that the major problem may lie in the left hemisphere. If this is true, then it might be the left limbic areas which are the primary site of the schizophrenic disease process.

SCHIZOPHRENIA RUNS IN FAMILIES

Ever since schizophrenia was first described in the early years of the nineteenth century, it has been noted that the disease sometimes runs in families. The brothers, sisters, and children of a person with schizophrenia, for example, have approximately a 10 percent chance of getting the disease. If it did not run in families, these close relatives would have only a 1 percent chance, the same percentage as in the general population. The fact that schizophrenia sometimes runs in families has been established beyond any doubt.

Less clear is how often this is true. Estimates of this vary widely, depending on the population group studied, the size of the families, and the definition used for schizophrenia. In my own work with large, inner-city families, I find that in almost half of all cases someone else in the family (mother, father, brother, sister, aunts, uncles, or grandparents) also has had schizophrenia. That also means, of course, that in half of the cases there is no family history of the disease.

The fact that schizophrenia runs in families means to most people that it is inherited. This may be true, but it is not necessarily true. Genetic theories could explain why schizophrenia runs in families (these will be discussed on page 000); however, other theories involving no genetic mechanisms could also explain it. For example, if some cases of schizophrenia were caused by an infectious agent, such as a virus, it might run in families because of transmission of the virus from mother or father to the child either before or after birth. Alternatively a child might be exposed to schizophrenia through a common dietary factor in the home or through common childhood experiences which were passed from generation to generation. In each theoretical case the disease would run in families but would not be inherited in the genetic sense of the word.

That schizophrenia sometimes runs in families is a fact. Transmission of the disease by genes is one theory to explain this fact, but it has not yet been proved. Other mechanisms of transmission are also possible which do not involve genes.

SCHIZOPHRENIA MAY BEGIN EARLY IN LIFE

Evidence has also accumulated that some, but not all, cases of schizophrenia begin with damage to the brain in early childhood, perhaps even while the child is still growing in the uterus. This may be true even in persons who show no symptoms of schizophrenia until they are in their late teens or twenties.

The fact that there is a skewed seasonality in the births of people who later become schizophrenic points strongly in this direction. In the northern hemisphere an excessive number of schizophrenics (5 to 10 percent more than could be expected) are born in the late winter and early spring months. This fact, which was ignored until the last ten years, has now been proved to occur in every northern hemisphere country in which it has been examined, including England, Ireland, Denmark, Sweden, Norway, Germany, Japan, the Philippines, and the United States. Studies in southern hemisphere countries have been less conclusive but have pointed in the same direction (i.e., a disproportionate number of schizophrenics are born during the winter months there). There also is evidence that the peak months for schizophrenic births have shifted over time, at least in Japan and the United States.

There are, of course, several possible explanations for the seasonality of schizophrenic births, including skewed patterns of conception, nutritional factors, infectious agents, and other environmental variables which differ by season. It is not yet known which of these explanations is the correct one. The important point to note is that *something* is going on during the conception, pregnancy or birth of these children which makes some of them more susceptible to schizophrenia later in their lives, and that this something has a seasonal occurrence.

Evidence pointing in this same direction comes from analysis of fingerprint patterns of persons with schizophrenia. Until recently it was thought that the formation of fingerprints was entirely genetically determined. Now it is known that disturbances in the first few months of the baby's growth in the uterus may alter the fingerprint pattern. Both rubella and cytomegalovirus infections, for example, can do this. Reports that persons with schizophrenia have an excessive number of unusual fingerprint (and palmprint) patterns date back at least to 1935. Such reports now cover more than 4,000 schizophrenics and come from England, Denmark, Sweden, Germany, Italy, Spain, Chile, Mexico, Australia, and the United States. It is not possible to say yet exactly what causes these unusual patterns. It does imply, however, that something significant is occurring before birth in some people who later become schizophrenic.

Another piece of the puzzle which points toward pregnancy as an important time for the development of schizophrenia is that children who later become schizophrenic are slightly lighter in weight at birth than, on the average, their brothers or sisters. There is also some evidence, although it is not conclusive, that children who eventually become schizophrenic have more birth complications and difficulty at the time of delivery. Similarly, it is interesting to note that women who have schizophrenia while they are pregnant give birth to more than an average number of stillborn children and children with congenital abnormalities. Most of the women who were studied were not taking medications, so the damage must be linked in some way to the schizophrenia itself.

Finally, the most important evidence that some cases of schizophrenia date to very early infancy or childhood comes from the histories provided by parents of schizophrenics. There is a definite subgroup of schizophrenics who, according to their parents, were never "like other children." It is not that they were frankly psychotic—that behavior usually does not begin until the late teens or early twenties. It is just that the child was different, usually shy, introverted and unable to relate to other people. It has been found that schizophrenic patients with abnormal CT scans as described above are more likely to have been this kind of child.

The fact that a subgroup of schizophrenic patients has a history of introversion and shyness was noted by psychiatrists early in this century. Kraepelin noted that many of his patients had made no friends as children, and Bleuler described such children's lack of interest in their environment. More recently Rachael Gittleman-Klein and other researchers have quantified this data in questionnaires. It is still not clear how large a subgroup of schizophrenic patients falls into this pattern. Many other schizophrenics, it should be emphasized, do not and have perfectly normal childhoods and normal relationships before the disease occurs.

It appears, therefore, that some, but not all, schizophrenics have antecedents of their disease in early childhood, perhaps even while still in the uterus, although they do not as a rule get the symptoms of the disease until they become young adults.

GENETIC THEORIES

We now leave the world of facts which are known about schizophrenia and enter the realm of theories. This is the realm of speculation about the ultimate causes of the disease. As new knowledge accumulates, some of these theories have dropped or will drop by the wayside and others may develop.

Genetic theories of the disease are probably the oldest and the most tested. Basically, these say that schizophrenia is an inherited disorder, passed on from generation to generation by way of the genes. The genes, of which we each have six million, are carried on chromosomes in the nuclei of all our body cells, and we receive half of them from our mother and half from our father. There are also diseases of the chromosomes themselves, but all these are accompanied by mental retardation and congenital abnormalities, so there is no reason to believe that schizophrenia is a chromosomal disorder.

In years past, genetic theories were relatively simple. Either the disease was inherited as a dominant gene (and would be activated whether inherited from either the mother *or* the father) or as a recessive gene (and would not be activated unless inherited from both parents). Inbreeding among families has long been discouraged because it tends to elicit otherwise recessive diseases even when the parents are distantly related. Neither dominant nor recessive inheritance patterns fit the facts of schizophrenia, however. Areas where schizophrenia is more prevalent do not necessarily have more inbreeding, and areas with more inbreeding do not necessarily have more schizophrenia.

There continues to be a general consensus among schizophrenia experts that genetics plays some role in the disease—the fact that schizophrenia runs in families suggests it—but its precise role is unclear. The offspring of nonschizophrenic parents has a 1 percent chance of developing the disease, of one schizophrenic parent a 10 percent chance, and of two schizophrenic parents a 39 percent chance. Twin studies also suggest it; the twin of a nonidentical (dizygotic) schizophrenic twin has only a 10 to 15 percent chance of developing schizophrenia (only slightly higher than other brothers and sisters), whereas the twin of an identical (monozygotic) schizophrenic twin has a 35 to 50 percent chance. It is important to note, however, that not all identical twins develop schizophrenia when one does. In fact, since these twins have identical genes, such studies prove conclusively that genetic inheritance cannot be the only cause of schizophrenia.

Genetic influences on schizophrenia are also suggested by the work on abnormal eye movements carried out by Philip Holzman and his colleagues. Not only were schizophrenics found to have the abnormal eye movements, but a study of nonschizophrenic relatives of these patients found that 45 percent of them *also* had abnormal eye movements, suggesting that something had been inherited in the family that produced schizophrenia in some family members but not in others.

Studies done in Denmark on children of schizophrenic parents who were adopted by other families at birth have added immeasurably to our knowledge of schizophrenia. The children were followed up after they had become adults, and it was found that children of schizophrenic parents retained their increased predisposition toward developing the disease despite the fact that they had been raised by nonschizophrenic parents. The conclusion drawn from these studies is that "something necessary but not sufficient for the development of a schizophrenic disorder is transmitted genetically." Or as summarized by Seymour Kety in a wry response to Thomas Szasz, "If schizophrenia is a myth, it is a myth with a strong genetic component."

Increasingly, it is being suspected that the disease schizophrenia is not itself inherited; rather, what is inherited is a predisposition of some people to react to environmental influences in a particular way which leads to schizophrenia. This is similar to current theories for many other chronic diseases of humankind, including diabetes, hypertension, heart disease, and some cancers. For diabetes, for example, Abner Notkins and his colleagues at the National Institutes of Health have developed a strain of mice which, when injected with a particular virus, develop diabetes. Another strain of mice is completely resistant and never develops diabetes. It is clear that the first strain has a genetic predisposition toward reacting with the virus in such a way as to produce diabetes. The mice do not inherit the diabetes but rather the predisposition.

This model may well be operant for schizophrenia as well. One may hypothesize any one—or more—of many possible precipitating causes in addition to viruses, including specific dietary factors, environmental contaminants, such as insecticides, or stress. Such a model is also compatible with schizophrenia research suggesting that individuals with certain genetic components (as measured by antigens found on white blood cells, known as the human leukocyte antigen or HLA system) are more susceptible to the disease.

Other genetic theories of schizophrenia include the idea that what is inherited is a specific defect in the brain that causes it to malfunction and thereby produce the symptoms of schizophrenia. For example, an inherited defect in the sensory-processing mechanism of the limbic system, or of the brain centers which integrate communication, could theoretically lead to schizophreniclike symptoms. A variant of this theory says that what is inherited is an abnormal or unusual blood supply to the limbic areas, thereby making them particularly liable to damage (e.g., too little oxygen at birth) or environmental insults (susceptibility to infections). Finally, it is possible to invoke complex models of genetic transmission, such as the disease being carried on more than one gene, to explain why schizophrenia is sometimes passed from generation to generation and sometimes is not.

It is clear, then, that genetic theories of schizophrenia fit comfortably with the facts known about the disease. The one major criticism which can be leveled at these theories is that schizophrenics themselves have a very low rate of reproduction. This was especially true in the past, for obvious reasons, when patients spent their lives in asylums on single-sex wards; it is less true now with large numbers of schizophrenics living in the community. Given the low reproductivity rate, schizophrenia should have died out, or at least become markedly less prevalent, if it is transmitted from affected individuals to their offspring.

The geneticists' response to this criticism is that schizophrenia could be simply one manifestation of a genetically related spectrum of personality disorders. If the spectrum also included individuals, such as antisocial personality types, these individuals might have a higher-than-average reproductivity rate and so transmit the disorder. In other words the schizophrenia-producing genes would be passed on through schizophrenia-spectrum individuals and not necessarily through schizophrenics themselves.

BIOCHEMICAL THEORIES

Many biochemical theories of schizophrenia assume a genetic basis as well. The biochemical mechanisms describe what is wrong in the brain but not how it got to be wrong. The ultimate cause is usually assumed to be genetic, such as an inherited error of brain metabolism leading to the biochemical defect.

Biochemical theories date back to the early years of this century, although they have become much more sophisticated in recent years as the technology for measuring the body's chemistry has improved. The center of attention throughout the last decade has been the neurotransmitter dopamine, one of the brain proteins in the class called catecholamines which transmit information between nerve cells. Dopamine has come under suspicion because amphetamines, when given in high doses, cause a rise in the dopamine level at the same time that they produce symptoms which resemble schizophrenia. Similarly, when L-dopa, a drug which the body may turn into dopamine, is given to persons with schizophrenia, it often makes them worse. Finally, it is now known that drugs which are effective in schizophrenia block dopamine action. For all of these reasons many researchers suspect that an excess of dopamine is one of the causes of schizophrenia.

Dopamine is broken down in the body to other compounds through the action of certain enzymes. One such enzyme is monoamine oxidase, known as MAO, and this enzyme has been the object of intensive research studies over the past decade. It has been reported, for example, that blood platelets of schizophrenic patients have a lower concentration of MAO than expected; recent findings suggest that this may be a drug effect, however, and the current status of MAO research is being reevaluated.

Other neurotransmitters which are under investigation in schizophrenia are serotonin and norepinephrine; the latter is suspected of playing a role in the causation of some depressions as well. Naturally occurring chemicals of the body, such as endorphins, prostaglandins, and prolactin (a hormone of the pituitary gland), have generated intense interest among some researchers. Perhaps all such efforts can be summed up by Joseph J. Schildkraut, a psychiatric researcher, who claims that we "have crossed the threshold into the era that I like to call psychiatric chemistry. . . . We are at a point in psychiatry today that is analogous to where our internist colleagues were in the 1950s. . . . I suspect that ten years from now we will probably view what we were doing here in the early 1980s as being as crude and primitive as what the endocrinologist was doing in his laboratory in the 1950s."

Just as there are different chemicals under investigation, so too there are different theories about how these chemicals might cause the symptoms of schizophrenia. These include the possibility of there being an excess (as is believed true for dopamine) or a deficit (as is believed true for MAO) of the chemical. Another theory suggests that the chemical may get changed into a toxic product and act as an internal brain poison; for example, it was widely believed for many years that chemicals such as dopamine might be changed to a mescalinelike compound and thus cause hallucinations. In recent years attention has been directed toward the branches of the nerve cells which send and receive neurotransmitters, and there has been speculation that blockage of the neurotransmitter may occur at that juncture.

How well do such biochemical theories fit the known facts about schizophrenia? They fit very well, especially when combined with the possibility of a genetically transmitted defect. Much of the structural and functional evidence of brain dysfunction is compatible with postulated biochemical defects. The limbic system would be a likely site for such defects since many of the neurotransmitters are concentrated there. The tendency for schizophrenia to run in families could be explained by a genetic transmission of the biochemical abnormality. And if there were biochemical abnormalities which were genetically inherited, it is possible that they might manifest themselves in childhood as altered personality traits even if the full disease did not develop until many years later.

NUTRITIONAL THEORIES

Nutritional theories of schizophrenia are really just a subset of biochemical theories. However, they have developed an identity of their own under the name of orthomolecular psychiatry.

Nutritional theories have had adherents ever since it was discovered that some B vitamin deficiency diseases (e.g., beriberi, pellagra, and pernicious anemia) may be accompanied by psychiatric symptoms. Then in the early 1950s, Drs. Humphrey Osmond and Abram Hoffer began treating schizophrenic patients with high doses of niacin (a generic name for vitamin B-3, which includes nicotinic acid and nicotinamide) along with electroconvulsive therapy (ECT), in an attempt to block the formation of adrenochrome, a toxic metabolite of the neurotransmitter epinephrine which they believed to be causing the symptoms of schizophrenia. They claimed remarkable therapeutic success, and orthomolecular psychiatry was born.

Since that time its theories have expanded and become more complex. Other scientists joined their ranks, most notably Dr. Linus Pauling, who had previously won a Nobel Prize in another area of research. They postulated that a genetically determined biochemical defect leads to subtle changes in the brain chemistry. This in turn leads to altered subjective experiences (such as those described in chapter 2) which are called "metabolic dysperception" in orthomolecular terms. The original treatment with niacin has expanded to include large doses of many other vitamins (thiamine, pyridoxine, folic acid, vitamin B-12, vitamin C, vitamin E) and minerals (e.g., zinc, manganese). Control of the diet has also been incorporated into therapeutic regimens, especially restricting the intake of carbohydrates, caffeine, and alcohol. Smoking is discouraged, and the person is urged to exercise regularly. The theories and combinations of these orthomolecular therapeutic elements have proliferated rapidly and now fill a textbook.

As this was occurring, orthomolecular psychiatry became separated from the mainstream of American psychiatry. No further evidence to support the adrenochrome theory was found, and attempts to replicate the original Osmond-Hoffer work with niacin were unsuccessful. Increasingly the orthomolecular adherents were regarded as cultists or food faddists by most American psychiatrists, and their claims were not taken seriously. Nonetheless, the orthomolecular group continued to grow, formed a network of patients and their families (the American Schizophrenia Association), and ridiculed the prevailing psychoanalytic and family interaction theories of schizophrenia which were prevalent in American psychiatry.

In retrospect, it appears that much of the controversy surrounding orthomolecular psychiatry has been not about the use of vitamins to treat schizophrenia but rather about the medical model of the disease. The orthomolecular followers have staunchly and loudly championed the view that schizophrenia is a *real* disease; this has probably been the main source of their appeal to schizophrenics and their families. Traditional American psychiatry, meanwhile, has been pursuing the psychoanalytic and family interaction theories of schizophrenia.

This view apart, when the specific theories of orthomolecular psychiatry are examined in a critical light, they are found to be lacking in supporting evidence. There are no studies comparable to the biochemical research referred to in the previous section, and the theories of vitamins, minerals, and dietary deficiencies remain completely unproven by generally accepted scientific standards. Since almost thirty years have passed since the original Osmond-Hoffer report, it is possible that proof for these theories never will be forthcoming. If this turns out to be the case, then orthomolecular psychiatry will be remembered as having been right on the big issue (the validity of the medical model of schizophrenia) long before the rest of American psychiatry but wrong on the smaller issue (vitamin deficiency as the specific cause). They will have been in the right church but in the wrong pew.

In addition to orthomolecular psychiatry's theories of vitamin deficiency, there are other nutritional theories of schizophrenia's causation. Gluten, for example, has been proposed by Dr. Curtis Dohan of Philadelphia as a likely dietary cause of the disease, and he pointed out that the decreased schizophrenia rate in Scandinavian countries during World War II closely paralleled the decrease in glutens in the diet. Some observers have claimed that maintaining schizophrenic patients on a gluten-free and milk-free diet improves their clinical condition, but other studies have found that it has no effect.

Disturbances of serine and glycine metabolism have been shown to occasionally cause a schizophrenialike psychosis, and recently there has been an interest in dietary lecithin as a possible treatment for both schizophrenia and mania. Since one of the most available sources of lecithin is a McDonald's milkshake, we have the remote possibility that one of the cures for schizophrenia might lie at the sign of the "Golden Arch." If so, it would not be any more bizarre than many of the other chapters in the history of nutritional theories of schizophrenia.

How well do nutritional theories fit what is known about schizophrenia? They could certainly account for structural and functional abnormalities in the brain. Furthermore, it is theoretically possible that specific dietary deficiencies or excesses might selectively affect the limbic system. Nutritional deficiencies, such as pellagra, run in families, and it is also possible to invoke genetic mechanisms to explain an inborn error of metabolism which would be passed down over several generations. Nutritional deficiencies or excesses would also be compatible with the beginnings of the disease prenatally or early in childhood and could theoretically be used to explain facts such as the seasonality of schizophrenic births (e.g., a dietary deficiency might be more common during certain months and affect the developing brain in the unborn child).

The problem with nutritional theories is the lack of data to support them. A recent search for food allergies among schizophrenic patients yielded negative results, and the analysis of schizophrenic spinal fluid for evidence of zinc or copper deficiency has been similarly unrewarding. Since the possible list of dietary substances is legion, however, it is still possible that such a substance will prove to be causal of schizophrenia for at least a subgroup of patients. The serendipitous finding that lithium, a trace metal in the body, improves some persons with schizophrenia (as well as persons with mania) suggests that we still know very little about the nutritional requirements of the brain. And one cannot help but be impressed by the stories of individual patients who claim to have an exacerbation of their schizophrenic symptoms whenever they ingest certain foods.

INFECTIOUS DISEASE THEORIES

During the early years of this century, there was considerable interest in infectious agents as the possible cause of schizophrenia. This interest was especially stimulated by the finding of a spirochete as the cause of brain syphilis, a disease which can closely resemble schizophrenia. Most of this early research centered on bacteria, as viruses were not well known at the time.

In the last thirty years there has been sporadic interest in viruses as a possible cause of schizophrenia. Viral particles in the spinal fluid of schizophrenic patients were first reported by several researchers in the 1950s. Many observers also noted the occurrence of schizophrenialike symptoms in known viral infections of the brain, especially in cases of encephalitis caused by the influenza virus, herpes viruses, and encephalitis lethargica. As far back as 1928 it had been noted that "encephalitis and schizophrenia are different diseases, but it seems that some factor common to both is sometimes present and accounts for the coincidence of identical symptoms."

Current infectious disease theories of schizophrenia claim that the "factor common to both" is a virus. Viruses are known to attack very specific areas of the brain while leaving other areas untouched; for example, the rabies virus and the herpes zoster virus will attack only one kind of cell in one part of the central nervous system. Viruses may also alter the function of brain cells without altering their structure; cell enzymes, for example, may be permanently disrupted by a viral infection yet the cell itself will continue to live and show no evident damage. This means that viruses could conceivably cause schizophrenia and leave no trace of their damage visible under a microscope.

Another intriguing fact about viruses as a possible cause of schizophrenia is that they may remain latent for many years at a time. This is true for some well-known viruses, such as those in the herpes family, but it is also true for a new group of viruses called "slow" viruses, which may not cause disease for twenty years or more after they originally infect the person. Thus, persons with schizophrenia could theoretically become infected while still in the uterus or shortly after birth and yet not show symptoms of the disease until their twenties or thirties.

If viruses are involved in the causation of schizophrenia, it may be that the timing of the original infection is critical. There are known viral diseases which cause brain damage if introduced at one stage of fetal brain development but not at another stage. German measles (rubella) is the best-known example of this, causing mental retardation and heart and other defects if it infects the baby in the first three months of pregnancy but often causing no damage if infection takes place a few months later.

Is there any evidence that schizophrenia might be caused by a virus?

Within recent years, such evidence has begun to accumulate. Some of the structural changes described in schizophrenic brains at autopsy look very much like viral changes. Alterations in the protein portion of schizophrenics' spinal fluid are also compatible with a viral infection of the brain. More specifically, antibodies against cytomegalovirus (CMV) have been found in the spinal fluid of one-third of schizophrenics examined, and additional tests for CMV suggest that this may represent a subgroup of the disease. CMV is a member of the herpes family of viruses and is known to have an affinity for the limbic system. Researchers in England have also found a viral-like activity in the spinal fluid of over one-third of schizophrenic patients, but the precise identity of this agent has not yet been ascertained. All these studies need to be replicated by others before they can be said to have proved anything, but the results to date are provocative.

How well does an infectious disease theory of schizophrenia fit the known facts? The answer is very well. It could easily account for the changes in brain structure and function described. The involvement of the limbic system as the primary site of the disease is also plausible since several viruses are known which have a special affinity for the limbic system. The fact that schizophrenia runs in families could be explained either by a genetic predisposition to the virus, by transmission of a virus on the gene itself (such as is known to occur in the mouse leukemia virus), or by transmission of the virus across the placenta from the mother (or the father, via the semen) during pregnancy. Finally, infectious agents would be compatible with damage to the brain early in life and could account for the seasonality of schizophrenic births (many viruses have a seasonal occurrence), the altered fingerprint patterns, the slightly lighter birthweight of children who become schizophrenic, and the stillbirths and congenital abnormalities sometimes found in offspring of mothers with schizophrenia. It should also be noted that some viruses have been shown to cause changes in neurotransmitters, such as dopamine in the brain, and so could theoretically account for some of the biochemical changes described in schizophrenia. The infectious disease theory is an appealing theory, though like the other theories it is still unproved.

PSYCHOANALYTIC AND FAMILY INTERACTION THEORIES

Psychoanalytic and family interaction theories of schizophrenia have been very important in the United States since the turn of the century, although less so in Europe. In recent years, they have gradually lost adherents because of the lack of any supporting data. They remain important from a historical perspective, however, and also because large segments of the American public (and media) continue to believe they are true.

Psychoanalytic theories began with Freud, who in 1911 published his analysis of a paranoid schizophrenic, the Schreber case. Working from the memoirs which Daniel Schreber had published in 1903 and never actually examining the patient, Freud concluded that Schreber suffered from "conflict over unconscious homosexuality" which led to an inverted Oedipus complex. Schreber had become attached to his father instead of to his mother, as occurs in a normal childhood Oedipal situation, and that in turn had produced schizophrenia. Prior to this Freud had acknowledged very limited experience with schizophrenics; in 1907 he wrote to Karl Abraham that "I seldom see dements [dementia] and hardly ever see other severe types of psychosis."

In the ensuing years Freud's followers began a lively debate about the cause of schizophrenia. Carl Jung and Karl Abraham made the debate public, with Jung favoring a chemical toxin and Abraham arguing for a massive blockage of libido. Freud sided with Abraham, ironically attributing Jung's views to his mystical tendencies. Much of the debate focused on when the psychic damage causing schizophrenia occurred. On one end of the spectrum were psychoanalysts who argued that the trauma may even have preceded birth and be related to "the unceasing terror and tension of the fetal night" while in the womb. Melanie Klein, an influential protégé of Freud, fixed the critical schizophrenia-producing period at 3 to 6 months of age, while others focused on later parts of the oral, genital, or Oedipal periods of development. Related to this were differences of opinion as to whether schizophrenia was primarily due to disorders of libido development (e.g., drives, such as sex), or due to disorders of ego development (the inability to differentiate the self from others).

The one thing on which virtually all psychoanalysts could agree was that the source of psychic trauma theoretically responsible for schizophrenia was the interactions of the child and the parents. Harry Stack Sullivan, one of the most important American psychoanalysts, believed that schizophrenia was caused by parental rejection of the child. According to Freedman and Kaplan's *Textbook of Psychiatry:*

> Others have described the mother of the potential schizophrenic as aggressive, rejecting, domineering, and insecure, and the father as inadequate, passive, and indifferent. Elsewhere in the literature these fathers have been depicted as directly threatening, assaultive, or brutal or as overwhelming the child. In contrast to those mothers who are described as either subtly or overtly rejecting, others are said to be fussy and overprotective, perpetuating the symbiotic union.

Mothers who caused schizophrenia by their coldness and rejection were termed "schizophrenigenic mothers." Silvano Arieti estimated that "the majority" of cases of schizophrenia were caused by such mothers, although more recently he revised his estimates down to only 25 percent. Theodore Lidz claimed that about half of all schizophrenics have mothers who are "strange, near-psychotic or even overtly schizophrenic." Earlier Lidz had characterized fathers of schizophrenics as exerting "an extremely noxious or pathogenic influence upon the family and the patient." All in all, it was not an attractive picture which the psychoanalysts painted of the parents of schizophrenics.

In the 1950s, psychoanalytic views of the cause of schizophrenia were supplemented by theories of pathological family interaction. Rather than just the mother or father being blamed for the disease, the pattern of communication and interaction within the entire family was cited as the important causative factors. The best-known of these theories was that of the double-bind, first introduced by Gregory Bateson. According to this theory, schizophrenia results when children are put into impossible heads-I-win-tails-you-lose situations by their parents. For example, a mother buys her son two ties for his birthday. He comes downstairs wearing one of the ties the next morning and his mother asks, "What's the matter, dear, don't you like the other tie I gave you?" Another example is:

> Momma goes out shopping leaving three-year-old Leo with Daddy. As she returns and opens the door, Leo runs over to greet his mother. Whereupon the woman involuntarily freezes. Leo sees this and stops. Whereupon his mother says, "Leo, baby, what's the matter, don't you love your Mommy? Come and give me a big kiss."
>
> If baby Leo ignores his first perception and runs up to the woman again, she freezes and takes his kiss in an off-hand, angry way. If baby Leo refuses to budge, she scolds him for being a bad boy. Because of his age or inexperience Leo can't comment on what is happening, or if he does, either his mother or father scolds him for being naughty: "Don't talk to your mother/father that way or you will be punished." The net result is that Baby Leo is reduced to an impotent rage whereupon he is sent to bed for being bad.

Several other theories of pathological family interactions causing schizophrenia followed the double-bind. Theodore Lidz and his coworkers studied the relationship between the husband and wife in several families with a schizophrenic child; "none of the marriages seemed normal or healthy" and all were marked by a significant degree of "marital schism" (open fighting) or "marital skew" (covert fighting). Lyman Wynne and his colleagues described "pseudomutual" relationships within families of schizophrenics in which there is an outward appearance of genuineness but much covert animosity beneath the surface. This group of workers also observed an unusual amount of fragmented thinking in the communications within these families.

It is worth noting that much of the thinking of "antipsychiatrists," such as R. D. Laing and Thomas Szasz, arose directly from these psychoanalytic and family interaction theories of schizophrenia. For example, Laing's follower, Joseph Berke, notes:

> Long before I ever heard of Mary Barnes, I had begun to realize that what is commonly called "mental illness" is not an "illness" or "sickness" (according to the prevailing medical-psychiatric use of the term), but an example of emotional suffering brought about by a disturbance in a whole field of social relationships, in the first place, the family. In other words, "mental illness" reflects what is happening in a disturbed and disturbing group of people, especially when internalized in and by a single person. More often than not, a person diagnosed as "mentally ill" is the emotional scapegoat for the turmoil in his or her family or associates, and may, in fact, be the "sanest" member of this group.

The person with schizophrenia is not really sick, but merely acting in a crazy way to insure his/her survival because of the pressures of the family and/or society. Similarly, Szasz is a traditional psychoanalyst and believes the behavior we call schizophrenic is simply due to impaired learning about relationships. If one believes that schizophrenia is merely a rational response to an irrational family, or an impaired learning about relationships, then it is a short (and logical) step to saying that schizophrenia is not a disease at all but merely an adaptation.

How well do psychoanalytic and family interaction theories fit what is known about schizophrenia? The answer is not very well. By themselves they shed no light on why the brains of persons with schizophrenia are different or how the limbic system becomes disordered. One must postulate a theory that the abnormal childhood experiences or the disordered family communications *cause* the brain to change, a Lamarckian view of evolution which has long since been discredited. Psychoanalytic and family interaction theories are ostensibly compatible with the fact that some cases of schizophrenia date to early childhood, although, as we have noted, explaining facts such as the seasonality of schizophrenic births with these theories is difficult to do.

Even more importantly, there are no supporting data for these theories and considerable data which refute them. The major outstanding problem is cause and effect. Does schizophrenia in a mother produce schizophrenia in a son by the behavior of the mother toward the son (as psychoanalysts and family interactionists would contend), or is the schizophrenia of both related to some third factor (e.g., genetic, biochemical, viral, or nutritional factors)? The adoption studies in Denmark previously described strongly support the latter explanation. Children who were adopted at birth and then followed up for schizophrenia many years later were found to have a schizophrenia rate consistent with their biological parents and not their adoptive parents. In other words, if you take the son of a schizophrenic mother at birth and adopt him into a family with normal parents, he will still be more likely to develop schizophrenia than his adoptive brothers and sisters. Similarly, if you take the son of normal parents and adopt him into a home where one parent becomes schizophrenic, the son will not acquire the predisposition to schizophrenia. These adoption studies are strong evidence against theories that child-rearing practices or family interaction cause schizophrenia.

There are also numerous methodological problems with these theories. Most of the psychoanalytic and family interaction studies include very few patients, do not include control groups for comparison, and fail to take into consideration the bias of the observer. They also fail to take into account the family chaos caused by having a schizophrenic member, so that communication and interaction problems *caused by* the schizophrenic are mistakenly perceived as problems *causing* the schizophrenia. Nor do these theories account for the wide variations in schizophrenia prevalence in different cultures in the world and the total lack of correlation between schizophrenia rates and child-rearing practices; if these theories are valid one would expect some such correlations. These theories also fail to explain how and why the vast majority of children who grow up in families with a schizophrenic father or mother turn out to be nonschizophrenic or why psychoanalysis or family psychotherapy in families with schizophrenics is such an unproductive mode of therapy; if the theories are correct it should work.

Given the absence of any confirmatory evidence for these theories, there is a further criticism of psychoanalytic and family interaction assumptions, which is the most troubling of all. Genetic, biochemical, infectious, and nutritional theories attribute the ultimate cause of the disease to agents beyond the control of the affected individual or family; nobody is responsible for causing it. Psychoanalytic and family interaction theories, in contrast, attribute the cause to the behavior of the mother and father. As such they generate guilt and blame within the families. The magnitude of this guilt and blame is enormous and has led to depression, divorce, and even suicide. It has been iatrogenic anguish (physician-caused), wholly generated by the psychiatric profession. As doctors we are charged to "first do no harm"; purveyors of these theories have violated that basic tenet.

For all of these reasons both the psychoanalytic and family interaction theories of schizophrenia have lost their importance and are becoming of largely historical interest. When a new book on the psychoanalytic treatment of schizophrenia by L. Bryce Boyer and Peter L. Giovacchini was reviewed in 1981 in the *American Journal of Psychiatry,* official organ of the American Psychiatric Association, it was overtly ridiculed:

> This book is anomalous, atavistic. While others demonstrate the cerebral
> pathology of schizophrenia with computerized tomography, Boyer and Gio-

vacchini employ dream analysis to uncover preoedipal symbiotic fusions. Do schizophrenic patients have cerebral atrophy, dilated ventricles, neurological deficits, dementia? No matter, just interpret the transference regression and everything will be set right again. In this netherworld of science fantasy the brains of schizophrenic patients are haunted by partially cathected psychotic introjects that loom menacingly out of the murky darkness, while a hideous throng of primitive, internalized, preoedipal dyads rush out forever and laugh but smile no more.

In the words of the reviewer, Richard Abrams, it is no longer possible to protect "the crumbling edifice of psychoanalysis from the advances of modern behavioral neurobiology." Family interaction theories have fared no better, with a recent review noting "the relatively small number of family [interaction] studies of schizophrenia in recent years is consistent with the sharp decline in family interaction studies from 1968 to 1975. . . ." Steven Hirsch, coauthor of an extensive analysis of these theories, concluded, "There is as yet no evidence to support the view that parents bring about, in the formative years, the tendency for their children to become schizophrenic in later life." Psychoanalytic and family interaction theories have not been *disproved,* of course; as Hirsch notes, "Neither has anyone ever proved that there are no unicorns; one could turn up at any time."

In terms of the current status of the Laing-Szasz antipsychiatry view that schizophrenia is a myth, a sane response to an insane world, or even a growth experience, it continues to be popular only with those who are romantically inclined and who have no exposure to patients with the disease. Perhaps the most succinct commentary on these views was that of Dory Previn, who herself underwent a psychosis which was probably manic-depressive illness: "Insanity is terrific on the 'Late Show' . . . but in the real world it's shit."

STRESS THEORIES

Perhaps the most widespread popular theory about the cause of schizophrenia is that the disease is caused by stress. This has been true since the early years of the last century and continues to be true. Overwork, too much pressure, family problems, and similar formulations are commonly heard as causal explanations by friends and relatives of persons who become schizophrenic. As described in one book about a schizophrenic, "The individual who is to become schizophrenic can do neither. He hangs on, digs in, breaks finally, unable to meet stress. What is stress? Stress is a situation which you have not learned to meet and which terrifies you, occurring in a place you cannot leave." Stress theories are invoked frequently by schizophrenics and recovered schizophrenics themselves. Judi Chamberlain, a leader of ex-patient organizations, wrote, "We believe that the kinds of behavior labeled 'mental illness' have far more to do with the day-to-day conditions of people's lives than with disorders in their brain chemistry."

The reasons why stress theories are so widely believed are multiple. It is known that stress can be a major cause of diseases such as ulcers, so it seems logical to suspect it of causing schizophrenia. More importantly, it is known that subjecting individuals to very large amounts of stress can produce bizarre behavior which may mimic schizophrenia. This is seen, for example, in wartime, when "combat neurosis" may produce a soldier with a sudden hysterical paralysis or an acute paranoid reaction; or in persons subjected to severe sensory deprivation that causes them to experience hallucinations. These kinds of reactions are usually called brief reactive psychosis and were discussed in chapter 3; they are not the same as schizophrenia, but may look very similar to it for a short period of time. Given these facts, it is not surprising that stress has been linked to schizophrenia in the minds of many people.

In recent years stress theories have been popular among schizophrenia researchers as well. Usually they assume a genetic predisposition (diathesis) in addition to stress, the so-called diathesis-stress theory. For example, one can postulate that some brains are genetically unable to handle stress and that, because of this inherited inability, such people develop schizophrenia under an amount of stress which others would find easy to handle. Alternatively, some brains may be genetically unable to process sensory input, thereby producing much stress when subjected to such input and eventually leading to schizophrenia. By mixing various genetic predispositions with childhood experiences and learning, one can create dozens of possible scenarios producing stress and, hypothetically, schizophrenia as well.

How well do stress theories fit what is known about schizophrenia? It is difficult to account for changes in brain structure or function with stress alone, although it can be done in theory (e.g., stress causes ulcers, which include changes in both structure and function of the stomach). Stress could also be said to run in families and to begin early in life in those who become schizophrenic.

The main trouble with stress theories of schizophrenia is that there are no supporting data. When studies have been done ascertaining the stresses in patients' lives prior to their schizophrenic breakdown, the stresses are found to be no greater than those in a random sample of a general population. As summarized by one reviewer: "The research evidence indicates a weaker relationship between life events and schizophrenia onset than the clinical literature suggests. . . ." Moreover, stress theories leave many important questions unanswered. If stress can cause schizophrenia, why don't we have epidemics of schizophrenia in prisons and concentration camps? Why did the schizophrenia rate go down in many countries during World War II rather than up? Why is the schizophrenia rate low in places like warring Northern Ireland, and yet much higher in the relatively peaceful western part of Ireland? Why would stress produce increased strength of character in many people yet produce schizophrenia in others?

It is not a question of whether stress can cause mental distress and disorder; that is known. Rather it is a question of whether stress is in any way causative of schizophrenia. And if so, is the stress an important cause, or merely the straw that breaks the camel's back, and of little consequence in the larger picture? The data for answering these questions definitely are lacking.

TOWARD THE FUTURE

Given the speed of current technological development for studying the human brain, it is likely that research knowledge about schizophrenia will accumulate rapidly in the coming decade. Many believe that new knowledge of brain diseases, such as schizophrenia, will outdistance new knowledge of all other diseases, including cancer, until the beginning of the next century. It is an exciting time for those in the field.

One of the limiting factors on such predictions, however, is the limitations on manpower and funds for schizophrenia research. Currently in the United States there are estimated to be only 300 psychiatrists engaged in full-time research on mental diseases, of a total pool of 27,000 psychiatrists. Of these 300, perhaps one-third are working predominantly on schizophrenia. These are complemented by approximately an equal number of PhD's (such as psychologists and biochemists) also working on schizophrenia. It is not a large number given the magnitude of the disease.

The reason for this paucity of researchers on schizophrenia is a parallel paucity of research funds. Researchers migrate to where the funds are. In fiscal year 1980 the federal government provided a total of $143 million to the National Institute of Mental Health (NIMH) for mental health research. Of this amount approximately $20 million went for research on schizophrenia (one-half for research grants and contracts and one-half for research actually done at the Institute). The $20 million spent on schizophrenia research was approximately the same amount which the federal government spent on research on tooth decay. The big research money went to such diseases as heart disease ($298 million) and cancer ($761 million).

One may criticize the National Institute of Mental Health for not putting greater priority on schizophrenia research. To spend only $20 million out of $143 million—14 percent—on a disease which occupies one-half of all psychiatric hospital beds in the nation seems sadly shortsighted. One may also criticize NIMH for not allocating more of its total resources to research. As the President's Commission noted in 1978, almost 50 percent of the NIMH budget went to research in 1955, but by 1977 that had decreased to 24 percent.

There is also very little money available for schizophrenia research from private sources. In contrast to cancer, diabetes, muscular dystrophy, and some other diseases, there is no national fundraising campaign, no door-to-door solicitation, no jars to put coins in next to the cash register. Neither is there any appreciable support for schizophrenia research by private foundations, with one important exception: since 1934, the Scottish Rite of Freemasonry, headquartered in Boston, has supported a modest schizophrenia research program. Currently this totals approximately $500,000 a year; given the fact that the total federal expenditure is only $20 million, the Scottish Rite grants have made a significant contribution to the field.

Why has schizophrenia research been short-changed? The basic answer is that nobody has fought very hard for it. There has been no schizophrenia lobby, no concerned citizens group, no pressure on legislators. Such things are possible, of course, as will be detailed in chapter 12. But to put it crudely, at least up to this point in history schizophrenia research has not been considered to be very chic.

6

THE TREATMENT OF SCHIZOPHRENIA

To be schizophrenic is best summed up in a repeating dream
that I have had since childhood. In this dream I am lying on a
beautiful sunlit beach but my body is in pieces. This fact causes
me no concern until I realize that the tide is coming in and that
I am unable to gather the parts of my dismembered body together to run away. The tide gets closer and just when I am on
the point of drowning I wake up screaming in panic. This to me
is what schizophrenia feels like; being fragmented in one's personality and constantly afraid that the tide of illness will completely cover me. I like to hope that one day medical science will
find a permanent cure.

Schizophrenic patient, quoted in Henry R. Rollin,
Coping with Schizophrenia

Contrary to the popular stereotype, schizophrenia is an eminently treatable
disease. That is not to say it is a curable disease, and the two should not be
confused. Successful treatment means the control of symptoms, whereas cure
means the permanent removal of their causes. Curing schizophrenia will not
become possible until we understand its causes; in the meantime we must
continue improving its treatment.

The best disease model to explain schizophrenia is diabetes, a disease
which has many similarities. Both schizophrenia and diabetes have childhood
and adult forms, both almost certainly have more than one cause, both have
relapses and remissions in a course which often lasts over many years, and both
can usually be well controlled, but not cured, by drugs. Just as we don't talk
of curing diabetes but rather of controlling its symptoms and allowing the
diabetic to lead a comparatively normal life, so we should also do with schizophrenia.

HOW TO FIND A GOOD DOCTOR

There is no easy answer to this question, one which is most frequently asked
by friends and relatives of persons with schizophrenia. There are very few

doctors in the United States who either know anything about, or have any interest in, schizophrenia. This is both shocking and sad, since it is one of the most important chronic diseases in the world. In Europe, especially the British Isles and Scandinavia, it is somewhat easier to find a good doctor.

Since schizophrenia is a true biological disease, and since drugs are the mainstay of treatment, there is no avoiding the doctor-finding issue. If schizophrenia is to be properly treated, sooner or later a doctor will need to be involved. He or she will be needed not only to prescribe the proper drugs but also to do an initial diagnostic work-up, including laboratory tests, in order to rule out other diseases which may be masquerading as schizophrenia. Before the schizophrenia is treated, one had better be certain that it is not really a brain tumor or herpes encephalitis in disguise. Only a doctor can do this.

The best way to find a good doctor for schizophrenia or any other disease is to ask others in the medical profession whom they would send their own family to if they had a similar problem. Doctors and nurses know who the good doctors are and pass the information freely among themselves; often they will tell you if you ask. If your brother-in-law has a sister who is a nurse, all the better. Use every contact and every relative you have, however distant, to locate and identify competent doctors who may know something about schizophrenia. It is an appropriate time to cash in all your IOUs, for the information is invaluable and may save you months of searching.

Another way to find a good doctor is through other families who have a schizophrenic family member. They can often provide a quick rundown of the local resources and save weeks of hunting and false starts. Sharing this information is one of the most valuable assets of organizations of relatives of schizophrenics. These support organizations, which are proliferating rapidly, provide bewildered relatives ready access to others who have faced identical problems and who may have invaluable ideas (see chapter 8 for a detailed account of these organizations, and appendix C for a list of them). Without such help one must flounder through the local mental health labyrinth until, by chance, the right resources are identified. The frustrations of such searches are well described by James Wechsler in *In a Darkness* and the Gotkins in *Too Much Anger, Too Many Tears.*

Distinctly *un*helpful in searching for a good doctor are referral lists maintained by local medical societies or the local chapters of the American Psychiatric Association. Anyone can call these organizations and obtain three names. The names, however, are taken from a rotating list of those doctors who are looking for additional patients. Since any doctor who wishes to pay the annual dues can belong to these organizations, there is no screening or ascertainment of quality of any kind. Even those doctors who are under investigation for malpractice will continue to be listed by such organizations until they are specifically removed from membership, which is an all-too-rare occurrence. Thus referral lists from medical and psychiatric societies are really no better than picking a name at random from the physicians' list in the Yellow Pages.

What should one look for in a good doctor who can treat schizophrenia? Ideally he/she should combine technical competence with an interest in the disease and empathy with its sufferers. Training in psychiatry or neurology is helpful but not mandatory; there are some internists and family practitioners who have an interest in schizophrenia and can treat it very competently. As a general rule younger physicians who have been trained recently are more likely to view schizophrenia as a biological disease. However, there are major exceptions to this rule: some older practitioners who will tell you, "I've said all along it was a real disease" and some younger practitioners who still believe that what is needed is psychoanalysis of the mother-child relationship.

In trying to find a good doctor it is perfectly legitimate to ask them questions, such as "What do you think causes schizophrenia?" and "Do you believe in drugs to treat it?" Such questions will usually elicit the relative biological orientation of the practitioner—or its absence—quite rapidly and save both time and money. The goal is to find a physician who views the schizophrenic, in the words of one psychiatrist, "as a suffering patient, not a defective creation of abstruse, mystical, psychic body parts."

How important is it for the physician to be "board eligible" or "board certified" in his/her speciality? "Board eligible" means that the physician has completed an approved residency program in that speciality. "Board certified" means that the physician has taken and passed an examination in the special-ity. Such board examinations are completely optional and are not required for licensure or for membership in any professional organization. They are simply a badge indicating that, at the time the boards were taken, the physician knew the theoretical knowledge required to be competent in that speciality area.

Unfortunately, there is relatively little relationship between success in passing board examinations and being a good physician capable of treating any disease, including schizophrenia. I have known many board-certified psychia-trists who were woefully incompetent to treat anyone with schizophrenia, and I have known some physicians—psychiatrists and otherwise—who have never taken board examinations who were excellent. Some physicians have refused to take the board examinations because of the belief that they are irrelevant; others (including me) have refused to take them on the grounds that they should be made mandatory in order to provide consumers with a guaranteed minimal level of knowledge. Until that time comes, it is probably wise for families to seek out "board eligible" (i.e., fully trained) physicians and to further favor those who are "board certified," but not to let this factor be an overriding consideration.

What about nonphysicians for treating schizophrenia? These include psychologists, psychiatric social workers, nurses (especially psychiatric or public health nurses), and mental health counselors of various kinds. These people may be perfectly appropriate for ongoing care of patients with schizophrenia *once* the person has been properly diagnosed by a physician and *if* a physician is overseeing the patient's medications. Such nonphysicians often do a better job of continuing contact and psychiatric assessment since they are usually more available and less hurried than physicians. You do need a medical degree to diagnose persons with schizophrenia and to prescribe drugs for them, but you do not need a medical degree to provide ongoing care. This has been demonstrated many times.

For those looking for a good doctor to treat schizophrenia, one final word of caution. Doctors are human beings and, as such, run a wide range of personality types. Throughout the medical profession can be found occasional physicians who are dishonest, mentally ill, addicted to alcohol or drugs, sociopathic, or who have some combination of the above. I have a sense that psychiatry attracts more than its share of such physicians, often because the physician has become interested in his/her own mental aberrations. Thus one should not make an absolute assumption that physicians who treat persons with schizophrenia are themselves beyond question. If the physician seems strange to you, move on quickly to another. There *are* occasional strange birds in the psychiatric aviary.

SHOULD THE PERSON BE HOSPITALIZED?

In most cases persons *acutely* ill with schizophrenia need to be hospitalized. Such hospitalization accomplishes several things. Most importantly it enables mental health professionals to observe the person in a controlled setting. Laboratory tests can be carried out to rule out other medical illnesses which might be causing the symptoms, psychological testing can be done, and medication can be started in an environment in which trained staff can watch for side effects. In addition, the hospitalization often provides the family with a respite from what have often been harrowing days and nights leading up to the acute illness.

Hospitalization is also often necessary to protect such patients. Some will try to injure themselves or others because of their illness (e.g., their voices tell them to do so). For this reason most hospitals utilize a locked ward for acutely agitated schizophrenics, and its use is often necessary. Even in a locked setting the person occasionally may be dangerous and require additional restraints. These may include wrist or ankle restraints (usually made of leather), a special jacket which keeps the arms next to the body (the famous straitjacket of popular lore), or a seclusion room. None of these measures should be necessary for more than a few hours if the person is being properly medicated. It is currently chic in some circles to condemn locked wards and all use of restraints as "barbaric" and antiquated; the people who make such statements have usually never been faced with the task of providing care for persons with acute schizophrenia. It certainly will be nice when we arrive at the point where medications are instantly effective in acutely disturbed patients and restraint is not necessary, but we have not reached that nirvana yet.

There are ancillary benefits of hospitalization for persons with schizophrenia. Well-functioning psychiatric units have group meetings for the patients; this often allows each of them to see that his or her experience is not unique. Occupational therapy, recreational activities, psychodrama, and other forms of group interaction often accomplish the same thing. For someone who has been acutely schizophrenic and who has experienced many of the disturbances described in chapter 2, it is usually a relief to learn that other people have experienced them too. None of the above activities are likely to be of much benefit, however, unless the person is also being properly medicated to relieve the acute symptoms.

There are several different types of hospitals available in which people can be treated for schizophrenia. Psychiatric wards in community hospitals have become increasingly common in recent years and are often satisfactory. Psychiatric wards in university (teaching) hospitals generally have good reputations. Private psychiatric hospitals run a wide gamut from those of excellent reputation to fly-by-night operations in which making a profit is the main incentive and quality of care is often sacrificed. Of special concern are private hospitals which are owned by the psychiatrists themselves; in these instances there is an inherent conflict of interest between the needs of the patient and the need of the psychiatrist to make money. This may be seen, vividly, in the frequent instances in which the length of hospitalization in such hospitals coincides with suspicious closeness with the maximum period covered by the patient's hospitalization insurance. When the insurance runs out, the patient is declared well and discharged.

In addition to community, university, and private hospitals, there are also state and Veterans Administration (VA) hospitals. The VA hospitals are very similar to state hospitals except that only those who have served in the armed forces are eligible for admission to them. State hospitals, by contrast, are open to everyone and run as wide a range in quality as do the private psychiatric hospitals.

In selecting a hospital for treatment, the most important factor by far is the competence of the treating psychiatrist. The type of hospital is relatively insignificant compared with this factor. Thus, in some state hospitals there are well-run wards with a competent psychiatrist offering excellent treatment for schizophrenia; and there are other wards in state hospitals which are still proverbial snake pits. The same can be said for private psychiatric hospitals and VA hospitals. As a general rule, community hospitals and university hospitals offer a more predictably high level of care than state, VA, or private hospitals, but this is not always so. I have treated patients who have received abysmal care in both community and university hospitals.

A measure of hospital quality which has become increasingly useful in recent years is accreditation by the Joint Commission on Accreditation of Hospitals (JCAH) in Chicago. At the invitation of a hospital, JCAH sends a survey team to evaluate it, as well as provide consultation and education. The survey is very thorough, focusing especially on patient care and services but also including such related issues as the therapeutic environment, safety of the patient, quality of staffing, and administration of the hospital. The survey team then recommends that the hospital receive full three-year accreditation, full accreditation with a contingency (which may necessitate a follow-up inspection to insure that the contingency has been corrected), or no accreditation. Full accreditation by JCAH probably means that the hospital is a good one although, since the accreditation is for the hospital as a whole, there may be individual wards in an accredited hospital which are below standard. The JCAH certification of accreditation is usually displayed by hospitals in the entryway or lobby; alternatively, anyone in the hospital administrator's office can tell you, or you can find out by writing to JCAH, 875 North Michigan Avenue, Chicago, Illinois 60611. Currently approximately one-half of the state psychiatric hospitals and three-quarters of the private psychiatric hospitals and general hospitals are accredited.

A yardstick for measuring hospital quality which is *not* very useful is the fees charged. People throughout the world have a strong inclination to equate higher cost with higher quality of medical care, but this is erroneous; in psychiatry, as in the rest of medicine, that which costs more is not necessarily better. Far more important is the JCAH accreditation status.

How, then, should a hospital be chosen? The answer is, again, first to identify a good doctor. Since doctors have admitting privileges in a limited number of hospitals, you will probably have to hospitalize the person where the doctor you choose has access. If you have a choice, because the doctor has more than one hospital affiliation, always opt for a JCAH-accredited facility.

ALTERNATIVES TO HOSPITALIZATION

Hospitalization is usually necessary for schizophrenic patients who are sick for the first time, for the reasons described above. For those who have already been clearly diagnosed and who have relapsed (usually because they have stopped taking their medicine), hospitalization can sometimes be avoided. There are several possible alternatives.

One such alternative is the use of drugs given by injection in an emergency room or clinic. A skilled physician can dramatically reduce the psychotic symptoms in approximately half of schizophrenic patients within six to eight hours, thereby allowing the person to return home. One problem with this technique, however, is that frequently the family members are so worn out by the person's recent behavior that *they* need the rest and understandably are not prepared to accept the schizophrenic home again immediately.

Another alternative is the treatment of the schizophrenic patient at home, using public health nurses or, rarely, physicians to make home visits. This technique is used much more often in England, with apparent success. It was also demonstrated to be feasible in a study done in Louisville by Benjamin Pasamanick and his colleagues, who concluded that "the combination of drug therapy and public health nurses' home visitation is *effective* in preventing hospitalization, and that home care is at least as good a method of treatment as hospitalization by any or all criteria, and probably superior by most." It has also been used successfully in a special treatment program in Madison, Wisconsin. I utilized it once when practicing in a rural village, when the family expressed a wish to keep the person at home if possible; it required home visits for injections twice a day for a week, but it was successful.

The use of partial hospitalization is another good alternative. Day hospitals, in which the patient goes to the hospital for the day and returns home at night, and night hospitals, in which the patient goes to the hospital only to sleep, can both be effective in selected cases. Since both cost less than full hospitalization they may be useful in communities in which they are available. They are usually affiliated with a full-time institution. Unfortunately both are much less available than they should be in the United States. When present, they are inspected by the JCAH accreditation team at the same time as the parent institution is surveyed.

Another theoretical alternative to hospitalization is the use of homes or hostels set up to provide care for acutely psychiatrically disturbed individuals in the community. There are only a handful of such institutions in the United States, the best-known being Soteria House in Palo Alto, California. It has accommodations for six patients (called residents) and two staff members. Medications are used only when absolutely necessary. The staff spends long hours talking with newly admitted schizophrenic patients about their symptoms, and the psychosis is used as "a growth experience" after the fashion popularized by R. D. Laing in London. I would never recommend such institutions for persons with schizophrenia, but others may feel differently and wish to utilize them.

COMMITMENT PROCEDURES: HOW TO GET
SOMEONE INTO A HOSPITAL

It is ideal when people with schizophrenia recognize that they are becoming sick and voluntarily seek treatment for their sickness. Unfortunately, however, this is often not the case. Schizophrenia is a disease of the brain, the body organ charged with the responsibility of recognizing sickness and the need for treatment—the same organ which is sick. Out of this unfortunate coincidence arises the frequent need for schizophrenic persons to be committed to psychiatric treatment settings against their will.

How does the commitment process work? All laws governing commitment of psychiatric patients are state laws, not federal laws. Therefore commitment laws vary from state to state, especially those governing long-term commitment. In addition, commitment is a legal area very much in flux, and the laws are currently being amended in several states. To keep up with developments in this field it is recommended that the *Mental Disability Law Reporter* be consulted; this is a bimonthly publication of the American Bar Association (see appendix D).

Legally there are two rationales for the commitment of mental patients. The first is referred to as *parens patriae* and is the right of the state to act as parent and protect a disabled person; it arose in early English law from the belief that the king was the father of all his subjects. The second is the right of the state to protect other people from a person who is dangerous. The first right may be invoked when persons are so disabled that they do not recognize their own need for treatment or cannot provide for their own basic needs and therefore may be dangerous to themselves. The second may be invoked when persons, because of their mental illness, are dangerous to other people.

The legal and ethical ramifications of commitment procedures are manifold and complex. Some of the ethical issues will be covered in chapter 9; this chapter will focus more on the actual mechanics of getting a person committed to a hospital and getting him or her out again. It should be noted, however, that there has been a broad swing in the last decade toward making the commitment of mental patients more difficult. In particular there has been a move to narrow the use of *parens patriae* in many states and a reliance on stricter "dangerousness" criteria instead. Since it is well known that the ability of psychiatrists to predict dangerousness accurately is very poor, this swing, in effect, insures that many fewer psychiatric patients will be committable in the future. Given abuses of commitment procedures in the past, many people believe that this swing is both corrective and helpful. Other people (including me) believe the swing is going too far, making it too difficult to get people into the hospital who need to be there and who can benefit from treatment. A healthy dialogue on commitment is under way and is likely to continue.

There are two kinds of commitment—emergency and long-term. The basic purpose of commitment laws is to enable persons who are psychiatrically ill to be put forcibly into hospitals so that they will not harm themselves or others and can be treated. This can be done as follows:

1. A petition for commitment of the person thought to be psychiatrically ill must be initiated. In most states this can be done by one of several persons; for example, Tennessee allows petitions to be filed by "the parent, guardian, spouse, or a responsible adult relative of the individual or by any licensed physician or licensed psychologist or by any health or public welfare officer, or by the head of any institution in which the individual may be, or by any officer authorized to make arrests in Tennessee."

2. The person initiating the petition asks a physician (not necessarily a psychiatrist) to examine the person for whom commitment is sought. Some states require two physicians to be examiners while others allow psychologists. If the examiner(s) conclude that the person is mentally ill and meets the grounds for commitment in that state (see appendix A), then the examiners' report is attached to the petition and it is filed.

3. The examination may take place anywhere, including in the person's home.

4. If the person for whom commitment is sought refuses to be examined, many states have a provision for the petitioner to file a sworn written statement. In, for example, Nevada, this says, "such person is mentally ill and, because of such illness, is likely to harm himself or others, or is gravely disabled."

5. Once the petition has been filed, a police officer can bring the person to the hospital for examination by a psychiatrist.

6. Alternatively, if any person is acting strangely in public, a police officer can bring the person to the hospital for examination by a psychiatrist.

7. The examining psychiatrist at the hospital decides on the basis of his/her examination whether the person meets the criteria for commitment in that state. If the person does, emergency commitment is effected and the person is kept at the hospital. If not, the person is released.

8. An emergency commitment lasts for seventy-two hours in most states, not including weekends and holidays. At the end of that period the person must be released unless either the director of the hospital or the family has filed a petition with the court asking for long-term commitment. If this has been filed, then the person can be held until the hearing.

9. The hearing for long-term commitment may be held in a room in the hospital or in a courtroom. The person alleged to be mentally ill is expected to be present unless a psychiatrist testifies that the person's pres-

ence would be detrimental to his/her mental state. The person is represented by a lawyer appointed by the state if necessary, and normal judicial rules of evidence and due process apply. Testimony may be taken from the examining psychiatrist, from family members, and from the person alleged to be mentally ill.

10. The hearing is held before a Mental Health Commission, judge, or similar judicial authority depending on the state. In nineteen states the person has the right to a jury trial if he/she so wishes (see appendix A).

The major differences in commitment procedures among states are the grounds which are used for commitment and the standard of proof. In states that utilize only dangerousness to self or others and define dangerousness stringently, it is generally more difficult to get a commitment than in states which define dangerousness vaguely (for example, Texas laws say a mentally ill person can be committed "for his own welfare and protection or the protection of others"). Similarly, in states in which "gravely disabled" or "in need of treatment" are grounds for commitment by themselves, it may be easier to get a commitment.

The standard of proof utilized by states is also a major source of variation, and these are summarized in appendix A. The most stringent level of proof is "beyond a reasonable doubt," the same standard used to judge persons charged with crimes. Currently eight states utilize this (California, Hawaii, Kansas, Kentucky, Massachusetts, New Hampshire, Oklahoma, and Oregon). If all other things are equal (see below), then it should be theoretically more difficult to commit a mentally ill person in these states. A lesser level of proof is "clear and convincing evidence," which is utilized in the rest of the states. In 1979 the United States Supreme Court ruled that the use of "clear and convincing evidence" was an acceptable level of proof under the Constitution and that "beyond a reasonable doubt" could be utilized by individual states if desired but was not required. The ruling in effect says that the same level of proof is not required to commit a person to a mental hospital as is required to convict a person of a crime and commit him/her to jail. Civil rights lawyers interested in the mentally ill continue to fight for more stringent standards of proof, whereas many psychiatrists and families of schizophrenics would prefer to see the standard of proof remain more flexible.

In the past some states utilized standards of proof more lenient than "clear and convincing evidence." Texas, New Jersey, and Mississippi, for example, required only "a mere preponderance of the evidence" for a person to be involuntarily committed; this was generally interpreted to mean that the evidence on each side was added up and the side with the "preponderance of the evidence" won. Since the 1979 Supreme Court ruling, however, these states have had to adopt stricter criteria.

Probably the most important variables in determining how easy or difficult it is to commit psychiatric patients to hospitals are the specific judge involved and the local community standards. As lawyers well know, laws are written one way but can be interpreted in many ways, and this is certainly true for those concerned with psychiatric commitment. Thus in the same state one judge may interpret dangerousness much more stringently than another, and what for one judge is "clear and convincing evidence" is for another judge not at all persuasive. The standards of the community vary as well, with some localities more inclined to "lock up all those crazies" whereas another part of the same state may be reluctant to commit people unless absolutely necessary. Also important is the current local milieu. For example, if a former psychiatric patient has recently been accused of murder in the local newspaper, the tendency may be to commit everyone with acute symptoms. If, on the other hand, the local newspaper is doing an exposé on the poor conditions in the state hospital, the tendency may be to commit nobody unless absolutely necessary.

What does all this mean for a family with a schizophrenic member who is in need of treatment and who refuses to go to the hospital? It means that the family must first learn the commitment procedures and criteria which apply in that state. The quickest way to do this is to telephone or visit the admission unit of the nearest state psychiatric hospital, whose personnel are usually experts in this area. Other potential resources for this information are the local or state Department of Mental Health, public defenders, psychiatrists, or policemen. The family must also know what kinds of evidence are necessary and admissible to prove dangerousness. Are threats to other people sufficient, or does the person actually have to have injured someone? Families who wish to can usually testify at the commitment hearing, and their knowledge of what proof is necessary will often determine whether the person with schizophrenia is or is not committed. Indeed, many persons with schizophrenic family members have become amateur lawyers in order to survive!

COMMITMENT PROCEDURES: HOW TO GET SOMEONE OUT OF A HOSPITAL

The other side of the commitment coin is protection of people's rights and getting those who have been committed out of the hospital. There is no question that commitment laws were too liberal in the past and that they were abused. Popular psychiatric literature in the last decade has abounded with horror stories of people committed indefinitely to mental hospitals on the strength of one person's signature.

Thanks to reformers in this field, especially Bruce Ennis of the American

Civil Liberties Union and Paul Friedman and Charles Halpern of the Mental Health Law Project, all this is changing. Psychiatric patients increasingly have the rights to counsel, the rights to a jury trial, and the rights to appeal which are guaranteed to other people before they are involuntarily incarcerated. This is the way it should be. The current push and pull between those fighting for more commitments and those fighting for fewer is a healthy struggle and a sign that the democratic process is well. For those who wish to keep up with the blow-by-blow account of this struggle, subscriptions to *Mental Disability Law Reporter* will be more than sufficient.

Psychiatric patients who are being, or have been, committed have several safeguards. Initially they can demand a "probable cause" hearing in some states, which is a preliminary assessment of whether the person should be held beyond the seventy-two-hour provision of the emergency commitment. This hearing can be conducted before a judge. The actual legal proceedings determining commitment are usually held before a mental health commission (a mixture of lawyers and psychiatrists) or a judge. In many states the patient now has the right to a jury trial (see appendix A), a right which should be extended to all states. Other basic legal safeguards, such as written advance notice of proceedings, prompt hearings, the right to be present at all proceedings, the right to call witnesses, the right to appeal, and the right to periodic review of all commitments, should also become incorporated into the laws of all states. Persons who have been committed, or relatives or friends on their behalf, may also petition for a writ of habeas corpus to question the legality of detention and request the court for release.

Most important is the right to be represented and defended by a lawyer at all commitment hearings. In the past this was often a sham, with the patient's lawyer not defending him/her at all. In recent years, with the growth of legal advocacy for the poor and of public defenders, this has improved dramatically. There now exist in many parts of the United States legal organizations specializing in defending the rights of mental patients. Some of these are public defender units funded by the local government or the Department of Justice. Others are local units of the National Legal Services Corporation, an independent federal corporation which underwent some reduction in funding during the Reagan administration but which continues to provide legal services for the poor. Still others are small groups of independent lawyers who have developed a special interest in the legal problems of psychiatric patients. For a patient with schizophrenia, or a relative or friend interested in the legal defense of such patients, the best way to identify the local resources is to telephone the local bar association. In addition, lists of these organizations on a state-by-state basis can be ordered for $15 from the National Legal Aid and Defender Association, 1625 K Street, N.W., Washington, D.C. 20006. An older listing is also included as an appendix in the excellent American Civil

Liberties Union handbook *The Rights of Mental Patients,* by Bruce J. Ennis and Richard D. Emery.

DRUGS: THE MOST IMPORTANT TREATMENT

Once a competent doctor has been located and the intricacies of hospitalization have been mastered, then the treatment of schizophrenia becomes comparatively simple. Drugs are the most important treatment for schizophrenia, just as they are the most important treatment for many physical diseases of the human body. Drugs do not *cure,* but rather *control,* the symptoms of schizophrenia—as they do those of diabetes. The drugs we now have to treat schizophrenia are far from perfect, but they work most of the time for most of the people with the disease if they are used correctly.

Drugs used to treat schizophrenia are usually called antipsychotics. They have also been called neuroleptics and major tranquilizers, but the best term is "antipsychotic" because that is what they are. They frequently do not produce tranquilization, so that term is a misnomer.

The fact that antipsychotic drugs work is now well established. They reduce symptoms of the disease, shorten the stay in the hospital, and reduce the chances of rehospitalization dramatically. Whereas persons with schizophrenia entering a psychiatric hospital used to stay for several weeks or months, the average stay with these drugs is now reduced to days. And the data on their preventing rehospitalization is even more impressive. John Davis, for example, reviewed twenty-four scientifically controlled studies testing whether antipsychotic drugs were effective. All twenty-four studies found that schizophrenic persons who took antipsychotic drugs were less likely to have to return to the hospital than those who did not take these drugs. The differences between the two groups were highly significant, especially for persons with chronic schizophrenia. On the average, a person who takes the drugs has a 3-out-of-5 chance (60 percent) of not being rehospitalized, whereas the person who does not take the drugs has only a 1-out-of-5 chance (20 percent) of not being rehospitalized.

When studies have been done on the long-acting, injectable form of antipsychotics (where compliance in taking the drug is assured), the results are even more impressive. In one study of chronic schizophrenic patients, only 8 percent of the patients who were taking the drug relapsed within one year, but 68 percent of those not taking the drug relapsed. In another study of schizophrenic patients taking injectable antipsychotics, 80 percent relapsed within two years when the drug was stopped. What all this means is that though taking the drugs does not guarantee you will *not* get sick again and not taking the drugs does not guarantee you *will* get sick again, their use improves the odds toward staying out of the hospital tremendously. The data on the effectiveness of drugs are so clear that any physician or psychiatrist who fails to try them on a person with schizophrenia is probably incompetent. It is not that drugs are the *only* ingredient necessary to treat schizophrenia successfully; they are just the most essential ingredient.

Antipsychotic drugs are not equally effective for all the symptoms of schizophrenia. They are most effective at reducing delusions, hallucinations, aggressive or bizarre behavior, thinking disorders, and the symptoms having to do with the overacuteness of the senses. For example, against auditory hallucinations, one of the most common and disabling symptoms of schizophrenia, antipsychotic drugs are 80 to 90 percent effective in being able to relieve the hallucinations, usually making them disappear altogether. The drugs are less effective (often completely ineffective) against symptoms such as apathy, ambivalence, poverty of thought, and flattening of the emotions.

Antipsychotic drugs were discovered in 1952 in France. Physician Henri Laborit noticed that a new drug synthesized as an anesthetic was unusual in its ability to sedate patients without loss of consciousness. He persuaded psychiatrist Jean P. L. Delay and his colleagues to try the new drug, chlorpromazine, on their schizophrenic patients. The results were remarkable, and its use spread rapidly all over the world. Although this original drug (better known by its trade name of Thorazine) is still in use, it has been largely superseded by better and more potent alternative antipsychotic drugs.

There are seven different types of antipsychotic drugs currently available in the United States. They are listed in table 1 by their chemical class, their generic name (the official name for that chemical compound), and their trade names (the brand names used by drug companies for that product; e.g., Thorazine and Largactil are both chlorpromazine, exactly the same drug chemically and marketed by two different drug companies under their own registered trade names).

Antipsychotic drugs are usually given as tablets or liquid. Tablets can be taken once or twice a day and are more effective if taken on an empty stomach. If taken at the same time as antacids containing aluminum or magnesium (information that appears on the lists of ingredients on their labels), their effectiveness is reduced. Some people believe that taking them with tea or coffee also reduces their effectiveness, but recent studies have not supported this idea. Tablets may usually be crushed for ease of administration. There is also a liquid form of many of the antipsychotic drugs, which can be mixed with juice and may be useful if there is a question whether the patient is really swallowing the tablets; the liquid form is usually more expensive. Many of these drugs can also be given as a short-acting intramuscular injection, and one (fluphenazine decanoate) can be given as a long-acting injection which lasts anywhere from

Table 1

Types of Antipsychotic Drugs

Type	Generic Name	Trade (Brand) Names*
Aliphatic phenothiazines	chlorpromazine	Thorazine, Chloramead, Chlorprom, Chlor-Promanyl, Largactil, Promachlor, Promapar, Promosol, Terpium, Sonazine
	promazine	Sparine, Norzine, Promabec, Promanyl
	triflupromazine	Vesprin
Piperidine phenothiazines	thioridazine	Mellaril, Novoridazine, Thioril
	mesoridazine	Serentil
	piperacetazine	Quide
Piperazine phenothiazines	fluphenazine	Prolixin, Permitil, Moditen
	trifluoperazine	Stelazine, Clinazine, Novoflurazine, Pentazine, Solazine, Terfluzine, Triflurin, Tripazine
	perphenazine	Trilafon, Phenazine
	prochlorperazine	Compazine, Stemetil
	carphenazine	Proketazine
	acetophenazine	Tindal
	thiopropazate	Dartalan
	butaperazine	Repoise
Thioxanthines	thiothixene	Navane
	chlorprothixene	Taractan
Butyrophenones	haloperidol	Haldol
	droperidol	Inapsine
Dibenzepines	loxipine	Loxitane, Daxolin
Dihydroindolones	molidone	Moban, Lindone

*The trade names of drugs can be found in the *American Drug Index* (Philadelphia: Lippincott, 1981) and the *U.S. Pharmacopeia Dispensing Information* (Rockville, Md.: U.S. Pharmacopeia, 1981).

one to six weeks. Injections are extremely useful for individuals who find it difficult (or refuse) to take pills; they have to return to the clinic for another injection only once every two weeks (on the average) in order to stay well. Injections are usually given in the buttocks, although they can be given in the arm if preferred.

Several other antipsychotic drugs are available in Europe but not yet in the United States. They include oral forms of flupenthixol (Fluanxol), which is a thioxanthine, and sulpiride (Dogmatil), which is said to have antidepressant, as well as antipsychotic, properties. Of particular interest are two butyrophenones available abroad, penfluridol (Semap) and pimozide (Orap), which are long-acting and effective when taken orally as infrequently as once a week; applications for their approval by the Food and Drug Administration for use in the United States have been pending for over ten years. Also of interest are other long-acting injectable preparations available in Europe, including the phenothiazines perphenazine enanthate and pipotiazine (said to be effective for four to six weeks), the thioxanthines flupenthixol decanoate

(Depixol) and cis-clopenthixol (Clopixol), and fluspirelene (Redeptin, Imap). The more such different antipsychotics there are available to treat schizophrenia, the greater the chances of finding a suitable one for any given patient.

There is currently no way to predict which drug is best for which person with schizophrenia, and the only way to find out is by trial and error. There are two clues to predicting response which should be noted, however. First, if a person responds well to a certain drug one time, then he/she is likely always to respond well to that drug. Second, if another person in the same family has been psychiatrically ill and responded well to a certain drug, then it is likely that other members of the same family who become ill will also respond well to that drug. This suggests that there is a genetic predisposition to how well one responds to these drugs. In practical terms, this means that all persons who have been treated for schizophrenia, and their families, should know which drugs they respond well to and which ones are ineffective. This can be extremely helpful and save weeks of trial-and-error medications, if the person becomes sick again or if another member of the family is stricken. It is also worthwhile for this information to be on a card in the patient's wallet or purse.

Persons with schizophrenia who do not respond to one type of drug at all may respond well to another type of drug, a very important fact. This is true even of those schizophrenic patients who have been sick for many years. I have treated patients who have been given chlorpromazine for twenty years with poor results and who, once they were switched to another type of drug such as haloperidol, improved dramatically. It is one of the major tragedies of schizophrenia that in the state hospitals the newer types of antipsychotic drugs have not been tried on many patients; some of them would certainly respond and some could then be released from the hospital. Patients and families of patients with this disease should insist that the treating physician or psychiatrist try each of the major types of antipsychotic agents. And if the doctor switches the patient from one drug to another drug of the same type (e.g., from fluphenazine to trifluoperazine) then he/she probably doesn't know what he is doing because, with rare exceptions, switching to different drugs within the same drug type makes no sense at all. Such treatment suggests that it is time to look for a new physician.

It has become clear only in recent years that different people require widely varying doses of these drugs to be effective. This is probably also a genetic trait and is not surprising in view of how differently our bodies handle other chemical compounds. One ounce of alcohol will make one person intoxicated and will not even be felt by another. Similarly, when 20 milligrams a day of fluphenazine was given to a group of schizophrenic patients and then the blood level of the drug was measured, the difference between the lowest and highest blood level was *fortyfold*. The absorption and excretion of antipsychotic drugs varies widely from person to person, so that one patient requires 10 milligrams and another patient 400 milligrams to achieve identical blood levels. The practical implication of this for doctors is the need to be very flexible in thinking about dosage. It also seems clear that many patients who have been tried on drugs and have not responded failed to respond because the drug was not tried in high enough dosage. This information is in conflict with a presently popular stereotype of mental hospitals which portrays all the patients as being overmedicated. The truth is quite the opposite, and in every state hospital I have been in I can find at least five *undermedicated* patients with schizophrenia for every one who is overmedicated.

But stereotypes die slow deaths, and the image of the overmedicated, "zonked-out," "zombied" schizophrenic patient is a very strong one. It has its principal origin in the fact that the *symptoms* of schizophrenia are often confused with the *effects* of the drugs used in its treatment. Thus families see their schizophrenic relatives sitting lethargically, apathetic and ambivalent, and suffering poverty of thought, and they assume that the drugs made them that way. All one has to do to prove that this is not so is to talk with anyone who had to care for schizophrenic patients *before* antipsychotic drugs were introduced in the 1950s; they will invariably tell you that *more* patients were "zonked-out" in the old days.

This is not to say that antipsychotic drugs are never abused or that patients are not sometimes overmedicated for the convenience of the hospital staff who want to calm them down. These things certainly do happen. But stereotypes to the contrary, this is a relatively minor problem in the treatment of schizophrenia compared with the number of patients with the disease who have never been given an adequate trial of available medications.

The other fact which has reinforced the stereotype of overmedicated schizophrenic patients is the reputation of drug companies in the United States. Drug companies have a comparatively bad reputation among many segments of the American public, a reputation which I believe they have earned and deserve. Through countless congressional hearings and investigations it has become clear that drug companies often make excess profits, sometimes falsify test data, and frequently put too little money into developing new and useful drugs. It is therefore easy to imagine that these companies are responsible for everything wrong which has anything to do with drugs, including the overmedication of schizophrenic patients. This is not true, however, and it is important not to confuse the two issues.

What is an adequate dose of antipsychotic medication? As mentioned above, this varies widely from person to person. On the average, however, it is at least 20 milligrams a day of fluphenazine or haloperidol, two of the most widely used and useful of the drugs. This dose is adequate to treat the acute symptoms of schizophrenia in many patients, although I have had patients get well on as little as 5 milligrams a day and others who required up to 200 milligrams a day. Fluphenazine and haloperidol provide the baseline against which other drugs should be judged for they provide the most antipsychotic effect with the least milligram dose. The equivalent dose of other antipsychotic drugs is seen in table 2.

Like the oral medication, the dose and frequency of the injectable preparations also varies widely. One patient may remain well on 25 milligrams every six weeks, another may require 200 milligrams a week or more. In recent years there has been a move to extend the dosage range on both ends of the spectrum. Thus there appear to be patients who remain well on as little as 5 milligrams every two weeks, and others who remain well only on massive doses of up to 900 milligrams a week; patients on the very high doses have been followed in Sweden for up to eight years with no more apparent side effects than at the medium dose range. Doses of all these drugs should be reduced in people who are over 50 years of age because changes in liver and kidney function make it more difficult for the body to excrete drugs. Therefore a lower dose of a drug usually has a comparatively greater effect on the older patients.

Decisions regarding drug use and dosage are ultimately physicians' decisions. Because there are not yet sufficient test data to prove that one particular approach is superior to another, methods of using antipsychotic drugs vary from physician to physician. A currently popular technique for treating a patient with acute schizophrenia is to begin with 5 to 20 milligrams a day of fluphenazine or haloperidol, then to increase the dosage rapidly at a rate of 10 to 20 milligrams a day for a few days until symptoms (such as the auditory hallucinations and delusions) have improved or until side effects force a reduction in dosage. When the symptoms have substantially abated, the dose of the drug can slowly be reduced to a maintenance level. Improvement is usually seen within a few days, and occasionally within a few hours (especially if the drug is given by injection). However, when trying a new drug type on a person with chronic schizophrenia, improvement is not seen as quickly, and the trial should last at least one month before it is given up as a failure.

How long should the drugs be taken by persons with schizophrenia? This is also an area where opinions outnumber facts. In general, antipsychotic drugs should be continued for only a short time if the person has only had schizophrenia for a short time and for a long time if the person has had schizophrenia a long time. Thus in someone who has been diagnosed and treated for schizophrenia for the first time, it is usually safe to discontinue the drugs a few weeks after the person has recovered. As described in chapter 4, one-third of these people will never get sick again.

If the person has had more than one attack of schizophrenia or if recovery has not been complete, then the drugs should probably be continued for longer periods of time. After the second or third attack, for example, I ask patients

Table 2

Equivalent Doses of Antipsychotic Drugs

The following list of antipsychotic drugs by drug equivalency is only approximate. Fluphenazine and haloperidol, the most potent (and among the most used) are taken as the baseline. To find out what an equivalent dose of another drug is, multiply by the number indicated. Thus 10 milligrams of fluphenazine is approximately equivalent to 20 milligrams of thiothixene ($\times$ 2), 50 milligrams of molindone ($\times$5), 100 milligrams of acetophenazine ($\times$10), 150 milligrams of mesoridazine ($\times$15), and 200 milligrams of chlorpromazine ($\times$20).

Generic Name	Trade (Brand) Names
Baseline	
fluphenazine	Prolixin, Permitil, Moditen
haloperidol	Haldol
droperidol	Inapsine
Multiply $\times$ 2	
thiothixene	Navane
trifluoperazine	Stelazine and others
Multiply $\times$ 5	
perphenazine	Trilafon, Phenazine
butaperazine	Repoise
molidone	Moban, Lindone
loxapine	Loxitane, Daxolin
thiopropazate	Dartalan
piperacetazine	Quide
Multiply $\times$ 10	
prochlorperazine	Compazine, Stemetil
carphenazine	Proketazine
triflupromazine	Vesprin
acetophenazine	Tindal
Multiply $\times$ 15	
mesoridazine	Serentil
chlorprothixene	Taractan
Multiply $\times$ 20	
thioridazine	Mellaril, Novoridazine, Thioril
chlorpromazine	Thorazine and others

NOTE: Adapted from R. I. Shader, ed., *Manual of Psychiatric Therapeutics* (Boston: Little, Brown & Co., 1975); J. M. Davis, "Comparative Doses and Costs of Antipsychotic Medication," *Archives of General Psychiatry* 33 (1976): 858–61; and R. J. Baldessarini, "The Neuroleptic Antipsychotic Drugs," *Postgraduate Medicine* 65 (1979): 108–19. Differences among the authors were averaged.

to continue taking drugs for several months after they are well, usually at a reduced dosage level. If they have had several episodes of the disease I advise them to continue taking the antipsychotic drugs for the rest of their lives, just as many diabetics have to take insulin for the rest of their lives.

Our understanding of how antipsychotic drugs work is still incomplete but is increasing rapidly. It is known that these drugs block the transmission of dopamine in brain cells. Exactly how this is related to the symptoms of schizophrenia is not yet understood (see chapter 5), but those drugs which can block the dopamine most effectively appear to be the best antipsychotic agents.

It is a research area of much current activity.

The question of addiction to these drugs is also frequently raised by patients and their families. There is no evidence to date that antipsychotic drugs cause addiction. The person's body does not slowly get used to them and therefore require higher and higher doses, and the stopping of these drugs does not cause withdrawal symptoms. Antipsychotic drugs for schizophrenia are exactly the same as insulin for diabetes or digitalis for heart failure—they are drugs needed by the body to restore the functioning of the respective organs (brain, pancreas, and heart) to more normal levels.

What if the antipsychotic drugs do not work and the patient remains severely schizophrenic? This, unfortunately, does occur in a small percentage of cases, probably less than 10 percent. Despite trials of all known anti-psychotic drugs in adequate doses, he/she may continue to hallucinate, be delusional, and behave strangely. For such people it is worth trying alternative drugs. Lithium, a standard drug for manic-depressive illness, is proving to be a very useful ancillary drug for schizophrenia as well, especially for those patients who fall into the schizoaffective diagnostic category (see chapter 3). It is usually used in combination with antipsychotic medication. Lithium is a more difficult drug to monitor than antipsychotics, however, and should be supervised by a physician who has experience with it and who also has access to a laboratory which can measure the blood level of the drug at regular intervals. Other ancillary drugs which are being used experimentally for some schizophrenic patients include tricyclic antidepressants such as imipramine (Tofranil) and amitriptyline (Elavil), new anti-epileptic drugs, such as car-bamazapine (Tegretol), and a drug primarily used for hypertension called propranolol (Inderal). Given the veritable explosion of knowledge about brain chemistry which is under way, it is likely that many new drugs for treating schizophrenia will become available over the next ten years.

What kinds of drugs are *not* effective in treating schizophrenia? The commonly used mild tranquilizer benzodiazepine (e.g., Valium, Librium, Serax, Tranxene) should be included in this category. Sleeping pills and bar-biturates are also ineffective. It is important that friends and relatives of schizophrenics do not offer their own medications to the patients in an attempt to be helpful; some of these drugs interact with other drugs being taken and may cause serious side effects.

DRUG SIDE EFFECTS AND TARDIVE DYSKINESIA

"The antipsychotic agents," says Dr. Ross J. Baldessarini, "are among the safest drugs available in medicine." As one of the foremost experts on these drugs, Dr. Baldessarini should know, yet his claim is at variance with popular stereotypes of the drugs. It is widely believed that antipsychotic drugs have terrible side effects, are dangerous, and almost invariably produce tardive dyskinesia (involuntary muscle movements) and other irreversible conditions which may be worse than the original schizophrenia.

Dr. Baldessarini is in fact correct, and the popular stereotype is wrong. Antipsychotic drugs are among the safest group of drugs known. It is almost impossible to commit suicide with them by overdosing, and their serious side effects are comparatively rare.

Then why is there such a strong misperception and fear of these drugs? Much of the reason can be traced to theories of causation of the disease. As we have noted, it is only in the past few years that the evidence for schizophrenia being a real biological disease has become clear. The resistance to this idea among mental health professionals, especially psychiatrists trained in the psychoanalytic or other psychogenic belief systems, has been impressive. And one of the ways this resistance is shown is by strongly opposing the use of drugs; implicitly, if the drugs are too dangerous to be used, then schizophrenic patients will again have to rely on psychotherapy and other nondrug modes of treatment. For this reason it is not uncommon to find psychiatrists who should be better informed warning schizophrenic patients about all kinds of terrible calamities which will befall them if they take antipsychotic drugs.

This is *not* to say that antipsychotic drugs are perfectly safe and have no side effects whatsoever. They do have side effects, sometimes so severe that the drug must be stopped. The side effects have on occasion even been fatal, but this is very rare. One of the main goals of the current search for newer antipsychotic drugs is to find effective compounds which will continue to suppress psychotic symptoms while producing minimal undesirable side effects. But it is important to repeat that the point to be remembered is that antipsychotic drugs, as a group, are one of the safest groups of drugs in common use and are the greatest advance in the treatment of schizophrenia which has occurred to date.

The side effects of antipsychotic drugs can be discussed as a group. Some side effects are more common with particular drugs, but the differences are not great. And, like side effects to all drugs used in medicine, it is not possible to predict ahead of time with any accuracy which person is likely to get which side effect. The side effects can be divided into five types: common and less serious; uncommon and less serious; common and more serious; uncommon and serious; and tardive dyskinesia.

1. *Common and less serious:* In this category are many side effects which people complain of when first starting to use these drugs. The most common

are dry mouth, constipation, and blurring of vision. Drowsiness occurs commonly with the aliphatic and piperidine phenothiazines (see table 1, page 113) but much less commonly with the other types. These side effects usually diminish or go away altogether after the first few weeks of use.

More frightening to the patient are side effects such as restlessness (called akathisia), stiffness and diminished spontaneity (called akinesia), slurring of speech, tremors of the hands or feet, and dystonic reactions. In the latter the neck muscles become rigid, it is not possible to turn the head, the eyes may become fixed, looking toward the ceiling, and it becomes difficult to talk. Some patients get none of these side effects; others get them all.

Dystonic reactions can be completely counteracted within minutes by giving the patient an anticholinergic drug, such as benztropine (Cogentin), biperiden (Akineton), procyclidine (Kenadrin), or trihexyphenidyl (Artane). It is known that these reactions occur more commonly among males and more commonly among younger patients. Generally it is felt that anticholinergics should not be given prophylactically to prevent these side effects from occurring, because they have side effects of their own and also some potential for abuse (it is possible to get high on them). Current theory holds that the doctor should wait to see whether patients develop these side effects, and then treat them with the anticholinergics. There are, however, times when it is useful to use the anticholinergics prophylactically and avoid the side effects. This is especially true when the main symptoms are paranoid delusions and the patients suspect that their doctor may be trying to poison them. If they develop a dystonic reaction they will be *sure* of it, and this may permanently jeopardize their trust in the doctor. Another reason for possibly using anticholinergic drugs to avoid these reactions is a recent study that suggests they may enhance the effectiveness of the antipsychotic medication

Restlessness, stiffness, slurring of speech, and tremors respond in varying degrees to anticholinergics. When they do not respond, it is often necessary to stop the drug and try alternative antipsychotic medication. Akinesia is especially difficult to evaluate because it includes not only stiffness but also diminished spontaneity of physical movements, gestures, and speech. As such it may be indistinguishable from residual schizophrenic symptoms in the patient or demoralization and depression as a reaction to illness. It takes an experienced clinician to evaluate such side effects and to try systematically to minimize them by using anticholinergics, reducing the drug dosage, trying other medications, or trying a drug-free interval.

The relationship between the patient and the physician is critical in this evaluation; the better the physician knows the patient, the easier and more accurate such evaluations become. It is not uncommon for mental health professionals to view these side effects as not serious in a medical sense whereas the patient may see them otherwise. As one patient described it:

I am unfortunate in feeling quite seriously affected, with symptoms ranging from a dry mouth and blurred vision to a terrible tension and restlessness and fears of "losing myself " completely and being entirely controlled by the drugs. These feelings are often hard to appreciate, and therefore doctors are inclined to prescribe medication without really being aware of the implications for the patient. . . . Somehow I think I prefer to be a little bit "mad" than overdosed by major tranquilizers.

Another patient felt the antipsychotic drugs had inhibited her thinking:

Whereas I lived in a fascinating ocean of imagination, I now exist in a mere puddle of it. I used to write poetry and prose because it released and satisfied something deep inside myself; now I find reading and writing an effort and my world inside is a desert.

This divergence between the physician's and patient's view of a drug's side effects is usually greatest when the patient has little memory for the more psychotic period of his or her illness and the doctor has a clear image of just how sick the patient was without the drugs. I have often wished that I had a videotape to show to patients in such instances, so that we could share the same information base. In the end, however, the decision as to whether to continue taking the antipsychotic drug will be the patient's, although the family often is intimately involved in these deliberations as well.

2. *Uncommon and less serious:* Side effects in this category are seen less often than the above. Menstrual changes in women can be caused by antipsychotic drugs; discharge from the breasts can also occur. Both are caused by the effect of the drugs on the pituitary gland and may be annoying, but they are rarely serious enough to stop the drugs. Rashes, loss of appetite, and increased salivation are other uncommon and nonserious side effects.

Changes in sexual functioning definitely occur as a side effect of antipsychotic drugs, but both their frequency and their seriousness are matters of dispute. Decreased sexual desire may be found in both sexes and impotence or retrograde ejaculation may occur in men; the latter occurs especially with thioridazine (Mellaril). It is difficult to evaluate how many of these effects are due to the drugs, how many are due to the schizophrenia, and how many antedated the disease altogether. For example, impotence is a common condition among men, and it is obviously inaccurate to blame all impotence in men taking antipsychotic drugs on these drugs.

It is similarly difficult to evaluate the seriousness of these symptoms since sexual functioning varies so widely in people who do not have schizophrenia. For some people, with comparatively little interest in sex, the decreased libido from antipsychotic drugs may not even be noticed. For others it may be a disaster of monumental proportions and they may insist on stopping the drugs for that reason. I have one patient, for example, who definitely is impotent when he takes antipsychotic drugs and who becomes acutely psychotic whenever he does not. He is faced with a painful dilemma; the role of the physician in such cases should be to outline the choices and consequences as clearly as possible and then support the person's choice. This kind of dilemma is fortunately not common.

3. *Common and more serious:* There are three side effects of antipsychotic drugs which are relatively common and potentially serious. One is oversensitivity to the sun (called photosensitivity) in which the person may become sunburned much more easily; it occurs most commonly with the aliphatic phenothiazines. Such people must wear wide-brimmed hats and be very careful when they are outside on sunny days; strong sunscreens also provide effective protection. Another potentially serious side effect is fainting whenever the person goes from a lying to a standing position; this is called orthostatic hypotension and is also seen most commonly with aliphatic and piperazine phenothiazines but rarely with the other drugs (see table 1, page 113).

Weight gain is another potentially serious side effect and may sometimes involve the gain of one hundred pounds or more. A large gain is always serious, for it can often be life-shortening and can also lead to other diseases. Antipsychotic drugs definitely cause weight gain in some people. In others it is less clear whether the weight gain is a direct consequence of taking the drugs or whether it is a consequence of inactivity due to the disease itself. Some schizophrenic patients may have symptoms, such as auditory hallucinations and delusions, which are relieved by the antipsychotic drugs, but continue to show apathy, withdrawal, and inactivity which then lead to weight gain. With all of these more serious side effects it is sometimes necessary to take the person off the drugs.

4. *Uncommon and serious:* Antipsychotic drugs can have serious and, rarely, even fatal side effects, but fortunately these are uncommon. Liver damage was seen more commonly in the past, especially with chlorpromazine, but is rarely observed now even when chlorpromazine is used; the reasons for this decline are not known. Damage to the blood-forming organs, thus decreasing the number of white cells, may occur, making the person very susceptible to infections. Damage to the eye lens or the retina has been reported, especially with thioridazine, as has also a worsening of glaucoma. Blockage of the urinary tract, especially in men who have enlarged prostates, and intestinal obstruction are also known to occur occasionally. Convulsions have been reported. Rarely, abnormalities in heart function or unexplained high fevers may lead to death.

Uncommon though all these serious side effects are, they must always be kept in mind when patients are being given these drugs.

5. *Tardive dyskinesia:* Much of the fear of using antipsychotic drugs is linked to a fear of tardive dyskinesia. This syndrome has received much publicity in recent years, and most persons with schizophrenia, and their families, have been warned about it. The condition usually develops in schizophrenics who are older and who have been on antipsychotic drugs for many years. It consists of involuntary movements of the tongue and mouth, such as chewing movements, sucking movements, pushing the cheek out with the tongue, and smacking of the lips. Occasionally these are accompanied by jerky, purposeless movements of the arms or legs, or rarely, even the whole body. It usually begins while the patient is taking the drug, but rarely may not begin until shortly after the drug has been stopped. Occasionally it persists indefinitely, and no effective treatment has been found to date.

The frequency and seriousness of tardive dyskinesia is one of the most hotly debated topics in current psychiatry. Estimates of frequency are confounded by the fact that the movements of tardive dyskinesia can be caused by schizophrenia, as well as by the drugs used to treat it. Kraepelin described such movements in patients as early as 1904; more recently researchers found involuntary movements in one-half of all chronic schizophrenics who had never been treated with antipsychotic medications. Thus, to say what portion of tardive dyskinesia is drug-caused and what portion is disease-caused is not really possible. The most informed estimate to date is that 13 percent of chronic schizophrenic patients suffer from some degree of drug-induced tardive dyskinesia. This also falls within the 10 to 20 percent range estimated by the American Psychiatric Association's 1980 task force on the subject. It occurs more commonly in women than in men.

In the great majority of cases the early symptoms of tardive dyskinesia will abate and the condition disappear when the antipsychotic medication is stopped; thus mental health professionals must be alert for it. In a minority of cases it will not. Its cause appears to involve abnormalities in the dopamine pathway, and it is likely that treatment will become available as these brain chemicals are better understood. In the interim it is good practice for physicians to use the lowest effective dose of antipsychotic medication, to discuss the problem openly with patients and their families, and to help them weigh the risks of tardive dyskinesia against the risks of recurrent schizophrenia. As the American Psychiatric Association task force concluded, "While the problem is serious, an alarmist view is unwarranted."

Antipsychotic drugs should not be taken by pregnant women unless absolutely necessary. While there is not yet strong evidence that these drugs directly damage the fetus, it is possible that they do. In individual cases it is sometimes judged necessary to give them to pregnant women who are acutely psychotic, and in such instances it is essential to weigh the possible damage of the drug to the fetus against the possible danger to the patient of remaining psychotic. Her family should be involved in such deliberations.

Finally, people with certain kinds of medical problems should be especially careful in taking antipsychotic drugs because the drugs may worsen their concurrent condition. Heart disease and strokes may be affected by the drugs, and people with epilepsy may get seizures more frequently. Those with serious liver disease and kidney disease may not be able to excrete an antipsychotic drug very well, causing it to build to toxic levels in the body, and persons with glaucoma or difficulty in urinating may find these conditions become worse. People being treated with guanethidine (Ismelin, Esimil) for hypertension should be given a different antihypertensive drug, for antipsychotics will interact with the guanethedine and render it ineffective.

For all these reasons it is important that a person with schizophrenia or his/her family give the treating physician a full medical history and that he/she have a complete physical examination before antipsychotic drug treatment is begun.

INDIVIDUAL PSYCHOTHERAPY

Insight-oriented psychotherapy, in which the therapist tries to make the patient aware of underlying unconscious processes, is now known to be not only useless in treating schizophrenia, but probably detrimental. Freud himself recognized that schizophrenic patients "are inaccessible to the influence of psychoanalysis and cannot be cured by our endeavors," but that observation has not stopped his followers from trying.

Five separate studies have now demonstrated that insight-oriented psychotherapy is of no value for schizophrenia. Probably the best-known of these studies was done by Philip R. A. May and his colleagues at Camarillo State Hospital, California. May randomly assigned 228 schizophrenic patients to five separate wards where they were treated by (1) psychotherapy alone, (2) psychotherapy plus drugs, (3) drugs alone, (4) milieu alone, and (5) electroconvulsive therapy. The patients who did best were those treated by drugs alone or psychotherapy plus drugs, and there were virtually no differences between the two groups; the patients who did worst were those treated by psychotherapy alone or milieu alone. The inescapable conclusion is that psychotherapy added nothing to the treatment regimen in this study. These patients were followed up for from three to five years after the initial treatment and the results did not change: "Analysis of variance indicated an extremely significant effect from drug . . . , no significant effect from psychotherapy."

May's study has been criticized by some for utilizing psychotherapists with limited experience. Another study therefore treated twenty schizophrenic patients for two hours a week for two years, with therapy provided by highly experienced psychotherapists. At the end of the study period the outcome was said to be that "psychotherapy alone (even with experienced psychotherapists) did little or nothing for chronic schizophrenic patients in two years." Such studies were summarized by Donald Klein, one of America's most respected psychiatrists: "There is no scientific basis for the affirmation of clinical benefit from the individual psychotherapy of schizophrenic patients." And Judd Marmor, former president of the American Psychiatric Association, has said that, given what we now know, to treat schizophrenic patients with psychotherapy alone without using drugs is malpractice.

Utilizing psychotherapy for the treatment of schizophrenia without also utilizing drug therapy is a sin of omission. There is some evidence that the use of psychotherapy may actually be detrimental and make some schizophrenic patients sicker; thus it would be a sin of commission as well. In the May study, for example, the "outcome for patients who received only psychotherapy was significantly worse than the outcome in the no-treatment control group." In other words, getting no treatment at all led to better outcomes than being treated with psychotherapy alone. This correlates with the individual experience of many psychotherapists who have given up treating schizophrenic patients because many of their patients seemed to get worse. In following up Freud's original formulation about unconscious homosexual impulses being the cause of paranoid schizophrenia, one psychiatrist "checked the therapeutic successes of psychoanalysts and found to our surprise that it is common experience, frequently admitted and often implied, that not only are 'paranoid' patients not improved by homosexual interpretations, but even made worse." Gerald Klerman, while director of the Alcohol, Drug Abuse and Mental Health Administration and thus the highest-ranking government psychiatrist, also acknowledged that "recent evidence suggests that high intensity psychotherapy may actually have negative effects in schizophrenia."

Given what we now know about the brains of persons with schizophrenia, it should not be surprising to find that insight-oriented psychotherapy makes them sicker. Such persons are being overwhelmed by external and internal stimuli and are trying to impose some order on the chaos. In the midst of this a psychotherapist asks them to probe their unconscious motivations, a difficult enough task even when one's brain is functioning perfectly. The inevitable consequence is to add insult to injury, unleashing a cacophony of repressed thoughts and wishes into the existing internal maelstrom. To do insight-oriented psychotherapy on persons with schizophrenia is analogous to directing a flood into a town already ravaged by a tornado.

It is remarkable, however, how many people (including people in the mental health professions) still believe that psychotherapy is effective in treating schizophrenia. One reason for this has been popular accounts of such treatment, especially *I Never Promised You a Rose Garden.* The problem with this account is that the patient was not really schizophrenic but rather hysterical. Moreover, it must be remembered that one-third of all first admission schizophrenics will get well spontaneously no matter what "treatment" is used —psychotherapy, drugs, dandelion extract, and pureed gumdrops are all equally "effective." Claims for the effectiveness of psychotherapy, or any other mode of treatment, must establish that it is more effective than this one-third spontaneous cure rate. To date, only drugs have convincingly and unequivocally so established themselves. Thus, it is apparent that thousands of families have spent large sums of money for a treatment modality which may have made the patient worse.

Insight-oriented psychotherapy should not be confused with a long-term supportive relationship between a person with schizophrenia and a mental health professional; this latter kind of relationship can be very helpful. It is sometimes called "supportive psychotherapy" but really consists primarily of friendship, advice, practical help in securing financial and supportive services, and caring. The mental health professional can be the same person who is monitoring the patient's medication or it can be another person—physician, psychologist, counselor, nurse, social worker, occupational therapist. Following a period of illness the relationship may consist of frequent meetings, but after an interval of time the contacts may become infrequent, sometimes reduced to only telephone calls or letters; they are nonetheless important. Dr. Werner M. Mendel, one of the few American psychiatrists who has followed individual schizophrenic patients for over twenty-five years, tells the story of one of his patients whom he treated for schizophrenia many years ago. The man, who still has residual symptoms but is able to function as an engineer abroad, flies to Los Angeles approximately once a year just to meet briefly with Dr. Mendel and get his chlorpromazine prescription refilled. The man only rarely has to take the chlorpromazine, but he carries it around in his pocket continuously and is reassured by the rattle of the pills. It takes about a year for the pills to turn to powder; the rattling stops, and so the man returns to Los Angeles for another refill. Mendel cites this as an appropriate and supportive long-term relationship, the pills being the daily reminder that Dr. Mendel will be there to help if the schizophrenia recurs.

There is scientific evidence that such a supportive relationship, when it is used *in addition to drug therapy,* is helpful in reducing the rehospitalization rate for schizophrenia. In one study patients were followed for one year after release from the hospital and offered one of four modes of follow-up: (1)

placebo* alone, (2) placebo plus supportive psychotherapy, (3) drugs alone and (4) drugs plus supportive psychotherapy. At the end of the year the rehospitalization rates were:

Treatment	Percentage of Patients Hospitalized
Placebo alone	72
Placebo plus psychotherapy	63
Drugs alone	33
Drugs plus psychotherapy	26

The "psychotherapy" used in this study included social services and vocational counseling provided by someone who was predictably available to the patients. The results suggest again that drugs are the single most important element in preventing rehospitalization but that a supportive relationship provides a measure of additional improvement.

Presumably such supportive relationships are effective by helping the person to accept the limitations of his/her illness and live more successfully in the community. In this sense supportive psychotherapy with a person with schizophrenia is similar to supportive psychotherapy with any person with a chronic disease which imposes limitations—polio, diabetes, kidney failure, etc. The person must learn to accept his or her disease and its limitations but to lead as normal a life as possible.

GROUP PSYCHOTHERAPY

Group psychotherapy, like individual psychotherapy, may run a broad range from insight-oriented groups to supportive meetings with an educational and/ or social focus. Traditional group psychotherapy with its emphasis on interpersonal processes (e.g., "Sam, why did you ignore Sally just now when she was talking to you?") or intrapersonal processes ("Edna, can you explain to the group why your self-esteem is so low?") is of no value for patients with schizophrenia. Of nineteen studies done on group psychotherapy with such patients, "sixteen either failed to demonstrate an effect or were uninterpretable or irrelevant . . . two showed possible but very dubious effects" . . . and "only one showed a minor clinical effect that was clearly not due to group therapy." Another reviewer of these studies concluded that "most controlled evaluations of group therapy with schizophrenics (especially long-term inpatients) showed meager, if any, therapeutic benefit from groups."

As with individual psychotherapy, there is some evidence that traditional

*A placebo is an inert or dummy medication with no physiological action.

group therapy with schizophrenic patients may even be detrimental. One study of aftercare centers for schizophrenics found that those centers which emphasized group psychotherapy had poorer results maintaining patients in the community compared with centers without this emphasis. Others have reported that group psychotherapy may precipitate the psychosis of persons who are becoming schizophrenic or bring about the relapse of those who previously have been sick.

Groups with a predominantly educational or social focus, on the other hand, may function like a long-term supportive relationship and may be helpful for some patients. As summarized by one reviewer of group psychotherapy studies, "It is tempting to conclude that the most effective types of psychosocial treatments for schizophrenia are those that provide the most comprehensive, corrective, and sustaining social support systems." Helpful groups may span a range from an in-hospital formal class on the nature of schizophrenia, such as has been tried at one Veterans Administration Hospital, to predominantly social and affiliative clubhouse atmospheres, such as are described in the following chapter.

SHOCK THERAPY, DIET, AND OTHER TREATMENTS

The use in schizophrenia of shock therapy, more formally called electroshock therapy (EST) or electroconvulsive therapy (ECT), is a controversial and unresolved issue in psychiatry. In the United States it is used very seldom, and most follow-up studies indicate that any benefits derived from it are transient. In Europe, in contrast, shock therapy is used frequently on patients with schizophrenia and follow-up studies are more sanguine. Its use has been vigorously opposed by ex-patient groups in the United States, and in states like California approval for its use must go through a special state-controlled board. In November, 1982, in a local referendum the city of Berkeley even voted to ban its use altogether, although this was later reversed by the courts. It is, therefore, not a realistic therapeutic alternative for most patients with schizophrenia.

No diet has been shown to be effective for schizophrenia, although many different diets utilizing vitamins have been advocated by proponents of orthomolecular theories (see chapter 5). Gluten-free diets have also been tried with contradictory results. Some families with schizophrenic members are convinced that the patient does better (or worse) when certain things are added to or deleted from his or her diet. My advice in such cases is to encourage the family to persist in the use of such a diet if it seems helpful and if the diet is nutritionally balanced and does not contain toxic amounts of any substance.

Other therapies are primarily of historical interest. Psychosurgery was utilized prior to the advent of antipsychotic drugs but no longer has a place in the treatment of schizophrenia. Similarly insulin shock therapy was commonly used during the two decades following World War II but is no longer thought to be of value. Newer therapies are tried from time to time, usually with great initial hopes and publicity; a recent example of this was hemodialysis, in which the blood of the schizophrenic patient is passed through a filter and returned to the body. Unfortunately, careful studies of this innovative attempt have failed to demonstrate that it has any effectiveness.

HOW TO PAY FOR TREATMENT

Schizophrenia is a very expensive disease. Many families have literally had their life savings wiped out in attempts to find adequate treatment for their schizophrenic member; Louise Wilson describes this vividly in *This Stranger, My Son*. Since the person with schizophrenia has often also caused chaos within the family unit, the financial burden exacerbates the strain between the schizophrenic and the family.

The best advice for families with a schizophrenic member is to spend what money is available early in the course of the illness to insure adequate diagnosis and trials of treatment. If this is done and the person afflicted is one of the unfortunate ones who do not recover, then do not continue bankrupting the family in a lost cause. Instead, utilize public hospitals and rehabilitative facilities, such as are described in chapter 7.

Exactly what does it cost to treat an episode of schizophrenia? If you were such a person in Washington, D.C., in 1982 and needed to be hospitalized for ten days, it would have cost approximately the following, depending on where you were admitted:

University hospital A	$3,100
University hospital B	2,500
Community hospital A	2,750
Community hospital B	2,080
Private, nonprofit hospital	2,200
Private, for profit hospital	3,740
Public hospital	(charges dependent on income)
Laboratory and psychological test fees	300
Drugs	50
Ancillary therapy fees (group, occupational, etc.)	300
Physician's fees	300

Thus the total bill would have been between $3,100 and $4,700 for the ten-day hospitalization, unless you went to the public hospital. Public hospitals charge patients only as long as they have assets to pay the costs.

The majority of people carry medical insurance which includes short-term psychiatric hospitalization. A recent survey found that 85 percent of Americans have some coverage for inpatient psychiatric care. Thus for a ten-day stay the majority of people are covered for some up to all of the hospital bill and for some up to 80 percent of the doctor's bills. The exact coverage varies from insurance plan to insurance plan, depending on whether one has purchased a plan with specific psychiatric options or not. Many plans have a ceiling on psychiatric hospitalization benefits in a single year (such as thirty days maximum); others pay only 50 percent of the doctor's fees; and others have a deductible. There has been a trend in recent years toward expanded short-term psychiatric hospitalization coverage under insurance plans; this is especially true if the hospitalization takes place in general hospitals (either on the psychiatric ward or on the general medical ward) as opposed to psychiatric hospitals. A family may therefore find that its insurance will cover hospitalization of the patient more effectively in a general hospital. There has also been a recent trend toward expanded insurance coverage for treatment in day hospitals (where the patient goes for the day and returns home at night), but a sharp countertrend toward restricting coverage for the number of patient's visits to psychiatrist's offices (outpatient visits). Another interesting insurance development has been the refusal by some companies to pay for orthomolecular treatment of schizophrenia or for psychoanalytic treatment unless antipsychotic drugs are also being used.

For individuals not covered by insurance, it may be possible to use Medicaid (for the indigent) or Medicare (for the elderly and disabled) to cover the costs of brief inpatient hospital care. Medicaid coverage varies from state to state, including the number of days of psychiatric hospitalization that Medicaid will cover. In some states Medicaid will pay for hospitalization on the psychiatric ward of a general hospital but not in a psychiatric hospital. Medicaid may also pay for care in nursing homes classified in either the "intermediate" or the "skilled" care category, allowing some elderly schizophrenic patients to be cared for in these facilities if they prefer. Medicaid does not cover halfway house costs, an omission which many people would like changed. Medicaid also covers outpatient psychiatric visits in some states, but the amount reimbursed to the psychiatrist varies widely from state to state.

Medicare also covers inpatient psychiatric costs for those who qualify but limits this to a maximum of 190 days for an entire lifetime. Therefore, for someone with schizophrenia who qualifies for Medicare, it may be most sensible to use the lifetime coverage early in the course of the disease in order to get a complete diagnostic assessment in a good hospital. Medicare also covers 50 percent of outpatient psychiatric costs up to a maximum of $250 in a single year. Thus if a psychiatrist charges $50 for a visit, Medicare will pay $25 of it. There is also a $60 annual deductible (i.e., the person must pay the first $60 in costs each year before the Medicare payments begin). These coverages and deductibles are those in effect in 1982 and are subject to change by congressional action. For physical illnesses Medicare pays 80 percent, rather than 50 percent, of outpatient visit costs, so the Medicare program discriminates against mental illnesses like schizophrenia—something which many people think should be changed.

In contrast to short-term psychiatric hospitalization coverage, there is virtually no insurance program which covers the cost of long-term care. Monthly fees for long-term care in private hospitals average about $5,000, making it prohibitive for all except the very wealthy.

The only realistic option open to most families with a schizophrenic member who requires long-term care is reliance on public hospitals and rehabilitative facilities. These vary widely in quality and availability, but some can be excellent, as will be described in the following chapter. Moreover, families *can* affect the quality of these institutions and facilities if they will work cooperatively and bring pressure on local and state governments.

7

WHAT COMES AFTER THE HOSPITAL

Schizophrenia is the cancer of psychiatry. People afflicted with
this disease are regularly in extreme difficulties. If they progress
to chronicity, they are in truly terrible trouble—socially, economically, vocationally, psychologically, emotionally, cognitively, and
you name it.

Donald F. Klein, *Schizophrenia Bulletin,* 1980

Among all the problems facing schizophrenic patients and their families in the
United States, none is greater than the problem of what comes after the
hospital. The problems of getting schizophrenic persons into the hospital and
the problems of getting appropriate treatment are relatively small compared
with the deplorable living conditions awaiting many patients after discharge.
Of all the blemishes on the face of American psychiatry, none is more conspic-
uous than this. When the history of human services is written, the plight of
discharged schizophrenics in the 1980s will surely be cited as a national
disgrace.

THE DEBACLE OF DEINSTITUTIONALIZATION

Up until the mid-1950s virtually nobody asked what came after the hospital
for one simple reason—almost nobody left the hospital. Schizophrenic patients
entered state hospitals with one-way tickets and stayed there until they died.
Even today, one of the hospitalized patients for whom I provide psychiatric
care has been in the hospital continuously since 1909, when he was 20 years
old. In the past this was a relatively common finding.

In the 1950s a shift took place and patients began to be released from
mental hospitals. The major reason for this was the introduction of antipsychotic drugs which effectively reduced the symptoms of schizophrenia in
many patients. Two-thirds of these released patients returned to live with their
families or relatives. In this manner the number of hospitalized mental patients
in the United States was reduced from a maximum of 557,000 in 1955, when
the releases began, to approximately 350,000 twelve years later. The majority
of the 200,000-patient reduction in the state hospitals were schizophrenics.

However, the first patients released were those who were comparatively easy to return to the community; they were the ones who responded best to the drugs, were least dependent on the hospital and, in a great many cases, had families to live with. So far so good.

But in the late 1960s there was a change. The word "deinstitutionalization" became a catchword. What had been a relatively orderly return to the community became a mass, disorderly exodus as the state hospital population was reduced by almost 200,000 additional patients. Whereas the first group had consisted of those who were relatively prepared for return to community living, the second group was woefully unprepared. They included those who responded poorly (or not at all) to the antipsychotic drugs, those who had become highly dependent on the state hospital, and those who had no family and nowhere to go. Many of them wanted to stay in the hospital. This group had not been prepared to leave and the community was not prepared to receive them.

The forces behind the deinstitutionalization movement have been a diverse mixture of judicial, political, and economic interests, and they have made strange bedfellows. Legal suits brought against states, such as the *Wyatt* v. *Stickney* suit in Alabama mandating better patient care (see chapter 9), frightened many states. Realizing that they could not provide better care, the states decided to discharge the patients instead and thus absolve themselves of the responsibility. Moreover, there was a powerful economic reality: the state mental hospital represented the largest, or next to largest, single budget item in most states. It did not take much persuasion for state legislators to vote to return patients to the community. While hospitalized, patients are the financial responsibility of the states alone, whereas in the community they receive much federal support, such as Medicaid, Medicare, Supplemental Security Income (SSI), and food stamps. By moving the patients from the hospital to the community the states saved money.

Finally, adding impetus to all this were liberal social and political forces which pictured hospitalized mental patients as mistreated captives needing to be liberated. A *One Few over the Cuckoos' Nest* mentality was in vogue throughout the 1970s and was shared by the media. Mental health professionals promoted the idea that many of the patients who had been hospitalized for years suffered primarily from the effects of institutionalization rather than from the symptoms of their disease, an idea which gained currency from sociological analyses, such as Erving Goffman's *Asylums*. It was radical chic to liberate the poor mental patients and return them to the community.

So the total state mental hospital population was reduced by almost 400,000 patients over twenty-five years. In California, a state which pioneered the deinstitutionalization movement, it was reduced most drastically, from 37,000 to 3,000 patients; in Massachusetts from 23,000 to 2,400. Despite these

massive transfers of patient responsibility from the state level to the community, however, there was no concomitant transfer of psychiatric staff or fiscal
resources to cope with them in the community. What the state politicians and
mental health planners expected to happen to all these patients loosed upon
the communities without resources is an abiding mystery. Moreover, in New
York State, the state hospital population shrank from 93,000 patients in 1955
to 24,000 in 1981. Yet, despite this reduction, not a single state hospital was
closed and the total state hospital employees during this period *increased* from
23,800 to 37,000. In 1955 there were four patients for each employee; in 1981
there were one-and-one-half employees for each patient.

Where did all the patients go? In fact we don't know the complete answer,
for many of them have been lost to follow-up. In New York State, for example,
of all the patients discharged from state mental hospitals in 1975, it is known
that 23 percent went to their own relatives' homes, 38 percent went to boarding
houses or hotels, and 11 percent went to nursing homes. The other 28 percent
vanished from the records. Some undoubtedly ended up on the streets living
as best they could. Such ex-patients can be found on the streets of every major
American city, often unable to care for their own needs. New York City is
estimated to have as many as 36,000 homeless vagrants living in its streets,
hallways, subways, waiting rooms, and heating ducts. Among this tide of
human flotsam, discarded by life's passing ships, are a large number of schizophrenics discharged from the state hospitals. In 1980 a psychiatric survey of
homeless individuals found that 60 percent of them were moderately or
severely mentally ill, and 7 percent in need of immediate psychiatric hospitalization. Even a smaller city, such as San Jose, California, has 1,100 former
mental patients living in a fifteen-square-block area downtown. As the homeless schizophrenics stand quietly in front of the vacant buildings in the inner
city, they have been likened to contemporary gargoyles. Future generations
will remember it as a disgraceful era in the history of human services.

It is important to note the different proportion of released patients who
went to their own homes in the first 200,000-patient reduction (1955 to 1968)
compared with the second 200,000-group (1968 to 1980). In the first group
two-thirds of the patients were released to their own or relatives' homes. In
the second group only one-quarter went to their own or relatives' homes. The
other three-quarters went to a variety of places, but especially to foster homes,
boarding houses, nursing homes, and cheap hotels.

Housing for released mental patients varies greatly. On one end of the
spectrum are small foster homes where each patient has a room, the food is
adequate, and the foster home sponsors watch over and worry about their
charges as if they were their own children. A larger version of this may be a
renovated hotel where the manager hires staff which organizes social activities
for the ex-patients, checks to be sure they are taking their medicine, reminds

them of dentist appointments, and helps them fill out applications for food stamps.

But at the other extreme are foster homes with sponsors who provide insufficient heat, blankets, and food, steal the patients' meager funds, use them as cheap labor, and sometimes even rape them or pimp them. The larger versions of these homes are old hotels that provide no services other than a rundown room and perform similar kinds of exploitations.

Predictably the deinstitutionalization movement has spawned many foster homes, boarding houses, and hotels on both ends of the spectrum and at all points in between. Exposés of abuses have been relatively infrequent, perhaps because the media are partly responsible for the deinstitutionalization movement itself and feel guilty about facing its failures. When the situation becomes abominable, however, word does reach the public, such as the released mental patients in New York living in private homes with broken plumbing, rotting food, roaches, no heat, and insufficient clothing. I have been in a similar home set up for twelve released mental patients which was located only five blocks from the White House. In another foster home that was closed in the nation's capital, according to a newspaper story, an unannounced inspection found dirty pans with mold growing on them and covered with roaches, "hundreds of roaches living in the oven feeding on a bag of prunes," multiple electrical and fire hazards, termites throughout the house, swollen cans of home-canned fruit, and for sleeping, only "one folding bed with a thin uncovered mattress which was urine stained and odorous." In Mississippi nine ex-patients were kept in a small wooden shed with no toilet or running water and only two mattresses and a cot for sleeping; "two vicious dogs chained outside the small room" insured that nobody left. In New York "the police found the decaying corpse of a former patient lying undisturbed in one home inhabited by six other residents." By no stretch of the imagination can it be argued that such people are better off than they were in the state hospitals.

Because the community living facilities are so poor in many places, the mental health professionals in charge of discharging patients from state hospitals are frequently caught in an ethical dilemma. Is the patient really better off in the community than in the hospital? Are the living conditions and exposure to potential victimization really an improvement? Though, as we have seen, the patients often do not want to leave the hospital, and the community, increasingly vocal against the released patients, does not want them to come, hospital administrators and state legislators often insist that they go. Whether this is a step forward or backward for the patients is frequently difficult to tell. Perhaps the back ward is merely being replaced by the back alley.

Unquestionably, the deinstitutionalization movement has proceeded without adequate planning for the needs of the patients. In most states they have been simply dumped onto the surrounding towns and cities and only after there is a predictable local backlash in the communities do the state officials become concerned. In only a few states, such as Massachusetts, has any serious planning for community facilities preceded the release of the patients.

By the early 1980s it had become clear that deinstitutionalization had been a debacle. The patients whose symptoms had been thought to be due primarily to the institutions were found to be just as sick in the community; rather than talking to voices in the ward dayroom they did so in downtown parks. The cost of maintaining the patients in the community was just as great as it had been in the state hospital; in fact, in 1980 the Massachusetts Commissioner of Mental Health announced that moving all the patients to the community and closing the state hospitals was turning out to be *more* expensive than the old system.

Moreover, many people were surprised to find that some of the released patients were trying to return to the state hospitals. Resistance in the communities where the patients had been placed was formidable and in some localities the existence of the patient clusters had become a major political issue. An article in the *American Journal of Psychiatry* castigated public officials and psychiatrists for not monitoring the massive changes more carefully:

> The failure to have evaluated adequately the effect of discharging hundreds of thousands of chronically ill patients from large public mental hospitals has been a major defect in the conduct of public policy. . . . Given the magnitude of social policy change entailed by deinstitutionalization and the two decades that have elapsed since it was put into motion, it is astonishing that so little productive effort has been put into evaluating the effects of the policy.

And *The New York Times* intoned an obituary for the movement: "Deinstitutionalization has become a cruel embarrassment, a reform gone terribly wrong, threatening not only the former mental inmates but also the quality of life for all New Yorkers."

It is against the bleak background of deinstitutionalization, then, that the needs of released schizophrenic patients must be assessed. These needs include psychiatric aftercare, housing, food, safety, medical care, employment, and social relationships.

PSYCHIATRIC AFTERCARE AND THE FAILURE OF COMMUNITY MENTAL HEALTH CENTERS

As was detailed in chapter 6, psychiatric aftercare is essential for schizophrenic patients who wish to minimize the symptoms of their illness and live in the community. Aftercare services should be readily available for such patients and should be organized so the patient sees the same mental health professional (or team of professionals) at each visit, to facilitate the proper evaluation of side effects and the forming of a supportive relationship.

How well have we done in providing aftercare psychiatric services for schizophrenic patients? The answer is very poorly. One summary of studies in this field estimated that no more than 25 percent of former schizophrenic patients get regular aftercare and less than half of them take medicine regularly. A 1977 General Accounting Office report described the failure in the state of Maryland:

> The mental hospital we visited had no formal procedure for referring patients to county mental health clinics. Only eight of the forty-seven patients we traced who were recommended for mental health clinic services went to the clinics as a result of a referral. The clinics had records on only five of the remaining thirty-nine patients.

Fortunately, not all hospitals do this badly. A review of patients released from hospitals in the states of Washington and Idaho found good follow-up compared with most of the United States. And the Canadian province of Saskatchewan has demonstrated what a good follow-up and aftercare program can accomplish. With 80 percent of released patients receiving continuous aftercare, the evidence shows that this not only can be done, but that it reduces the frequency of return to the hospitals, and improves the quality of life for the released patients.

The failure to provide aftercare for released schizophrenic patients in the United States is intimately connected with the failure of the community mental health centers. These institutions were a product of the brave new world of the early 1960s, an era when money for new social programs was plentiful and federal largesse was exceeded only by the optimism of the good ship Government. It was believed that building community mental health centers would really improve the life of mental patients, especially those in the state hospital system, by making psychiatric services available to them closer to home. No longer would it be necessary for queer old Aunt Polly to be taken off to the state hospital every few months for treatment, for she could go down to her local Community Mental Health Center (CMHC) instead and be treated as an outpatient. The CMHC program, thus, was basically a good idea put together by people with good intentions.

Since 1963 a total of 789 CMHCs have been funded by the federal government. The total amount of federal money invested in them is over $3 billion, and they theoretically provide at least five essential services (inpatient, outpatient, partial hospitalization, emergency, and consultation) for over half of the nation's population. But from the point of view of the schizophrenic patients in the United States, the CMHC movement must be regarded as an abysmal failure.

The major problem is that the CMHCs have never been interested in patients with schizophrenia. In 1975, for example, only 10 percent of all patients seen at CMHCs were diagnosed with schizophrenia. This should be contrasted with 21 percent of the patients diagnosed with neuroses and personality disorders and 22 percent with social maladjustments of various kinds. In short the CMHCs have served those with neuroses and problems of living of various kinds, but they have not served the schizophrenics. This is really an extraordinary deficiency, considering the original intent of the CMHC program and the magnitude of schizophrenia as a problem. It is as if the federal government had set up a system of cancer treatment centers and, seventeen years later, said that the centers hadn't gotten around to treating many cancer patients yet but they had treated a lot of patients with acne. It is not that patients with acne don't need help; it is just that the program was set up to treat patients with much more serious conditions.

But the news is even bleaker than this history indicates, for it shows that the trend is getting worse. In 1970, of all admissions to CMHCs, 19 percent had schizophrenia; in 1974 this had decreased to 11 percent; and this downward trend has continued. Conversely the percentage of CMHC admissions with social maladjustments increased during these same years from 5 percent to 20 percent. Just at the time when thousands of chronic schizophrenic patients were being released from state hospitals into the communities, the CMHCs were seeing proportionately *fewer* of them. Dr. Donald Langsley, president of the American Psychiatric Association 1979–80, acknowledged this deplorable state of affairs: "Many programs are moving from treating the most seriously and chronically mentally ill to providing care more oriented to social services—that is, care for patients with less serious illnesses and also assistance with their housing and sociocultural problems. . . ." And Dr. Gregory B. Leong of Los Angeles stated:

> The majority of mental health workers in these centers [CMHCs] prefer not to treat patients with mental disorders, but only healthy, insightful clients with problems in living. This seems ironic, since a primary reason for the development of the community mental health center was to treat patients returning to their communities as a result of the deinstitutionalization movement.

Supporters of CMHCs object to these figures and say they are misleading. The absolute number of schizophrenic patients seen in CMHCs has risen sharply, they maintain, from 51,000 admissions in 1970 to 92,000 admissions in 1975. The decrease in the *percentage* of schizophrenics seen was caused by an opening of many new CMHCs (from 255 in 1970 to 528 in 1975) and a resulting dilution of the percentage of schizophrenic patients by that of other patients. This seems to be grasping for straws. To defend CMHCs on these grounds is like saying that the centers set up to treat cancer are seeing more cancer patients now, but proportionately they are a smaller percentage because they are seeing an even greater number of patients with acne. One would certainly have hoped that the newly opening CMHCs during this period would have focused on the thousands of released schizophrenic patients more than they apparently did.

How could a program fail in its primary mission so colossally? As will be detailed in chapter 12, it failed mostly because there is no status in American psychiatry in providing care for schizophrenic patients. CMHCs rather quickly adopted the middle-class, psychotherapeutic coloration of private psychiatry, where the most desirable patients are those who can talk about their neuroses and problems of living. Schizophrenic patients are viewed as dull and uninteresting, needing only a prescription refill, and undesirable for the milieu of the waiting room because of their peculiar habits. The schizophrenic patients and their families got the message: they were not wanted.

Added to this was an incomprehensible failure of state systems to refer patients discharged from state hospitals to CMHCs. In 1969, in fact, one-third of all schizophrenic patients discharged from state hospitals were not referred to *any* outpatient follow-up facility. This was, of course, perfectly all right with CMHCs, who didn't want the schizophrenic patients anyway. As recently as 1979 I met a social worker employed full-time at a northern Virginia CMHC who not only never saw schizophrenic patients but did not even know which one of the three Virginia State Hospitals was supposed to refer its discharged patients to her center.

The National Institute of Mental Health must accept a large share of the responsibility for the failure of the CMHC program. NIMH, like many parts of the federal government, has proven itself adept at handing out money but less than interested in determining whether it is being spent wisely. From the earliest days of the CMHC program there has been abundant evidence that the centers were not providing care for patients with schizophrenia and other serious mental diseases. NIMH has chosen to ignore the evidence and do nothing. The reports of NIMH staff who visited the centers over the years contain many references to shortcomings of the program, but very little corrective action has been recommended. For example, a 1970 NIMH report on a CMHC in Minneapolis that was woefully deficient and seeing virtually no patients with schizophrenia stated: "The Center is not in complete compliance with the law and its applications in that it is obviously not providing all residents of its catchment area with the five basic services. . . . No follow-up by NIMH is necessary at this time." The centers were not doing the job and

NIMH staff preferred not to notice. It was a minuet of mutual deception.

During the early years of the CMHC program, NIMH also claimed that it was largely because of the CMHCs that the state hospital population was declining. Since the hospital population was in fact declining, this rhetoric was very effective in eliciting ever-increasing funds for CMHCs from Congress each year. The centers were seeing virtually no schizophrenic patients, and thus it was difficult to figure out how the centers could be responsible; but these minor details were brushed aside in the need to present effective public relations. Beginning in the early 1970s, however, a series of internal NIMH studies threw serious doubt on the official rhetoric. In areas where CMHCs had been started there was no more decline in the state hospital population than in areas where CMHCs had not been started. As summarized by one report: "No large consistent relationship appears between initiation of federally funded centers and change in inpatient rate in state mental hospitals."

By the mid-1970s it was clear to many people that the CMHC program would either have to change or it would go the way of the brontosaurus. Accordingly, Congress passed the Community Mental Health Centers Amendments in 1975 specifying that discharged state hospital mental patients, among others, *must* be given aftercare services by CMHCs; everyone politely ignored the fact that the same goal had been the intent of the original CMHC legislation more than a decade earlier. In 1977 NIMH initiated another new program called the Community Support Program (CSP), which provides funds to states and local communities to develop comprehensive support systems for chronically ill psychiatric patients. In 1982 alone almost $6 million was spent on this program. The funds are not to be used to begin services as such but are to be used to coordinate existing services for economic assistance, housing, vocational training, and education. Much of the rhetoric about what it is intended to accomplish is reminiscent of the CMHC goals of earlier years, and there is no reason to believe that it will be any more effective.

If CMHCs are not providing psychiatric aftercare for released schizophrenics, who is doing so? For some patients it is provided by a variety of local clinics run by cities, counties, university medical centers, or state hospitals. These clinics are frequently organized in such a way that the schizophrenic patient does not see the same professional or team of professionals on successive visits. A few released schizophrenic patients utilize private psychiatrists under Medicaid, but many psychiatrists will not accept Medicaid patients. The fact is, the majority of released schizophrenics receive no psychiatric aftercare, eventually relapsing and returning to the state hospitals. There medication is resumed, they improve, and they are again released to start the revolving door cycle over again. This cycle is the hallmark of schizophrenia over the past decade.

HOUSING AND FOOD

As mentioned previously, only 25 percent of released schizophrenic patients return to live with their families. According to a California study another 11 percent are able to live alone in their own home or apartment; those most likely to do this are those who lived by themselves prior to becoming sick and those who have not been hospitalized for a long period.

That leaves the majority of released schizophrenic patients, who live neither with their families nor alone. They live in boarding houses, single-room-occupancy hotels (New York City has an estimated 10,000 patients in such hotels), board-and-care homes, foster homes, halfway houses, nursing homes, YM and YWCAs, hostels such as the Salvation Army, jails, hallways, abandoned buildings, and on the heating grates of city streets. Of these alternatives, halfway houses have emerged as the most humane accommodation for a majority of patients.

The concept of halfway houses dates back six hundred years to Geel, Belgium, when mental patients were first put into homes associated with the "hospital" and given supportive services. Basically it assumes that the person requires more than just shelter and food; he or she also needs social companionship, work, and social support. Halfway houses provide a wide range of services for their residents; and for many persons with schizophrenia, they provide an ideal mix of support and independence. Some halfway houses include both released patients and other residents who have never been mentally ill (e.g., Conrad House in San Francisco and Wellmet in Cambridge, Massachusetts). In most halfway houses, however, the vast majority of residents have been diagnosed with schizophrenia. Some houses offer day programs only, although most provide living accommodations for at least some of their clients. Halfway houses differ in their primary emphasis (e.g., work, social activities, and companionship), in the strictness of their rules (visitors, alcohol), and in the length of stay of their residents (six months, indefinitely). In almost all of them the residents of the house share responsibilities for shopping, cooking, and cleaning.

Until recently there were very few halfway houses in the United States. Fountain House in New York City was among the first, and its excellent programs have continued for over thirty years. In 1950 there was only 1 other halfway house in the whole country. By 1960 this had grown to 40, and by 1970 to 200. A grant from the National Institute of Mental Health to Fountain House in 1976 permitted more persons to be trained to set up similar institutions, and in the past five years 117 more such houses have been established. Compared with the magnitude of the need, however, the present supply is still pathetically small. In New York City, for example, approximately 1,000 mental patients use the facilities of Fountain House each month, yet at least forty times that number live on the streets and in rundown hotel rooms. It is interesting to speculate how much better off chronic mental patients would be in this country if the federal dollars that have been put into Community Mental Health Centers had been put into halfway houses instead.

Income to pay for housing and food is also a basic need which must be solved by persons with schizophrenia. It has been estimated that approximately 25 percent of such patients are self-supporting. The largest source of income for the remainder is Supplemental Security Income (SSI), a federal program with supplements provided by some states. The SSI program provides income for needy aged, blind, and disabled persons and is administered by the Social Security Administration. It defines disability as "an inability to engage in any substantial gainful activity by reason of any medically determined physical or mental impairment which . . . has lasted, or can be expected to last, for a continuous period of not less than twelve months."

In the United States at the end of 1980 there were 550,000 mentally disabled individuals receiving monthly checks through the SSI program; the total cost of this support was $2.25 billion for the year. It is not known exactly how many of these mentally disabled individuals had a diagnosis of schizophrenia, but it would certainly be a majority. The amount of the monthly check varies, as approximately half of the states supplement the federal money with additional funds from state treasuries. The federal SSI payment is also tied by law to the cost of living and so has risen progressively in recent years.

Applications to establish disability and receive SSI funds should be made at the local Social Security office. The person's assets and other income are taken into consideration in computing eligibility. If he or she has assets worth more than $1,500 he may not be eligible; in computing assets a home and basic household goods do not count toward the $1,500. Income from a job of over $65 a month will also reduce the amount of the SSI payment. Thus a person with schizophrenia who is trying to go back to work must compute work income carefully to be certain that this income offsets the loss of SSI benefits.

The application for SSI is evaluated by a team consisting of a disability examiner and a physician; they may request additional medical information or even request an examination of the applicant in selected cases. In evaluating the application they pay special attention to evidence of a restriction of daily activities and interests, deterioration in personal habits, marked impairment in relating to other people, and the inability to concentrate and carry out instructions necessary to hold a job. Assessing eligibility for SSI is necessarily a subjective task, and studies have reported disagreement among SSI reviewers as much as 50 percent of the time.

If the applicant is denied SSI, he/she has the right to appeal. This must be done within sixty days of the denial, and additional evidence of disability can be included at that time. The initial reconsideration of the appeal occurs in the local Social Security office and results in approval only 15 percent of the time. However, the applicant may appeal again, and this time the hearing is before an administrative law judge of the Bureau of Hearings and Appeals of the U.S. Department of Health and Human Services. At this level 58 percent of appeals were approved in 1980. Further appeals are possible to a Department of Health and Human Services appeals council and then to a U.S. district court. It is clear that persistence in pressing a legitimate claim for SSI benefits will result in success most of the time. In 1982, however, the traditional success in the appeals process was brought into question when the Reagan administration tightened standards for SSI approval and review, and in many states some SSI recipients were removed from the rolls. Protests by families of schizophrenics and by psychiatric organizations mounted quickly; and the long-term outcome of this budget-cutting government initiative is yet to be determined.

Schizophrenics usually require assistance with SSI applications and, when necessary, with the appeals processes. Social workers who are doing these on a regular basis are often very helpful, especially in insuring that the correct clinical information is included so that the person's degree of disability can be assessed fairly. Persons applying for SSI for psychiatric disability for the first time would be wise to utilize the services of a knowledgeable social worker. Application forms and appeals processes are confusing even for persons whose brains are working perfectly; to a schizophrenic they must appear completely Kafkaesque.

SSI payments are reduced by one-third when the disabled recipient lives with his/her family. In theory this takes account of the room and board the person receives, but in fact it penalizes schizophrenics for living at home. Many families of schizophrenic persons resent this discriminatory living aspect of the SSI program and claim that they have expenses for the person just as surely as a boarding house operator does. SSI payments are also stopped if a person is hospitalized for more than thirty days. A portion of the SSI monthly payment is intended for the disabled person to use as spending money for clothes, transportation, laundry, and entertainment. This must be at least $25 a month (the federally designated payment), but is supplemented in most states and so usually is more.

It is important for persons with schizophrenia to establish eligibility for SSI benefits if they can. Even if they have other income, thereby reducing the monthly SSI check to a very small amount, it is still worthwhile. The reason is that eligibility for SSI may also establish eligibility for several other assistance programs which can be worth much more than the SSI benefits by themselves. Such programs include Medicaid, vocational rehabilitation services, food stamps, and some housing and rental assistance programs of the Department of Housing and Urban Development.

Persons with schizophrenia who are not self-supporting and not receiving SSI may utilize other sources of income. In some cases their families support them. Others may utilize public assistance and welfare payments. If the person is fortunate enough to have worked before becoming ill, he/she may be eligible for Social Security Disability Insurance (SSDI), which is more liberal than SSI because it allows the recipient to also work part-time without losing benefits. Schizophrenics who were in the military at the time they first became ill often qualify for disability payments from the Veterans Administration; these are often very generous and may total over $1,000 a month when all benefits are included.

Food stamps are another supplementary source of support for persons with schizophrenia and are under-utilized. To be eligible a person must have an income below the poverty level; this level includes many or most persons with schizophrenia. When the food stamp program first started, persons who were eligible were required to contribute some money of their own to get the food stamps (e.g., for $20 a person could purchase food stamps worth $50). This requirement was dropped in 1977 so that food stamps are now free to those who are eligible. The amount of food stamps a person can receive varies by state and with income. It also varies with the cost of food and so has been rising as food prices have been rising. Food stamps can be obtained through local welfare or social services offices.

MEDICAL CARE AND SAFETY

Discharged schizophrenic patients often encounter great difficulties in obtaining medical care. Medicaid and Medicare are the two programs which have been most useful. Medicaid, the federal program to pay medical costs for the indigent, is run by the states and eligibility and benefits vary considerably from state to state. In most states, a person who is eligible for SSI is automatically eligible for Medicaid, as well. Medicare, the federal program for the aged and disabled, covers most inpatient and some outpatient medical expenses for individuals aged 65 and over.

Theoretically Medicaid and Medicare should enable most discharged schizophrenics to obtain adequate medical care. In fact, however, it often does not work out that way. Negotiating the bureaucratic maze to establish eligibility can be beyond the person's intellectual and functional resources. Once eligibility is achieved, the person frequently loses his/her card, without which services cannot be obtained. General hospital emergency rooms can discourage schizophrenics from utilizing their facilities because waits of several hours are frequent; and private physicians often will not accept Medicaid or Medicare patients. The result is that the majority of discharged schizophrenic patients receive little or no medical care.

The failure to consider the safety of discharged patients has been a very serious omission of deinstitutionalization. Patients are placed in community facilities as if they were as capable of defending themselves and calling the police as are any other citizens. Because of the residual symptoms of their schizophrenia, however, self-defense is often a myth and incidents of robbery, rape, and serious bodily harm are routine among released patients. These assaults occur with greater frequency because of the placement of many boarding houses, halfway houses, and foster homes in the areas of the inner city with the highest crime rate. When schizophrenic patients do call the police or attempt to bring charges, they may be confronted by their inability to explain to the police what happened, skepticism on the part of the police, and the reality that if the case should go to court the patient would be a very poor witness. Most released schizophrenic patients learn these facts of life soon after leaving the hospital and are forced to accept assaults as a part of life if they wish to remain in the community. Many cite it as a major reason for wishing to return to the hospital, the "asylum," where they feel safer.

EMPLOYMENT AND FRIENDSHIP

Schizophrenic persons who have continuing or residual symptoms of the disease usually cannot work at full-time jobs. Hallucinations, delusions, problems in thinking, poor concentration, and impaired interpersonal relations, all present formidable obstacles for successful employment. This is further exacerbated by stereotypic prejudices of potential employers about the undesirability of having a "psycho" working for them. The number of chronic schizophrenics who are potentially capable of holding full-time jobs is not high; one study estimated it was only 6 percent, although others have claimed that it was higher. Past employment is the best single predictor of future employment for a person with schizophrenia; a person who becomes sick after having a job is more likely to be able to return to work than a person who becomes sick without ever having worked.

Vocational rehabilitation efforts in the United States have traditionally excluded the mentally handicapped. The major focus of Department of Labor programs has been the poorly educated members of society, especially minority groups. Department of Health and Human Service programs concentrate heavily on the physically disabled, and sheltered workshops set up for them have shunned the mentally disabled like lepers. There is no program, then, to rehabilitate those schizophrenics who are capable of returning to the work force at least part-time.

Some other countries do a much better job of providing job opportunities for schizophrenics. Sweden, England, and the Netherlands, all have a greater availability of sheltered workshops for long-term partial employment of psychiatric patients. In the Soviet Union employment of schizophrenics in sheltered workshops is the rule and not the exception; such workshops work closely with psychiatric hospitals.

Work provides several potential benefits for schizophrenics, not the least of which is additional income. Improved self-esteem is equally important, for to hold a job is evidence that one is like other people. Schizophrenics will often work very hard to control their psychiatric symptoms in work situations because work is so important to them. It has been observed, for example, that "in the morning, at the day center, the same person is fulfilling the role of patient and acts like a patient, exhibiting symptoms and bizarre behavior never seen in the workshop the same afternoon." Some patients, like some nonpatients, prefer not to work at all, of course, and all efforts to rehabilitate them will be futile.

It is ironic that the civil rights efforts which led to the release of so many patients from psychiatric hospitals also led to sharply decreased availability of jobs for them. In the past many of these patients had worked on the hospital farms, on the grounds, and on housekeeping and kitchen details. Undoubtedly there was some abuse of this captive work force, and civil rights lawyers went to court with cases of "peonage." The result was a pendulum which swung too far in efforts to correct the situation; hospitals became reluctant to employ patients at all because they could not afford to pay them the minimum wage and other employee benefits. The consequence is thousands of patients in hospitals and in the community who are capable of, and enjoy, working for brief periods but who are not capable of full-time employment. The jobs of the past which were often tailored to their needs are gone.

The only significant efforts to assist schizophrenics in partial employment are those now being carried out by some halfway house programs. The staff locates entry level jobs, then contracts with the employers to fill them. One arrangement which is often successful is the sharing of a single job by two or more schizophrenic patients with each of them working part-time. The number of such efforts, however, is minuscule compared with the magnitude of the need.

Social companionship is needed by persons with schizophrenia just as it is by everyone. There are major obstacles for such persons to obtain companionship, however. The greatest of these is the stigma attached to the disease. Once labeled as "crazy," a schizophrenic is likely to be shunned by former friends and relatives. Another obstacle to companionship is the symptoms of the disease itself. One young man I provided care for recovered from most of his symptoms and was living at home. He attempted to return to his social group of peers, going to taverns and drinking with them as he had done prior to his illness. He found this very difficult, however, complaining that "I can't make out their words, I don't know what to say. It's just not like it used to be." Another patient complained that in social situations "I get lost in the spaces between words in sentences. I can't concentrate, or I get off into thinking about something else." In view of such difficulties it is not surprising that many schizophrenics often respond inappropriately in social situations and eventually withdraw. Studies of schizophrenic patients living in the community report that 25 percent are described as very isolated, 50 percent as moderately isolated, and only 25 percent as leading active social lives. Almost half have no recreational activity whatsoever other than watching television.

MODEL PROGRAMS: THE GREEN DOOR AND FELLOWSHIP HOUSE

Given all the problems outlined above, it is clear that only a comprehensive program will meet the needs of schizophrenics released from the hospital. There have been several models of comprehensive programs which offer viable alternatives. They include the Lodge Model developed by George Fairweather and his associates (the Fairweather Lodge); the Training for Community Living Program in Madison, Wisconsin; the Missouri Foster Community Program; the Sacramento County (California) mental health system; and the clubhouse model patterned after Fountain House in New York City. Each has certain advantages and may be more suitable for some population groups than for others. The success of most such programs is intimately tied to an individual or group of individuals who are caring, energetic, and dedicated, and without such key individuals it is often impossible to transplant such model programs to new environments. For the same reason model programs such as these change over time, depending on their leadership.

The two examples of the clubhouse model which follow illustrate that good programs *can* be created for persons with schizophrenia and that there *can* be something after the hospital besides loneliness and cockroaches.

The Green Door, Washington, D.C.

Jerry is arguing about potato chips. He insists that they go onto the dinner menu for tonight because he is responsible for this week's menu and he wants them. Eve is not persuaded and reminds Jerry that the menu was made out several days before and baked potatoes were selected. The fact that Jerry purchased the potato chips does not give him the right to change the menu at the last minute. Besides, Eve adds, she has already put the baked potatoes into the oven. Milton walks into the midst of the fray and works out a quick compromise: baked potatoes for dinner and the potato chips as a late evening snack. He reminds them both that when they are living in their own apartment they will have to resolve such differences without his help.

The scene is the transitional living apartment of the Green Door. It is a row house in a modest middle-income and racially mixed neighborhood in Washington, D.C. Jerry and Eve both have schizophrenia and have been hospitalized for most of the last decade in St. Elizabeths Hospital, the local federal psychiatric hospital. They will live in the apartment for several months, supervised by Milton and other staff counselors, until they are ready for the next step into an unsupervised apartment. Six schizophrenics live in the transitional living apartment at a time, and another thirty are living nearby in the unsupervised apartments.

Most of these people can be found at the Green Door clubhouse sometime during the day. The clubhouse, which is a short bus-ride away, down Sixteenth Street in an aging but elegant large house, once provided shelter for Washington's rich and socially aspiring families. Its mahogany vestibule, beamed ceilings, and marble fireplace bespeak gentility and quiet; it is a pleasant sanctuary from the outside world. What was once the ballroom now functions nicely as a large dining room for Green Door members who eat lunch there. Other rooms are used for ping-pong, pool, listening to music, or classes.

Much of the clubhouse is given over to the various daily activities of its members. These are divided into kitchen, clerical, and maintenance duties and community relations. Typically a patient who is still living in St. Elizabeths Hospital comes to the Green Door four days a week, works on one of these activities, and returns to the hospital in the late afternoon. Other members live in foster homes or boarding homes, and still others live in the transitional living apartment or independent apartments of the Green Door itself. Most members are in their twenties and thirties, and almost all of them have been diagnosed with schizophrenia. On any given day approximately 100 individuals are served by the clubhouse.

The single most important facet of the Green Door is its ability to integrate services for the schizophrenics who use it. Skills needed for working and skills needed for living outside the hospital are blended into a program of social activities and mutual support among the members. Work skills are developed in the activities within the clubhouse (e.g., receptionist, telephone operator, Xerox operator), in a Green Door-operated thrift store several blocks from the clubhouse, which is managed by the members, and in a transitional employment program. In this program the Green Door contracts with local employers for entry-level jobs, such as drugstore clerk, gas station attendant, stockroom clerk. Some of the persons so placed are then able to move into permanent positions, while others gain experience and move to other employers. Small group discussions, called work adjustment groups, provide support for the members in solving the inevitable on-the-job problems faced by persons with schizophrenia.

Social activities are often educational in nature and are targeted toward developing the skills and confidence needed to function in the community. Formal and informal teaching takes place on hygiene and grooming, budgeting and money management, shopping, menu planning and food preparation, household maintenance, use of public transportation, use of leisure time, use of community resources, applying for food stamps and Medicaid, and socialization skills. For example, one clubhouse discussion focused on how to find the best grocery buys. A typical grocery list was developed and pairs of members were sent out with identical lists to price the items in different stores. The pair of members who were able to find the best buys (i.e., had the lowest total grocery bill) received a free lunch that day.

Evening and weekend programs augment the weekday socialization program. Members operate a snack bar for other members who drop in. Volunteers run a Saturday field trip program with bowling, hiking, movies, picnics, and museum tours. The emphasis is on utilizing community resources which are inexpensive or free and on getting there by public transportation. Members who have been part of the program in the past but who have moved on to more independent living are encouraged to return for social activities. They are told strongly that once a member, always a member, and they provide role models of successful adaptation for people still in the program.

Perhaps the most important benefit of the program, however, is the social support and friendships which develop. Persons with schizophrenia can share their joys and frustrations with each other in a way that they cannot do with nonschizophrenics. If a member is responding to auditory hallucinations within the clubhouse, it does not cause any problems. Other members can sympathize, for most of them have also been plagued with such hallucinations at one time or another. The shared experience of having schizophrenia and having gone through a hospitalization experience is a strong bond.

Programs such as the Green Door are also an effective means to achieve deinstitutionalization of schizophrenics who have been in the hospital for many years. Such patients are guided through the step-by-step process of relearning to do things themselves. When your day has been completely regulated for twenty years, when you have been told when to get up and when to go to bed, when your food and laundry have been taken care of, it is difficult suddenly to have to reassume responsibility yourself. The Green Door is extremely successful in helping such persons take responsibility for their own lives again.

The staff of the Green Door consists of twenty full-time persons. Half are social workers and the other half have college degrees in a variety of fields. The program was begun in 1977 by two women, Gail Marker and Ellen McPeake, who had been working with the Mental Health Law Project and who had been impressed with Fountain House in New York. In less than three years it grew to the program described above. Its original funding was a small foundation grant, which was then supplemented by contract money from St. Elizabeths Hospital, other government grants (such as the Department of Labor CETA program and the Department of Housing and Urban Development), and by public fund raising and benefits.

Fellowship House, Miami, Florida

Mark was describing how he used to think he was Tarzan. He would stand in the middle of the street, take off his clothes, and stop the traffic light in the middle of Miami. Having spent two years in the Marines before becoming both schizophrenic and Tarzan, he acquired some karate and other skills that stood him in good stead as Tarzan until he was sent off to the state hospital in a straitjacket.

He recalled his days as Tarzan with a touch of humor. All that was in the past, he said. He was standing in the open courtyard of Fellowship House, where he had been coming daily for three months. "This time I'm going to make it here," he said. He had tried once before but had "gotten crazy" again. "Stopped taking my medicine and bang I was right back in the hospital." Now he was on 30 milligrams of Haldol a day and swore he was going to continue it. He liked Fellowship House very much and hoped that he would eventually get a job as a mechanic. He claimed to be a good one and clearly took much pride in his skills.

Mark is one of over three hundred former mental patients being served by Fellowship House. Almost all have been diagnosed schizophrenic and almost all are veterans of numerous psychiatric wards and state hospitals. They come by bus and van to the refurbished warehouse in South Miami which serves as the clubhouse and main focus of the program. It is just a few yards off the Dixie Highway, right next to the Eagle Family Discount Store, in a semi-industrial area.

Jason is another regular. Having spent over twenty years in the state hospital and long since having been abandoned by his family, he comes to Fellowship House because he is wanted there. It has become his family. Staff members and other House members greet Jason affectionately. He really *is* wanted; there is no mistaking it or putting it on. Jason knows it, too, negotiates a loan to cover his lunch, and quietly mingles with the other members. It has been a long, long time since Jason had a place to go where he was really wanted.

When asked what he likes about coming to Fellowship House, Jason says the activities. And activities there are. On any given day it takes on the appearance of a community recreation center with pool, ping-pong, a piano, television, and volleyball and basketball in the courtyard. Then there are the regular monthly trips, and special nights, such as a talent show, a Hispanic festival, black culture night, and a four-day camping trip. The day before I visited they had had a rummage sale of donated items to raise money. The members, of course, do most of the work getting ready for these events. Jason also likes it because he will soon have a regular job at the House cataloguing and caring for the teaching materials and videotapes being developed. It is not a paying job, but it recognizes Jason's talents and his worth, which is more than anyone else had done for him for over twenty years.

Many other members like Fellowship House because it also arranges for a place for them to live. There are a variety of options spread out around Miami. The most supervised of these is Fellowship Manor, a transitional house for fifteen residents with a staff person always present. This is often the first place a person lives in when leaving the state hospital, and most are ready to move to a less supervised setting within a few months. A member may also move back to Fellowship Manor on a temporary basis if he/she is getting sick or needs more individual supervision.

There are also two kinds of apartments under the aegis of Fellowship House. Seven supervised apartments, each housing four persons, are in downtown Miami with a staff person living nearby. The staff person assists the residents with cooking, cleaning, marketing, bus travel, and interpersonal relationships. Fifteen other satellite apartments, each with four members, are clustered around town and have only on-call supervision. Rent money for the apartments comes from the members' SSI and welfare checks. Altogether, then, one-third of the Fellowship House members live in housing maintained by the organization. The remainder live with their families, in boarding houses, or alone.

Because the program has been so successful and because Miami is so spread out, Fellowship House recently opened a satellite center on the northern edge of the city. It is a converted house, sitting in a middle-class housing development, with a day program for members who live nearby. It is also only a few minutes' drive from the state hospital. Under a contract with Fellowship House, the state brings several patients being readied for discharge to the satellite house each day; this gives the patients a chance to make a more gradual transition from the hospital back to the community. Such a program stands in sharp contrast to the abrupt dumping of patients that goes on in most communities in the United States.

Another important facet of the Fellowship House program is its vocational rehabilitation program. For those members who are capable of working, there is a program of graduated responsibilities with guidance and supervision. This begins in the main center, where members are assigned regular responsibilities in one of the work units such as food service (cooking, waiting on tables for the daily lunch), plant care, housekeeping and maintenance, clerical, data processing, and video. The last group utilizes a closed-circuit television for a daily news show and a newspaper for distribution to the satellite center, Fellowship Manor, and the apartments. For those who are capable of moving to regular employment there is a transitional employment program for approximately forty persons. The staff seeks entry-level positions throughout Miami. Members work half-time, so full-time jobs are filled by two persons. Fellowship House guarantees job performance and reliability by training two persons for every position (thus if one is sick the other can fill in) and also by assigning staff to work closely with the newly assigned worker at no additional expense to the employer. Entry-level job opportunities offered are as dishwasher in the University of Miami student union and as warehouseman. Members may hold the transitional job for three to six months, at which time they turn it over to (and help train) a new member. The person who has completed the job successfully receives a letter of recommendation for regular employment, as well as the regular wages for the period worked. It is possible for members to have several different transitional employment jobs if they need to broaden their experience and increase their employability.

> Marie, a Cuban refugee, became schizophrenic at age 17; she is now 23 and about to begin transitional employment in a cafeteria. She had worked on the data processing work detail for six months, then switched to the food service unit. She is excited about the possibility of getting a real job; her shyness and residual schizophrenic symptoms would have made it impossible for her to have done so on her own. Yet when talking to her there seems little doubt that she will make an excellent employee, for her motivation is exceptionally high.

All of these programs were put into operation over a period of seven years. Fellowship House began in 1973 when a parent of a schizophrenic volunteered to help organize a halfway house. The local Miami chapter of the Mental Health Association and a helpful local psychiatrist, Dr. James Sussex, provided early support. A social worker from New Jersey, Marshall Rubin, was hired and Fellowship House was under way. Mr. Rubin has provided skilled leadership during its rapid growth, and it now has sixty staff members. As in most of these programs, the staff is a mix of social workers, college graduates, and people generally committed to human services. The atmosphere is similar to that found on a Vista or Peace Corps project, where the staff knows that they are performing a useful function and are proud of it.

Funding for Fellowship House has come from a variety of sources. Initially $35,000 in seed money was obtained from the U.S. Department of Health and Human Services, and this was later supplemented by county, state, and federal funds. Long-term funding of such programs is problematical, with neither the local, state, or federal government prepared to commit themselves.

A unique and exciting aspect of Fellowship House is the support it receives from the South Miami Kiwanis Club. Individual Kiwanis members have assisted it with a variety of professional problems, such as legal advice in obtaining apartments or a mortgage on the satellite day facility. A Kiwanis physician offered his services without charge for a few hours a week, and this has now grown into a panel of fifteen physicians and dentists which Fellowship House members can utilize. Mr. Rubin is a member of Kiwanis, and Kiwanis members are on the governing board of Fellowship House. When a new Fellowship House facility needed painting, members of Kiwanis helped out, and when the Kiwanis had their annual pass-the-can fundraising drive the Fellowship House members assisted them. Many other projects are being explored, including transitional employment in Kiwanis-supported jobs and the shifting of Kiwanis bulk mailing (labeling, stamping, etc.) from a commercial firm to Fellowship House. In the support and opportunities it is providing for the members of Fellowship House, Kiwanis has demonstrated what community service really means; it is a model which could profitably be adopted elsewhere.

Another unusual feature of Fellowship House is its training program. Under a state contract, twelve other Florida communities are sending people to Fellowship House to be trained in how to set up and run similar programs. To assist with this, Fellowship House has prepared a series of videotapes which potentially could be used by communities anywhere. By utilizing such teaching aids it is hoped that the wheel will not have to be invented independently by each community.

Finally, it should be stressed that the recurring theme of the program, made explicit by Marshall Rubin, is the message which the members receive daily: "We need you." Fellowship House depends on its members to operate, just as the members depend on Fellowship House for their social needs and often their housing and vocational needs as well. On the day I visited, one member announced excitedly that she had been coming to Fellowship House for exactly one year on that day. Everyone sang "Happy Birthday" to her.

8

WHAT THE FAMILY CAN DO

Psychiatrists who insist that their patient choose parents for
whom life has been a never-never land of tranquility would be
conspicuously underemployed.

J. A. Wechsler, *In a Darkness*

Schizophrenia is a devastating illness not only for the person afflicted but for
the person's family as well. There is probably no disease, including cancer,
which causes more anguish. After interviewing eighty families in which one
member was afflicted with schizophrenia, Clare Creer and John Wing concluded, "Of all types of handicapping conditions in adults, chronic schizophrenia probably gives rise to the most difficulties at home."

The family atmosphere is often like the interval waiting for a time bomb
to explode. The patient is faced with "seemingly endless questions and doubts.
Needing motives for almost every action, comment, or even hobbies. Having
to curb one's natural emotions, fearing they may be misconstrued as symptoms. . . ." As described by one patient, "One lives closeted with the appalling
picture of oneself out of control, while relations and some friends in their
kindness try to pretend the thing never happened." On the other side the
family lives with the constant fear that the symptoms will recur. "Because it's
happened before you always fear it will happen again so you are constantly
trying to avoid saying the wrong thing. You're like a taut string, not knowing
what will set him off next."

In such an atmosphere trivial problems become magnified and substantial
problems become overwhelming. Family members blame the patient, one
another, and themselves. Family schedules, social life, and finances are frequently put into total disarray. The needs of other family members are neglected. And at the beginning of each day the same recurring question presents
itself to both the patient and the family: is this the day the symptoms will recur
or get worse? It is this element of unpredictability which is the most difficult
aspect of schizophrenia and the source of the greatest tension.

Several studies have been done on family problems caused by schizophrenics. The problems which recur most frequently are the person's failure
to care for his/her personal needs (e.g., to take a bath); inability to handle

money; social withdrawal; strange personal habits (wandering around talking to himself in the middle of the night); suicide threats; interference with the family's work, school, and social schedule; and fears for the safety of both the schizophrenic and the family members. Clearly there is no shortage of serious problems.

WHERE SHOULD HE/SHE LIVE?

The most important decision to be made by most schizophrenics and their families is where the schizophrenic should live. This was not always an issue. Thirty years ago brother John and Aunt Kate were sent off to the state hospital when they became schizophrenic, never to be seen again. The question of where they should live never came up—it was simply assumed that they would remain at the hospital. That has all changed, and now brother John and Aunt Kate will probably be on their way home from the hospital within a few weeks. The question of where they will live is a very real one.

As a general rule, I believe that most persons with schizophrenia do better living somewhere other than at home. I have come to this conclusion after working with many schizophrenic persons and their families for several years; but it is a fact often learned painfully, and at great emotional cost, by families. The reasons for living elsewhere are complex. They include the facts that most people who are not schizophrenic do better living away from the family home once they are grown and that schizophrenic persons often function at a higher level living away from home. Most schizophrenics I have known do better, and are happier, in a halfway house or similar setting.

This does not mean that *no* persons with schizophrenia should live at home. A minority can, and it may work out well. This is true for females more often than it is for males. Nor does it mean that the schizophrenic family member who is living elsewhere should not come home to visit overnight or for weekends; this arrangement is often mutually satisfactory. Such persons may also live at home temporarily while they are waiting, for example, for an opening in a halfway house.

Regardless of whether the schizophrenic is living at home, coming home for weekends, or just coming by for an occasional meal, families of schizophrenic persons have many problems, of their own and in connection with the patient, which must be resolved. These include problems of blame and shame; anger and depression; how to behave toward the schizophrenic; independence and money management; guardianship; religion and cults; alcohol, drugs, and sex; and violence, suicide, and homicide threats.

BLAME AND SHAME

The problems of blame and shame dwarf all others which arise between schizophrenics and their families. They lie constantly just beneath the surface, souring relations between family members and threatening to explode in a frenzy of finger-pointing, accusations, and recriminations. Blame and shame are the Scylla and Charybdis of schizophrenia.

As should be clear from chapter 5, feelings of blame and shame are completely irrational. There is no evidence whatsoever that schizophrenia is caused by how people have been treated either as children or as adults; it is a biological disease of the brain, unrelated to interpersonal events of childhood or adulthood. But many families believe otherwise, and their feelings have often been based on what a mental health professional has said (or at least implied) to them. An excellent description of this process is recounted by Louise Wilson in *This Stranger, My Son:*

> Mother: "And so it is we who have made Tony what he is?"
> Psychiatrist: "Let me put it this way. Every child born, every mind, is a tabula rasa, an empty slate. What is written on it"—a stubby finger shot out, pointed at me—"you wrote there."

The consequences are predictable, with the mother lying awake at night remembering all the things she did that might have caused the schizophrenia.

> We had moved too often during his early years. . . . My tension during the prenatal period when his father was overseas. . . . His father's preoccupation with his profession. . . . No strong companionship and father image. . . . A first child, and too many other children coming along too rapidly. . . . Our expectations were too high. . . . He had been robbed of his rightful babyhood, had grown up too fast. . . . Inconsistent handling. . . . Too permissive. . . . Too much discipline. . . . Oedipal fixation. . . .

There is, of course, not a mother, father, brother, or sister in the world who has not done things he or she regrets in past relationships with other family members. We are, after all, rather imperfect human beings, and it is not surprising when at times we all speak or act impulsively out of jealousy, anger, narcissism, or fatigue. But fortunately we have resilient psyches, capable of absorbing random blows without crumbling or being permanently damaged. People do not cause schizophrenia; they merely blame each other for doing so.

Moreover, not only do the well family members blame each other for causing the schizophrenia in the family but the person with schizophrenia may also do so. James Wechsler's son, in *In a Darkness,* once turned to him and angrily exclaimed, "You know, Dad, I wasn't *born* this way." And in *This*

Stranger, My Son Louise Wilson recounts the following conversation with her son:

> "I read a book the other day," Tony said. "It was in the drugstore. I stood there and read it all the way through."
>
> We waited, alarmed by the severity of his expression.
>
> "It told what good parents ought to be. It said that people get . . . the way I am . . . because their parents weren't qualified to be parents."
>
> "Oh Tony," I began, but Jack's signal silenced me.
>
> "I'm a miserable wreck, because both of you are, too. You're queers and you never should have had a child."
>
> "In what way are we queer?" Jack asked quietly.
>
> "You never played ball with me. All you ever wanted to do was tramp around looking at birds or read. Or work in the damned hospital."
>
> "Well, maybe it would have been more fun for you if I'd been an athlete. I can see that. But I really don't see why that should make me such a terrible father."
>
> "Read the book!" Tony exclaimed.
>
> "Tony, there are a lot of things written in books, a lot of opinions that are inaccurate, distorted, or just plain wrong. Besides, I'm sure the book—"
>
> "Listen, even the doctor that I've got here agrees! He says nobody's born with problems like mine!"

The blaming of one another for the illness magnifies the tragedy of schizophrenia manyfold. By itself it is a chronic disease of the brain and a personal and family disaster of usually manageable proportions. But when family members add blame to its burden, the disease spreads its roots beneath the whole family structure and becomes a calamity of boundless dimensions. The pain blame causes in such circumstances must be seen to be believed. One woman wrote to me:

> My mother died twelve years ago tormented by my sister's illness. After reading every book and article published on the subject, she decided that she was to blame. My father, who is in his seventies, brought my sister home from the state hospital for five years following my mother's death, in memory of my mother, trying to prove that she wasn't sick. My sister was so sick he finally had to return her to the hospital.

Few members of the mental health profession have focused on the amount of harm that has been done by the idea that parents and families cause schizophrenia. Psychiatrists especially, as members of the medical profession, see themselves as unlikely to cause harm. We now know that this is not so, and it is likely that in the twentieth century psychiatrists as a group have done more harm than good to schizophrenics. The harm has not been done maliciously; indeed I know of few psychiatrists who could be characterized as mean spirited. Rather the harm has been done inadvertently because of prevailing psychodynamic and family interaction theories of the disease (see chapter 5). But it is harm nonetheless. William S. Appleton is one of the few professionals who have written about this, and he has analyzed the undesirable consequences that follow when professionals blame the families for causing the disease:

> Badly treated families retaliate in ways that are detrimental to the patient. They become less willing to tolerate the problems he causes, are less agreeable to changing their behavior toward him, do not give much information when interviewed, and pay few visits to the hospital.

There is one type of family which, although not common, presents special problems. This is the family which *enjoys* guilt and blaming one another. They savor and at times appear to wallow in this, always pleased when a new reason can be found to point their fingers. One or more members of such families are usually in long-term psychoanalysis, and exploring their personal guilt has become a principal pastime. In such families I encourage the schizophrenic to minimize time spent within the family setting because it is detrimental to his other progress and to getting on with life despite a handicap.

The obverse of blame is shame. Inevitably, if families believe that they have somehow caused the schizophrenia, they will try and hide the family member affected, deny the illness to their neighbors, and otherwise dissociate themselves from the victim in a multiplicity of ways. Persons with schizophrenia sense this and feel more isolated than ever. It is not unusual for the patient then to react angrily toward the family, retaliating by making less effort to control bizarre behavior, and perhaps disrobing in front of elderly Aunt Agatha. Such behavior generates more shame in the family, producing more isolation and anger in the patient, and the downward spiral of shame and anger continues.

There is now evidence that families in which blame and shame are conspicuously prevalent are very difficult milieus for schizophrenic patients to live in. Studies in both London and Los Angeles found that schizophrenics had to be rehospitalized more frequently when their families were excessively hostile, critical, and/or emotionally overinvolved with them. This should not be surprising, and is certainly true for other chronic disabling diseases, such as multiple sclerosis, in which adults must remain dependent on their families.

Education is the resolution to the problem of blame and shame. When family members come to understand that they did not cause the disease, the blame and shame felt by them are usually markedly reduced and the living situation for the schizophrenic member improved. A recent highly publicized study by Ian Falloon and his colleagues in Los Angeles attempted to show that teaching schizophrenic patients and their families "better methods of coping with stressful events" and encouraging the families to be less critical of the patient led to reduced hospitalization for the patient. Unfortunately the study failed to control adequately for medication compliance, and the reduced hospitalization that occurred may simply have been because the patients in the study took their medicine more often. The study also made the mistake of calling its work with families a "family treatment approach": families of schizophrenic patients do not need to be "treated," but rather *educated*. "Treating" such families reinforces the ingrained idea that they are somehow responsible for the schizophrenic's illness.

Education of families of schizophrenic patients can be remarkably effective in reducing blame and shame. The question of who is responsible for the disease should be asked of all family members, and the schizophrenic person should participate in the discussion if possible. Once this is asked, the beliefs and fears that will sometimes emerge in the ensuing discussion are extraordinary. And once the issue of blame and shame is resolved and put to rest, schizophrenia becomes much easier to live with. One parent expressed it this way:

> Once you have unloaded your guilt, laid upon you by well-meaning professionals, the next step is easier. If you have done nothing wrong and have been doing the best you can, then you have nothing to be ashamed of. You can *come out of the closet*. The relief experienced by this act gives you strength to go on, and support starts coming out of the woodwork.

ANGER AND DEPRESSION

Some families with schizophrenics skillfully steer a course between the twin dangers of blame and shame only to run aground on the shoals of anger and depression. The anger is usually directed at the patient for becoming schizophrenic, at God for creating a world in which diseases like schizophrenia exist, or at fate for loading the dice against them. It varies from being a mild resentment which bubbles to the surface when social activities must be curtailed because of the schizophrenic to a more virulent bitterness which flows beneath the surface of their daily activities like a caustic acid. Occasionally the anger does not get expressed overtly but rather is turned inward; it is then seen as depression.

Resolution of feelings of anger is often made more difficult because of questions of the patient's responsibility for his or her own behavior. Clearly patients cannot be blamed for getting sick *per se,* but what portion of their sick behavior can they control? In a few cases the answer is zero; but in the majority the schizophrenic has some control at least some of the time. Moreover, this control may fluctuate. John Wing expressed this dilemma for the family:

Part of the peculiar difficulty in managing schizophrenia is that it lies somewhere between conditions like blindness which, though severely handicapping, do not interfere with an individual's capacity to make independent
judgments about his own future, and conditions like severe mental retardation, in which it is clear that the individual will never be able to make such
independent judgments. There is frequently a fluctuating degree of insight
and of severity.

When the patient disrobes in front of Aunt Agatha, is it because his voices
told him to, or because he is angry at his family for a real or imagined slight?
Some persons with schizophrenia become highly skilled at utilizing their
symptoms to manipulate those around them and get what they want. Patients who are placed where they do not want to live, for example, know
exactly what to do behaviorally to insure that they will be returned to the
hospital or wherever they were living previously. And I have had many patients improve and tell me explicitly, "Doc, I'm a little better but I'm not
well enough to go to work."

It is important for families to assess and talk through their feelings about
the schizophrenic's degree of responsibility for his/her own behavior; this is
most useful if done with the patient present. The professional caretakers and
families can then set limits on what behavior will not be acceptable. The disease
affects a random selection of personality types, and families should remember
that persons who were lazy, manipulative, or narcissistic before they got sick
are likely to remain so as schizophrenics. This problem is very similar to that
faced by families of physically handicapped, diabetic, or otherwise chronically
disabled patients who may utilize their condition to manipulate their families
and environment.

Once the responsibility issue has been resolved, then anger and its somber
handmaiden, depression, can be addressed. Family support groups (see page
246) will often facilitate this and families will find that anger is a common
reaction to having a schizophrenic family member. It can be acknowledged
and explored, and in the process will lose some of its virulence and its capacity
to destroy lives.

HOW TO BEHAVE TOWARD A SCHIZOPHRENIC

In general, the people who get along best with schizophrenics are those who
treat them most naturally as people. This can be verified by watching the
nursing staff in any psychiatric hospital. The staff who are most respected by
both professionals and patients treat the patients with dignity and as human
beings, albeit with a brain disease. The staff who are least respected treat the

patients in a condescending manner, frequently reminding them of their inferior status. Often this is because the staff person does not understand schizophrenia or is afraid of it. The simple answer, then, to the question, How should I behave toward a schizophrenic? is, Kindly.

Beyond this, however, there are certain aspects of schizophrenia as a disease which do modify to some degree one's behavior toward a person who has it. These modifications arise directly and predictably out of the nature of the brain damage and the symptoms of the disease as described in chapter 2. Persons with schizophrenia have great difficulty in processing sensory input of all kinds, especially two or more simultaneous sensory stimuli. If this is kept in mind, then determining how to behave toward a schizophrenic becomes much easier.

Make communications, for example, brief, concise, and unambiguous. As explained by one family member: "Look at the person. Talk in short, concise, adult statements . . . be clear and practical . . . give one set of directions at a time with no options."

Another mother described how she communicates with her adult son with schizophrenia:

> My son seemed to have difficulty dealing with all the stimuli around him. He responded slowly and said that he had difficulty with "everything coming at me." At those times it was important for me to speak in simple, slow sentences. Requests were made for one thing at a time. Keeping down complexity was very important. Strong emotion increased his difficulty in processing what I was saying. However much in a hurry I felt, there was no way to hurry him. Patience was absolutely necessary.
>
> I learned finally the futility of arguments. When S. was in more acute stages, it was easy to get into impossible rounds of arguments. Often he could not be reasoned with, but I didn't know how to back off. I learned to choose carefully what had to be done, plan ahead how I would handle the situation, and not respond to all the objections. For example, I might say in a clear, firm, simple statement, "You must be ready to leave at 8:00 o'clock." Then I stood expectantly, even handing him his coat, and opening the door.
>
> Sometimes leaving requests by way of memo or over the telephone seemed to work better than face to face—I am not sure why—sometimes he seemed to be overstimulated by my presence.

Ask the schizophrenic questions one at a time. "Did you have a nice time, dear? Who went with you?" may seem like a straightforward two-part question for a normal person, but for a person with schizophrenia it may be overwhelming.

It is also counterproductive to try to argue schizophrenics out of their delusional beliefs. Attempts to do so often result in misunderstanding and anger, as described by John Wing:

Patients tended to develop sudden irrational fears. They might, for instance, become fearful of a particular room in the house. Maybe they would tell the family the reason for their fear. "There's a poisonous gas leaking into that room" or "There are snakes under the bed in that room." At first relatives are baffled by this. Some admitted they had grown frustrated with a patient's absolute refusal to abandon some idea, despite all their attempts to reason with him, and had lost their temper. But they found this only resulted in the patient becoming very upset, and in any case the idea continued to be held with as much conviction as ever.

Rather than arguing with the patient, simply make a statement of disagreement; this can be done without challenging or provoking him or her. Thus a reasonable response to "There are snakes under the bed in that room" is "I know you believe there are snakes there, but I don't see any and I doubt that there are," rather than a peremptory "There are *no* snakes in that room." The patient has some reason for believing that there are snakes there—perhaps he/she heard them or even saw them. It is often useful for the family member to acknowledge the validity of the patient's sensory experiences without accepting the person's interpretation of the experiences. Such a statement might be "I know you have some reason to believe there are snakes there, but I think that the reason has to do with the fact that your brain is playing tricks on you because of your illness."

Family members and friends of schizophrenic patients are often tempted to deal with the patient's delusional beliefs in a sarcastic or humorous manner. The statement about snakes, for example, might be responded to as follows: "Oh yes, I saw them there too. And did you see the rattlesnakes in the kitchen as well?" Such statements are never useful and are often very confusing for the patient. Humor is difficult for most schizophrenics to understand, and they become the butt of jokes which they cannot fully comprehend. It also reinforces their delusional belief and makes it more difficult for them to separate their personal experiences from reality. One patient, who believed he had a rat in his throat and asked the doctors to look at it, was told sardonically by the doctors that the rat was too far down to see. When the patient recovered he recalled that "I would have been grateful if they had stated quite plainly that they did not believe that there was a rat in my throat." This is good advice.

Another useful way to handle the delusional thinking of schizophrenic patients is to encourage them to express such thinking only in private. Talking about snakes being under the bed is not harmful within the context of family and friends, but if said in a crowded elevator or announced to the saleslady in a store, it can be embarrassing for everyone concerned. Discuss this frankly and straightforwardly with the patient and it will often be appreciated. As

Creer and Wing point out: "A more realistic aim is to try to limit the effect of such ideas upon the patient's public behavior. Many patients were well able to understand this and to limit odd behavior, such as talking to themselves, and the expression of odd ideas, to private occasions."

An impediment to communicating with schizophrenics is their frequent inability to participate in normal back-and-forth conversation. "One patient returned home each evening from the day center, ate in complete silence the meal her aunt provided, and then went straight to her room. . . . Her aunt, who was lonely and elderly, would have been very glad for a chat in the evenings. She was puzzled by the patient's almost total lack of communication." Such patients often are aware of conversations around them but are unable to participate. "One young man generally sat in silence, or muttering to himself, while his parents were conversing about family matters. Later, however, they learned that he had quite often spoken to a nurse at the hospital about such topics of conversation at home and had clearly been taking in what was said despite all appearances to the contrary." Many such schizophrenic patients like to have other people around them but do not like to interact with them directly. "One lady said she had been surprised to hear from a friend that her nephew suffering from the disease liked to come and visit her. 'I would never have guessed it because when he comes he just sits in a chair and says absolutely nothing.' "

An analogous problem families have in their efforts to relate to persons with schizophrenia is their impaired ability to express emotions. Frequently the patient will relate to even close family members in what appears to be a cold and distant way. This emotional aloofness is quite normal for many persons with this disease and should be respected. Difficult though this coldness may be, do not take it personally. The schizophrenic may find it easier to express emotion or verbal affection toward a family pet, and it is often a good idea to provide the person with a cat or dog for this purpose.

Give persons with schizophrenia a quiet place to go to. This is an important need for them. This was one mother's solution:

We have come to realize how very important quiet is to Jim. Since we live in a rather small house and there are young people around and often noisy grandchildren visiting, we now make sure the noise level is kept down as much as possible. Jim doesn't want to make this demand for quiet. It is often a deep need for him. Not long ago, we bought a small trailer to keep in the driveway, and this has been a godsend. Either Jim can escape there or the noisy children can play and even sleep there! I know this is not a practical solution for many families, yet some answer to the noise problem is important.

Schizophrenics need such places in order to withdraw and to be alone. We all have such a need at times, but in persons with schizophrenia it is much more pronounced. Relatives often find such behavior discomfiting and difficult to understand: "In the evenings you go into the sitting room and it's in darkness. You turn on the light and there he is, just sitting there, staring in front of him."

Because they need places to which they can withdraw, it is important to provide schizophrenics with their own bedrooms if at all possible. The patient can use the bedroom as a sanctuary. "One mother said her son spent most of his time closeted in his room, only coming out at night when everyone was in bed. Usually he was talking to himself and moving about, but every few weeks there would be complete silence for a few days." I once had a similar patient who only emerged from her room at night to cook her own food; often many days would go by without her family seeing her. This behavior is related to the fact that schizophrenics often have grossly disrupted sleep-wake cycles, being up all night and sleeping during the day. This also makes it difficult for them to share a bedroom with another person.

It can be puzzling to know what to do in these cases of social withdrawal. Should you insist that the person emerge from the bedroom and interact socially, or should you leave him or her alone? The answer is, as a general rule, to leave the person alone. If the withdrawal seems excessive or too persistent, it is possible it may herald the recurrence of more severe symptoms and will require evaluation by the patient's psychiatrist. But in most cases the withdrawal is being used as a means for coping with the internal chaos in the patient's brain and is an appropriate response. Family members should remind themselves not to take such withdrawal as a personal rejection but should keep themselves available. As described usefully by the mother of a schizophrenic: "When our son was acutely ill we managed best by not being too intrusive, by not trying too hard to draw him out of his world and into ours, but by always being available at the times when he needed our support and tried to communicate."

Minimize the number and scale of social events in the house in order to relieve pressure on the schizophrenic. Patients can often handle one visitor at a time, but groups are usually overwhelming to them. Similarly, taking the schizophrenic to group gatherings or parties outside the home is often a difficult and confusing experience for the person.

Provide as predictable and simple a daily routine as possible. One mother said:

> I found structure was very important during the more difficult days. Things were done similarly each day and at designated times, and every day of the week had its individual character which was kept as consistent as possible.

This seemed to give him a sense of order, that life was predictable, and also established a sense of time.

In *Autobiography of a Schizophrenic Girl* the patient also comments on the importance of routine in counteracting hallucinations and other abnormal sensory stimuli:

> What saved me that day was activity. It was the hour to go to chapel for prayer, and like the other children I had to get in line. To move, to change the scene, to do something definite and customary, helped a great deal.

Routine exercise and routine chores or jobs which the person is expected to do daily can also be helpful in this regard. Sweeping, dusting, or weeding a garden are all appropriate examples. Remember, however, that instructions should be given one at a time. Do not say, "Sweep the kitchen, then take the garbage out, and clean out the garage." The chances are that none of the three will get done.

At the same time that routines are established, realize that the person with schizophrenia may deviate from them for no apparent reason. This is especially true of sleeping and eating routines. One father complained about his son, "My wife will cook a meal, and then he doesn't want it. Then two hours later he suddenly decides he does." An admirable solution to this kind of problem was outlined by this mother:

> The second practical suggestion concerns the schizophrenic's need for a sudden intake of food. At least in the case of our son, available wholesome snacks are very important. I've learned to keep yogurt, cheese, cold meat, etc., in the refrigerator; fruit on the table; and quick canned meals on the shelves. All this has seemed more important than a regular schedule of meals, although three good meals a day helps, too. The strict time doesn't matter. If Jim fixes himself a can of stew at four in the afternoon, I simply leave his dinner ready for him to heat up when he's ready."

Experiment to find leisure time activities which are enjoyable. Those with a single (or dominant) sensory input are usually most successful. Thus a person with schizophrenia will often enjoy cartoons or a travelogue on TV but will not be able to understand a show with a plot. A boxing match may be preferable to a baseball game. Visual spectacles, such as a circus or ice show, are often very enjoyable, while a play is usually a total failure. Individuals are, of course, different in this regard, and it is necessary to explore different possibilities. The fact that people enjoyed something before they became ill does not mean that they necessarily will enjoy it after they become ill.

Above all, cultivate the art of being unflappable. Radiate quiet confidence that you can handle any idea, however strange, that your schizophrenic relative may come up with. One parent said, "The most remarkable lesson I have learned about managing a schizophrenic at home is to try to stay as calm as possible. The upsets and delusions have not been caused by me and being calm keeps my son that way also. I might be heaving inside but my behavior on the outside is controlled."

INDEPENDENCE AND MONEY MANAGEMENT

A recurring problem for almost all families with a schizophrenic member is how much independence to give him or her. The battles are most often fought over the issues of medication, traveling alone, staying out, safety, chores, and money management.

Management of a schizophrenic's medication is exceedingly important. Since continuation of the medication is often essential for remaining out of the hospital (see chapter 6), I encourage families to be very conservative in giving responsibility for taking medication to their relative. Many mental health professionals and families have defined "self-medication" as a highly desirable goal, a milestone to be achieved by schizophrenic persons on the road toward greater autonomy. I realize that I am in a minority on this issue, but I do not include self-medication as an important target. There are some patients who can handle it, but they are relatively infrequent. I have been much more impressed by the tragic relapses of those who were doing well but then decided by themselves that they did not need the medicine any more.

Traveling alone, staying out late, and the schizophrenic's personal safety raise similar kinds of problems. As a general rule persons should be given as much autonomy and independence as they can handle, and this should be done in a graduated series of steps. For example, a schizophrenic who believes he or she should be able to travel alone to a concert and stay out late should be given the opportunity to demonstrate readiness by successfully going to the store regularly, traveling alone to the halfway house during the day, avoiding street drugs, and not getting into trouble in public because of bizarre behavior. I have known families who have discreetly followed their schizophrenic family member on initial forays into the community to insure that no harm befell the patient. When the patient asks for more autonomy, the family should set up a series of conditions which must be met before the autonomy can be granted; for example, a patient who asks to travel home alone from the halfway house might be told that this can be tried once the patient has demonstrated familiarity with the bus route and has successfully gone for two weeks without forgetting to lock the door of the house.

Chores are another means by which schizophrenics can demonstrate their readiness for more independence. Sweeping, cleaning, doing the dishes, taking out the garbage, feeding the dog, and weeding are all examples of chores which may be appropriate to assign to the schizophrenic family member. Families are sometimes reluctant to assign such chores, fearing that any stress will cause a recurrence of the patient's symptoms. Patients who are lazy may encourage such fears, pleading illness whenever there is work to be done. One mother described the resentment which is an inevitable consequence of this situation: "It's so annoying when you've got lots of housework to do, and there he is, a fine healthy-looking young man, and he just *sits* there doing absolutely nothing." Doing chores will not cause a patient to become sicker, and such chores are used extensively in halfway house settings and model programs, such as those described in chapter 7. They are an ideal way for patients to assume more independence and they increase the person's self-esteem at the same time. I have seen some extremely psychotic patients doing chores quite nicely and feeling better for having done so.

The management of the patient's money may cause the most difficulty of all. Many patients know that a portion of their SSI check is earmarked for their personal needs, and they believe they should have the right to spend it however they please. They should be reminded, however, that the personal portion of the check is intended to cover necessities, such as clothes, as well as cigarettes and sodas.

Occasional persons with schizophrenia can take total responsibility for their money and can manage it with minimal difficulties. I know one severely affected paranoid schizophrenic, for example, who is very delusional much of the time but is able to take monthly trips to the bank and manage her funds. Predictably, she will not tell the doctors or nurses how much money she has. More common, however, is the schizophrenic who cannot manage money at all; some patients, for example, will repeatedly give away any money they have to the first person who asks for it. For such persons it may be useful to link autonomy in money management to other behavior indicating independence. For example, if patients have difficulty with personal hygiene and grooming, it may be appropriate to agree to give them more money to spend as they wish every week that they successfully take a shower without being told. The successful performance of chores is another way that schizophrenics can demonstrate that they are ready for greater financial responsibility.

Issues of independence and money management may also cause problems for families because of the family's inability to understand that their schizophrenic member is getting better. When one has lived with a severely psychotic individual who may have even needed help in dressing himself, it is often difficult to recognize a few weeks later that the person is now able to travel by bus alone and manage a weekly allowance. Families have often been both scared and scarred, and their ability to respond and adapt sometimes becomes constricted.

Some parents are reluctant to give autonomy to their schizophrenic children because they themselves need to continue their parental role. This is, of course, true for some parents of nonschizophrenics as well, and it often leads to retarded maturity in the young adult. It is another reason why living away from home is preferable for most released schizophrenic patients.

GUARDIANSHIP

When a schizophrenic patient is unable to make rational decisions for a long period of time, a guardian is sometimes appointed by the courts. The guardian may be either a relative or friend of the patient or, if none is available or appropriate, another person selected by the judge. The appointment of a guardian occurs most frequently when the patient owns large amounts of money or property or is likely to inherit some. Guardianship is a legal relationship authorizing one person to make decisions for another and is based upon the same *parens patriae* tenet of English law which permits involuntary hospitalization. When the guardian has jurisdiction only over the property of the patient, it is frequently referred to as a conservatorship. When both property and personal decisions are involved it is called a guardianship.

Guardianship (and conservatorship) laws are remarkably outmoded in most states. In many instances no distinction is made between personal and property decisions, and a guardian automatically is granted decision-making permission for both. Personal decisions affected by a guardianship may include where the patient may reside, the right to travel freely, and the right to consent to medical or psychiatric treatment; property decisions may include the right to sign checks or withdraw money from a bank account. Most guardianship laws are all-or-nothing affairs and fail to take into account the ability of schizophrenic patients to manage some areas of their lives but not others. The laws are often extremely vague: the law in California, until recently changed, said that a guardian could be appointed for any "incompetent person . . . whether insane or not . . . , who is likely to be deceived or imposed upon by artful and designing persons." This could include most of us! The actual appointment of a guardian is usually done without legal due process and without the patient present; nor is there periodic review to determine whether the guardianship is still necessary.

For all these reasons the family of a schizophrenic should only initiate a guardianship procedure if absolutely necessary and after consultation with the patient's psychiatrist. The benefits which accrue to a patient by having a guardian should clearly outweigh the loss of decision-making ability and independence. Since state laws on guardianship and conservatorship vary widely and are in the process of changing, consultation with a good lawyer is mandatory. States also vary considerably on how much money, if any, goes to the state out of inheritances to patients in the state hospitals. For schizophrenic patients who are likely to inherit substantial amounts of money or property, it behooves the family to check the legal situation before the bequest is made.

Enlightened guardianship laws have been established in some states in recent years; those in California, Minnesota, Illinois, and North Carolina are especially commendable. The Mental Health Law Project and the American Bar Association have also promulgated model statutes which can be used to revise state laws; these include notification for the patient of the hearing, the right to counsel, the right to a jury trial, and a mandatory periodic review. Families of schizophrenics can be helpful in encouraging the update of their state laws in this area.

RELIGION AND CULTS

Like all human beings, persons with schizophrenia have a need to relate to a god or philosophical worldview which allows them to place themselves and their lives within a larger context. For schizophrenics this can be particularly problematical for many reasons. For one thing, the onset of the disease often occurs during the same period of life when religious and philosophical beliefs are in great flux, thus making resolution extremely difficult. Another complicating factor is that many persons with this disease undergo intense heightened awareness, or "peak experiences" (as described in chapter 2), during the early stages of their illness and conclude that they have been specially chosen by God. When auditory hallucinations are experienced, these usually reinforce such a belief. Still another impediment to resolutions of religious concerns is the schizophrenic's inability to think metaphorically and in symbols, which most formalized religious belief systems require.

It is therefore not surprising that religious concerns continue to be important for many persons with this disease throughout the course of their illness. Most psychiatric hospitals provide chaplains to assist the patients; schizophrenics living in the community frequently utilize ministers, priests, and rabbis in their neighborhoods. I have been impressed by the quality of the spiritual ministrations shown by many of these people and their patience in answering the schizophrenics' questions.

Occasionally schizophrenics resolve their religious concerns by joining a religious cult of one kind or another. The variety of available cults is wide and includes the Unification Church ("Moonies"), Hare Krishna, Divine Light Mission, Jesus People, Scientology, and many smaller groups. One study reported that 6 percent of members from the Unification Church and 9 percent of members from the Divine Light Mission had been previously hospitalized for psychiatric problems. However, psychiatrists who have studied such groups believe that most of these previously hospitalized members were severely neurotic rather than schizophrenic. The groups themselves tend to exclude seriously disturbed individuals as too disruptive to the closely cooperative living and working conditions demanded by the groups.

For schizophrenics who are accepted into these cults there may be some advantages. A highly structured belief system and life style are inherent in such groups, as is also a sense of belongingness and community. These in turn lead to increased self-esteem in the member. Some cults also value unusual religious experiences, and in such settings a schizophrenic may feel more comfortable with his/her "peak experiences" or auditory hallucinations.

The cults also pose potential dangers for schizophrenics, however. Many such groups emphasize the desirability of not taking any drugs; schizophrenics who are doing nicely on maintenance fluphenazine or haloperidol may be encouraged to stop the drug, with resultant relapse. The groups may also encourage the schizophrenic to deny the reality of his or her illness, casting problems such as delusional thinking and auditory hallucinations into the mold of spiritual shortcomings rather than acknowledging that they are products of a brain disease. Some groups may also encourage paranoid thinking in schizophrenics who are already inclined in that direction, as there is often a siege mentality in the cults, a "we-they" feeling that the world is out to persecute them as a group. Finally, a few religious cults may exploit the money or property of schizophrenic members, as they sometimes do of nonschizophrenic members as well.

ALCOHOL, DRUGS, AND SEX

Many clinicians urge persons with schizophrenia not to drink alcohol at all, saying that the alcohol will make their symptoms worse and/or interact adversely with their antipsychotic medicine. It has been my experience that the majority of schizophrenics living in the community take a drink now and then and discover that the dire warnings of adverse effects do not materialize. Most schizophrenics can, in fact, have a social drink, and they appreciate doing so because it makes them feel more like "normal" people.

Like all life's pleasures, however, alcohol is best used in moderation and this may be as difficult for some schizophrenics to do as it is for some nonschizophrenics. This is especially true if the schizophrenic gets symptom relief from the alcohol (e.g., a decrease in auditory hallucinations), and such patients frequently abuse alcohol. I have found it useful to set specific, well-defined *maximum* amounts of alcohol which may safely be consumed; for example, in any twenty-four-hour period I tell patients not to exceed two cans of beer, two small glasses of wine, or one ounce of alcohol. For persons with a low tolerance to alcohol even this may be too much. Excess drinking by persons taking antipsychotic drugs usually leads to increased sedation, because both alcohol and the antipsychotic have sedative properties. If schizophrenics cannot control the amount of alcohol they drink, then they should not drink at all.

There is one group of psychiatric patients for whom alcohol is absolutely forbidden. These are patients who are taking the type of antidepressant medication known as MAO (monoamine oxidase) inhibitors; phenelzine (Nardil) and tranylcypromine (Parnate) are examples. These drugs are rarely used in schizophrenia but commonly used in severe depression. If patients on this medication drink even small amounts of alcohol, they may suffer very serious side effects, including a sharp increase in their blood pressure.

In contrast to alcohol, street drugs are like poisons for many schizophrenics. Even marijuana may set off psychotic symptoms in an unpredictable way, and it may take days to recover from them fully. One young man I treated remained virtually symptom-free on medication except when he smoked marijuana; he then became floridly psychotic for several days. Not all schizophrenics react this dramatically, of course, but as a general rule the use of street drugs by schizophrenics should be strongly discouraged.

Sex is a problem for many schizophrenics just as it is for many persons who do not have the disease. The fact that the onset of the disease commonly occurs in late adolescence, at the same time that the person's sexual identity is being resolved, tends to confuse the issue still further. The number of delusional ideas about sex found among schizophrenics is impressive. I have one patient who regularly announces that she is pregnant although she has not had intercourse; she is convinced that sex is not a necessary precondition to pregnancy. Another patient claims she has been continuously pregnant for five years and may deliver any week.

Some patients with schizophrenia enjoy sexual intercourse and engage in it for the same reasons that nonschizophrenics do: physical pleasure, sharing, and intimacy. Others avoid it for a variety of reasons, including my delusionally pregnant patient who avoids it so as "not to hurt the baby." Some patients avoid it because of the emotions and complexity of the interpersonal relationships which it entails; as described by one patient, "I find emotions tremendously complex, and I am quite acutely aware of the many over- and undertones of things people say and the way they say them. Generally I like direct, honest, kind people, and I have difficulty handling social situations that require me to be artificial or too careful." Still others avoid it because their libido is depressed either by the disease process itself or as a side effect of their antipsychotic medication. This contrasts sharply with patients with manic-depressive illness, who usually have increased libido as a symptom of their disease.

Families who are faced with a sexually active schizophrenic member will encounter many problems. One is embarrassment that the patient has an interest in sex at all; mentally ill persons are consigned in our imaginations to the realm of nonlibido inhabited by some elderly persons and by some with chronic physical illness. Initially, then, the family must confront and accept the reality of normal sexual desire in the person. That acceptance alone may alleviate some of the tension within the family.

The next problem is how to assess whether the patient is a consenting adult or is being taken advantage of in the sexual situation. This usually applies to women, although occasionally schizophrenic men will be taken advantage of by homosexuals. Questions which the family should ask itself include: Is she able to say no to men in nonsexual situations? Is her judgment reasonably good in other areas of her day-to-day functioning? Is she discreet, which suggests good judgment, in her sexual encounters? Is she trying to avoid men or is she seeking them out? Is she agreeing to sex primarily to obtain specific payment, most often cigarettes or food?

Consultation with the patient's psychiatrist and/or nursing staff at the halfway house or the psychiatric ward where the patient is known in a sustained situation will often clarify the consent issue for the family. The family of one woman, for example, became upset when they found that she was having intercourse regularly at the halfway house and she told her parents she was being taken advantage of. Discussion with halfway house staff established that the woman was seeking out the sexual encounters, and her claim of being taken advantage of was designed to assuage the disapproval of her parents. If a woman really is being taken advantage of, however, increased supervision and restrictions in her activity may be indicated. Women who are consenting to intercourse merely to acquire cigarettes or food need a plan formulated by the families and psychiatric staff to provide these items reliably so the schizophrenic will be less tempted to prostitute herself.

Women with schizophrenia become pregnant surprisingly infrequently. This may be due in part to a lower libido and lower rate of sexual exposure, but it is probably also due to some malfunction in pituitary hormones which is tied to the disease process in the brain. Nonetheless a family with a sexually active schizophrenic woman is always and understandably concerned about pregnancy. The best means for avoiding it are education of the patient regarding sexual functioning, times of maximum fertility, and contraception. The choice of a contraceptive should be made collaboratively with the patient, the patient's psychiatrist, family doctor or gynecologist. Many schizophrenics are unable to plan ahead well enough to use condoms or diaphragms. Oral contraceptives are effective but assume a degree of responsibility in taking a pill each day (there are no known adverse interactions between oral contraceptives and antipsychotic drugs). The I.U.D. loop is effective and requires no planning once inserted, and I have seen it used effectively by many schizophrenic women. In all cases the wishes of the patient must be considered, and the possible side effects of each method weighed against its merits.

VIOLENCE, SUICIDE, AND HOMICIDE

The schizophrenic's threats of violence, suicide, and homicide probably cause more sleepless nights among families than any other problems. The possibility lurks as a specter on the periphery of their consciousness, never completely out of view, quietly repeating "what if," "what if," "what if . . . ?" In fact schizophrenic patients as a group are remarkably nonviolent. Timidity is characteristic of them far more often than is aggression. Wandering the streets of the inner cities, schizophrenics are routinely preyed upon and assaulted; they are usually victims, not assailants.

Despite this fact, the arrest rate of schizophrenics has climbed in recent years. Given the release of large numbers of them from state institutions and their poor psychiatric follow-up (see chapter 7), this increased arrest rate should not be surprising. As their schizophrenic symptoms recur, such persons do things or behave in ways which bring them to the attention of the police, who frequently arrest them in order to return them to the hospital. One man smashed a store window because he saw a dinosaur jumping out at him. Another was arrested for repeatedly following two men who he believed were CIA agents and had kidnapped his imaginary benefactress. A woman was arrested for repeatedly eating in restaurants and then refusing to pay; she said she was the reincarnation of Jesus Christ and was therefore not required to pay. Patients I have known have been arrested for throwing stones at cars, attacking a telephone booth with an ax, and walking nude on public streets. One study found that 94 percent of arrested schizophrenic patients were not receiving psychiatric aftercare.

Occasionally, schizophrenic patients turn aggressive impulses upon themselves and commit suicide. Estimates of how frequently this occurs vary in different studies from 2 per 100 (over a twenty-year follow-up) to 6 per 100 (ten-year follow-up) to 10 per 100 (forty-year follow-up). One researcher estimates that in the United States 3,800 persons with schizophrenia commit suicide each year. The majority of such suicides occur in the first year or two of the onset of schizophrenia and are more likely to occur in patients with depression as a symptom.

The suicide rate for schizophrenia is misleading, however. Many schizophrenic suicides are a consequence of delusional thinking and thus should be more properly classified as accidental deaths than as suicides. One of my patients jumped from a third story window believing he could fly; another jumped from a window because his voices commanded him to do so. Fortunately neither was seriously injured. Daniel Paul Schreber reflects such delusional thinking in the autobiographical account of his sickness:

> If for instance I were to fall into water or wished to put a bullet through my head or chest . . . I would expect temporary signs corresponding to those of death by drowning or unconsciousness following a bullet wound which would be fatal in other people. But as long as contact with rays [magical protectors] remains, it can hardly be denied that I would be revived again, the action of the heart and circulation restarted and the destroyed inner organs and bones restored.

Other schizophrenic suicides may also be a result of a direct, conscious will to die, just as occurs in nonschizophrenic individuals, as was the death of Michael Wechsler in *In a Darkness*. One young man I knew shot himself to death because he was plagued with auditory hallucinations and did not wish to live with them; another drowned himself for similar reasons. An elderly gentleman I treated had been living alone with only his "devils" (auditory hallucinations) for companionship for many years. After carefully adjusting his medication we were able to get rid of the "devils," at which point he fully realized how lonely and isolated he was and he drowned himself. Given the symptom-caused torment and social isolation which many schizophrenics must endure, in truth I find it surprising that the suicide rate among them is not higher than it is.

Suicide is just one component of the elevated mortality rate found among schizophrenics, compared with the nonschizophrenic population. Another component is accidental deaths which are also related to the disease. One man I knew had difficulty concentrating because of his "voices" and walked in front of a bus, with fatal consequences. Another patient I had known stopped taking his medicine and, while acutely psychotic, made menacing gestures at a young woman on a crowded bus. The terrified woman struck him with a knife from her purse, piercing his heart and killing him.

Still another factor in this increased mortality rate is death due to medical causes. Once released from the hospital, schizophrenics often receive little medical care (see chapter 7); even when they do see a doctor they may be unable to describe their symptoms and/or the doctor may attribute their medical symptoms to their schizophrenia. Further, as noted in chapter 2, many schizophrenics have an elevated pain threshold and are unaware of warning symptoms, so they do not seek medical help until their illness is far advanced. For all of these reasons schizophrenics have been found to have relatively high mortality rates not only from suicide and accidental death but from medical conditions (especially infections) as well.

Homicide, although rare among schizophrenic patients, does occur. Most often it is a product of paranoid delusions, an attempt to get "them" before "they" get him/her. Parents and spouses of paranoid schizophrenics live in a special circle of Hell, which must be experienced to be believed. As one parent phrased it, "I often live in fear that one day he might act on his persecutory ideas and that when he does I'm going to be the target." Always at the back of one's mind are the rare but dramatic cases of such acts: for example, the man who believed his neighbors were persecuting him, made a list of whom to kill, and proceeded then to fatally shoot thirteen persons in twenty minutes.

Rarely, nonparanoid schizophrenics also attempt homicide. One of my patients, instructed by her voices, walked into a city hospital nursery and attacked a newborn baby; fortunately the baby survived. Another patient went home for the Christmas holidays; when her husband announced that he was going out to see another woman (which he had done many times before) on Christmas Eve, the patient shot him. (This is an instance in which she might have shot him whether or not she was schizophrenic.) Such examples are very uncommon, but newspaper accounts always prominently display the "mental patient" aspect when reporting cases like these, and this is the source of the erroneous impression that schizophrenics as a group are violent, homicidal maniacs. The truth is quite the reverse.

What should families do when faced with a schizophrenic relative who may be violent or assaultive? First, it should be stressed that such problems *invariably* have forewarnings through threats and other signs of impending trouble; placid, withdrawn schizophrenic patients do not suddenly metamorphose into violent, homicidal individuals. Paranoid schizophrenics are the group which merit most concern, and if patients with this diagnosis start talking about "I'll get them before they get me," then an immediate reevaluation by a psychiatrist is mandatory.

When faced with threats of violence, the family of a schizophrenic patient should not ignore them but rather should discuss them openly. Is the patient simply seeking attention and/or trying to intimidate the family? Are the threats based upon rational manipulation, or do they arise in irrational, usually delusional, thought processes? Does the patient have a past history of violence, which is the single best predictor of future violence? Has the patient ingested street drugs or been drinking heavily? The family should usually consult with the patient's psychiatrist, who may help them assess the seriousness of the threat. If such threats are being heard for the first time, reevaluation of the patient by the psychiatrist is probably indicated. In all instances the family should convey to the patient that violence of any kind will not be tolerated, and the penalty for acting out the threats may well be expulsion from the home. Families with such problems often learn to "schizophrenia-proof" their homes as well, including locking up sharp objects and weapons, removing the inner locks from the schizophrenic's bedroom and bathroom, and insuring that sufficient help is nearby if the person appears to be disturbed. The mother of one assaultive patient has a college student stay in the house as a companion when her son is at home; it gives her protection which she feels she needs and it gives her son somebody to spend time with who is closer to him in age.

Families in which the schizophrenic patient has been assaultive or violent are particularly poignant. Family members are often afraid of the patient, yet at the same time feel sorry for him/her and recognize that the behavior was a product of abnormal brain function. The ambivalence inevitably felt by the family members is formidable; fear and love, avoidance and attraction rest uneasily side by side. No matter how well the patient subsequently gets, no matter how much time elapses, the memory of the past assault or violence never fully recedes.

EXPECTATIONS FOR THE FUTURE

Perhaps the hardest task for families with a schizophrenic member is to accept the reality of the disease and modify their expectations for the patient's future. When a person has been sick only once or twice for a few months, this is not necessary. But if and when there have been recurrent episodes or illness, or hospitalization for long periods, then it is essential and desirable for the family to assess the future realistically.

This is especially difficult to do for a family in which the schizophrenic person had been unusually promising prior to becoming ill. Such families tend to hang onto the hope, year after year, that the schizophrenic will someday become normal again and resume his or her career. Grossly unrealistic plans are made, money is saved for college or a big wedding, and family members fool each other with the shared myth of "when he gets well again."

The problem with the myth is that the chronic schizophrenic knows it is a myth, and it puts him/her in a no-win situation. There is nothing the schizophrenic can do to please the family except to get well, and that is beyond his or her control. Several observers have noted this problem and have urged families to lower their expectations for the person. If this is done, the families themselves become happier. Creer and Wing noted in their interviews with such families:

> Several relatives mentioned that giving up hope had paradoxically been the turning point for them in coming to terms with their unhappiness. "Once you give up hope," one mother said, "you start to perk up." "Once you realise he'll never be cured you start to relax." These relatives had lowered their expectations and aspirations for the patient, and had found that doing this had been the first step in cutting the problem down to manageable size.

Another parent said, "You've got to reach bedrock, to become depressed enough, before you are forced to accept the reality and the enormity of the problem. Having done that, you don't allow your hopes to become too high and thus leave yourself open to disappointment when they are not fulfilled."

This does not mean that families should have no expectations at all of the person with schizophrenia. H. Richard Lamb, one of the few psychiatrists who have worked assiduously on the rehabilitation of schizophrenic patients, has said, "Recognizing that a person has limited capabilities should not mean that we expect nothing of him." Expectations must be realistic, however, and consonant with the capabilities of the schizophrenic. Just as the family of a polio victim should not expect the person's legs to return to complete normality, so too the family of a schizophrenic should not expect the person's brain to return to complete normality. Psychiatrist John Wing wrote:

> A neutral (not overemotional) expectation to perform up to *attainable* standards is the ideal. This rule, if difficult for the specialist to adopt, is a thousand times more difficult for relatives. Nevertheless, we should be humbled to recognize that a large portion of relatives, by trial and error, do come to adopt it, without any help from professionals.

The effect of lowering one's expectations is often to be able to enjoy and share things with the schizophrenic for the first time in many years. Thus if someone who was an accomplished flutist prior to becoming ill takes up the flute again to play simple pieces, both the person and the family can enjoy that accomplishment. It no longer is going to be seen, implicitly or explicitly, in the light of when-you-are-well-you'll-be-able-to-give-concerts-again-dear. Similarly, if the person is able to ride a bus for the first time alone or go to the store by himself or ride a bicycle, these accomplishments can also be celebrated for what they are—often magnificent accomplishments for a person whose brain is not functioning properly. The person with schizophrenia and the family need to be able to find joy in such accomplishments just as a polio victim finds joy in relearning to walk. As long as families deny the reality of the illness, however, they are also denying themselves and the person the few pleasures they can obtain from accomplishments.

BROTHERS AND SISTERS

The brothers and sisters of schizophrenics are often forgotten in the confusion of getting care for their sick sibling. Their needs are very real, however, and should be addressed both by the family and by mental health professionals working with the family.

The problems brothers and sisters face are manifold. If there is a belief within the family that psychosocial events caused the disease, then the brother or sister may share the family guilt. Which of us has not done things to our own siblings which we did not later regret? When looking for "causes" of the person's schizophrenia, all of these past misdeeds and memories may be dredged up, accompanied by the barnacles of guilt encrusted on them. Another source of guilt, often not conscious, is the survivors' syndrome, in which persons who survive a disaster feel guilty for not having perished with the others; well siblings may similarly feel guilty that they have escaped the disease and are able to lead normal lives.

Embarrassment is another common and understandable feeling among brothers and sisters of schizophrenics, especially prominent during the teen years when peer pressure and social concerns are at their peak. Imagine a sixteen-year-old, for example, walking with a schizophrenic sibling through a park when the schizophrenic suddenly "jumped on one of the statues and yelled, 'I'm the king of the castle and you're all the dirty rascals.' " And the sister of one of my patients never asks anyone to visit when the patient is home because he unpredictably takes off his clothes. The embarrassment felt by the brother or sister is also likely to be greater if the parents, too, are embarrassed.

Siblings almost invariably feel anxiety as well, especially if they are younger than the affected person and still in an age range where the possibility of sickness is plausible. Comments such as "I often wonder if they think I'm likely to be as mad as my brother" or "We all do stupid things when we're with friends, but I can't help feeling that every odd action or word that I say is taken as evidence that I could develop into a schizophrenic" are not uncommon. The specter of the disease, of becoming insane, lurks in the minds of these young people throughout their formative years.

Jealousy is sometimes a problem. The well siblings may be jealous of the attention and concern being focused on the person who is sick. This may become exacerbated if large amounts of the family's financial resources, such as the money set aside for college for the well children, must be commandeered in order to pay for treatment of the schizophrenic. Louise Wilson expresses this dilemma from the mother's point of view in *This Stranger, My Son* when told that her son's care will cost $50,000 a year.

Surely you will do anything for your child. But you have to live along the way. You have to take care of your other children who are not sick. They are entitled to their share, too. How much ought you to spend on the sick one? How ought you to apportion what you have? . . . Some will say: "Everything for the sick one because the healthy can take care of themselves." Others will say: "The well have a future, therefore give to them; don't sacrifice them for the sake of the hopelessly ill."

The only solution to problems posed by the brothers and sisters of schizophrenics is facts, education, and more of the same. As schizophrenia is understood as a disease, many of these problems will resolve themselves. The allocation of family resources is a family problem and should be discussed openly as such; siblings should be included in such decision-making. It is they, after all, who are likely to have long-term responsibility for their schizophrenic brother or sister after the mother and father have died, and it is only fair that they be involved in decisions whose consequences they will have to live with.

FAMILY SUPPORT GROUPS

The single biggest advance in coping with schizophrenia since the introduction of antipsychotic drugs has been the advent of family support groups. These groups existed sporadically in earlier years, but in the mid-1970s began to proliferate rapidly. In September 1979, approximately 300 representatives from 80 such groups met in Madison, Wisconsin, and formed the National Alliance for the Mentally Ill (National AMI). Since that time the number of family support organizations has mushroomed to over 300 and National AMI has opened a national office in Washington, D.C.* A current listing of family support groups by state may be found in appendix C.

Family support groups vary in character and purpose. Almost all of them include mutual support and education. Either in large group meetings or in smaller groups (such as "sharing nights"), the families exchange information about psychiatrists, financial resources for patients, commitment laws, places for schizophrenics to live, and problems they are encountering with their schizophrenic relatives. One study of such groups found that it was this sharing of common experiences and problems, not merely practical information, which was their most useful function. Most family support groups supplement this private information exchange with a monthly newsletter, and some have even undertaken public education. San Mateo AMI in San Mateo, California, for example, sponsored a public conference at the College of San Mateo

---

*National AMI, 1234 Massachusetts Ave., N.W., Washington, D.C. 20005.

entitled "Schizophrenia Through the Eyes of Families."

Advocacy for legislation affecting schizophrenics is another activity these groups have undertaken. In one such effort the Fox Valley Alliance for the Mentally Ill in Oshkosh, Wisconsin, worked to modify the state involuntary commitment laws. Other groups have lobbied for legislation affecting housing and consumer representation on local and state mental health advisory boards.

A few family support groups have themselves opened and maintained halfway houses, group homes, or apartments for schizophrenics. Examples of groups which have had experience with this include the Oasis Fellowship in East Lansing, Michigan; Families for Mental Recovery in Davis, California; Families and Friends of the Mentally Ill in Boulder, Colorado; San Mateo AMI in San Mateo, California, and Thresholds in Kensington, Maryland. An innovative family support group has been the Marin Parents for Mental Recovery in Marin County, California, which not only opened a group home but also opened a successful coffeehouse in which recovering schizophrenics could work. California's then governor Jerry Brown visited the coffeehouse and provided publicity. The Marin County group grew out of an original four families who had young adults with schizophrenia; the group home and coffeehouse were in operation within five years of its founding.

Most family support groups are started by family members of schizophrenics, and are affiliated with National AMI. In the past some began with a commitment to promoting an orthomolecular approach to treating schizophrenia (see chapter 6); these are usually identified as chapters of the American Schizophrenia Association or the Huxley Institute. A few were begun under the auspices of the local chapter of the Mental Health Association (MHA) although, as will be discussed in chapter 12, the MHA at the national level has been disappointingly oblivious to the needs of schizophrenic patients. A few also have been started by community mental health centers (e.g., NEWW Center in Newton, Massachusetts), psychiatric hospitals (Clarke Institute of Psychiatry in Toronto) or halfway houses (Thresholds in Chicago).

Outside the United States family support groups have also developed quickly in the last decade. The National Schizophrenia Fellowship in Britain* has been especially active. It was founded in 1970 and now has 150 chapters and over 3,000 members. It provides a good model for the National Alliance for the Mentally Ill to follow in the area of public education, for it produces high quality pamphlets available at very modest cost. The National Schizophrenia Fellowship has sponsored studies of problems schizophrenic persons have living at home and has run residential weekend study seminars for families of schizophrenics. It raises money through concerts, television appeals, and selling its own Christmas cards and has begun an annual National

*78/79 Victoria Road, Surbiton, Surrey, England KT6-4NS.

Schizophrenia Day. It has also opened secondhand book stores to both raise money and provide sheltered employment for schizophrenics.

The National Schizophrenia Fellowship has taken an active role in promoting research as well. It has arranged for the brains of deceased schizophrenics to be made available for research, and some of the studies referred to in chapter 5 utilized this material. It has also set up its own Research Advisory Group to give out small research grants.

Family support groups have also been formed in several other countries within the last few years. The Schizophrenia Fellowship of New Zealand has been especially active and is following the model of its English counterpart. Australia and Canada also have many active groups. Other countries with family support groups now forming include Argentina, Austria, Chile, France, Ireland, Israel, Japan, Malta, the Netherlands, Sweden, South Africa, and West Germany.

9

LEGAL AND ETHICAL DILEMMAS
IN SCHIZOPHRENIA

When I tell them that I suffer from schizophrenia I often get blank
looks and sometimes a wary one. I have often felt that the mad
cannot explain and the sane cannot comprehend.
                    Schizophrenic patient, quoted in Henry R. Rollin,
                                        Coping with Schizophrenia

Providing care for someone with a chronic illness is a difficult task. Diseases
such as polio, multiple sclerosis, kidney failure, and slowly progressive cancer
can drain a family physically, emotionally, and sometimes also financially.
When the chronic illness affects the person's brain, however, then the task
becomes herculean. It has no-win qualities, so that whatever the relative or
friend does, there is always the lingering feeling that it wasn't enough or it
wasn't right. Like Sisyphus condemned forever to roll a huge stone uphill, only
to have it roll down again, the unremitting process of caring for someone with
schizophrenia will tax the inner resources of even the strongest person.

One major reason for this is the many legal and ethical dilemmas raised
by this disease. Relatives and friends of people with schizophrenia are caught
frequently in damned-if-you-do and damned-if-you-don't situations. They
want to be helpful and do the right thing for the patient, but often when they
try they are confronted by these dilemmas. This chapter will not solve the
dilemmas, but it will at least articulate them forthrightly, and thus allow them
to be thought through as rationally as possible.

INVOLUNTARY HOSPITALIZATION

The most common of the legal and ethical dilemmas posed by people with
schizophrenia is if and when to hospitalize them against their will. Consider
the following case:

A young woman is observed to be living in a train station for several
days. She asks passers-by for money but otherwise does not bother

them. She is often seen talking to herself or to imaginary people. A newspaper reporter talks with her and discovers that she is a college graduate who has been recently released from a psychiatric hospital. The woman's conversation does not make sense. A policeman takes her to the local psychiatric hospital but the psychiatrists there refuse to admit her because they say she has done nothing to suggest that she is a danger to herself or others. She also indicates unwillingness to go back into the hospital voluntarily. She returns to the train station. A few days later she is found raped and murdered nearby.

This woman represents all the dilemmas of involuntary hospitalization. On one side are those who would argue against hospitalizing her against her wishes. Opponents of involuntary hospitalization include psychiatrists, such as Dr. Thomas Szasz, civil liberties lawyers, such as Bruce Ennis of the American Civil Liberties Union, and many ex-patient groups. Szasz has been working for the abolition of involuntary psychiatric hospitalization for over two decades, and in 1970 helped found the American Association for the Abolition of Involuntary Mental Hospitalization (AAAIMH). His many books, especially *Law, Liberty and Psychiatry* and *Psychiatric Slavery,* articulately expound the case against involuntarily hospitalizing persons with strange behavior or strange beliefs. Ennis, the forerunner of an increasingly large group of civil liberties lawyers concerned with mental illness, in 1972 published *Prisoners of Psychiatry*, in which he said, "The goal should be nothing less than the abolition of involuntary hospitalization." And ex-patient groups publish periodicals, such as the *Madness Network News,* which offers "all the fits that's news to print" and vividly describes the many injustices perpetrated on incarcerated mental patients.

The arguments used by these people against involuntary hospitalization include the deprivation of civil liberties and the violation of various constitutional rights guaranteed us as individuals. They cite thinkers such as John Stuart Mill and Thomas Jefferson, and argue that the state has no right to protect people from themselves. We allow people to smoke, drink, climb mountains, race automobiles and do many other things which clearly are dangerous to themselves. Doesn't one have the right to do what one wishes with one's own body provided no one else is harmed? Furthermore, dangerousness is a vague and relative concept, and what one person finds dangerous the next person may call pleasurable. And to confine people because they *might* do something to hurt themselves or hurt others is just preventive detention; if we can confine people for what they *might* do, then we must confine all criminals forever because we know that when they are released their dangerousness is much greater than the dangerousness of mental patients. Opponents of involuntary psychiatric hospitalization also point to the lifelong stigma which accrues to psychiatric hospitalization and to the accompanying loss of the right to vote, the right to make a contract, and the right to drive an automobile, which may accompany such hospitalization in some states.

Another argument against involuntary hospitalization is its potential for abuse. If the state has the right to hospitalize people against their will, then it may create arbitrary criteria for such hospitalization and thereby use it to remove dissenters and political opponents. This has in fact happened in the Soviet Union and other East European bloc countries and is well described by Sidney Bloch and Peter Reddaway in *Psychiatric Terror: How Soviet Psychiatry Is Used to Suppress Dissent.* Such hospitalizations are doubly effective as political tools because they not only incarcerate dissenters with indeterminate sentences but tinge them with the brush of insanity, thereby discrediting them.

The strongest arguments put forth against involuntary psychiatric hospitalization, however, are the horror stories of individual cases. There is no doubt that there has been much abuse of involuntary commitment, so there is much ammunition which can be used in the battle. People have indeed been locked up for thirty, fifty, even seventy years for strange behavior. Combine with this the fact that conditions in public psychiatric hospitals where they are locked up are so often grim, and you have the ingredients necessary for lurid testimonials of beatings, forced labor, and other inhumane conditions.

What about the young woman at the train station? Opponents of involuntary psychiatric hospitalization would argue that it was correct to let her remain free. Her behavior, they would say, may have been strange but then behavior is a relative concept. As long as she was not harming anyone she should have been left free. They, too, would mourn her death but would say that the price you must pay for liberty is the possibility that a few people may be killed.

Supporters of involuntary psychiatric hospitalization include most psychiatrists, many other mental health workers, the policemen and social workers who face these crises on a daily basis, and large segments of the general public. The major argument for hospitalizing people against their will is that they are unable to care for themselves because of their illness or because they are dangerous to themselves or to others. The idea of *parens patriae* (see chapter 6) says that the state has an obligation to protect people who cannot protect themselves and that mentally ill individuals have a right to be both protected and treated so that they will get well. Temporarily confining them and restricting their liberties is a small price to pay for this protection and treatment.

Another reason used to hospitalize patients against their will is the protection of others. A few psychiatric patients are genuinely dangerous. The problem arises when you try to quantify dangerousness. How dangerous do they have to be? What must they have done? Is a threat enough? I recently had a young man under my care who had threatened the life of one of the nation's leaders. In addition to the threat, a rifle with a telescopic sight and dozens of rounds of ammunition were found in his car. Do we require actual dangerous acts to justify incarceration, or is circumstantial evidence sufficient? These are real dilemmas faced daily in the admissions departments of the nation's psychiatric hospitals.

The key to resolving the dilemma of involuntary hospitalization is the nature of schizophrenia. If it is nothing other than a euphemism for unusual behavior, then it is hard to justify involuntary hospitalization. If schizophrenia is really one or more brain diseases, however, then the justification becomes much easier. When the brain is diseased, it does not function properly and one could not reasonably expect a person with a diseased brain to be able to make accurate judgments. When you say to persons with schizophrenia, "Look, I think you are getting sick again and you need to go back to the hospital," and they answer that they are not sick and refuse to return, then the refusal does not necessarily have to be taken as an absolute. The brain which is causing the sickness is the same brain deciding on the need for treatment. In one study of chronic schizophrenic patients, for example, it was found that only 13 percent of them understood that they were mentally ill. Even though we know that the entire brain is not sick in such persons, we have no way of knowing which of its parts are ailing and which are functioning normally; to say that the person's refusal of hospitalization is coming from the healthy parts is absurd. Thus the concept of a diseased brain provides sufficient rationale for invoking the *parens patriae* role of the state and hospitalizing persons against their will when necessary. Using such reasoning, the young woman in the vignette at the beginning of this chapter could be hospitalized against her will, at least until it was ascertained whether she could be improved with medications. To let such people alone, perhaps to die because they cannot take care of themselves, is to let them "die with their rights on."

Now that we are on the threshold of delineating the biological underpinnings of schizophrenia, the dilemma of involuntary hospitalization may become easier. Even Szasz has said that he would permit involuntary hospitalization *if* there was something wrong with the body which could be measured objectively. As an example of what he means, he gives the measurement of abnormal chemicals in the body in a person withdrawing from alcohol addiction. Schizophrenia is now developing such measurements (see chapter 5), and it will be interesting to watch the development of scientific criteria for involuntary hospitalization.

If people with schizophrenia really have a brain disease, then the medical model also provides justification for involuntary hospitalization to protect other people. We do not argue against the regulation that persons with smallpox and tuberculosis can be confined involuntarily to protect others. So can persons with epileptic attacks or brain tumors that cause them to strike out at other people.

I believe the pendulum in many states has swung too far in our efforts to

protect people's civil liberties. It is becoming increasingly difficult to hospitalize people involuntarily, and the cost to schizophrenics and their families is
great. As noted in chapter 6, the use of the *parens patriae,* the state's obligation
to protect those who cannot defend themselves, is being narrowed in many
states, and often the only acceptable justification for involuntary hospitalization is evidence of dangerousness of the person. It was poignantly summarized
by one observer of the scene: "Patients wander our streets, lost in time, as if
in a medieval city. We are protecting their civil liberties much more adequately
than we are protecting their minds and their lives."

The current situation engenders frequent hypocrisy in courts of law.
Psychiatrists, including me, sometimes testify that patients are more dangerous than we really believe them to be so we can keep them in the hospital and
treat them. Stretching the truth is often not sufficient, however, and patients
are released daily who are treatable but who demonstrate no legal grounds for
commitment. It is admittedly difficult to strike the correct balance between the
patient's right to freedom and society's obligation to protect those who cannot
protect themselves, between the patient's right of self-expression and society's
obligation to protect other citizens from the consequences of that self-expression. We must continue striving to achieve this balance.

A reasonable compromise to this dilemma was proposed by Dr. Loren
Roth. He suggested that schizophrenics judged by psychiatrists to be incapable
of caring for themselves should be involuntarily hospitalized for a limited
period of time (no longer than twelve weeks), during which time treatment
could be tried. At the end of this time they would have to be released unless
they agreed to stay or were found by a court (judge and/or jury) to be
genuinely dangerous to other people. This would be using the *parens patriae*
obligation of the states to protect those who cannot protect themselves for a
defined and limited period of time, and using dangerousness-to-others criteria
as the only one allowed for longer term of commitment.

THE INSANITY DEFENSE

The responsibility of schizophrenic persons for criminal acts becomes a problem for their families if they break the law. Most persons with schizophrenia
are not dangerous and do not commit major crimes. Minor violations of the
law are not uncommon, however, when the person becomes confused or
psychotic. Often such persons are judged not competent to stand trial. In the
past, incompetency to stand trial was used as grounds for long-term commitment to a psychiatric hospital, but in recent years there has been a tendency
for courts to either bring the person to trial or drop the charges.

If the person is brought to trial the lawyer may plead him/her not guilty by reason of insanity. This is the insanity defense. It dates back to the thirteenth century, when it was known as the "wild beast test" (insofar as persons are like wild beasts they cannot be held accountable). In England in the nineteenth century it was modified in the M'Naghten case to the "right or wrong test" (insofar as persons do not know right from wrong they cannot be held accountable). In the United States in recent years this has been replaced in many states by the "product test" (insofar as their acts were a product of mental disease persons cannot be held accountable) or by various modifications and compromises between the "right or wrong test" and the "product test." Indeed the insanity defense has attracted more attention than any other issue in criminal law over the past hundred years.

Among the arguments for using the insanity defense for persons accused of crimes is the fact that it protects them from being simply convicted and punished as if they had been fully responsible. Thus, a schizophrenic who steals a car with the key in it because he thought it was his car or because voices told him to do so is not treated in the same way as a car thief who steals it to sell to others.

Arguments against use of the insanity defense are impressive, and many people have suggested that it be abolished. Deciding whether a person's behavior is a "product" of his or her mental illness is an exceedingly difficult and subjective task. As one observer has noted, "Almost all crimes, by definition, involve transgressions of societal norms that could be called insane." Such judgments are made even more difficult by the fact that they are retrospective. Who can really know what was in a person's mind when a criminal act was being committed months before he or she comes to trial?

The biggest problem with the insanity defense is that, because it is so imprecise, it has been widely abused. The well-publicized trials of Sirhan Sirhan, in which psychiatrists tried to convince the jury that Sirhan had hypnotized himself with mirrors before he shot Robert Kennedy, or of Patty Hearst, who was said to have been brainwashed prior to holding up a bank, strongly discredited the insanity defense. More recently the finding of John Hinckley not guilty by reason of insanity in his attempted assassination of President Reagan unleashed a torrent of criticism, both public and governmental, and calls for reform or abolition of the insanity defense. Prior to the Hinckley trial Idaho had become the first state to eliminate the insanity defense altogether; Wisconsin and California had passed laws restricting its use and six other states (Michigan, Kentucky, Illinois, Indiana, Georgia, and New Mexico) had instituted an alternate plea of "guilty but mentally ill." Since the Hinckley trial there have been congressional hearings on limiting the insanity defense in federal cases, and in late 1982 President Reagan formally proposed changing these laws. Virtually every state legislature has considered proposals to restrict its use.

Many proposals to change the insanity defense have included a two-part trial in which the issues of guilt for the crime and extenuating circumstances (including insanity) would be separated. In the first part the only question addressed would be whether or not the accused actually committed the crime. If the person was found guilty, *then* psychiatrists and other witnesses would be allowed to testify on the person's mental state and other extenuating circumstances; this testimony would be used to help decide where the person should be sent (prison or psychiatric hospital) and for how long.

If the second part of the trial specifically addressed the question of responsibility, such a system would be a definite improvement over the current legal quagmire engendered by the insanity defense. The insanity defense as currently practiced includes an assumption that persons are either responsible or not responsible for their actions. Sane persons are considered to be responsible, insane persons to be not responsible; it is an all-or-nothing determination. Such simplistic thinking, however, contradicts the experience of everyone who has ever lived with or taken care of persons with schizophrenia. As discussed in chapter 8, schizophrenics are almost never wholly responsible or wholly irresponsible; further, their level of responsibility may fluctuate over time. Included in the second part of the trial, therefore, should be a determination by a jury of the level of responsibility that they believe the person had at the time of the crime. For example, a schizophrenic who kills another man because he believed he was an alien creature from another planet may be judged to have a very low level of responsibility, whereas a schizophrenic who kills her philandering husband out of anger may be judged to have a high level of responsibility. No longer would a defendant like John Hinckley be said to be totally responsible or totally not responsible.

THE RIGHT TO TREATMENT

For the 1970s, the emerging issue in law and psychiatry was the right to treatment. It came to the forefront in 1971 when Judge Frank Johnson in Alabama issued a court order in the case of *Wyatt* v. *Stickney*. This order dealt with the deplorable conditions in Alabama's mental hospitals and mandated that the conditions must be improved so that treatment of the patients could take place. As Judge Johnson phrased it: "To deprive any citizen of his or her liberty upon the altruistic theory that the confinement is for humane and therapeutic reasons and then fail to provide adequate treatment violates the very fundamentals of due process." He then went on to recommend specific staff-to-patient ratios and minimal conditions which were to be implemented. It was the first time the courts had entered mental hospitals and legally mandated that things must be improved.

The next major thrust in this direction came in 1975 when the United States Supreme Court ruled in favor of Kenneth Donaldson in the case of *Donaldson* v. *O'Connor.* Donaldson had been a patient in a Florida state hospital for many years and sued the hospital superintendent, Dr. O'Connor, for failing to treat him and failing to discharge him since he was not being treated. Lower courts had found in favor of Donaldson and had awarded him monetary damages. The Supreme Court ruled that a psychiatric patient who is not dangerous to himself or others, who can survive safely outside the hospital, and who is not getting treatment must be released from the hospital. It reversed the award for monetary damages and did not rule specifically on the right to treatment *per se.*

Also in 1975, a judge in Washington, D.C., ruled in favor of psychiatric patients in the case of *Dixon* v. *Weinberger.* This suit had been raised in behalf of patients at St. Elizabeths Hospital, a federal psychiatric facility serving the District of Columbia, in the name of Dixon (a patient) against Weinberger (then Secretary of the Department of Health, Education and Welfare, which had jurisdiction over the hospital). It stated that patients not only have a right to treatment but have a right to treatment in the least restrictive setting. This meant that patients who don't require full-time hospital care must be moved to alternative facilities, such as foster homes, halfway houses, and nursing homes. The right to treatment had been carried an additional step.

Most recently, in 1982, the Supreme Court ruled on the rights of a mentally retarded man, Nicholas Romeo, in a Pennsylvania state institution. It ruled that the patient had a right to safety, to a reasonable amount of physical freedom, and to training to improve his level of function. Although the ruling was specifically aimed at institutions for the mentally retarded, it is generally assumed that it will be invoked in court actions for the mentally ill as well.

What relevance do these legal suits have for schizophrenic patients and their families? Most importantly, they illustrate how the courts may be used to promote better treatment in state hospitals and better community facilities for chronic mental patients. It is not yet clear whether they will be successful, however. The courts can mandate minimum staff ratios, as they did in Alabama, but the courts cannot magically produce nurses and psychiatrists to work in the hospitals and improve the ratios. The courts can mandate alternative community facilities, as they did in Washington, D.C., but the courts cannot build the foster homes or halfway houses if the local government refuses to do so. Most disturbingly, the suit for monetary damage by Donaldson against the state hospital superintendent in Florida might have the reverse effect and frighten away psychiatrists from working in the state hospital system. It may also be argued that one of the effects of these legal proceedings has been to increase the speed of deinstitutionalization, with the states dumping unprepared ex-patients onto unprepared communities, so that the staff-to-patient ratios in the state hospitals will be improved.

Right-to-treatment suits are an exciting and potentially valuable tool which may force improvement in the facilities available for treating schizophrenic patients over time. In the short run, however, the suits may have some undesirable effects, and this should be monitored closely. Organized groups of patients' families can be invaluable in assisting the legal groups to initiate and then follow up the suits. It is a legal area in flux and one which will almost certainly evolve further in the 1980s.

THE RIGHT TO REFUSE TREATMENT

If the right to treatment was the emerging forensic psychiatric issue of the 1970s, then the right to refuse treatment is the issue of the 1980s. The issue was joined in 1979 in the United States District Court in Boston when Federal Judge Joseph L. Tauro, in the case of *Rogers* v. *Okin,* ruled that psychiatric patients in state mental hospitals could no longer be required to take medicine except in emergency situations "when there is a substantial likelihood of extreme violence, personal injury, or attempted suicide." Since then similar cases have come to public attention in New Jersey, Oklahoma, Wisconsin, and Utah and promise to emerge in other states as well. Supporters of Judge Tauro have hailed his decision as a landmark on the road to patients' rights, while his detractors have viewed it as leading only to patients' "right to rot" as they languish without necessary treatment. The United States Court of Appeals for the First Circuit modified Judge Tauro's decision somewhat, but the issue is clearly headed for the Supreme Court for a definitive decision.

The arguments in favor of patients having the right to refuse treatment are several. It may be argued that forcing medication on patients violates constitutional rights, such as the right to privacy, freedom from harm, freedom of speech and thought; and it may also represent cruel and unusual punishment. Forcing medication on patients, insofar as medication sedates them or impairs their thinking, may also impair their ability to defend themselves at legal hearings and may influence the judge or jury by making them appear to be unable to think clearly. The potential for abuse of forced medication is enormous, and in the Soviet Union many political dissidents have described having been involuntarily given antipsychotic and sedative drugs which made clear thinking very difficult. Even in the United States, the newspaper of the American Psychiatric Association ran an advertisement for liquid concentrate haloperidol (Haldol), encouraging its surreptitious use in tea, coffee, milk, et cetera, in which it could not be tasted by the person drinking it.

Proponents of the right to refuse treatment have used medication side effects as their strongest argument. They cite those studies showing that antipsychotic medications cause frequent and irreversible tardive dyskinesia (see chapter 6) and other unpleasant or undesirable side effects. In response to the argument that schizophrenic patients cannot make rational judgments on these matters, they counter that even if such persons were thinking completely normally, they would decline to take such drugs because of the threat of these side effects.

Arguments on the other side of the question are equally numerous. The loss of civil rights, such as privacy, can be balanced by the right to be free of disease. Such freedoms are meaningless if the person is sick. As articulated by one observer, psychiatric patients "will suffer if a liberty they cannot enjoy is made superior to a health that must sometimes be forced on them." It can also be argued that giving schizophrenic patients medication improves their thinking and their ability to defend themselves at hearings. The dangers and frequency of tardive dyskinesia and other side effects of these drugs vary widely in different studies, and for every report showing the drugs to be dangerous, another report can be brought forth showing that they are relatively safe drugs.

Other arguments supporting the right of psychiatrists to administer medications involuntarily to schizophrenic patients focus on benefits to society as a whole. With medications dangerous persons with this disease may be rendered nondangerous. And the drugs usually allow patients to leave the hospital and return to the community much sooner; this not only is better for the patient (by avoiding institutionalization) but also saves society the cost of long-term hospitalization of individuals too sick to be released untreated. Advocates of this position are collecting horror stories about the effects of Judge Tauro's decision and related cases, such as the patient in Massachusetts who could not be medicated for seven months while the court was securing a guardian, or the patient in New Jersey whose refusal to take medication cost an additional $35,350 for extra time in the hospital and legal fees.

Finally, it can be argued that because people with schizophrenia have diseases of the brain, they cannot give informed consent and cannot make an informed judgment on their own need for medication. Supporting this position is a study of chronic schizophrenic patients showing that only 27 percent of them understood that they needed medication.

The issue is complex and compelling, and families of schizophrenic patients will become drawn into the arguments increasingly often as courts move into this area. Psychiatrists will ask families more and more frequently for permission to give their relative antipsychotic medication against his or her wishes. This may put the relatives in an awkward position, but court mandates may make it necessary.

I myself come down strongly on the side of being able to give schizophrenic patients medication against their will if they need it. Checks and balances should certainly be built into the system to protect the patient in the same way that involuntary hospitalization should be periodically reviewed. But the fact is that persons with schizophrenia are really sick, and to withhold medication usually hurts them rather than helps them. I would urge those who advocate an elaborate court proceeding before involuntary medication can be given to spend a day on an acute psychiatric admission ward for schizophrenics where the patients have not been medicated; it will be an unforgettable experience. Finally, I would recommend that the process of involuntary commitment to a psychiatric hospital should automatically include the right to administer medications involuntarily if needed. To commit a patient to a hospital but say simultaneously that drugs cannot be given involuntarily, as some courts have done, is illogical and unworkable.

EXPERIMENTATION AND RESEARCH

Mental patients confined to institutions have occasionally been used to test new procedures and experimental drugs. This practice came into sharp public focus in the early 1970s when it was disclosed that mentally retarded patients in New York's Willowbrook Hospital had been experimentally infected with hepatitis virus. Since then public awareness of the issue has increased, and the 1978 *Report of the President's Commission on Mental Health* contains a concise and enlightening summary of the problem.

There are three kinds of experimentation or research which are theoretically possible. The first is the use of procedures or drugs which have little or no direct relationship to the illness for which the person is confined. Experimentally infecting retarded patients with hepatitis is an example of this. Hepatitis is a disease which is widespread in society and, while it occurs among retarded institutionalized patients more frequently than in the general population, it cannot be said to be a major threat to the health or life of such patients. Most importantly, hepatitis is not the reason these patients are hospitalized; retardation is the reason. Thus there is no justification for experimenting on retarded patients with the hepatitis virus or with any other procedure which is not directly related to their underlying condition. As stated by the President's Commission: "Experimentation which is neither directly beneficial to individual subjects nor related to subjects' mental condition and which poses any degree of risk to such subjects should not be permitted with institutionalized mentally handicapped individuals."

The second kind of experimentation is the use of procedures or drugs which may be directly beneficial to the person with schizophrenia. This possibility arises frequently with chronic schizophrenic patients on whom all the generally accepted modes of therapy have been tried to no avail. A conscientious psychiatrist will not be satisfied at this point but may want to go on and try newer and more experimental approaches. If this is done in a reputable hospital, it should be encouraged by the patient's family, for the alternatives are usually continued psychosis and indefinite hospitalization. Reputable hospitals insure that all experimental procedures have passed a research review board and that experimental drugs are used only under protocols approved by the Food and Drug Administration. The protection of the patient's rights under such procedures is adequate, usually insuring that there has been a careful consideration given to the benefits weighed against the risks to the patient, and that the risks have been explained to the patient and/or family. Even if the patient objects, it may be legitimate to try the experimental drug if the patient is not competent to decide and if the family gives consent.

The third kind of experimentation is directly related to finding the cause or treatment of schizophrenia but which realistically is unlikely to benefit that particular patient. For example, I perform lumbar punctures on many schizophrenic patients under my care in an attempt to find the causes of the disease. Such a procedure is virtually harmless and causes little more discomfort than drawing blood. For a 20- or 25-year-old patient I can honestly say that the procedure might be of direct benefit if it helps find the causes of schizophrenia. But for a 50-year-old patient direct benefit is much less likely. Is it justifiable to use experimental procedures or unproven drugs on such a patient?

Such a question raises the general problem alluded to previously of informed consent in psychiatric patients. Patients who are legally competent can give informed consent in such instances and pose no problem. Patients who are legally incompetent, however, raise further issues, for it is illogical to call a patient incompetent in some matters (e.g., understanding the need for medication) yet competent in other matters (understanding the risks in an experimental procedure). If the experimental procedure includes any substantial risk, therefore, it is desirable to obtain consent from the patient's family. Furthermore, schizophrenic patients who are sickest are precisely the ones we should be studying to learn what causes the disease, and those who are sickest are frequently the best candidates for experimental drugs because they may not have responded to traditional antipsychotics. Families of schizophrenics are likely to be asked increasingly often to give consent for the incompetent family member, and they should weigh all aspects of the question in giving their decision.

In general, the current situation regarding experimentation and research approaches a reasonable balance between protecting the rights of patients and allowing worthwhile experimentation and research to go forward. The trend, however, is toward increasing restrictions on psychiatric research, so that it will become virtually impossible to do this in the future. Real and well-publicized research abuses in the past, the vociferous defense of patients' rights by civil liberties lawyers, and the continuing rhetoric by Szasz, Laing, et al. that "mental illness is not really a disease," are all acting to swing the pendulum past the point of adequate protection toward an end which specifies overprotection. It is certainly possible to protect schizophrenic patients' rights so zealously that research on causes of the diseases and on new treatments will be effectively terminated, and in some psychiatric hospitals research has already become a dirty word. It is urgent that this be guarded against, and families of schizophrenic patients can help in this regard. There is little enough research going on as it is; if it is made more difficult to perform, then the amount done will decrease further. What we will then have is a generation of well-protected schizophrenic patients and the guarantee of more generations of similar patients to follow.

GENETIC COUNSELING AND OTHER DILEMMAS

There are other ethical and legal dilemmas connected with schizophrenia, but these concern families of the patients less frequently. Psychiatrists, for example, are frequently put into positions of having a conflict of interest between the patients in their care and society. Patients often give information to the psychiatrist which they think is being given in confidence (e.g., hearing voices, believing that people are after him/her) only to hear the psychiatrist repeat the information publicly at a judicial hearing for involuntary commitment. The patient has incriminated him/herself in a sense. Yet there is often no way to measure schizophrenic psychosis other than by using what the patient has said. Psychiatrists are also put into difficult dilemmas by the conflicting needs of the patient and the family. What should be done about the patient who doesn't quite qualify for involuntary commitment, yet who whenever out of the hospital harasses his/her family unmercifully with telephone calls all night, broken windows, and generally obnoxious behavior? Other children in the family often suffer significant damage in these situations. The family will often plead with the psychiatrist to keep the patient in the hospital, at least for a brief period.

Finally, sterilization, abortion, adoption, and genetic counseling may present legal and ethical dilemmas for schizophrenic patients and their families. In the past it was common to sterilize chronically psychotic female patients routinely so that they would not become pregnant. Legal suits and consequent court decisions have made this much less common, so that now most schizophrenic patients are able to procreate. Since impairment of judgment is often a symptom of their diseases, it is not surprising that unwanted pregnancies sometimes follow sexual intercourse. A decision must then be made whether to interrupt the pregnancy or let it proceed; if the latter, another decision will ensue as to whether the woman is able to care for the baby or whether it should be put up for adoption. Like so many dilemmas associated with schizophrenia, the questions of competency and informed consent arise in these matters and may be difficult to resolve. It is easy to empathize with, for example, a 36-year-old schizophrenic woman who has just been released from the hospital after fifteen years and wants to have a baby before it is too late; it is also easy to empathize with the infant who is born into such a situation and who is totally dependent for care on its mother. The relatives of schizophrenics may become involved in the dilemmas surrounding pregnancy and childbirth; responsible decisions frequently involve consultation with the psychiatrist, family physician, lawyer, religious adviser, and social worker. Often from such consultations a consensus will emerge on the best course of action, and this sharing of decision-making will alleviate the burden on both the patient and the patient's family. It is my experience that many women with schizophrenia do not wish to bear children; they find that taking care of themselves is difficult enough in our society, and to care for an infant as well may be completely overwhelming. In such instances the termination of pregnancy or prophylactic sterilization may be indicated.

Occasionally a person who has had schizophrenia will decide to marry and will seek genetic counseling regarding the chances of having a child who will also develop schizophrenia. If such a person has a child by a mate who does not have schizophrenia, the chances of the child developing schizophrenia are 10 percent. This contrasts with a 1 percent risk in the general population for children of parents neither of whom has had schizophrenia. If the person has a child by a mate who has also had, or still has, schizophrenia, then the chances of the child developing schizophrenia are 35 percent. Thus, if a person with schizophrenia strongly wants to have a child, he/she should be counseled to select a mate other than another schizophrenic. The high risk of schizophrenia in the offspring of two schizophrenic parents would also suggest that therapeutic abortion might be considered in the early months of pregnancy if the woman is agreeable.

10

THE DISTRIBUTION OF SCHIZOPHRENIA

The greatest proportion of insanity is in the northeast, in New
England and the Middle States.
William A. White, "The Geographical Distribution of Insanity
in the United States," 1903

Although it is commonly said that schizophrenia exists everywhere and is
distributed evenly around the world, this is not true. There are wide variations
in distribution of this disease, with some countries having a rate which is much
higher than other countries. Even in the United States there are variations in
schizophrenia's distribution, with an especially high concentration of it among
poor people and in the inner city. These facts should yield some clues to the
causes of the disease if they are pursued. To date, however, they have been
largely ignored.

UNITED STATES

As far back as 1840, it was recognized that the northeastern states in the
United States had a higher rate of insanity than the midwestern or the southern
states. Early figures were, of course, very unreliable, but it is noteworthy that
this same pattern of distribution has been cited repeatedly up to the present.
In 1903, for example, a well-known American psychiatrist surveyed the distribution of schizophrenia by states. He found that the greatest concentration was
in the northeast and "if from this center of greatest prevalence of insanity we
draw a line in any direction—west, south, or southwest—we see that no matter
which way we go we find a steady decrease until we strike the Pacific Slope."
More recent data on schizophrenia admission rates to American mental
hospitals support these earlier studies. The states with the greatest population
density and with most people living in cities have approximately twice as high
a schizophrenia rate as states with low population density and most people
living in rural areas. Thus in 1960, for example, the rate of first admissions for
schizophrenia per 100,000 population was 32 in Massachusetts and 16 in
Maine, 22 in Illinois and 11 in Arkansas. When the figures for the different

decades of the twentieth century are examined, there is an impression that the differences are becoming less over time; the difference between highest and lowest states in 1840 was fourfold, in 1903 it was threefold, and it now appears to be twofold.

There are, of course, many explanations for these differences. One which is certainly true is that people who develop schizophrenia tend to migrate away from their hometowns and go to cities to live. San Francisco and New York are well known as having collected more than their share of strange people, and the same thing is true of most major American cities. Therefore, in terms of the examples cited above, schizophrenic patients in Maine are more likely to migrate to Boston to live, thus inflating the Massachusetts rate, and schizophrenic patients in Arkansas are more likely to migrate to Chicago and thus inflate the Illinois rate.

Another commonly cited explanation for these differences is that it is easier for persons with schizophrenia to live in rural areas; thus they do not get taken to the hospital and counted in the statistics. It is said, for example, that a schizophrenic family member on a farm can remain there for longer than a schizophrenic family member in the city and that this produces the differences in the statistics. Though this may have been true one hundred years ago when rural America was truly isolated, it is much less clearly true today. People living in small towns and on farms are now constantly in touch with each other by telephone and automobile, and it is doubtful whether a schizophrenic family member can really be assimilated any more easily on the farm than in suburban or urban areas. Farm work is increasingly mechanized, and the farmer's wife is now quite likely to have a job in a small nearby factory or business.

Even with explanations, such as the migration of schizophrenic persons from rural to urban areas, and the possibility that schizophrenics can be more easily assimilated in rural areas, important differences in the distribution of schizophrenia still remain. There is clearly a disproportionate number of schizophrenics who come from the cities, and especially from those portions of cities where the poor live. This was noted over a twenty-year period in a well-known study of New Haven, Connecticut, and has been shown to be true in many other studies. One of the foremost researchers in this field reported: "The evidence that there is an unusually high rate of schizophrenia in the lowest socioeconomic strata of urban communities seems to me to be nothing less than overwhelming." Furthermore the association of schizophrenia with lower socioeconomic class status appears to be strongest for the largest cities and to be less clearly evident in smaller cities.

Since large numbers of blacks live in the poorer sections of large cities, it is not surprising to find that blacks as a whole have a higher rate of schizophrenia than whites. Five separate studies have confirmed this in highly urbanized states such as New York, Maryland, and Ohio. The higher rate of schizophrenia among blacks holds up even when corrections are made for the age distribution of the population; thus in a very careful study in Rochester, New York, blacks still had a schizophrenia rate one and one-half times that of whites.

When blacks who live in rural areas are compared with whites who live in rural areas, however, the results are different. This was done in Texas and in Louisiana and no differences were found. This argues strongly against race as being the cause of the difference. Rather it suggests that it is because blacks live in the inner city, and not because they are black, that they have a higher schizophrenia rate. Others have claimed that blacks appear to have a higher rate of schizophrenia because most psychiatrists are white and unconsciously (or consciously) racist; such psychiatrists would more readily label a black patient than a white patient as schizophrenic. This may well be so and is impossible to measure. Even if it were so, however, it would explain only a small portion of the differences and we are left with the fact that poor people in inner cities, whatever their race, have a disproportionately high schizophrenia rate.

Further evidence that the schizophrenia prevalence rate is lower in rural areas of the United States came from a study of the Hutterite population. These people, a religious sect who migrated from Europe and settled in rural villages in the north-central and mountain states, as well as in Canada, were surveyed extensively for schizophrenia in 1951 in a well-known study. Out of the total Hutterite population of 8,542, only 9 cases of schizophrenia were found.

All of these differences are, of course, only statistical. Schizophrenia does occur much more commonly among poor, inner city people than among wealthy rural people. But it does occur in all social and economic classes in all parts of the United States, and if you happen to be the relative or friend of a well-to-do, rural schizophrenic person, the statistics may be of theoretical interest, but they are of little consolation.

WORLDWIDE SCHIZOPHRENIA RATES

If the United States as a whole is averaged, most surveys have found between 2 and 4 cases of schizophrenia per 1,000 population at any given time. (This should not be confused with the generally accepted estimate that at least 1 out of every 100 people will develop schizophrenia sometime during their lifetime.) This prevalence figure of 2 to 4 per 1,000 is only an average, of course; the Hutterite rate will be a low 1.1 per 1,000 and poor inner city populations probably reach 6 per 1,000 or even higher.

When the United States rate is compared with the rest of the world it is found to be in the middle. There are many countries with approximately the same rate, some countries with higher rates, and some with lower rates.

Countries with approximately the same schizophrenia rate as the United States include Japan, England, Denmark, and Germany. Japanese national surveys in 1954 and again in 1963, covering a total of 68,000 people, found identical rates of 2.3 per 1,000. This rate is virtually identical with the 2.2 per 1,000 found in a survey in Tokyo and the rate of 2.1 per 1,000 found for a small Japanese town. Only surveys of one relatively isolated island have found higher rates in Japan. It is also interesting that the rates of schizophrenia (and other psychoses) are higher in lower socioeconomic population groups in Japan just as they are in the United States.

Comparisons of schizophrenia prevalence rates between the United States and most other countries are made more difficult because there are different diagnostic practices in different places. American psychiatrists tend to use the label "schizophrenia" more broadly than their colleagues elsewhere in the world. Thus a rate of 2.3 per 1,000 in Japan (where the diagnosis of "schizophrenia" is used more narrowly) and a rate of 3.7 per 1,000 in the United States (where it is used more broadly) may in fact represent identical rates of actual disease. This must always be kept in mind when comparing prevalence figures.

In England the best survey done to date is of a working-class district of London, where the schizophrenia rate was found to be 3.4 per 1,000. The disease has also been shown to be more prevalent in lower socioeconomic classes in England. In Denmark a recent survey found a rate of 2.2 per 1,000. In Germany two surveys of villages in the 1930s reported rates of 1.9 and 2.6 per 1,000.

AREAS WITH HIGH SCHIZOPHRENIA RATES

There are several countries, or parts of countries, which definitely have higher schizophrenia rates than the United States. Foremost among these are some of the Scandinavian countries, Ireland, and northern Yugoslavia. We do not know yet why these differences exist, but they do; and studying such areas, we may gain additional clues to the cause of this disease.

Ever since W. Charles Hood published his *Statistics of Insanity* in 1862, it has been clear the northern European countries have high rates of schizophrenia. A large survey in Finland, for example, found a rate of 4.3 cases of schizophrenia per 1,000 population. In Norway a study of a small fishing village found a rate of 5.3 per 1,000. And in Sweden six separate studies have been done and averaged 5.8 cases of schizophrenia per 1,000 people. Since

Scandinavian psychiatrists are known to use a very narrow definition of schizophrenia, these numbers contrast even more sharply with those in the United States than first appears. Thus Swedish psychiatrists, counting only clearly schizophrenic individuals, found twice as many cases of schizophrenia as American psychiatrists did in most American studies, and the American psychiatrists were counting cases which would not have been counted in Sweden. From such comparisons it seems safe to conclude that Sweden, Norway, and Finland probably have at least twice as much schizophrenia as such countries as the United States, England, Germany, and Japan.

Probably the best-known Swedish study was the one done by Book in a rural area in the far northern part of the country. Between 1946 and 1949 he surveyed the area and found a schizophrenia prevalence rate of 9.5 cases per 1,000 people. In 1976 he again surveyed the same population and found that there had been no change. This is the highest schizophrenia rate found anywhere in the world to date and is probably at least five times higher than the United States average when differing diagnostic patterns are taken into consideration.

(It is also interesting that a study in Norway found schizophrenia to be more common among lower socioeconomic population groups. This was also reported to be true in Iceland, a north Atlantic island with close ties to Scandinavia. Thus Norway and Iceland join England, Japan, and the United States as countries in which this pattern has been noted.)

Another area in which schizophrenia appears to be unusually high is the northwestern corner of Croatia in Yugoslavia. The affected area lies on the Adriatic just south of Trieste and is popular with tourists. It is an area of mixed genetic stock (Croats, Italians, Austrians, Hungarians, and Rumanians), very little inbreeding, and one which has had shifting political fortunes over the years as empires rose and fell. By Yugoslav standards it is comparatively prosperous.

Yet there, on the shores of the Adriatic and on the adjacent islands, it has been reported that insanity has been especially prevalent for at least one hundred years. Because of such reports an American-Yugoslav survey team conducted careful studies between 1961 and 1972 to ascertain the truth of these reports. For comparison they used other areas of Croatia, which were not thought to have an unusually high rate. The study consisted of comparing the hospitalization rates for schizophrenia, doing a house-to-house survey of a village (Labin) in the suspected high prevalence area and three villages in the low prevalence area, and then comparing Labin with other parts of the suspected high prevalence area. The results confirmed the local belief which had been handed down from generation to generation: schizophrenia was more than twice as common in this part of Yugoslavia as it was in the other regions studied. Manic-depressive illness was also elevated, being almost four times higher than expected. Because of differences in techniques, it is difficult to compare the Yugoslav findings with those for other countries, but it would appear that the overall schizophrenia rate in the high prevalence part of Croatia is about the same as the rate in countries like Sweden, Norway, and Finland.

In 1978 I traveled through the high schizophrenia prevalence area of Yugoslavia. It is an attractive region, with villages clinging to hillsides overlooking the sea and old men in dark suits timelessly tilling the fields as their ancestors did. Wandering the back streets of Labin, where small houses are surrounded by ancient brick walls, I wondered what made these villages different. Why should they have twice as much schizophrenia as their counterparts one hundred miles across the hills? If Labin and villages like it will yield their secret, we will have gone a long way toward understanding and, hopefully, preventing this disease.

The other area of the world known for its high rate of schizophrenia is Ireland, and especially western Ireland. As in Yugoslavia, the story also goes back over one hundred years, and many nineteenth-century observers were impressed by the number of insane in Ireland. In 1808 Sir Andrew Halliday noted that in Ireland "insanity is a disease of as frequent occurrence among the lower classes of the people as in any other country in Europe." Others made similar observations. In 1845 the disastrous famine began in Ireland, resulting in mass emigration to America and elsewhere. By 1864 it was noted that "it is remarkable that during the last ten years no perceptible diminution has taken place in the number of the insane, notwithstanding the decrease of population in that period." By the turn of the century it was claimed that "the insane have all but doubled, and the cry is, Still they come!"

Contemporary studies of the high Irish schizophrenia rates were begun in 1963 by Walsh, O'Hare, and their colleagues. They found that the number of schizophrenic patients resident in Irish mental hospitals was higher than anywhere else in the world. The rate was almost three times higher than neighboring England and Wales. The rates were highest for the westernmost counties, for example, Galway and Mayo. Not only was the schizophrenia rate high but the rates for manic-depressive psychosis and alcoholism were also high.

The question next arose whether the schizophrenia rate in Ireland was high only because more patients were hospitalized there. To answer the question a community survey was begun in three counties in 1973. Preliminary results from this survey confirm that schizophrenia is very common in Ireland, with a prevalence in the western region of 7.1 per 1,000. This is higher than any other place yet studied except for northern Sweden. Ireland as a whole appears to have a schizophrenia rate roughly equivalent to that of Sweden as a whole. But for the western counties, Walsh has estimated that 4 percent of the people will develop schizophrenia during their lifetime. This is approximately four times higher than in the United States.

I have visited western Ireland several times and lived there for six months in 1982 in order to do research on schizophrenia in this fascinating area. The winding sloughs and rocky hills are inhospitable to crops, and the people poorer than in most other parts of Ireland. They live quietly in an area of bleak beauty. The prevalence of schizophrenia was confirmed to be very high; also high was the prevalence of manic-depressive illness. The distribution of schizophrenia and manic-depressive illness is not uniform but occurs in pockets across the countryside; the pockets correspond to the areas in which the people are poorest.

Many of the Irish in these areas are themselves aware of their unusual number of "mad people." In the high prevalence areas almost everyone has a relative or friend who has been "over at the county hospital," great old stone asylums dating to the middle of the nineteenth century. Many confided to me that the cause of the problem was "close marriages," and this is a common local belief. The problem with this theory is that there is no evidence that there are any more marriages between close relatives in western Ireland than in any other rural area in the world, and the Catholic Church strongly discourages such marriages. Neither are the Irish an unusually inbred population, as multiple invasions of Celts, Spaniards, Scots, and English in centuries past insured a broad genetic mix. Since schizophrenia sometimes runs in families, however, it is possible that the tendency to have large families in Ireland is contributing to the higher prevalence of schizophrenia if the families which are genetically predisposed to the disease are also having disproportionately large families.

Emigration is the other commonly heard explanation for the high Irish schizophrenia rates. When the nineteenth-century famine came, the story goes, all the healthy young people left to go to America and the weak ones stayed behind. They in turn begat weak offspring, and the high schizophrenia rate is one consequence.

There are several problems with this explanation, too. First, the high Irish schizophrenia rate was clearly noted before the mass emigration began. More important, an equally high rate of schizophrenia was noted among those who left Ireland as among those who stayed behind. As early as 1850 a high rate of insanity was reported among Irish immigrants in Massachusetts. By 1913 in the same state it was said that "in the Irish we find a higher ratio of insanity than in any other people." In New York State in 1920 it was observed that "the Irish-born had then the highest age-standardized rates for schizophrenia in either sex among the eleven immigrant groups differentiated." Subsequent studies of immigrants in the 1930s and 1940s showed a continuing high rate for the Irish, but one which decreased over time. The children of the Irish immigrants had a lower schizophrenia rate than their parents. Clearly it is not possible to explain the high schizophrenia rate in Ireland by saying that the healthiest people went to America and only the weak remained behind.

There are four other aspects of schizophrenia in Ireland which should be noted. First, there is no evidence that the large number of schizophrenics there is decreasing; recent figures show an 8 percent increase in first admissions for schizophrenia between 1965 and 1974. Second, it has been found that, as in so many other countries, schizophrenia in Ireland occurs much more frequently among lower socioeconomic groups. (This may be why it is more prevalent in Ireland's western counties, which are generally poorer.) The Irish "far larger increase of alleged insanity among the poorer than the wealthy classes" was noted as far back as 1894. Third, several people have remarked that schizophrenia appears to have a later onset in Ireland; this is seen in the larger numbers of people in older age groups being admitted to hospitals for the first time. Finally, the high schizophrenia rate in Ireland is not shared by her neighbor, Northern Ireland, which was found to have a lower rate in 1911 and has continued to have a low rate up to the present. Given the history of constant turmoil and strife in Northern Ireland over the years, this would argue against stress being an important causative factor of the disease. On the other hand, Northern Ireland has always been wealthier than the rest of Ireland, and this socioeconomic difference may be a factor in the lower rate there.

AREAS WITH LOW SCHIZOPHRENIA RATES

Just as there are many areas of the world with more schizophrenia than the United States, so there are also many areas with less schizophrenia. These include most southern European countries and most of the developing nations.

For southern European countries there is little hard data, but impressions over the years have consistently cited less insanity there. In 1848 and again in 1852, surveys of all European countries for insanity found Italy and Spain to have very low rates. One hundred years later Italy was still noted to have a very low rate of mental hospitalization. Italian immigrants in New York, Massachusetts, England, and Australia were all noted to have low hospitalization rates for schizophrenia compared with other immigrant groups, and an Italian-American community in Pennsylvania was found to have only half as much schizophrenia as nearby communities of other European immigrants.

But it is to developing countries that we must turn for truly low rates of schizophrenia. The impression that insanity is rare in developing areas goes back well into the nineteenth century. In 1828, for example, Sir Andrew

Halliday observed that "we seldom meet with insanity among the savage tribes of men; not one of our African travelers remark having seen a single madman." In 1835, J. C. Prichard added that "insanity belongs almost exclusively to civilized races of man; it scarcely exists among savages, and is rare in barbarous countries." Similar observations continued throughout the nineteenth century, so that one hundred years later the same theme was being sounded. In 1929 a German noted that schizophrenia was rare among isolated Soviet tribes and had been virtually nonexistent prior to "contact with civilization." And in 1932 C. Lopez reported no schizophrenia among the "true primitives" in the interior of Brazil but said it did occur occasionally among the urbanized "natives" on the coast.

Beginning in the 1930s there was a steady stream of studies from African countries noting the relative infrequency of schizophrenia. Independent observations from Zaire, Malawi, Kenya, Tanzania, Ghana, and Ethiopia have continued up until the present to verify the fact that schizophrenia is relatively infrequent and that when it does occur, it is more likely to be in Africans who have been exposed to western technology and cultures.

Perhaps the most striking example of these observations was the work of anthropologist Meyer Fortes and his psychiatrist wife, Doris Mayer. From 1934 to 1937 Fortes lived with and studied the Tallensi people in northern Ghana. During that period he observed only 1 possibly schizophrenic individual among the population of approximately 5,000 people. In 1963 Fortes returned with his wife. In the same villages where twenty-seven years earlier there had been a single schizophrenic, there were now thirteen definite cases.

Drs. Mayer and Fortes themselves were convinced that the dramatic rise in schizophrenia in the twenty-seven-year period was real, and that it could not be explained by population growth:

> What was quite startling, from my point of view, is that several of these cases occurred in families which were especially well known to me in 1934–37 and which were basically the same in structure in 1963 as in the early period. I knew some of the patients as young wives or youths or children. These were the families of my best friends and informants, some of whom are still living. Had such cases occurred among them in 1934–37 I could not have missed them.

Tallensi elders were also convinced that there had been a sharp rise in insanity.

The authors reject the possibility that cases of schizophrenia had simply been missed in the earlier study. "I doubt this, since sufferers are never hidden from public knowledge." Similarly they reject the explanation that schizophrenic patients in the earlier period had simply been allowed to starve. "This view is not tenable, for then, as now, food and shelter were always available to a madman even if he was so violent as to require putting 'in log' " (putting his foot through a log so that he could not run around and be destructive).

The village under study had, of course, become much more developed and exposed to technology in the interim between the studies. Schools and missions had increased, and bicycles, radios, canned goods, and gin had all become prevalent. In addition to this influx of technology and western culture into the Tallensi area, the authors note that an unusual number of those who became psychiatrically ill had traveled to southern Ghana (the more urbanized and technologically advanced area) prior to the onset of their illness.

Two contemporary studies from Southeast Asia confirm that schizophrenia is uncommon in many developing parts of the world. On Taiwan, between 1949 and 1953, Taiwanese psychiatrists did surveys of four tribes of Formosan aborigines who lived by themselves in remote mountain villages and who, compared with the Chinese on Taiwan, had been much less influenced by western technology. The methodology of the study has been cited as the best of any such study done to date. Among 11,442 aborigines only 10 cases of schizophrenia were found, yielding a rate of 0.9 per 1,000. This rate was less than half that found for the Chinese living in Taiwan, who had a schizophrenia rate of 2.2 per 1,000. The Formosan aborigine rate is also less than half the rate found in most American studies.

Studies of schizophrenia have also been carried out in Papua New Guinea, probably the least developed country remaining in the world. More than one million people living in the highlands there were not even known to exist until just prior to World War II, and cannibalism has not yet completely died out. In 1973 I undertook an analysis of all psychiatric records from 1970 to 1973 and surveyed the highlands for cases of schizophrenia. The disease was found to be very uncommon in the country as a whole and to be rare in the highlands. Although precise estimates of prevalence are difficult, it appeared that the highlands of Papua New Guinea had less than one-fiftieth as much schizophrenia as the United States. Compared with an area such as northern Sweden, there is probably at least a hundredfold difference.

In response to all such studies of schizophrenia in developing countries, it is common to reply that all the schizophrenic individuals were probably killed off by fights, famine, or neglect. This is simply not true. No doubt a few have so died, especially if they were violent or attacked other people. Most schizophrenic patients in virtually all these cultures are relatively harmless, however, and are treated humanely. They are given food by the extended family and often allowed to forage in the village gardens. If they become too much of a nuisance, they may be chained to a log or confined in huts, but they are not usually allowed to starve to death. Another myth which needs to be dispelled is that schizophrenic individuals in other cultures are given special roles, such as shamans or medicine men. This idea is, in a word, nonsense, and I have discussed it in detail elsewhere. There is no evidence at all that schizophrenics in other cultures are used systematically in these special roles. Undoubtedly there is the occasional schizophrenic who becomes a shaman by chance, but then in our own culture there is also an occasional schizophrenic who becomes a psychiatrist.

There is one part of the developing world which, contrary to the general rule, does not appear to have a lower schizophrenia rate than the United States. This area is India and Sri Lanka. Studies of schizophrenia rates in these countries have varied from 2.3 to 5.6 per 1,000 in India and from 3.7 to 5.2 per 1,000 in Sri Lanka. In addition there have been six separate studies in India showing schizophrenia to be more common among the upper castes, who are more educated and who have had more exposure to western technology. If we understood such patterns, we would probably understand the causes of schizophrenia much better than we do.

11

HISTORY: IS SCHIZOPHRENIA
OF RECENT ORIGIN?

I doubt if ever the history of the world, or the experience of past
ages, could show a larger amount of insanity than that of the
present day
John Hawkes, "On the Increase of Insanity," 1857

"Schizophrenia" is a new term, dating back only to 1911, and schizophrenia
may be a relatively new disease as well. This possibility, which has been
ignored by traditional textbooks of psychiatry, might shed important light on
causes of the disease. In order to explore it in depth, it is necessary to review
ancient concepts of mental disease, trace them through the ages, and then focus
on the last 180 years of history, in which schizophrenia clearly has been
present.

MENTAL DISEASE IN ANCIENT TIMES

Nobody would argue with the fact that there have been people with severe
mental disorders since earliest recorded history. Even the cavemen, with their
fondness for hitting each other over the head with clubs, inevitably caused
some permanent brain damage. This would have produced retarded and de-
mented individuals who would look identical to their counterparts today. It
is also important to recall that modern obstetrics is of recent origin and that
in centuries past many more individuals must have been brain damaged by
difficult births. This would have produced proportionately more retarded individuals, even allowing for the most severely retarded, who probably would
not have survived. To trauma and difficult births must be added other known
insults to the brain which existed then and which can produce mental disease
—strokes, tumors, malaria, syphilis, poisonings, vitamin deficiencies, hypothyroidism, temporal lobe epilepsy, viral infections—and a sizable group of
mental patients would have been inevitable.

Thus it is not surprising to find references to severely psychiatrically disturbed individuals in ancient sources. An early Hindu text from the fifteenth century B.C. described a man who was "gluttonous, filthy, walks naked, has lost his memory, and moves about in an uneasy manner." In the Old Testament there is a warning that "the Lord will smite you with madness and blindness and confusion of mind" if you disobey His commandments. In the New Testament there are numerous references to madness, seeing visions, and hearing voices, although these are attributed to God. And in ancient Greece Horace described a man who sat daily in an empty theater, claiming he could hear actors talking on the empty stage and applauding their nonexistent theatrical performances. He was subsequently said to have been cured and then complained at having had his imaginary productions taken away from him.

Undoubtedly such individuals as these were mentally ill. However, they might have had any one of a number of brain diseases, and there is nothing in their known history which would point to schizophrenia as opposed to any of the others. The more one peruses these ancient sources, moreover, the more striking it becomes that nobody clearly described the disease that we now call schizophrenia. Nowhere is there a picture of a person who was normal until early adulthood, then developed schizophrenic symptoms, and proceeded to either a recurrent course or a chronic course.

The absence of schizophrenia in early writings stands in sharp contrast to the presence of several other mental diseases. Depression (called melancholia) was described and was broken down into several subtypes. Senile dementia, hysteria, hypochondriasis, and alcoholism were all clearly depicted. Hippocrates gave good descriptions of postpartum psychosis, epilepsy with psychiatric symptoms, and transvestism (called the Scythian disease), all of which are much rarer than schizophrenia. And manic-depressive illness, which is only one-third as common as schizophrenia, was clearly described by the sixth century A.D.

There are some people who have claimed that schizophrenia was described in these ancient texts. Knowing now that many other diseases of the brain can produce schizophreniclike symptoms, it would indeed be surprising if there was no schizophrenialike disease at all. What is surprising is that there are few descriptions which even remotely resemble true schizophrenia. Philosopher Karl Jaspers once attempted to show that the prophet Ezekiel, for example, had schizophrenia, although medical historian George Rosen noted that "it cannot be said that the attempt was successful." Another interesting ancient case study was that of Alexarchos, a Greek who was diagnosed by one observer as schizophrenic on the basis of a single letter which he is alleged to have written. George Rosen also disputes this, saying the evidence is inadequate and that Alexarchos may not even have been mentally ill.

The most interesting claim of an early case of schizophrenia is undoubtedly that concerning Jesus. In the early years of the twentieth century four books were published in German purporting to prove that Jesus was a paranoid schizophrenic. In 1905 *Jesus Christ from the Standpoint of Psychiatry* and *Jesus: A Comparative Study of Psychopathology* appeared. These were followed in 1911 by *The Insanity of Jesus* and in 1912 by *Conclusions of a Psychiatrist.* All focused on the auditory hallucinations and delusions of grandeur of Jesus and cited various biblical texts in support of this claim. They were shown to be on very weak ground both clinically and historically, however, by Dr. Albert Schweitzer, who in 1948 published *The Psychiatric Study of Jesus* and demonstrated convincingly that there are really no solid grounds for suspecting that Jesus was schizophrenic. Rather, what the authors were doing was trying to discredit Jesus by tarring him with the brush of a psychiatric diagnosis, a practice which has subsequently become widespread in the Soviet Union.

In the final analysis there is no single case in ancient texts which can be pointed at with any conviction and called schizophrenia.

THE MIDDLE AGES AND THE POSSESSION OBSESSION

Until recent years there were only two major theories about why people became mad. The first was a medical theory having to do with disorders of the body. In ancient Greece this centered on the humors of the body, so that depression, for example, was thought to be caused by an excess of bile. A variant medical theory concerned the displacement of organs, and hysteria (from the Greek word for uterus) was thought to be due to the person's uterus wandering to other parts of the body. Symptoms of mental disorder were almost invariably attributed to either imbalanced humors or wandering organs.

The other major theory was the religious theory. This explained diseases in general, and mental diseases in particular, as due to religious and supernatural causes. Throughout ancient history this theory was important, but it became more visible in the Middle Ages. Possession by devils and demons had been widely believed to be a cause of mental illness for many centuries, but in the Middle Ages the incubi and succubi were organized and categorized on a more systematic basis. This does not mean that the Middle Ages were intellectually the Dark Ages as many historians have claimed; Dr. Jerome Kroll has pointed out correctly that the degeneration of religious views of mental illness into mass witchburnings did not occur in the Middle Ages but rather during the ensuing Renaissance.

Descriptions of mental illnesses continued during the Middle Ages with medical and religious theories often being commingled. Maimonides produced detailed accounts of depression, and Rhazes and Avicenna added careful clinical observations of a variety of psychiatric conditions. It was also during the Middle Ages that insane patients were first gathered together. Initially they were herded onto ships and sailed from port to port (the "ships of fools"), but later they were placed in asylums or hospitals. One of the first such hospitals was opened at Geel, Belgium, in the thirteenth century; shortly thereafter others were begun in Spain and England. The earliest hospital in England, Bethlem Hospital, gave rise to the term "bedlam," meaning noisy confusion.

With the collection of the mentally ill in one place the opportunity for good clinical descriptions of diseases multiplied tremendously. Over the next three centuries some excellent accounts of other mental diseases were published, such as those by Bartholomaeus Angelicus and Johann Weyer, but none of schizophrenia. In 1570 Johann Kaspar Lavater described delusions and hallucinations in great detail in a publication called *Of Ghosts*. And by the early years of the seventeenth century Shakespeare was incorporating these ideas into his plays. Shakespeare was clearly intrigued by mental illness; he has Hamlet feign lunacy, Lear develop a senile psychosis (he was over 80 years of age), and Ophelia become mad when she discovers that her father has been killed by the man she loves.

In 1656 Georg Trosse, an English minister, published an autobiographical account of his mental breakdown with delusions and auditory hallucinations at age 25. Some of his behavior sounds catatonic: "For several days I would neither open my eyes nor my lips." He was hospitalized for several months in an asylum and then recovered. This may be the first actual description in literature of what we now call schizophrenia. Some schizophreniclike symptoms were also described by Thomas Willis shortly thereafter. He differentiated mental retardation from "deteriorating illnesses" which may have referred to schizophrenia; in addition he described thought processes which some have interpreted as loose associations. Because of this some have proposed that Willis was the first to describe schizophrenia in psychiatric literature.

In the eighteenth century there are also a few scattered references to conditions which might have been schizophrenia, but they are remarkably few considering the magnitude of the disease as we know it. Dr. Samuel Johnson, who was a keen observer of the century's philosophy and politics, had a special interest in madness and believed that insanity was increasing in frequency. The increase, he believed, was due to a *decrease* in smoking, which was apparently becoming less fashionable. Smoking was thought to tranquilize the mind and as it decreased, Johnson reasoned, madness would increase. In his *Rasselas* in 1759 Johnson wrote: "Of the uncertainties of our present state, the most dreadful and alarming is the uncertain continuance of reason." The idea of increasing insanity was to become very important one hundred years later.

ENTER SCHIZOPHRENIA

Up until 1800 descriptions of possible cases of schizophrenia are scattered and uncertain. Suddenly, however, it appeared. Simultaneously (and apparently independently) John Haslam in England and Philippe Pinel in France both described cases which were almost certainly schizophrenia. These were followed by a veritable outpouring of descriptions continuing throughout the nineteenth century and also by evidence that schizophrenia was increasing in frequency. It was a dramatic entrance for a disease. Haslam's publication in 1809 was an enlarged second edition of his 1798 book, *Observations on Insanity.* It is a remarkable book, with descriptions of delusions, hallucinations, disorders of thinking, and even autopsy accounts of abnormalities in the brains of some of the patients. His descriptions of patients leaves no doubt that he was describing what we now call schizophrenia:

... there is a form of insanity which occurs in young persons; and, as far as these cases have been the subject of my observation, they have been more frequently noticed in females. Those whom I have seen, have been distinguished by prompt capacity and lively disposition: and in general have become the favorites of parents and tutors, by their facility in acquiring knowledge, and by a prematurity of attainment. This disorder commences, about or shortly after, the period of menstruation, and in many instances has been unconnected with hereditary taint; as far as could be ascertained by minute enquiry. The attack is almost imperceptible; some months usually elapse before it becomes the subject of particular notice; and fond relatives are frequently deceived by the hope that it is only an abatement of excessive vivacity, conducing to a prudent reserve, and steadiness of character. A degree of apparent thoughtfulness and inactivity precede, together with a diminution of the ordinary curiosity, concerning that which is passing before them; and they therefore neglect those objects and pursuits which formerly proved sources of delight and instruction. The sensibility appears to be considerably blunted; they do not bear the same affection towards their parents and relations; they become unfeeling to kindness, and careless of reproof. To their companions they show a cold civility, but take no interest whatever in their concerns. If they read a book, they are unable to give any account of its contents: sometimes, with steadfast eyes, they will dwell for an hour on one page, and then turn over a number in a few minutes. It is very difficult to persuade them to write, which most readily develops their state of mind: much time is consumed and little produced. The subject is repeatedly begun, but they seldom advance beyond a sentence or two: the orthography becomes puzzling, and by endeavouring to adjust the spelling the subject vanishes. As their apathy increases they are negligent of their dress, and inattentive to personal cleanliness. Frequently they seem to experience transient impulses of passion, but these have no source in sentiment; the tears, which trickle down at one time, are as unmeaning as the loud laugh which succeeds them; and it often happens that a momentary gust of anger, with its attendant invectives, ceases before the threat can be concluded. As the disorder increases, the urine and feces are passed without restraint, and from the indolence which accompanies it, they generally become corpulent. Thus in the interval between puberty and manhood, I have painfully witnessed this hopeless and degrading change, which in a short time has transformed the most promising and vigorous intellect into a slavering and bloated idiot.

Here for the first time was true schizophrenia clearly described, with normal development in childhood, an onset in young adulthood, and a steadily downhill course.

At the same time as Haslam was making his observations in London, Pinel was making similar observations in Paris. His *Traite Medico-Philosophique sur l'Aliénation Mentale* was published in 1809, the same year as Haslam's book, and also described cases of classical schizophrenia. He called it the *démence* syndrome, a name which was to stick until Bleuler changed it to "schizophrenia" 102 years later. Because of the simultaneous first clear descriptions of the disease by Haslam and Pinel, one psychiatric historian has recommended changing the term "schizophrenia" to the Pinel-Haslam syndrome.

It was as if a floodgate had been raised. Burrows, Rush, Morel, Hecker, Kahlbaum and finally Kraepelin added variations to the *démence* theme and expanded its dimensions. Even better descriptions appeared in general literature, such as Balzac's story *Louis Lambert,* which was published in 1832 (see chapter 2). Balzac even had his fictitious character go to Paris to be treated by Pinel's famous pupil, M. Esquirol. Unfortunately M. Esquirol declared him incurable and sent him home to his chronic deteriorative fate. A few years after Balzac's account, John Perceval in England published an autobiographical account of a mental breakdown which sounds like schizophrenia. Such descriptions and autobiographical accounts continued throughout the century.

THE RAPID INCREASE IN SCHIZOPHRENIA

At the same time as Haslam and Pinel were describing schizophrenia for the first time, they and many others were also expressing concern that insanity was becoming much more common. This was not wholly a new idea, as the quote by Samuel Johnson above illustrates, but from 1800 onward it became a subject of lively debate and speculation in both medical and philosophical circles.

In the preface to his 1809 book Haslam sounded a note which was to be heard increasingly often as the century progressed: "The alarming increase of insanity, as might naturally be expected, has incited many persons to an investigation of this disease." In the previous year the English House of Commons had passed a County Asylums Act establishing mental hospitals in many counties.

By 1829 Sir Andrew Halliday noted statistics "which not only show that insanity, in all its forms, prevails to a most alarming extent in England, but that the numbers of the afflicted have become more than tripled during the last twenty years." This was confirmed by J. C. Prichard, who said, "The apparent increase is everywhere so striking that it leaves in the mind a strong suspicion that cases of insanity are far more numerous than formerly."

As the century wore on, the increase in insanity was noted throughout the British Isles. By 1857 John Hawkes in England wrote, "I doubt if ever the history of the world, or the experience of past ages, could show a larger amount of insanity than that of the present day." Similar observations were made in Scotland, and in Ireland the apparent increase in insanity had produced a rapid building of asylums and much debate. W. J. Corbet, a member of the Royal Irish Academy, noted:

> I have written elsewhere on several occasions during the last twenty years pointing out that, account for it how we may, as time progresses the stream of insanity broadens and deepens continually. The great central fact stares us in the face, it cannot be hidden, no effort of obscurantism can conceal it. The figures given from official records indisputably prove it. The ominous word "increase" is written large upon every page of the annual reports for the last forty years, and it is surprising how the commissioners apparently fail to see the significance of their own figures or the emphatic language they themselves have used.

On the Continent similar pronouncements were being made. Pinel himself believed that the increased number of insane was a product in some way of the French Revolution. By 1856 Renaudin had published extensive data showing the increase in insanity in France. He noted that the increase had been most marked in younger age groups, which would be compatible with a diagnosis of schizophrenia: "Formerly insanity of early age was a very rare exception; now, on the contrary, we observe a marked precocity . . . it happens in all ranks of society and seems to be on the increase." He also noted the increased insanity was three times more common in urban areas compared with rural areas, an observation which was subsequently confirmed (see chapter 10). Other European countries which explicitly noted the increase in insanity during this period were Denmark, Greece, Germany, and Russia.

In the United States there was apparently less interest shown in the increase in insanity. It was noted, to be sure, by leaders such as Dorothea

Dix and Isaac Ray, but it did not seem to evoke the alarm it did in Europe. Perhaps the main reason for this was that large numbers of immigrants were arriving in America during those years, and it was widely assumed that the increase in insanity, and many other diseases, was simply due to them. There were also major shifts of population within the United States as it pushed westward, which could make it more difficult to perceive changes in any given area.

What figures exist, however, certainly point to a rapid increase in insanity in this country during the nineteenth century. The first American mental hospital opened in Williamsburg, Virginia, in 1773, but no more opened until 1816. Then suddenly there was an explosion of them, with eight more opened between 1816 and 1828 and another fourteen opened by 1846. Census figures suggest that between 1840 and 1880 there was a threefold increase in the number of the insane. The number of those hospitalized rose from 2,561 in 1840 to 38,047 in 1880, and by 1904 this number had skyrocketed to 150,151. The 1871 Report of the United States Commissioner of Education included the following observations:

> The successive reports, upon whatever source or means of information pro-
> cured, all tend to show an increasing number of the insane. In the United
> States, Great Britain, Ireland and other civilised nations, so far as known
> there has been a great increase of provision for the insane within forty years
> and a very rapid increase within twenty years. Hospitals have been built
> seemingly sufficient to accommodate all the lunatics within their respective
> States, counties, or districts. These have been filled, and then crowded and
> pressed to admit still more. They have been successively enlarged, and then
> other institutions created, and filled and crowded as the earlier houses were.

Since the beginning of the twentieth century the number of schizophrenics in the United States has remained steady. One analysis of seven separate states found no evidence of an increase between 1910 and 1950. And another study found no change between the 1930s and the 1950s. Thus it would appear that the rapid increase in schizophrenia which took place in the nineteenth century flattened out and remained steady in the twentieth century, at least in the United States.

There is, of course, no way to be certain that the increase in insanity noted in Europe and in the United States was specifically due to schizophrenia. Theoretically it could have been due to manic-depressive psychosis or to other brain diseases. The great bulk of the evidence is against this, however. Not only do we have observations by people, such as Renaudin, who noted that the increase was occurring in the younger age groups, but examination of the old hospital charts of these patients suggests that schizophrenia was the correct diagnosis. I have studied such charts in two of the oldest mental hospitals in the United States and found that the clinical data supported a diagnosis of schizophrenia in most cases.

Overall it is a strange history for a disease. Virtually unknown or at least undescribed for centuries, it suddenly appears all over the western world simultaneously and is noted to be increasing rapidly. The increase continues for a hundred years before leveling off. Why has this dramatic rise of schizophrenia been virtually ignored by both medical historians and psychiatrists?

There are at least two reasons. First there is a widespread belief that schizophrenia was probably present throughout the centuries and just wasn't recognized as such. This view holds that the urbanization and industrialization of the nineteenth century brought people together and forced society to build institutions for the mentally disabled. The schizophrenic patients came out of heretofore scattered closets, so to speak. This view is perfectly valid as a theory. However, there is no evidence to support it except for one book, *Psychosis and Civilization,* which analyzes Massachusetts mental hospital admission statistics between 1840 and 1940 and concludes that "there has been no increase in the frequency of the psychoses during the past one hundred years." A close reading of the book and its voluminous tables, moreover, makes it difficult to understand how the authors arrived at the conclusion they did. Their own data show an age-corrected first admission rate for 20- to 29-year-olds of 50 per 100,000 population in 1840–44, 85 in 1885, and approximately 107 in 1940. Thus the rate apparently doubled over the one hundred years. The authors append a series of qualifiers to their figures and attempt to explain them as artifacts. These attempts are not successful, and we are left with further evidence that the rise in schizophrenia was real despite the authors' conclusion to the contrary. William W. Eaton, in a recent reanalysis of *Psychosis and Civilization,* came to a similar conclusion.

Another problem with the "closet" theory of schizophrenia is that it denigrates the observational ability of many astute clinicians down through the ages, from Hippocrates onward, in that it assumes that the disease was missed. How could it have been missed if it affected 1 percent of the population, as it does now? Diseases which are far rarer were clearly described by these clinicians. It also assumes that there were a lot of closets full of schizophrenics for hundreds of years before the mental hospitals were built in the nineteenth century. I find this difficult to believe.

The other major reason why the apparent rapid rise in schizophrenia has been ignored is the assumption that it was a product of social changes. Insofar as schizophrenia is thought to be caused by such changes—as has been widely believed in the United States (see chapter 5)—then a rise in the prevalence of the disease would be assumed to simply reflect these same changes. This view was brought to full fruition by David J. Rothman in *The Discovery of the*

Asylum, in which he argued that the rapidly changing social, familial, and technological changes of the nineteenth century created more insanity and that asylums were then built to accommodate the increase. Similar views were expressed in Europe, where the increase in insanity was attributed to such events as the French Revolution or, in England, to the introduction of train travel.

This view is also valid as a theory but lacks evidence to support it. It implies that the social, familial, and technological changes of the nineteenth century were unique. Yet why wouldn't schizophrenia have been produced by the ancient world or by the radical tumult of the Inquisition and Renaissance or by the civil wars and strife of Europe in the seventeenth and eighteenth centuries? Nor is this view consistent with reported *decreases* in first admissions for schizophrenia during World War II in Europe. From all this, the possibility that schizophrenia did increase rapidly during the nineteenth century must be seriously considered.

EARLY TWENTIETH CENTURY

Schizophrenia entered the twentieth century as dementia praecox. Its meteoric rise in the nineteenth century had not gone unnoticed, and as a disease it was controversial. But it *was* almost universally considered to be a disease. The leaders in psychiatry of the nineteenth century—men like Wilhelm Griesinger in Germany, Henry Maudsley in England, and Benjamin Rush in the United States—had all made that assumption. The insane clearly had something wrong with their brains. For this reason Rush and the other psychiatrists used treatments like spinning chairs to relieve the brain of congested blood, thought to be one of the causes. There was at that time no belief that schizophrenia was caused by bad mothering, bad fathering, repression of libido, or mixed communication within families.

That was destined to change after the entrance of psychoanalytic theory in the early years of this century. The watershed year was 1911, during which Bleuler changed the name of dementia praecox to schizophrenia and Freud published his analysis of the Schreber case. Henceforth schizophrenia was regarded as within the legitimate province of psychoanalysis.

The spread of psychoanalytic theory in the United States during the first half of the twentieth century was impressive. The social sciences, literature, and the arts all incorporated Freud's ideas, and so too did the departments of psychiatry in America's medical schools. This spread increased exponentially in the 1930s as large numbers of psychoanalysts left Germany and Eastern Europe and settled in the United States; by the late 1940s virtually every important department of psychiatry in America was dominated by psychiatrists claiming psychoanalytic allegiance.

In many areas of normal development and human personality, psychoanalysis was making significant contributions. Psychoanalytic therapy also appeared to be helping some persons suffering from psychoneuroses. But at the same time as it was recording success in these areas, it was failing to contribute anything of importance to either the theory (see chapter 5) or the therapy (see chapter 6) of schizophrenia. The disease remained a mystery despite elaborate psychoanalytic theories regarding its possible cause by distorted early parent-child relationships. And despite ambitious attempts by psychiatrists like Harry Stack Sullivan and William Alanson White to utilize psychoanalytic therapy for schizophrenia, it was almost universally regarded as a failure for such patients.

The results were predictable. Psychoanalysis and the rest of American psychiatry turned their attention more and more toward normal personality development and the neuroses, and schizophrenia receded into the background. Psychiatrists who wanted to get ahead in their profession quickly learned that schizophrenia was not the way to do it, and serious research dropped off to almost zero. Psychiatrists in training were no longer taken to the wards of the asylum for their training with schizophrenics as they had been in the past; rather training took place in the antiseptic offices of the university hospital clinic where neurotic ladies and gentlemen patiently explained to the novitiate psychiatrists how their feelings about mother had shaped their lives. Schizophrenia became a neglected disease by the psychiatric profession, and as such it entered the contemporary era.

12

MOTHERS MARCH FOR MADNESS

There has been no effective public constituency for the severely and chronically mentally ill . . . without it the fate of the most neglected of society's children will continue to be in the hands of politicians and the press rather than the citizenry.

John A. Talbott, *The Death of the Asylum,* 1978

The contemporary history of schizophrenia in the United States is a history of neglect. Here is a disease which affects 1 out of every 100 Americans, with 100,000 new cases diagnosed each year. Yet what do we offer the sufferers of this disease? Frequently, mediocre psychiatric care in state hospitals. Eviction from the hospitals to live in vermin-infested boarding houses and fear-infested back alleys. Minimal psychiatric and medical follow-up. Virtually no sheltered workshops or opportunities for partial employment. Inadequate research budgets to pursue the causes of the disease. And psychiatrists who are at best indifferent to the disease and at worst blame the families for having caused it. This is not a record to be proud of.

Who is responsible? Given the magnitude of the neglect, it is not surprising that there is no shortage of persons and organizations to blame: America's psychiatrists and their parent American Psychiatric Association; the National Institute of Mental Health and its overseer, the Department of Health and Human Services; the Mental Health Association and other ostensible consumer groups. All these have played major roles in bringing about the tragic current state of affairs.

It is only because schizophrenics have the kind of disease which they have that this state of affairs is allowed to persist. They are often poor, always stigmatized, and have some degree of brain dysfunction. As such, they cannot organize themselves and demand adequate services. They are, in the words of the President's Commission on Mental Health, "a minority within minorities. They are the most stigmatized of the mentally ill. They are politically and economically powerless and rarely speak for themselves. . . . They are the totally disenfranchised among us." If schizophrenics had polio or cancer instead, if they could organize themselves, if schizophrenia were predominantly a disease of higher socioeconomic groups, then the neglect would not have been tolerated.

THE POLITICS OF NEGLECT

Until World War II there was little to offer persons with chronic schizophrenia except custodial care in state hospitals. The quality of this care ranged from relatively humane conditions to dehumanized warehousing. Dorothea Dix, Clifford Beers, and a long list of other reformers periodically castigated the asylums and kept them from sliding even further downhill.

After World War II conditions were propitious for improvement and reform. Alarmed by the high rate of schizophrenia and other mental illnesses discovered among inductees to the army, President Harry S. Truman signed the National Mental Health Act creating a National Institute of Mental Health (NIMH). Federal funds were allocated for training psychiatrists, who numbered only 3,000 at the time. In 1950 the National Committee for Mental Hygiene, founded by Clifford Beers in 1909, merged with the National Mental Health Foundation and Psychiatric Foundation to form a united front as a mental health consumer group, now known as the Mental Health Association. Then, two years later, effective antipsychotic drugs were discovered which, for the first time, allowed many persons with schizophrenia to be released from hospitals to live in more humane surroundings. One would have thought that the days of neglect were over, and that days of comparative wine and roses had arrived.

Unfortunately the wine turned out to be watered and the roses all died. Except for the advent of antipsychotic drugs, it is very doubtful whether persons with schizophrenia are any better off in the United States today than they were thirty years ago. What became of improvement and reform? What happened to all those fine words and promises to the chronically mentally ill, words spoken by politicians and psychiatrists and written large into the legislation authorizing the millions of dollars to be spent? It is a question that families and friends of persons with schizophrenia should be asking.

First, the National Institute of Mental Health grew and grew. From its modest beginning budget of $5.1 million in 1948, it ballooned to $885 million by 1977. In the meantime it had absorbed alcoholism and drug abuse, split three-for-one like any good growth stock, and spawned a parent Alcohol, Drug Abuse and Mental Health Administration to administer the three component institutes. It accepted all of society's problems as its proper function: drug abuse, alcoholism, child-rearing practices, poverty, malnutrition, racism, terrorism, even the effects of floods and earthquakes on people. This was all very interesting, providing jobs for an increasingly large number of mental health professionals and producing many papers for mental health journals. The only problem was that the original purpose of the Institute—the large number of schizophrenic and other severely mentally ill individuals—was forgotten.

Schizophrenic patients were also forgotten in the early decision of where to house NIMH. The grounds of St. Elizabeths Hospital, the federal psychiatric hospital in Washington, were the logical place, affording contact with seriously ill mental patients. Instead NIMH chose to locate in Washington's affluent suburbs as far away from St. Elizabeths as possible; out of sight meant out of mind.

In terms of research, NIMH has allocated relatively meager funds to schizophrenia research given the magnitude of the problem (see chapter 5). No research priority was ever assigned to schizophrenia; consequently NIMH has never acted as a catalyst to stimulate the kind of research effort which has taken place with such diseases as arteriosclerosis and cancer.

The lack of importance of schizophrenia in the National Institute of Mental Health can also be measured by the Institute's uninspired record on Community Mental Health Centers as detailed in chapter 7. Over $1.8 billion in federal funds have been spent, yet only 10 percent of all patients seen in CMHCs have schizophrenia. Even worse, this percentage has been dropping in recent years. NIMH has done little to monitor the CMHCs or try to insure that they provide the care for persons with chronic schizophrenia that was originally intended when the CMHCs were set up.

In the area of psychiatric training NIMH has also been negligent from the point of view of schizophrenic patients. For over thirty years NIMH has provided federal funds for the training of American psychiatrists. No medical speciality except psychiatry has enjoyed this special federal program to support residency training. During 1979 a total of $11 million was spent on this program; in previous years it had been as high as $20 million.

What do the psychiatrists do once they have been trained with public money? They do a variety of things, but the one thing they do *not* do is provide care for persons with schizophrenia. The majority of their time is spent in private practice caring for persons who have neuroses, personality disorders, and various problems in their interpersonal relationships. A survey of private psychiatrists in 1975 found that only 11 percent of the patients psychiatrists see in private practice had schizophrenia; by contrast 69 percent had neuroses or personality disorders. Nor are many poor or minority group members included among these private psychiatric patients; over 96 percent of private psychiatric patients are white. Among psychoanalytic patients, almost two-thirds have incomes over $20,000 per year.

The geographical distribution of psychiatrists also reflects their proclivity for treating the "worried well" who can afford private fees:

> The distribution of psychiatrists is as uneven today as it was twenty years ago. Psychiatrists concentrate in places like New York, Massachusetts, Illinois, and California, and in the District of Columbia, where the ratio is 1

to 5,000. In rural states such as Alabama, Mississippi, North Dakota, and West Virginia, few psychiatrists are available, and the ratio is 1 to 34,000.

Few American-trained psychiatrists are available in public, tax-supported facilities. There has been a dramatic decrease in the past decade in the number of psychiatrists in staff positions in community mental health centers. Many other psychiatrists now work there only part time.

All of this has gone on, and continues to go on, with the assistance of federal (public) funds to support the training of these psychiatrists. With over thirty years of such support the number of American psychiatrists has increased from 3,000 to 27,000, but persons with schizophrenia are no better than they were thirty years ago. The public funds have produced a group of psychiatrists who primarily treat affluent private patients.

NIMH has sanctioned this over the years by doing nothing about it. There are periodic ceremonial hand-wringings, of course, most often occurring around the time of budget requests. At such times there is general agreement that *something* must be done, but nothing ever is. In 1979, as a final irony, NIMH even instituted a *new* training grant program to train psychiatrists for public practice. It funded seventeen such programs, with a total of over $800,-000. Since NIMH had theoretically been training psychiatrists for public practice for the last thirty years, one must marvel at the gall of adding yet another program to make up for the failures of the preexisting one. This is exactly the mentality which led to the creation of the Community Support Program to make up for the failures of the CMHCs (see chapter 7). The principle seems to be: if your first program fails to work, just keep adding new programs on top of it.

A STITCH IN TIME GATHERS NO MOSS

If schizophrenics in the community are just as badly off now as they were thirty years ago in terms of finding good psychiatric care, schizophrenic patients in state hospitals may be worse off. At the end of World War II there were only 3,000 psychiatrists, but most of them were American-trained and a majority worked in state hospitals. As psychiatry moved into its era of largesse, American psychiatrists abandoned state hospitals for more lucrative careers in private practice and more prestige in teaching. The vacuum in the state hospitals was filled by importing doctors from developing countries and putting them to work in the state institutions.

This situation continued until the late 1970s, when Congress passed the Health Profession Educational Assistance Act restricting the number of foreign medical graduates who could enter the United States. At that time it was estimated that half of all state hospital psychiatrists were foreign medical graduates from developing countries, and in twelve states they comprised over 70 percent of the psychiatric staff. This is a description of Ohio's state institutions in 1979:

> Three-fourths of all full-time physicians in the department were foreign-born graduates of foreign medical colleges. Between 1970 and 1975 only four of 29 institutions had been able to recruit and retain a full-time psychiatrist who graduated from an American medical college. Only five of the 29 institutions had full-time physicians who had graduated from an American medical college within the past 14 years. Eighty-eight of 94 psychiatric residents in training were foreign-born graduates of foreign medical colleges.
>
> Only one of the full-time U.S. medical college graduates in the department was under age 40, and 35 percent of all full-time physicians were older than 60. Two institutions had no physician under the age of 65. Forty-one physicians practicing in the department had no Ohio license. Thus the department for years had been almost totally unable to recruit graduates of U.S. medical colleges. It was surviving almost entirely with foreign graduates and U.S. graduates recruited many years ago.

This aspect of American psychiatry has been well documented. The problem from the point of view of patients hospitalized with schizophrenia is that it becomes difficult to get high-quality psychiatric care. Some of the foreign medical graduates are unquestionably excellent and will make major contributions to psychiatry. There is evidence, however, that others are mediocre at best and in some cases incompetent. Some have had no training whatsoever in psychiatry yet are allowed to practice as psychiatrists by the state. The two foreign medical schools which contributed the greatest number of psychiatrists to American state hospitals both had very low pass rates on the Education Council for Foreign Medical Graduates (ECFMG) examination. Some of the foreign graduates who cannot pass basic licensing exams are given special exemptions by the state to practice only in the state institutions. In essence the state is saying that it does not consider them competent to treat the "worried well" in private practice but will accept them if they treat the truly sick in the state hospitals.

The most disturbing aspect of utilizing large numbers of foreign medical graduates to treat America's schizophrenic patients is the inevitable difficulties in communication. Verbal language skill is only one part of this; beyond it are many other levels of communication which involve nonverbal language, shared ideals and values, and other components of what is called culture. Communication between a psychiatrist and a schizophrenic is difficult enough even when they share a common language and culture; when they do not share these things, communication becomes virtually impossible. Delusions must be assessed in the context of the patient's culture. Affect which may appear appropriate within one culture context may be inappropriate within another. The evaluation of subtle disorders of thinking assumes a complete command of the idioms and metaphors of a language. One psychiatrist, for example, was observed asking a schizophrenic patient the following proverb: "What does mean, a stitch in time gathers no moss." That kind of psychiatric interview would inspire neither confidence nor clarity of thought in a schizophrenic patient.

The image of state mental hospitals as the dregs of American psychiatry persists. The patients who end up there are considered dull and unimportant, the psychiatrists who end up there as lazy and incompetent. In a recent public opinion poll two-thirds of the public viewed state hospital psychiatrists negatively. The private segment of American psychiatry utilizes the state hospital as a dumping ground for those patients who cannot pay their bills or who are not "good" patients. According to Dr. Miles Shore:

> Unfortunately it is widely accepted that state hospitals are consistently substandard. A culture of poverty, ineptitude, and stagnation pervades the institutions and takes on a life of its own. That culture extends to most institutions, including community mental health centers that are run by governmental bureaucracies and are expected to take all patients regardless of the availability of resources.
>
> Worse, both society and organized psychiatry need such institutions in order to maintain their own customary functioning. That was demonstrated recently when a university-affiliated state facility set up a waiting list to keep admissions at a level consistent with the staff available to provide adequate care. The outrage that this action generated in colleagues in private institutions was a measure of the tacit social contract that exists between the private and public sector. The contract holds that the private institutions maintain their fiscal integrity and their quality of care by moving to the public institutions patients who do not fit fiscally or clinically, or patients for whom they lack space. The public institution's responsibility is to take the patient regardless of the availability of resources, so that each new patient dilutes further the quality of care.
>
> On the whole, the public has successfully ignored the institutions and their clientele. It is only during periodic investigations of scandals that the plight of the hospitals surfaces in the public consciousness. Once the immediate furor is over, cost containment sets in, public amnesia reasserts itself, and the situation slides back to its customary disgraceful level.

This same point is made by Dr. John Spiegel who, as recent president of the American Psychiatric Association (APA), went around the country to talk to groups of psychiatrists on the ten key problems facing American psychiatry. The last problem on the list was the problem of the chronic mental patient. Dr. Spiegel noted that "although audiences tended to respond to the other points vigorously, on this issue, except for a rare complaint that something ought to be done about it by the leaders of psychiatry, there was a numbing silence."

Dr. Spiegel's findings are not surprising in view of the recent record of the APA on the care of persons with chronic schizophrenia. It was not always so; indeed the American Psychiatric Association was first founded in the 1840s as an association of superintendents of state hospitals. Up through World War II, the primary focus of the APA was on chronic mental patients.

Since that time, however, the APA's interest in schizophrenia and chronic mental illness has steadily waned, and the major focus and prestige of the organization have shifted to private practice and academic psychiatry. This can be seen in the selection of presidents of the organization. Of the past twenty presidents of the APA only two have had substantial responsibilities for state psychiatric hospitals, Dr. Daniel Blain with the Philadelphia State Hospital and Dr. Jack Weinberg with the Illinois State Psychiatric Institute. One other, Dr. Donald Langsley, developed a model treatment program for schizophrenics in the community, and another, Dr. Daniel X. Freedman, has been active in schizophrenia research. The remainder have been identified primarily with academic posts, private practice, or other areas of psychiatry.

In the last decade the APA has moved even further away from the concerns of schizophrenic patients and has evolved into a Washington lobbying organization for the interests of private psychiatry. It has spawned a political arm, hired lobbyists, and generally taken on the veneer of a professional union for the protection of the psychiatrists' income and their prerogatives. Occasionally it has spasms of guilt and convenes a conference on chronic mental patients. This occurred most recently in 1978 and was brought about primarily by Dr. John Talbott, one of the few psychiatrists who have consistently championed the cause of the schizophrenic patient. The conference concluded with a predictable set of exhortations (e.g., "the APA should take the lead in undertaking programs to elevate the prestige and value of work with chronic mentally ill patients") but, just as predictably, nothing has come or will come of it. In view of all this it is not surprising that the APA, and American psychiatrists in general, have an "image problem" and are regarded as increasingly irrelevant to the real issues of psychiatric illness in this country.

What about other mental health professionals—psychologists, psychiatric social workers, and psychiatric nurses? If American psychiatrists will not take the lead in championing the cause of the seriously mentally ill, why cannot these other professionals do so? In fact, they could if they wished. Unfortunately, however, virtually all of them look to psychiatry for their standards and try to emulate the psychiatric profession. Status within all these mental health disciplines accrues to the private practice model; taking care of schizophrenic or otherwise seriously disturbed patients is indicative of second class professional status. There are individual psychologists, psychiatric social workers, and psychiatric nurses who defy the laws of social gravity and devote their careers to the seriously ill, just as there are psychiatrists who do so. They stand out as the exceptions, however, always considered somewhat aberrant by their peers. And when the official organizations of these professions take public stands apart from psychiatry, it is usually on issues of pay and insurance compensation, not on issues like quality of care for schizophrenic patients.

What about the Mental Health Association? This is a private consumer organization founded by Clifford Beers, who was one of the original crusaders for improving conditions in state hospitals. Headquartered just across the Potomac from Washington, it claims 850 local chapters, one million members, and an annual budget of over $23 million. Theoretically it could have played an important role in reversing the neglect of schizophrenic patients.

Unfortunately, it has done almost nothing in this direction. It has instead supported the private practice, problems-of-living model of American psychiatry, acting as a handmaiden for psychiatrists and other mental health professionals and strongly supporting NIMH. On issues such as the coverage of individual psychotherapy under national health insurance, the Mental Health Association became very active, mobilizing volunteers to visit and write their congressmen and otherwise lobbying for the rights of the worried well. Much of its rhetoric focuses on the need for good mental health, a concept as nebulous as it is all-inclusive. Its interest in the needs of schizophrenics and other seriously ill mental patients has been limited to official platitudes of concern. It also gave one of its recent research achievement awards to two researchers whose work focused on the thesis that families might cause schizophrenia.

If the Mental Health Association is really a lobby for the providers of mental health services, what about other mental health organizations whose offices dot the Washington landscape? The National Association of State Mental Health Program Directors, for example, is interested in the plight of schizophrenic patients since this group is composed of the state directors of mental health programs. By itself, however, it has limited power. It also suffers from political eunuchism insofar as the state governors can dictate deinstitutionalization needs to their state mental health directors; few such directors have risked their jobs by standing up to the governor or state legislators and saying that hospitalized patients would not be released until adequate community aftercare facilities were in place first. Other Washington mental health lobby groups, such as the National Council of Community Mental Health Centers, the National Association of Private Psychiatric Hospitals, and the Association of Mental Health Administrators, have functioned primarily to help secure a larger slice of the federal pie for their clients and have been irrelevant as far as the needs of schizophrenics are concerned.

THE NEED FOR A SCHIZOPHRENIA LOBBY

Nothing is going to change for persons with schizophrenia in the United States until an effective lobby begins to fight for their interests. Schizophrenia will continue to get less than its share of research funds to find the causes of the disease and better treatments for it. Psychiatrists will continue to be trained with public money and go into private practice, leaving the schizophrenics without care. Community Mental Health Centers will continue failing to provide psychiatric follow-up for schizophrenics released from state hospitals. Sheltered workshops and transitional employment programs will continue to be deplorably meager. Housing conditions for released schizophrenics will continue to be wretched. The conditions in the state hospitals will continue to slide downhill, accelerated by further budget cuts. And the families and friends of persons with schizophrenia will continue to sit quietly and ask why things must be this way.

In retrospect, it is remarkable that an organized lobby has not existed for schizophrenia. Consumer groups have organized to fight for diseases far rarer than schizophrenia. For example, Jerry Lewis runs an annual telethon for muscular dystrophy. Sara Lee once donated five cents to the Muscular Dystrophy Association each time you bought one of its cheesecakes. Your Fiat dealer donated one dollar to the Association if you test-drove a Fiat. Reynolds Aluminum donated one cent to the Association for every pound of aluminum cans brought in for recycling. McDonald's is covered with muscular dystrophy literature during the annual drive. All this is well organized and very effective —yet muscular dystrophy is only one-fortieth as common as schizophrenia; for every person with muscular dystrophy there are forty with schizophrenia. That provides some idea of how effective a lobby for schizophrenia could be if it ever got organized.

The National Association for Retarded Citizens is another effective lobby. Founded in 1950 by parents and friends of mentally retarded persons, it now claims 1,900 local units, over 250,000 members in the United States, and an annual budget of $130 million. It works to educate the public (and thus reduce stigmatization of the retarded), improve services and housing, ensure legal rights, encourage employment opportunities, and reduce mental retardation through implementing known methods of prevention (e.g., adequate prenatal care). It provides an effective model for what an organization devoted to chronic brain dysfunction can accomplish.

The recently organized National Alliance for the Mentally Ill may well become a comparably effective lobby for schizophrenia, but it will only do so if the families and friends of schizophrenics become active participants. In addition to public education and lobbying for better services, housing, employment opportunities and legal rights, such an organization might work toward many other objectives which could benefit persons with schizophrenia:

- Establishing right-to-treatment laws for state hospitals mandating minimum staffing standards (a useful guide for lobbying at the state or federal level is *Guide for Legislative Action,* National Alliance for the Mentally Ill, 1234 Massachusetts Ave., N.W., Washington, D.C. 20005
- Amending state mental health laws to reflect contemporary standards (a model state mental health code was developed by the American Psychiatric Association Task Force on Mental Health Commitment in 1980 and is available from the APA, 1400 K St., N.W., Washington, D.C. 20005)
- Establishing laws mandating treatment in the least restrictive setting and thus encouraging states to fund halfway houses and other suitable alternatives to long-term state hospital care
- Amending state laws on guardianship so that they are more helpful for schizophrenics (a model law on guardianship can be obtained from the Mental Health Law Project, 2021 L St., N.W., Suite 800, Washington, D.C. 20036)
- Tying public funds for CMHCs to a minimum percentage of persons with schizophrenia and/or who have been released from state hospitals who must receive follow-up care at the CMHC
- Monitoring CMHC services to schizophrenics and offering to testify at congressional hearings on their funding
- Amending Medicaid and Medicare so that they are not discriminatory against persons with schizophrenia, and so that they cover persons living in halfway houses
- Amending SSI so that persons with schizophrenia may receive as much money living at home as they do when living in a boarding home
- Encouraging the setting up of halfway houses by working against restrictive zoning ordinances and changing federal regulations (through the Department of Housing and Urban Development, etc.)
- Encouraging sheltered workshops and transitional employment by legislating tax credits for employers
- Bringing legal suits against city and state governments, insisting that they provide psychiatric aftercare and shelter for released mental patients (in 1982 examples of such class-action suits were initiated in Denver by the Legal Aid Society and in New York City by the Coalition for the Homeless)
- Working with the media to clarify public thinking about schizophrenia (a guide on how to do this is *Anti-Stigma: Improving Public Understanding of Mental Illness,* National Alliance for the Mentally Ill, 1234 Massachusetts Ave., N.W., Washington, D.C. 20005)
- Identifying local physicians and psychiatrists who provide good care for persons with schizophrenia and putting out consumers' guides (see *How to Compile a Consumer's Directory of Doctors and Their Fees,* Health Research Group, 2000 P Street, Washington, D.C. 20036)

- Tying public funds used to train psychiatrists to an obligatory period of public service payback
- Lobbying for increased schizophrenia research funds

These are only a sampling of what could be accomplished. With a constituency of two million families and friends, the possibilities for improving the care and treatment of schizophrenics are limitless. Tactics which could be employed include writing letters and visiting state legislators and congressmen in their offices to educate them. On the more activist end of the spectrum are picketing and sit-ins; a sit-in by schizophrenics and their families of key legislative offices or the American Psychiatric Association headquarters, for example, would be eminently newsworthy. Each member of Congress and member of the media with a schizophrenic relative should be identified and targeted as a potentially valuable ally.

None of this will happen, however, until enough people get angry and organize. Schizophrenics will continue to be fourth-class citizens, leading twilight lives, shunned, ignored, neglected. The mad will be liberated only when those fortunate enough to have escaped the illness become mad as well.

APPENDIX A

COMMITMENT LAWS BY STATE

The following compendium of long-term commitment laws by state is a composite of information from A. L. McGarry, R. K. Schwitzgebel, P. D. Lipsitt, and D. Lelos, *Civil Commitment and Social Policy* (Cambridge, Mass.: Laboratory of Community Psychiatry, Harvard Medical School, 1978); *Mental Disability Law Reporter*, May/June, 1979; National Association of State Mental Health Program Directors, *Status Report on Current Mental Health Legislation* (Washington, D.C.: January 1, 1979); the files of the Commission on the Mentally Disabled of the American Bar Association; and a solicitation for current information from each state in 1982, to which I received an 80 percent response rate. However, legislation to modify commitment laws is pending in several states, and the laws are likely to continue undergoing changes (emergency commitment procedures, which vary little from state to state, are discussed in chapter 6). Where quotation marks are used they indicate the language is taken either from the existing statutes or from a summary furnished by a state official.

ALABAMA

Grounds for commitment: The person must be dangerous to self or others; gravely disabled if no less restrictive alternative is available. Dangerousness must be demonstrated by recent overt act. Commitment must be to least restrictive alternative.
Standard of proof: Proof must be "clear, unequivocal, and convincing evidence."
Jury trial: There is no right to a jury trial.
Duration of commitment order: Duration is unspecified.

ALASKA

Grounds for commitment: "Respondent is reasonably believed to present a likelihood of serious harm to himself or others or is gravely disabled as a result of mental illness." Persons have the right to be "treated in the least restrictive alternative environment consistent with their treatment needs" and "as close to the individual's home as possible." "Persons who are mentally ill but not dangerous to others" can be committed "only if there is a reasonable expectation of improving their mental condition."
Standard of proof: There must be "clear and convincing evidence."

Jury trial: There is the right to a jury trial at time of 90- or 120-day commitment hearing, but not at 21-day commitment hearing.

Duration of commitment: Commitment may be for 21 days, 90 days, 120 days, or multiples of 120 days.

ARIZONA

Grounds for commitment: The patient is, as a result of mental disorder, a danger to self or others and in need of treatment; or the patient is, as a result of mental disorder, gravely disabled.

Standard of proof: Proof must be "clear and convincing evidence" that the proposed patient is, as a result of mental disorder, a danger to self or others and in need of treatment, and that there are no available or appropriate alternatives to court-ordered treatment.

Jury trial: There is no right to a jury trial.

Duration of commitment: If a danger to self, commitment can be up to 60 days; if a danger to others, up to 180 days; if gravely disabled, up to 1 year.

ARKANSAS

Grounds for commitment: Person must be homicidal, suicidal, or gravely disabled.

Standard of proof: "Clear and convincing evidence" must be presented that the person sought to be committed is either homicidal, suicidal, or gravely disabled.

Jury trial: There is no right to a jury trial.

Duration of commitment: Initial commitment is for 45 days with a possible extension of one 120-day period. After that time the person is to be released or, if necessary, a new original petition filed.

CALIFORNIA

Grounds for commitment: Person must be dangerous to self or others due to mental disorder or gravely disabled due to mental disorder.

Standard of proof: To prove dangerousness, the individual should have threatened, attempted to inflict, or actually inflicted physical harm on another after being taken into custody for evaluation or was taken into custody because of such behavior, and as a result of a mental disorder, presents an imminent threat of substantial physical harm to others. Proof for gravely disabled must be "beyond a reasonable doubt" and a conservatorship may be used for long-term commitment.

Jury trial: The right to a jury trial is mandatory in two situations. One is in the case of an action to establish a conservatorship and the other is in the situation of a 90-day postcertification for dangerousness.

Duration of commitment: Commitment is 90 days for dangerousness due to mental disorder; 1 year is the maximum period of time for a conservatorship established on the basis of grave disability due to mental disorder.

COLORADO

Grounds for commitment: The person is "Mentally ill and, as a result of mental illness, a danger to others or to himself or gravely disabled."

Standard of proof: Evidence must be "clear and convincing."

Jury trial: Patient has the right to a jury trial to contest either a short-term or a long-term commitment.

Duration of commitment: Initial commitment is for 3 months; this may be renewed and may be reviewed by a court. After 5 consecutive months of short-term treatment, a professional may file a petition with the court for long-term care and treatment. An order for long-term care and treatment is not to exceed a period of 6 months. Extension of long-term care and treatment, for additional periods of 6 months, may be made by the court as many times as is necessary.

CONNECTICUT

Grounds for commitment: The person exhibits mental illness and dangerousness to self or others or is gravely disabled.

Standard of proof: There must be "clear and convincing evidence."

Jury trial: There is no right to a jury trial.

Duration of commitment: Commitment is for indefinite time, but periodic reviews required.

DELAWARE

Grounds for commitment: Person is dangerous to self or others, gravely disabled, or in need of treatment. Commitment must be to the facility which "imposes the least restraint." Dangerousness includes harm to property.

Standard of proof: There must be "clear and convincing evidence."

Jury trial: There is no right to a jury trial.

Duration of commitment: Period of commitment is indefinite but must be reviewed every 6 months.

DISTRICT OF COLUMBIA

Grounds for commitment: Person is dangerous to self or others.

Standard of proof: There must be "clear and convincing evidence."

Jury trial: All persons have the right to a jury trial.

Duration of commitment: Commitment period is indefinite, but review (by hospital, not court) is mandatory 90 days after initial commitment and every 6 months thereafter.

FLORIDA

Grounds for commitment: Person is mentally ill and because of this illness, likely to injure himself or others if allowed to remain at liberty; or in need of care or treatment which, if not provided, may result in neglect or refusal to care for himself, and such neglect or refusal poses a real and present threat of substantial harm to his well-being.
Standard of proof: There must be "clear and convincing evidence."
Jury trial: There is no right to a jury trial.
Duration of commitment order: The maximum period is 6 months.

GEORGIA

Grounds for commitment: Patient shows mental illness and "presents a substantial risk of imminent harm to himself or others as manifested by either recent overt acts or recent expressed threats of violence which present a probability of physical injury to himself or to other persons or who is so unable to care for his own physical health and safety as to create an imminently life-endangering crisis."
Standard of proof: "Proof shall be by clear and convincing evidence."
Jury trial: There is no right to a jury trial.
Duration of commitment: Original commitment is for maximum of 6 months; thereafter orders for continued hospitalization may be for a maximum of 12 months.

HAWAII

Grounds for commitment: Person exhibits dangerousness to self or others or is in need of treatment.
Standard of proof: Proof must be "beyond a reasonable doubt." Dangerousness may include harm to property. There must be no suitable alternative which is less restrictive.
Jury trial: There is no right to a jury trial.
Duration of commitment: Initial commitment is for 90 days.

IDAHO

Grounds for commitment: Person is mentally ill and dangerous to self or others or gravely disabled.
Standard of proof: There must be "clear and convincing evidence."

Jury trial: There is no right to a jury trial.

Duration of commitment: Commitment is for up to 3 years.

ILLINOIS

Grounds for commitment: Person is mentally ill and because of the mental illness is "reasonably expected to inflict serious physical harm upon himself or another in the near future" or "unable to provide for his basic physical needs so as to guard himself from serious harm."

Standard of proof: Evidence must be "clear and convincing."

Jury trial: All persons have the right to a jury trial.

Duration of commitment: Initial commitment is for 60 days maximum; renewal is for 60 days the first time, thereafter for 180 days each renewal.

INDIANA

Grounds for commitment: Person is dangerous to self or others or gravely disabled or "in need of continued custody, care, and treatment."

Standard of proof: No standard is specified, but it is implicitly "clear and convincing evidence" because of a 1979 U.S. Supreme Court decision.

Jury trial: The right to a jury trial is not specified.

Duration of commitment: Duration is not specified.

IOWA

Grounds for commitment: The person "must be found to be afflicted with a mental illness, consequently to lack sufficient judgment to make reasonable decisions with respect to his or her hospitalization or treatment and to be likely, if allowed to remain at liberty, to inflict physical injury on himself or others or to inflict emotional injury on the designated class of persons."

Standard of proof: There must be "clear and convincing evidence."

Jury trial: There is no right to a jury trial.

Duration of commitment: Duration is unspecified. "In Iowa, the respondent does not have a right to periodic state-initiated recommitments. After commitment and hospitalization, the Iowa Act requires periodic reports on the patient's condition be made by the chief medical officer of the hospital." However, the patient can initiate a judicial review by requesting a commission of inquiry, appealing to the State Supreme Court, or filing a writ of habeas corpus.

KANSAS

Grounds for commitment: Person must be dangerous to self or others or gravely disabled or in need of treatment. Courts must consider reasonable alternatives to inpatient treatment.

Standard of proof: Proof must be "beyond a reasonable doubt."
Jury trial: All persons have the right to a jury trial.
Duration of commitment: Duration is unspecified.

KENTUCKY

Grounds for commitment: "No person shall be involuntarily hospitalized unless
such person is a mentally ill person (1) who represents a danger or threat of
danger to self, family or others as a result of a mental illness; (2) who can
reasonably benefit from treatment; and (3) for whom hospitalization is the less
restrictive alternative mode of treatment presently available."
Standard of proof: Proof must be "beyond a reasonable doubt."
Jury trial: All persons have the right to a jury trial.
Duration of commitment: There is a 60-day and a 360-day commitment.

LOUISIANA

Grounds for commitment: Person must show "dangerousness to self or others or
is gravely disabled as a result of substance abuse or mental illness." Commitment should be to the facility "least restrictive of the patient's liberty."
Standard of proof: There must be "clear and convincing evidence."
Jury trial: Any person "shall have the right to demand a judicial hearing" before
the court but there is no right to a jury trial.
Duration of commitment: There is mandatory review after 60 days, then 120 days,
then every 180 days thereafter.

MAINE

Grounds for commitment: The person must be found to be mentally ill with recent
actions and behavior demonstrating that "his illness poses a likelihood of
serious harm." This likelihood "means a substantial risk of physical harm to
the person or to others or reasonable certainty that physical or mental injury
will result to the person as a result of recent actions or behavior."
Standard of proof: There must be "clear and convincing evidence."
Jury trial: There is no right to a jury trial.
Duration of commitment: Initial commitment must not exceed 4 months. "If further
hospitalization is sought, commitment may be ordered for a period not to
exceed one year."

MARYLAND

Grounds for commitment: Person must be dangerous to self or others or gravely
disabled or in need of treatment. Dangerousness includes the property of
others. There must be no less restrictive alternative available.

Standard of proof: Evidence must be "clear and convincing."

Jury trial: There is no right to a jury trial.

Duration of commitment: Period of commitment is unspecified.

MASSACHUSETTS

Grounds for commitment: There is a "likelihood of serious harm by reason of mental illness." Dangerousness must include threatened or attempted suicide or homicide, violent behavior, or serious physical harm.

Standard of proof: Proof must be "beyond a reasonable doubt."

Jury trial: There is no right to a jury trial in either the district courts or the probate courts.

Duration of commitment: Long-term commitments by district courts are for 1 year; new orders may be issued from year to year. Long-term commitment by probate courts, in which guardians are appointed, are indefinite, "subject to mandatory periodic review requirements at the hospital (once in the first three months; once in the second three months; and, thereafter, once every year), but not subject to further court orders unless a habeas corpus petition is brought."

MICHIGAN

Grounds for commitment: Person must be dangerous to self or others or gravely disabled or in need of treatment.

Standard of proof: There must be "clear and convincing evidence."

Jury trial: All persons have the right to a jury trial.

Duration of commitment: Period is unspecified.

MINNESOTA

Grounds for commitment: A "mentally ill person means any person who has a substantial psychiatric disorder of thought, mood, perception, orientation, or memory which grossly impairs judgment, behavior, capacity to recognize reality, or to reason or understand, which (a) is manifested by instances of grossly disturbed behavior or faulty perceptions; and (b) poses a substantial likelihood of physical harm to himself or others as demonstrated by (i) a recent attempt or threat to physically harm himself or others, or (ii) a failure to provide necessary food, clothing, shelter or medical care for himself, as a result of the impairment." Dangerousness is defined as "a clear danger to the safety of others as demonstrated by the facts that (i) the person has engaged in an overt act causing or attempting to cause serious physical harm to another; and (ii) there is a substantial likelihood that the person will engage in acts capable of inflicting serious physical harm on another."

Standard of proof: There must be "clear and convincing evidence."

Jury trial: There is no right to a jury trial.

Duration of commitment: For mentally ill but not dangerous persons initial commitment is for a maximum of 6 months and subsequent extensions limited to 1 year. For mentally ill and dangerous persons the commitment is for an indeterminate period.

MISSISSIPPI

Grounds for commitment: Person must be dangerous to self or others or gravely disabled or in need of treatment.

Standard of proof: There must be "clear and convincing evidence."

Jury trial: There is no right to a jury trial.

Duration of commitment: Period is unspecified.

MISSOURI

Grounds for commitment: Person must show dangerousness to self or others or be gravely disabled or in need of treatment "and, because of his mental condition, lacks sufficient insight or capacity to make responsible decisions with respect to his hospitalization."

Standard of proof: Evidence must be "clear and convincing."

Jury trial: All persons have the right to a jury trial.

Duration of commitment: Period is indefinite.

MONTANA

Grounds for commitment: Person must be dangerous to self or others. Dangerousness to self includes "the inability to adequately care for oneself." Dangerousness to others is injury "or the imminent threat thereof."

Standard of proof: Proof must be "beyond a reasonable doubt" with respect to any physical facts or evidence and "clear and convincing evidence" as to all other matters.

Jury trial: All persons have the right to a jury trial at the initial commitment but not at hearings for renewal of the commitment.

Duration of commitment: Initial commitment is for maximum of 90 days; first renewal is for 6 months, thereafter yearly.

NEBRASKA

Grounds for commitment: "The person presents (a) a substantial risk of serious harm to another person or persons within the near future, as manifested by evidence of recent violent acts or threats of violence or by placing others in reasonable fear of such harm; or (b) a substantial risk of serious harm to himself within the near future, as manifested by evidence of recent attempts at, or threats of, suicide or serious bodily harm or evidence of inability to provide for his basic human needs, including food, clothing, shelter, essential medical care, or personal safety." A less restrictive alternative is not available.

Standard of proof: There must be "clear and convincing evidence."

Jury trial: There is no right to a jury trial.

Duration of commitment: Term is unspecified.

NEVADA

Grounds for commitment: "Person is mentally ill and, because of such illness is likely to harm himself or others or is gravely disabled."

Standard of proof: Proof is not specified in statute but is implicitly "clear and convincing evidence" because of a 1979 U.S. Supreme Court decision.

Jury trial: There is no right to a jury trial.

Duration of commitment: Commitment is for 6 months; it may be renewed for 6-month intervals thereafter.

NEW HAMPSHIRE

Grounds for commitment: Person must exhibit dangerousness to self or others.

Standard of proof: Proof must be "beyond a reasonable doubt."

Jury trial: There is no right to a jury trial.

Duration of commitment: Commitment is for up to five years.

NEW JERSEY

Grounds for commitment: Person is "a danger to himself or others or property if he is not so confined and treated."

Standard of proof: Evidence must be "clear and convincing."

Jury trial: There is no right to a jury trial.

Duration of commitment: Initial commitment is for maximum of 3 months; first renewal is for 6 months, thereafter yearly.

NEW MEXICO

Grounds for commitment: "As a result of a mental disorder, the client presents a likelihood of serious harm to himself or others; the client needs and is likely to benefit from the proposed treatment; and the proposed commitment is consistent with the treatment needs of the client and with the least drastic means principle."

Standard of proof: There must be "clear and convincing evidence."

Jury trial: "The client has a right to a trial by a six-person jury if requested by the client."

Duration of commitment: Commitment is for "a period not to exceed 6 months."

NEW YORK

Grounds for commitment: Person is mentally ill and "in need of involuntary care and treatment." This has been interpreted by New York courts to mean that a person must, as a result of mental illness, be either likely to engage in violence or unable to live safely outside the hospital with the help of family or friends.

Standard of proof: Proof is not specified in statute but is implicitly "clear and convincing evidence" because of a 1979 U.S. Supreme Court decision.

Jury trial: All persons have the right to a jury trial.

Duration of commitment: Initial commitment can last up to 60 days; "continued commitment can be authorized for an additional year, and subsequent orders of commitment can be for two year periods."

NORTH CAROLINA

Grounds for commitment: There must be dangerousness to self or others.

Standard of proof: There must be "clear, cogent, and convincing evidence."

Jury trial: There is no right to a jury trial.

Duration of commitment: Commitment is for up to one year.

NORTH DAKOTA

Grounds for commitment: Person must be mentally ill "and, as a result of his condition, can reasonably be expected to harm himself or others or is unable to take care of his basic needs and that serious harm would result if not attended."

Standard of proof: Evidence must be "clear and convincing."

Jury trial: There is no right to a jury trial.

Duration of commitment: Commitment period is indefinite.

OHIO

Grounds for commitment: "A mentally ill person who, because of his illness: (1) represents a substantial risk of physical harm to himself as manifested by evidence of threats of, or attempts at, suicide or serious self-inflicted bodily harm; (2) represents a substantial risk of physical harm to others as manifested by evidence of recent homicidal or other violent behavior, evidence of recent threats that place another in reasonable fear of violent behavior and serious physical harm, or other evidence of present dangerousness; (3)

represents a substantial and immediate risk of serious physical impairment or injury to himself as manifested by evidence that he is unable to provide for and is not providing for his basic physical needs because of his mental illness and that appropriate provision for such needs cannot be made immediately available in the community; or (4) would benefit from treatment in a hospital for his mental illness and is in need of such treatment as manifested by evidence of behavior that creates a grave and imminent risk to substantial rights of others or himself."

Standard of proof: There must be "clear and convincing evidence."

Jury trial: There is no right to a jury trial.

Duration of commitment: Initial commitment is for maximum of 90 days; subsequent commitments are for maximum of 2-year periods.

OKLAHOMA

Grounds for commitment: "A person who has a demonstrable mental illness and who as a result of that mental illness can be expected within the near future to intentionally or unintentionally seriously and physically injure himself or another person"; or "a person who has a demonstrable mental illness and who as a result of that mental illness is unable to attend to those of his basic physical needs such as food, clothing, or shelter that must be attended to in order for him to avoid serious harm in the near future and who has demonstrated such inability by failing to attend to those basic physical needs in the recent past." To prove dangerousness there must have been a recent overt act.

Standard of proof: Proof must be "beyond a reasonable doubt."

Jury trial: All persons have the right to a jury trial.

Duration of commitment: Duration is unspecified.

OREGON

Grounds for commitment: Person must be dangerous to self or others or gravely disabled.

Standard of proof: Proof must be "beyond a reasonable doubt."

Jury trial: There is no right to a jury trial.

Duration of commitment: Commitment is for up to 180 days.

PENNSYLVANIA

Grounds for commitment: Person must exhibit dangerousness to self or others; the dangerousness to self can include the inability to care for oneself. Evidence of dangerousness must be a specific act within the past 30 days.

Standard of proof: There must be "clear and convincing evidence."

Jury trial: There is no right to a jury trial.

Duration of commitment: Initial commitment is for up to 90 days; subsequent commitments may be for up to 180 days.

RHODE ISLAND

Grounds for commitment: "Person is in need of immediate care and treatment and is one whose continued unsupervised presence in the community would create an imminent likelihood of serious harm by reason of mental disability." The likelihood of serious harm means "(1) a substantial risk of physical harm to the person himself as manifested by behavior evidencing serious threats of, or attempts at, suicide or by behavior which will result in serious bodily harm, or (2) a substantial risk of physical harm to other persons as manifested by behavior or threats evidencing homicidal or other violent behavior."
Standard of proof: Evidence must be "clear and convincing."
Jury trial: There is no right to a jury trial.
Duration of commitment: Commitments may be for up to 6 months.

SOUTH CAROLINA

Grounds for commitment: The person "is mentally ill, needs treatment and because of his condition (1) lacks sufficient insight or capacity to make responsible decisions with respect to his treatment, or (2) there is a likelihood of serious harm to himself or others."
Standard of proof: Evidence must be "clear and convincing."
Jury trial: There is no right to a jury trial.
Duration of commitment: Period is unspecified.

SOUTH DAKOTA

Grounds for commitment: Person must be dangerous to self or others or in need of treatment.
Standard of proof: Evidence must be "clear and convincing."
Jury trial: There is no right to a jury trial.
Duration of commitment: Period is unspecified.

TENNESSEE

Grounds for commitment: Person "is mentally ill and, because of this illness, poses a likelihood of serious harm, and is in need of care and treatment in a mental hospital or treatment resource." Likelihood of serious harm is defined as: "(1) a substantial risk of physical harm to the person himself as manifested by evidence of threats of, or attempts at, suicide or serious bodily harm; (2) a substantial risk of physical harm to other persons as manifested by evidence of homicidal or other violent behavior or evidence that others are placed in a reasonable fear of violent behavior and serious physical harm to them; or (3) a reasonable certainty that severe impairment or injury will result to the person alleged to be mentally ill as manifested by his inability to avoid or protect himself from such impairment or injury and suitable community resources for his care are unavailable."

Standard of proof: There must be "clear, unequivocal and convincing evidence."
Jury trial: All persons have the right to a jury trial.
Duration of commitment: Period is unspecified.

TEXAS

Grounds for commitment: Person is "mentally ill and in need of hospitalization for his own welfare and protection or the protection of others."
Standard of proof: There must be "clear and convincing evidence."
Jury trial: All persons have the right to a jury trial unless waived.
Duration of commitment: Period is indefinite. Most civil commitments are for a maximum of 90 days, however.

UTAH

Grounds for commitment: Person must be dangerous to self or others or gravely disabled or in need of treatment. There must be "no appropriate less restrictive alternative to a court order of hospitalization."
Standard of proof: Evidence must be "clear and convincing." Proof must be "beyond a reasonable doubt."
Jury trial: There is no right to a jury trial.
Duration of commitment: Period is indefinite, but the commitment must be reviewed every 6 months.

VERMONT

Grounds for commitment: Person must be dangerous to self or others or gravely disabled. Dangerousness includes "by his action or inactions he has presented a danger to persons in his care."
Standard of proof: There must be "clear and convincing evidence."
Jury trial: Right to trial is unspecified by the statutes. No one has ever requested one.
Duration of commitment: Initial commitment is for maximum of 90 days; any subsequent extension is indefinite.

VIRGINIA

Grounds for commitment: "Person is mentally ill and presents imminent danger to himself or others." "There is no less restrictive alternative to institutional confinement."

Standard of proof: Proof is not specified in statute but is implicitly "clear and convincing evidence" because of a 1979 U.S. Supreme Court decision.

Jury trial: All persons have the right to a jury trial.

Duration of commitment: Commitment is for up to 180 days.

WASHINGTON

Grounds for commitment: Person is dangerous or gravely disabled. Dangerousness is defined as "likelihood of serious harm to others or himself or substantial damage to the property of others." Gravely disabled is defined as a condition "in which a person, as a result of a mental disorder, is in danger of serious physical harm resulting from a failure to provide for his essential human needs of health or safety or manifests severe deterioration in routine functioning evidenced by repeated and escalating loss of cognitive or volitional control over his or her actions and is not receiving such care as is essential to his or her health and safety."

Standard of proof: There must be "clear, cogent and convincing evidence" for the 90-day or 180-day commitment. For the shorter 14-day emergency commitment the standard of proof is the "preponderance of the evidence."

Jury trial: All persons have the right to a jury trial.

Duration of commitment: Initial commitment is for 90 days; subsequent commitments are for 180 days.

WEST VIRGINIA

Grounds for commitment: Person is mentally ill and because of his illness "is likely to cause serious harm to himself or to others if allowed to remain at liberty." Commitment should not be used if there is a less restrictive alternative which is appropriate.

Standard of proof: There must be "clear, cogent, and convincing proof."

Jury trial: There is no right to a jury trial.

Duration of commitment: Commitment is for up to 2 years.

WISCONSIN

Grounds for commitment: Person is mentally ill and dangerous. Dangerousness is indicated when the person "(1) evidences a substantial probability of physical harm to himself or herself as manifested by evidence of recent threats of or attempts at suicide or serious bodily harm; (2) evidences a substantial probability of physical harm to other individuals as manifested by evidence of recent homicidal or other violent behavior or by evidence that others are placed in reasonable fear of violent behavior and serious physical harm to them, as evidenced by a recent overt act, attempt or threat to do serious physical harm; (3) evidences such impaired judgment, manifested by evidence of a pattern of recent acts or omissions, that there is a substantial probability of physical impairment or injury to himself or herself . . . (4) evidences behavior manifested by recent acts or omissions that, due to mental illness, he or she is unable to satisfy basic needs for nourishment, medical care, shelter, or safety without prompt and adequate treatment so that a substantial probability exists that death, serious physical injury, serious physical debilitation, or serious physical disease will imminently ensue unless the individual receives prompt and adequate treatment for this mental illness."

Standard of proof: There must be "clear and convincing evidence."

Jury trial: All persons have the right to a jury trial.

Duration of commitment: Initial commitment is for maximum of 6 months, subsequent commitments are for 1 year.

WYOMING

Grounds for commitment: Mental illness in "a person who presents an imminent threat of physical harm to himself or others as a result of a physical, emotional, mental or behavioral disorder which grossly impairs his ability to function socially, vocationally or interpersonally and who needs treatment and who cannot comprehend the need for or purposes of treatment and with respect to whom the potential risk and benefits are such that a reasonable person would consent to treatment."

Standard of proof: There must be "clear and convincing evidence."

Jury trial: All persons have the right to a jury trial.

Duration of commitment: Period is indefinite but the "head of the hospital" must examine every committed patient every 6 months to ascertain whether he/she still needs hospitalization.

APPENDIX B

COMPARATIVE COST
OF ANTIPSYCHOTIC DRUGS

The following table compares the cost of a thirty-day supply of selected, commonly used antipsychotic drugs. The dose of each drug is equivalent to that of each other drug as calculated in table 2 (see page 117); thus they are comparable in dose. A maintenance dose of 10 milligrams a day of fluphenazine or haloperidol is used as the baseline.

All calculations have been done assuming that the pharmacy is buying in bottles of 100 tablets or capsules. Some large retail pharmacies and many hospital pharmacies buy in bottles of 1,000, which would reduce the price. Calculations also assume a once-daily dose; all of these antipsychotic agents can be given this way. If the dose is split into two or more lower-dosage units and given more than once a day, the cost increases.

As is true for most pharmaceuticals, the least expensive antipsychotics are generics. The use of generics in place of brand names is controversial but generally accepted by most doctors. Occasionally generics have been marketed which have been found to be less effective than the brand name equivalents, due to such factors as different absorption or excretion of the drug. To date no study has been done comparing the efficacy of generic antipsychotic drugs with their brand name counterparts. I do not hesitate to prescribe them.

Table 3

Equivalent Doses of Antipsychotic Drugs

Generic Name	Trade Name	Maintenance (dose per day)	Cost for 30-day Supply*
Fluphenazine, 10 mg. tablets	Prolixin	10 mg./d.	$13.85
Fluphenazine, 10 mg. tablets	generic	10 mg./d.	4.15 to 6.70 (depending on company)
Fluphenazine, concentrate liquid	Permitil concentrate	10 mg./d.	7.80
Fluphenazine, long-acting injectable	Prolixin Deconoate	25 mg. every two weeks	10.20
Haloperidol, 10 mg. tablets	Haldol	10 mg./d.	11.85
Trifluoperazine, 10 mg. tablets	Stelazine	20 mg./d.	13.25
Thiothixene, 20 mg. tablets	Navane	20 mg./d.	11.65
Molindone, 50 mg. tablets	Moban	50 mg./d.	8.45
Loxapine, 50 mg. tablets	Loxitane	50 mg./d.	12.45
Perphenazine, 16 mg. tablets	Trilafon	48 mg./d.	25.65
Acetophenazine, 20 mg. tablets	Tindal	100 mg./d.	16.50
Triflupromazine, 50 mg. tablets	Vesprin	100 mg./d.	13.50
Mesoridazine, 100 mg. tablets	Serentil	150 mg./d.	10.25
Thioridazine, 200 mg. tablets	Mellaril	200 mg./d.	10.05
Chlorpromazine, 200 mg. tablets	Thorazine	200 mg./d.	3.15
Chlorpromazine, 200 mg. tablets	generic	200 mg./d.	1.20 to 1.80 (depending on company)

*The prices quoted are the *cost to the pharmacist* as reflected in the average wholesaler price (AWP) in *Drug Topics Redbook 1982* (Oradell, N.J.: Medical Economics). The cost to the consumer will vary, depending upon the pharmacy mark-up; it averages 30 to 40 percent more.

FAMILY SUPPORT GROUPS BY STATE

The following family support groups are those known to the National Alliance for the Mentally Ill (National AMI) or the author at the time of publication. Since these groups are proliferating rapidly the list should be considered to be incomplete. For information on recently formed groups contact the National Alliance for the Mentally Ill, 1200 15th St., N.W., Washington, D.C. 20005.

The majority of listed groups are affiliated with National AMI. Those which are listed as chapters of the American Schizophrenia Association or the Huxley Institute are oriented toward an orthomolecular (vitamin and diet) treatment of schizophrenia (see chapters 6 and 8). A few groups are affiliated with the local chapter of the Mental Health Association (MHA) (see chapter 12).

ALABAMA

Jefferson-Blount St. Clair
MH/MR Authority
3820 Third Ave., South, Suite 100
Birmingham, AL 35222

Huntsville Support Alliance for the
   Mentally Ill
403 Westburg Ave.
Huntsville, AL 35801

Mobile Family Support Group
4508 Kingsway Ct.
Mobile, AL 36608

ALASKA

Kenai AMI
P.O. Box 301
Soldotna, AK 99669

REACH
c/o Alaska MHA
2611 Fairbanks St.
Anchorage, AK 99503

Fairbanks AMI
P.O. Box 2543
Fairbanks, AK 99707

Juneau AMI
Box 31147
Auke Bay, AK 99821

ARIZONA

Arizona AMI
4109 E. Catalina
Phoenix, AZ 85018

Family AMI–Maricopa Co.
4109 E. Catalina
Phoenix, AZ 85018

AMI of Southern Arizona
5055 E. Broadway C-214
Tucson, AZ 85711

ARKANSAS

Help and Hope, Inc.
Arkansas Families and Friends of the
   Mentally Ill
4313 W. Markham
Little Rock, AR 72201

Help and Hope, Inc.
503 Cheri Whitlock Dr.
Siloam Springs, AR 72761

CALIFORNIA

State Organization

California AMI
5820 Yorkshire Ave.
La Mesa, CA 92041

Alameda Co.

American Schizophrenia Assoc.
2409 Le Conte Ave.
Berkeley, CA 94709

Butte Co.

AMI of Butte Co.
P.O. Box 385
Oroville, CA 95965

Contra Costa Co.

Contra Costa Alliance for the Mentally Ill,
Inc.
P.O. Box 2357
Walnut Creek, CA 94595

Desert Community

Desert Mental Health Advocates
81–492 Francis Ave.
Indio, CA 92201

East San Gabriel Valley AMI
319 No. Broadmoor Ave.
West Covina, CA 91790

Fresno Co.

Family Support Group
MHA of Greater Fresno
1759 Fulton, Suite 146
Fresno, CA 93721

Humboldt Co.

Families for Mental Recovery
Alliance for the Mentally Ill
P.O. Box 6404
Eureka, CA 95501

Kern Co.

Alliance for the Mentally Ill of Kern Co.
3017 Pomona
Bakersfield, CA 93305

Los Angeles

Westside and Coastal Friends
P.O. Box 241576
Los Angeles, CA 90024

Advocates for the Mentally Ill
3139 Colby Ave.
Los Angeles, CA 90066

Glendale AMI
5124 Eagle Rock Blvd.
Los Angeles, CA 90041

Marin Co.

Marin Parent Advocates for Mental
Health
Box 1039
Ross, CA 94957

Modesto

Alliance for the Mentally Ill
P.O. Box 1903
Modesto, CA 95353

Monterey Co.

AMI of Monterey Co.
1012 Forest Ave.
Pacific Grove, CA 93950

Napa Valley

Family Alliance for the Mentally Ill of
Napa Valley
P.O. Box 3494
Napa, CA 94558

North Inland San Diego Co.

Family Alliance for the Mentally Disabled
P.O. Box 27386
Escondido, CA 92027

Northern California

AMI of Napa State Hospital
2716 Henry Ave.
Pinole, CA 94564

Norwalk

AMI of Norwalk
11400 So. Norwalk Blvd.
Norwalk, CA 90650

Oakland

Families of the Mentally Ill of the Mental
Health Association
1801 Adeline St., Rm. 203
Oakland, CA 94607

Orange Co.

Orange County AMI
17341 Irvine Blvd., Suite 105
Tustin, CA 92680

Southcoast AMI
2775 Mesa Verde Dr., #X-102
Costa Mesa, CA 92626

Pasadena

Relatives and Friends of the Mentally
   Disabled
595 E. Washington Blvd., #K
Pasadena, CA 91104

Placer–Nevada Cos.

AMI, Placer–Nevada Cos.
P.O. Box 930
Auburn, CA 95603

Riverside Co.

Friends and Families of the Mentally
   Disabled
5499 Grassy Trail Dr.
Riverside, CA 92504

Friends and Families of the Mentally
   Disabled
44981 Viejo Dr.
Hemet, CA 92344

Sacramento

Sacramento AMI
P.O. Box 2154
Fair Oaks, CA 95628

San Diego

San Diego AMI
5820 Yorkshire Ave.
La Mesa, CA 92041

North Coastal Unit SDAMI
7111 Santa Barbara St.
Carlsbad, CA 92008

San Francisco

San Francisco AMI
631 Myra Way
San Francisco, CA 94127

San Francisco Schizophrenia Association
290 Seventh Ave.
San Francisco, CA 94118

San Gabriel Valley

AMI
1495 Bedford
San Marino, CA 91108

San Joaquin Co.

AMI San Joaquin Co.
Mental Health Center
1212 N. Calif. St., Box C
Stockton, CA 95202

San Mateo Co.

San Mateo AMI
P.O. Box 3333
San Mateo, CA 94403

Santa Clara Co.

Parents Alliance for the Mentally Ill
44 S. 5th St.
San Jose, CA 95112

Santa Cruz Co.

Mental Health Alliance
Santa Cruz Co.
1515A Capitola Rd.
Santa Cruz, CA 95062

Sonoma Co. Affiliate

Sonoma Co. AMI
415 Pythian Rd.
Santa Rosa, CA 95405

South Bay

South Bay AMI
30137 Avenida Tranquila
Rancho Palos Verdes, CA 90274

Stanislous Co.

AMI of Stanislous Co.
1039 Princeton
Modesto, CA 95350

Tulare Co.

Tulare Co. AMI
1325 W. Center St.
Visalia, CA 93291

Van Nuys

AMI, Van Nuys
6740 Kester Ave.
Van Nuys, CA 91405

Ventura Co.

AMI of Ventura Co.
P.O. Box AH
Ventura, CA 93002

Yolo Co.

AMI of Yolo Co.
615 J St.
Davis, CA 95616

COLORADO

State Organization

Colorado AMI
P.O. Box 28008
Lakewood, CO 80228

Boulder

Boulder AMI
980 6th St.
Boulder, CO 80302

Colorado Springs

Pikes Peak AMI
14425 Timberedge Lane
Colorado Springs, CO 80908

Denver

Denver AMI
P.O. Box 31001
2022 S. Univ. Blvd.
Denver, CO 80210

Jefferson Co.

Jeffco Alliance for the Mentally Ill
7005 W. 33rd Ave.
Wheat Ridge, CO 80033

Lakewood

Support Inc.
11335 W. Exposition Ave.
Lakewood, CO 80226

Larimer Co.

Friends and Families of Adult Mentally Ill
636 S. College Ave., Suite 123
Ft. Collins, CO 80524

Midwestern

Midwestern Colorado Mental Health
  Center
195 Stafford Ln.
Delta, CO 81416

CONNECTICUT

Pathways Inc.
40 Doubling Rd.
Greenwich, CT 06830

Families of the Mentally Ill Group
262 Battis Rd.
Hamden, CT 06514

DELAWARE

New Castle Co. AMI
2117 Largo Rd.
Wilmington, DE 19803

Sussex Co. AMI
RD # 2, Box 177
Georgetown, DE 19947

DISTRICT OF COLUMBIA

Threshold—D.C.
2200 S. Dakota Avenue, N.E.
Washington, DC 20018

FLORIDA

Brevard Co.

AMI of Brevard Co.
2718 Hillcrest Ave.
Titusville, FL 32796

Broward Co.

Broward Advocates for the Mentally Ill
16771 Harbor Ct.
Ft. Lauderdale, FL 33326

Collier Co

REACH
660 9th St., N.
Naples, FL 33940

Ft. Myers/Lee Co.

REACH (Reassurance for Each)
P.O. Box 06137
Ft. Myers, FL 33906

Hernando Co.

Family Support Group
11331 Ponce de Leon Blvd.
Brooksville, FL 33512

Miami

Community Advocates for the Mentally Ill
c/o Fellowship House
5711 S. Dixie Hwy.
Miami, FL 33176

Martin and St. Lucie Cos.

Martin and St. Lucie Co. AMI
1501 Burning Court
Port St. Lucie, FL 33452

Naples

REACH
660 9th St., N., Suite 37
Naples, FL 33940

North Central

AMI of North Central Florida
2224 N.W. 15th Ave.
Gainesville, FL 32605

North West

LOMI (Loved Ones of the Mentally Ill)
MHA of Bay Co., P.O. Box 2245
1316 Harrison Ave., Suite 203
Panama City, FL 32401

Palm Beach Co.

Alliance for the Mentally Ill of Palm
   Beach
666 Laconia Cir.
Lake Worth, FL 33463

Huxley Institute for Biosocial Research
900 N. Federal Hwy., Suite 3301
Boca Raton, FL 33432

Tamarac

Concerned Relatives and Friends of
   South Florida State Hospital, Inc.
9109 N.W. 81st Ct.
Tamarac, FL 33321

Venice

Families Together for Mental Health
1355 Cambridge Dr.
Venice, FL 33595

GEORGIA

Atlanta

Georgia Friends of the Mentally Ill
1390 DeClair Dr.
Atlanta, GA 30329

Central Georgia

Central Georgia MH/MR Consortium
   Adult MH SubCommittee Central State
   Hosp.
P.O. Box 325
Millegeville, GA 31062

Northeastern

Northeast Georgia CMH/MR
1247 Prince Ave.
Athens, GA 30606

Northern

Georgia Friends of the Mentally Ill
1563 Hidden Hills Pkwy.
Stone Mountain, GA 30088

Southeastern Coastal

AMI Chatham Area
30 Chatuachee Circle
Savannah, GA 31411

HAWAII

Hawaii Families and Friends of
   Schizophrenics, Inc.
P.O. Box 10532
Honolulu, HI 98616

IDAHO

Idaho Alliance for the Mentally Ill
321 Buchanan
American Falls, ID 83211

Canyon County AMI
1821 Howard Ave.
Caldwell, ID 85605

ILLINOIS

State Organization

AMI Illinois State Coalition
P.O. Box 2363
Glenview, IL 60025

Arlington Hts.

Northwest Suburban AMI
P.O. Box 1778
Arlington Hts., IL 60006

Boone/Stephenson/Winnebago Co.

Northern Illinois AMI
P.O. Box 6971
Rockford, IL 61125

Champaign Co.

Supportive Families of the Mentally Ill
702 W. Illinois
Urbana, IL 61801

Dyle/Lee/Whiteside/Carroll Co.

Sauk Valley AMI
1038 N. 8th St.
Rochelle, IL 61068

Greater Chicago

Illinois AMI
P.O. Box 1016
Evanston, IL 60204

Normal

REACH *
c/o Faye J. Townsend
612 Hilltop Ct.
Normal, IL 61701

Peoria

Tri-County AMI
705 Whippoorwill
Washington, IL 61571

Rock Island/Mercer Co.

AMI of Rock Island and Mercer Co.
P.O. Box 933
Rock Island, IL 61201

South Cook/Will Co.

AMI of the South Suburbs (AMISS)
P.O. Box 275
Olympia Fields, IL 60461

Springfield

Focus on Families
c/o MHC
710 Eighth St.
Springfield, IL 62702

Vermilien Co.

Vermilien Mental Health and
 Development Center
605 N. Logan
Danville, IL 61832

West Suburban Chicago

Schizophrenia Association of West
 Suburban Chicago
P.O. Box 237
Downers Grove, IL 60515

INDIANA

Ft. Wayne

Ft. Wayne AMI
909 East State Blvd.
Ft. Wayne, IN 46805

Marion Co.

Marion Co. TLC
(Together We Learn to Cope)
555 Sunset Blvd.
Greenwood, IN 46142

San Joseph Co.

South Bend AMI
1140 E. Ewing
South Bend, IN 46613

IOWA

State Organization

Iowa Alliance for the Mentally Ill
520 S.E. First St., Box 334
Eagle Grove, IA 50533

Cedar Rapids

REACH for Family and Friends of the
  Mentally Ill
c/o MH Advocates of Linn County
1118 First Avenue, N.E.
Cedar Rapids, IA 52402

Dubuque Co.

Dubuque AMI
723 5th St., S.E.
Dyersville, IA 52040

Johnson Co.

Johnson Co. Family Support Group
505 E. College
Iowa City, IA 52240

Northern Iowa

Northern Iowa AMI
Beeds Lake
RR2
Hampton, IA 50441

Northwestern Iowa

Northwest Iowa Family Support Group
201 E. 11th St.
Spencer, Iowa 51301

Scott Co.

The Advocates for Mental Health
311 E. 2nd St.
Davenport, IA 52801

KANSAS

Harvey, Marion and McPherson Cos.

Prairie View Community Support Program
Box 467
Newton, KS 67114

Johnson Co.

Families for Mental Health, Inc.
P.O. Box 2452
Shawnee Mission, KS 66201

Shawnee Co.

Families for Mental Health, Shawnee Co.
4538 N.E. Meriden Rd.
Topeka, KS 66617

Wyandotte Co.

Wyandotte Co. Families for Mental
  Health
36th at Eaton
Kansas City, KS 66103

KENTUCKY

Schizophrenia Association of Louisville
7702 Brownwood Dr.
Louisville, KY 40218

LOUISIANA

Greater New Orleans

Friends Alliance for the Mentally Ill
6028 Magazine St.
New Orleans, LA 70118

Lafayette

Families and Friends for Mental Health
178 Ronald Blvd.
Lafayette, LA 70503

New Orleans

Family Support Group
500 Walnut St.
New Orleans, LA 70118

Shreveport

Caddo-Bossier AMI
159 Bruce Street
Shreveport, LA 71105

Westwego

Association for Research in Children's
  Emotional Disorders (ARCED)
P.O. Box 511
Westwego, LA 70094

MAINE

Androscoggin Co.

Relatives and Friends Together for
  Support (RAFTS)
Star Route, Box 390
Poland, ME 04273

Bath

Brunswick SEA
348 Washington St.
Bath, ME 04530

Eastern

Citizen's Interest Group, Inc.
P.O. Box 108
Bangor, ME 04401

Kennebec Co.

Alliance for Troubled Families, Inc.
RFD #1, Box 4420
Oakland, ME 04963

Northern Aroostook Co.

Valley Family Support Group, Inc.
97 13th Ave.
Madawaska, ME 04756

Northern Oxford/Southern Franklin Co.

AIMED (Alliance Involved with the
  Mentally and Emotionally Disabled)
RFD 1, Box 470
Dixfield, ME 04224

Portland

AMI of Maine
P.O. Box 5196, Station A
Portland, ME 04101

Southern Aroostook

Southern Aroostook Family Support
  Group
59 Elm Street
Houlton, ME 04730

MARYLAND

State Organization

AMI of Maryland, Inc.
P.O. Box 336
Kensington, MD 20895

Baltimore

Mental Health Association of
  Metropolitan Baltimore, Inc.
323 E. 25th St.
Baltimore, MD 21218

AMI of Baltimore, Inc.
P.O. Box 16277
Baltimore, MD 21210

Carroll Co.

Springfield Hospital Family Support
  Group
c/o Martin Gross Service Bldg.
Springfield Hospital Center
Sykesville, MD 21784

Howard Co.

Threshold of Howard Co.
P.O. Box 2484
Columbia, MD 21045

Montgomery Co.

AMI of Montgomery Co., MD
7300 Whittier Blvd.
Bethesda, MD 20817

Prince Georges Co.

Threshold Families and Friends of the
  Mentally Ill, Inc.
7509 Newberry Ln.
Lanham, MD 20706

Southwestern Area Baltimore Co.

HOPE (Help Others Perform Equally)
  AMI
P.O. Box 21060
Catonsville, MD 21228

Towson

Next Step, Inc.
P.O. Box 5567
Towson, MD 21204

Wheaton

Schizophrenia Association of Greater
  Washington, Inc.
Wheaton Plaza Off. Bldg. N. #404
Wheaton, MD 20902

MASSACHUSETTS

State Organization

AMI of Massachusetts, Inc.
227 Mt. Hope Rd.
Somerset, MA 02726

Beverly

PSALMS (People Support/Advocacy
  Liberating Mental Sickness)
14 Colgate Rd.
Beverly, MA 01915

Boston

Mass. Assoc. of Social Clubs, Inc.
   (Former Patients' Group)
P.O. Box 9216
Boston, MA 02114

Ayer

Support–Advocacy Group for Families of
   Adult Mentally Ill
15 Maple St.
Ayer, MA 01432

Brockton

Self-Help Group for Families of the
   Mentally Ill at Massasoit Community
   College
1 Massasoit Blvd.
Brockton, MA 02402

Cambridge Middlesex Co.

AMI Cambridge Middlesex Co.
P.O. Box 165
Somerville, MA 02144

Cape Cod

Amicus of Cape Cod
P.O. Box 962
Osterville, MA 02655

Coastal Area

Coastal AMI
P.O. Box 149
Accord, MA 02018

Concord

Concord Area AMI
26 Concord Road
Bedford, MA 01730

Eastern Middlesex Co.

AMI of Eastern Middlesex Co.
22 Kensington Ave.
Reading, MA 01867

Fall River

Area Citizens Concerned with Ensuring
   Support Services (ACCESS)
P.O. Box 1865
Fall River, MA 02722

Greater Lynn

Mental Illness Network for Direction and
   Support (MINDS)
12 York Ter.
Lynn, MA 01904

Martha's Vineyard

AMI of Martha's Vineyard
c/o Mrs. Marion Trotter
West Chop, MA 02568

Middlesex Co.

AMI of Middlesex Co., Inc.
P.O. Box 3009
Framingham, MA 01701

Montachusett

ECHOES—Each Caring Heart Offers
   Endless Support
P.O. Box 442
Fitchburg, MA 01420

New Bedford

Greater New Bedford AMI
20 Woodville Way
Wareham, MA 02571

Newton-Wellesley

Alliance for the Mental Health of
   Newton-Wellesley
190 Hickory Rd.
Weston, MA 02193

Norfolk Co.

Medfield State Family Alliance, Inc.
35 Bicknell St.
Foxboro, MA 02035

North East Essex District

North East Essex District AMI
Whitehall Rd.
Amesbury, MA 01913

Northeastern

Merrimack Valley Advocacy for Mental
   Health
1018 Osgood St.
N. Andover, MA 01845

Quincy

Citizens Organization Assisting Mental
    Patients, Inc.
4 Ocean St.
N. Quincy, MA 02171

South Norfolk

South Norfolk AMI
82 Pleasant St.
Medfield, MA 02052

Western

Western Mass. AMI Citizens, Inc.
P.O. Box 500
Agawam, MA 01001

MICHIGAN

Cass Co.

Care-Action-Share-Support
Cass Co. Community Mental Health
109½ School St.
Cassopolis, MI 49031

Detroit

Neighborhood Serv. Org.
51 W. Warren
Detroit, MI 48201

Health and Nutrition Awareness
P.O. Box 36331
Detroit, MI 48236

Residential Care Alternatives
Family Support Group
24920 Hickory
Dearborn, MI 48124

Suburban West Support Group
c/o Peggy Spitzig
17331 Fairfield
Livonia, MI 48152

Flint

Family Support for Mental
    Recovery
P.O. Box 1320
Flint, MI 48501

Grand Haven

SHARE
1111 Fulton St.
Grand Haven, MI 49417

Grand Rapids

Self-Help Association for Relatives
    Enlightment (SHARE)
P.O. Box 1405
Grand Rapids, MI 49501

Kalamazoo

SHARE of Kalamazoo
c/o Edison Neighborhood Center
1331 Race St.
Kalamazoo, MI 49001

Lansing Area

Oasis Fellowship
12284 Cutler Rd.
Eagle, MI 48822

Citizens for Action in Mental Health Inc.
    (CAMH)
855 Grove St.
E. Lansing, MI 48823

Midland

Citizens for Action in Mental Health, Inc.
    (CAMH)
1202 Corrinne St.
Midland, MI 48640

Wayne/Oakland/Macomb Co.

AMI of Michigan
17596 Meadowood
Lothrup Village, MI 48076

MINNESOTA

Mental Health Advocates Coalition of
    Minnesota, Inc.
265 Ft. Rd. (W. 7th St.)
St. Paul, MN 55102

Schizophrenia Association of Minnesota
6950 France Ave. So.
Minneapolis, MN 55435

MISSISSIPPI

Families and Friends of the Mentally Ill
P.O. Box 1286
Hattiesburg, MS 39401

MISSOURI

Columbia

AMI of Columbia
c/o Carol Yoder
384 Maple Grove Way
Columbia, MO 65203

Greater Kansas City

Greater Kansas City Chapter AMI
P.O. Box 33086
Kansas City, MO 64114

Jefferson Co.

Care and Share
P.O. Box 353
Crystal City, MO 63019

Southwest

AMI of Springfield Missouri Chapter, Inc.
1504 N. Roberson
Springfield, MO 65803

St. Louis

AMI St. Louis
135 W. Adams
St. Louis, MO 63122

American Schizophrenia Association of
St. Louis
10426 Lackland Rd.
St. Louis, MO 63114

MONTANA

Cascade Co.

Great Falls AMI
North Central Montana MHC
P.O. Box 3048
Great Falls, MT 59403

Kalispell

FLAME (Families Loving Allied for
Mental Health)
640 Conrad Drive
Kalispell, MT 59901

Lewis and Clark Co.

Helena AMI
479 S. Park
Helena, MT 59601

Missoula

A New Beginning for the Mentally
Disordered
2405 39th St.
Missoula, MT 59807

Stevensville

Genesis House, Inc.
P.O. Box 350
Stevensville, MT 59870

NEBRASKA

AMI of Nebraska, Inc.
Lincoln Center Bldg.
1715 S. 22nd St.
Lincoln, NE 68502

NEVADA

Nevada Alliance for the Mentally Ill
3229 Anacapa
Las Vegas, NV 89102

NEW HAMPSHIRE

State Organization

NAMI in New Hampshire
P.O. Box 544
Peterborough, NH 03458

Concord

Concord AMI
Box 7122, Heights Station
Concord, NH 03301

Nashua

Greater Nashua MHA
c/o Bea Rosen
20 Cabot Dr.
Nashua, NH 03060

Sullivan Co.

High Hope Mental Health Support Group
c/o Counseling Ctr., Sullivan Co.
18 Bailey Ave.
Claremont, NH 03743

Winnipesaukee Co.

Winnipesaukee Advocates for the
Mentally Ill
35 Ridgewood Ave.
Gilford, NH 03246

NEW JERSEY

Atlantic City

Atlantic Co. MH Family Support Group
c/o CCP
1125 Pacific Ave.
Atlantic City, NJ 08401

Bergen Co.

Family Organization of the Mid-Bergen
  Community MHC
11 Park Pl.
Paramus, NJ 07652

MH Advocacy Group
340 12th St.
Palisades Park, NJ 07650

Burlington Co.

Focus Mental Health
Delaware House
Wood and Pearl Sts.
Burlington, NJ 08016

FACE
P.O. Box 1322
Delran, NJ 08075

Camden Co.

Pioneers for Mental Health
19 E. Ormond Ave.
Cherry Hill, NJ 08034

Elizabeth

Concerned Citizens for Chronic
  Psychiatric Adults
27 Prince St.
Elizabeth, NJ 07208

Essex Co.

Concerned Families for Improved Mental
  Health Services
424 Main St.
E. Orange, NJ 07018

Middleton

Concerned Citizens for Chronic
  Psychiatric Adults
521 Hayward St.
Bound Brook, NJ 08805

Monmouth Co.

Schizophrenia Foundation of New Jersey
138-B West Amberly Dr.
Englishtown, NJ 07726

Ridgewood

West Bergen MHC
74 Oak St.
Ridgewood, NJ 07450

Salem Co.

TLC (Together, Learning, Coping) of
  Salem Co.
RD 2, Box 346
Woodstown, NJ 08098

TLC
52 Mahoney Rd.
Pennsville, NJ 08070

So. Amboy

Family and Friends of the MI
200 S. Feltus St., #35
So. Amboy, NJ 08879

NEW MEXICO

State Organization

State Alliance for Mental Illness, New
  Mexico (SAMI, NM)
819 Bishops Lodge Road
Santa Fe, NM 87501

Albuquerque

Community Alliance for Mental Health
12712 Mountain View, N.E.
Albuquerque, NM 87123

Santa Fe

Community Alliance for Mental Health
819 Bishops Lodge Rd.
Santa Fe, NM 87501

Silver City

Community Alliance for MH
P.O. Box 1827
Silver City, NM 88062

NEW YORK

State Organization

AMI of New York State
42 Elting Ave.
New Paltz, NY 12561

Albany

Relatives
920 Myrtle Ave.
Albany, NY 12208

Brooklyn

APRIL (Association of Parents for
   Rehabilitation and Independent Living)
75 Livingston St., #11A
Brooklyn, NY 11201

Friends United to Help the Mentally Ill
50 Nevins St.
Brooklyn, NY 11217

Cortland

REACH
17 Charles St.
Cortland, NY 13045

Dutchess/Ulster/Orange Co.

Mid-Hudson Chapter NAMI
Mill House
Marlboro, NY 12542

Erie Co.

REACH (MHA of Erie Co.)
1237 Delaware Ave.
Buffalo, NY 14209

Jamestown

Families As Partners
c/o Jamestown General Hospital
   Psychiatric Unit
Jamestown, NY 14701

Mt. Vernon

Families (Family Advocates of the
   Mentally Ill Linked in Encouragement
   and Support)
21 N. Terrace
Mt. Vernon, NY 10552

Nassau Co.

People Acting Together with Hope
   (PATH)
307 Lido Blvd.
Lido Beach, NY 11561

Caring Families of the Mentally Ill
11 Brook Ln.
Manhasset, NY 11030

Long Island Schizophrenia Association
1691 Northern Blvd.
Manhasset, NY 11030

Growth and Rehabilitation
   Advocates for the Mentally Ill
   (GRAML)
c/o Progress House
3095 Hempstead Tpke.
Levittown, NY 11756

Peninsula Counseling Center
League for the Advancement of MH
   Programs (LAMP)
124 Franklin Pl.
Woodmere, NY 11598

New York City

Friends and Advocates of the Mentally Ill
   (FAMI)
c/o HAI (Hospital Audience, Inc.)
220 W. 42nd St., 13th Fl.
New York, NY 10036

Friends of the Psychiatric Institute
722 W. 168th St.
New York, NY 10032

Manhattan State Citizens Group
350 E. 54th St.
New York, NY 10022

Niagara Co.

Niagara AMI
610 Sandlewood Dr.
Lewiston, NY 14092

Northern Westchester

Alliance for Mental Health of
  Northern Westchester
Box 275
Katonah, NY 10536

Onondaga Co.

Parents and Friends of the Mentally Ill
  Supporting Each Other (PROMISE)
c/o Transitional Living Service
423 W. Onandaga St.
Syracuse, NY 13202

Queens Co.

Long Island Regional Council, Inc.
  Federation of Parents Org. for NYS
  Mentally Disabled, Inc.
80-45 Winchester Blvd.
Queens Village, NY 11427

Concerned Citizens of Creedmore
P.O. Box 42
Queens Village, NY 11427

Rochester

Family and Friends of the Mentally Ill
  and Emotionally Disturbed
c/o Reformation Church
111 N. Chestnut St.
Rochester, NY 14605

Rockland Co.

The Family Support Group of
  Rockland Co.
10 Hester St.
Piermont, NY 10968

Saratoga Springs

Alliance for the Mentally Ill of Saratoga
  Springs (AMISS)
c/o T. M. Smith
15 Elizabeth Ln.
Saratoga Springs, NY 12866

Schenectady Co.

Schenectady Co. Relatives Group
1444 Dean St.
Schenectady, NY 12309

Suffolk Co.

Suffolk Relatives of NYS AMI
37 Hawthorne St.
Mt. Sinai, NY 11766

Sullivan Co.

Friends and Advocates for Mental Health
9 Maple St.
Liberty, NY 12754

Westchester Co.

Advocacy League for the Mentally Ill of
  Westchester (ALMI)
P.O. Box 1138
White Plains, NY 10602

NORTH CAROLINA

Cabarrus AMI
3807 Dakeita Circle
Concord, NC 28025

Greensboro AMI
P.O. Box 10557
Greensboro, NC 20704

NORTH DAKOTA

REACH
1113 10 St., N.W.
Minot, ND 58701

OHIO

State Organization

Ohio Family Coalition for the Mentally Ill
199 S. Central Ave.
Columbus, OH 43223

Allen Co.

Family Resource Centers
799 S. Main St.
Lima, OH 45804

Butler Co.

Families in Touch
c/o Mental Health Association of
  Butler Co.
111 Buckeye St.
Hamilton, OH 45011

Cincinnati

SOS–CAMI
P.O. Box 37004
Cincinnati, OH 45222

Dayton

Families in Touch
Mental Health Association
184 W. Salem Ave.
Dayton, OH 45406

Franklin Co.

Families in Touch
MHA of Franklin Co.
634 Wager St.
Columbus, OH 43206

Greene Co.

Families in Touch
Mental Health Association
130 W. Second St.
Xenia, OH 45385

Hancock Co.

REACH
Hancock Co. Mental Health Clinic
2515 N. Main St.
Findley, OH 45840

Lake Co.

Supportive Services for Mental Health
1657 Mentor Ave.
Painesville, OH 44077

Licking Co.

Families in Touch
Mental Health Association
65 Messimer Dr.
Newark, OH 43055

Northeastern

Northeast Ohio AMI
P.O. Box 217
Chagrin Falls, OH 44022

Summit Co.

Kevin Coleman MHC, Inc.
P.O. Box 724
275 Martinal Dr.
Kent, OH 44240

OKLAHOMA

REACH
5104 N. Francis, Suite B
Oklahoma City, OK 73118

OKLAHOMA

Families in Touch
MHA in Tulsa
5 W. 22nd St.
Tulsa, OK 74114

OREGON

State Organization

Oregon Alliance for Advocates of the
    Mentally Ill
P.O. Box 47
Thurston, OR 97482

Coos Co.

Family And Friends Support Group
Rt. 1, Box 1135
Bandon, OR 97411

Eugene

Save A Mind
2981 Willamette
Eugene, OR 97405

Florence

SOS (Save Our Sanity)
P.O. Box 821
Florence, OR 97439

Jackson Co.

Southern Oregon AMI (SOAMI)
P.O. Box 924
Medford, OR 97501

Josephine Co.

Options for Josephine Co.
202 N.W. A St.
Grants Pass, OR 97526

Linn Co.

Mid Valley AMI
3308 Southview Dr.
Albany, OR 97321

Marion/Polk Co.

PREMED
3324 Glen Creek Rd., N.W.
Salem, OR 97304

OREGON

Portland

AMI of Multnomah Co.
718 W. Burnside, #310
Portland, OR 97209

Homestreet
233 S.E. Sixth St.
Hillsboro, OR 97123

PENNSYLVANIA

State Organization

Pennsylvania AMI
840 Grandview Blvd.
Lancaster, PA 17601

Allegheny Co.

Peoples Oakland
231 Oakland Ave.
Pittsburgh, PA 15213

Bridgeville

Chartiers Family Support Group
437 Railroad St.
Bridgeville, PA 15017

Cumberland Co.

AMI Cumberland Co.
1110 Cocklin St.
Mechanicsburg, PA 17055

Eastern

Families Unite for Mental Health
Box 126
Oreland, PA 19075

Main Line Mental Health Group
582 Cricket Ln.
Radnor, PA 19087

Lancaster Co.

Threshold of Lancaster PA
41 Londonvale Rd.
Gordonville, PA 17529

Northeastern

Families and Friends for the Mentally Ill
504 Union St.
Peckville, PA 18452

Northern Allegheny Co.

Families of the Adult Mentally Ill
c/o Betty Holder
9361 N. Florence Rd.
Pittsburgh, PA 15237

Northwestern

Family Support for Mental Health
721 E. Grandview
Erie, PA 16504

Philadelphia

The Family and Friends Association of
   Norristown State Hospital
8008 Gilbert St.
Philadelphia, PA 19150

Pittsburgh

Families of the Adult Mentally Ill—Living,
   Interacting and Sharing (FAMILIAS)
1623 Denniston Ave.
Pittsburgh, PA 15217

Southwest Pittsburgh

Parents of the Adult Mentally Ill
2333 Los Angeles Ave.
Pittsburgh, PA 15216

University Park

Alliance for Families of the Mentally Ill,
   Rm. 112
Nursing Consultation Center,
Human Development East
Penn. State University
University Park, PA 16802

York Co.

Mental Illness Needs Devoted Support
   (MINDS)
RD 4, Box 942
Harrisburg, PA 17112

RHODE ISLAND

East Bay Advocates
c/o Alice L. Tupaj
19 Barney St.
Warren, RI 02885

Families and Advocates for the Mentally Ill
of Newport Co. (FAMI)
P.O. Box 837
Newport, RI 02840

MHA Project Reach Out
89 Park St.
Providence, RI 02908

SOUTH CAROLINA

Families and Friends of the Mentally Ill
P.O. Box 32084
Charleston, SC 29417

Mid-Carolina FFMI
P.O. Box 61075
Columbia, SC 29260

Piedmont Family and Friends of the
Mentally Ill
112 Robin St.
Clemson, SC 29631

SOUTH DAKOTA

Northeastern MHC Family Support Group
703 3rd Ave., S.E. Box 550
Aberdeen, SD 57401

Brookings Area MHA
Box 273
Brookings, SD 57006

Sioux Falls REACH
P.O. Box 618
Sioux Falls, SD 57101

TENNESSEE

Hamilton Co.

Mental Health Association of Hamilton
Co./Families in Touch
921 E. Third St.
Chattanooga, TN 37403

Knox Co.

Families in Touch
c/o Mental Health Association of Knox
Co.
6712 Kingston Pike
Knoxville, TN 37919

Memphis

AMI of Memphis
P.O. Box 17304
Memphis, TN 38187-0304

Nashville

Families in Touch
c/o MHA in Nashville
250 Venture Cir., #204
Nashville, TN 37228

TEXAS

Dallas

Dallas Alliance for Mental Recovery, Inc.
P.O. Box 816264
Dallas, TX 75381

Houston

Alliance for Mental Recovery
4415 Breakwood
Houston, TX 77096

Citizens for Human Development
2123 Oak Creek
Houston, TX 77017

Friends of Pyramid House and the
Houston Lodge, Inc.
3904 Austin
Houston, TX 77004

San Antonio

Reclamation, Inc. (Former Patients'
Group)
2502 Waterford
San Antonio, TX 78217

Victoria

Victoria Alliance for Mental Recovery
702 Kelly Crick
Victoria, TX 77904

UTAH

Utah Alliance for the Mentally Ill Salt
Lake City Chapter
P.O. Box 26561
Salt Lake City, UT 84126

AMI, Ogden
P.O. Box 1427
Ogden, UT 84402

VERMONT

AMI, Vermont
9 Andrews Ave.
So. Burlington, VT 05401

VIRGIN ISLANDS

St. Croix Concerned Citizens for Mental
  Health, Inc.
P.O. Box 937, Kings Hill
St. Croix, VI 00850

VIRGINIA

Augusta Co.

We Care
1245 Chatham Road
Waynesboro, VA 22980

Charlottesville

Blue Ridge Family Alliance for the
  Mentally Ill
1602 Gordon Ave.
Charlottesville, VA 22903

Farmville

Southside Affiliate—Town House Friends
127 North St.
Farmville, VA 23901

Harrisonburg

Massanutten Family Support Group
276 W. Market St.
Harrisonburg, VA 22801

Norfolk

Norfolk Community Services Board
201 Granby Mall, Suite 103
Norfolk, VA 23510

Northern

Pathways to Independence
P.O. Box 651
McLean, VA 22101

Northwestern

Northwestern VA Family Support Group
  for the Mentally Ill
315 Wood Ave.
Winchester, VA 22601

Richmond

Richmond Area Schizophrenia
  Foundation (RASF)
4010 W. Franklin St.
Richmond, VA 23221

Virginia Beach

Schizophrenia Foundation of VA
Box 2342
Virginia Beach, VA 23450

WASHINGTON

State Organization

Washington State Coalition of Family
  Assoc.
906 E. Shelby
Seattle, WA 98102

Bainbridge Island

Bainbridge Island Advocates for the
  Mentally Ill
c/o Helpline House
282 Knechtel Way
Bainbridge Island, WA 98110

Benton/Franklin Co.

Tri-Cities Advocates for the Mentally Ill
P.O. Box 1135
Richland, WA 99352

Clallum Co.

Peninsula Advocates for the Mentally Ill
  (PAMI)
87 Garden Club Rd.
Nordland, WA 98358

Clark Co.

Clark AMI
P.O. Box 5353
Vancouver, WA 98668

Cowlitz Co.

Cowlitz AMI
P.O. Box 385
Kelso, WA 98626

Eastern

Spokane AMI
P.O. Box 141141
Spokane, WA 99214

Ft. Steilacoom

Citizens' Guild of Western State Hosp.
P.O. Box 94999
Ft. Steilacoom, WA 98494

King Co.

Washington Advocates for the
    Mentally III
119 N. 85th
Seattle, WA 98103

Pierce Co.

Family Action for the Seriously
    Emotionally Disturbed (FASED)
P.O. Box 297
Puyallop, WA 98371

Seattle

Well Mind Association
4649 Sunnyside Ave. N.
Seattle, WA 98103

Snohomish Co.

SnoAmi/Snohomish Co. Advocates for
    the Mentally III
4526 Federal Way, P.O. Box 2484
Everett, WA 98203

Yakima Co.

Yakima Advocates for the Mentally III
217 N. 25th Ave.
Yakima, WA 98902

WEST VIRGINIA

Charleston AMI (CHAMI)
5453 Kingswood Ln.
Charleston, WV 25313

AMI of Eastern Panhandle
404 Edgemont Ter.
Martinsburg, WV 25401

WISCONSIN

State Organization

AMI of Wisconsin, Inc.
Rt. 8, 1997 Hwy. PB
Verona, WI 53593

Ashland

AMI of Chequameson Bay
Rt. 3, Box 237
Ashland, WI 54806

Central

AMI of Central Wisconsin
1120 Third St.
Port Edwards, WI 54469

Dane Co.

AMI of Dane Co.
P.O. Box 1502
Madison, WI 53701

Eau Claire

AMI of Eau Claire
RR 2, Box 267A
Mondovi, WI 54755

Fond du Lac Co.

AMI of Fond du Lac
P.O. Box 1007
Fond du Lac, WI 54935

Green Bay

AMI of Brown Co.
1024 Mt. Mary Dr.
Green Bay, WI 54302

La Crosse Co.

AMI of La Crosse County
4062 Terrace Dr.
La Crosse, WI 54601

Marathon Co.

AMI of Marathon Co.
201 N. 7th Ave.
Wausau, WI 54401

Marinette

AMI of Marinette
1428 Mary St.
Marinette, WI 54143

Manitowoc Co.

AMI of Manitowoc Co.
3505 Schroeder Dr.
Manitowoc, WI 54220

WISCONSIN

Milwaukee Co.

AMI of Greater Milwaukee
4011 W. Capitol Dr., P.O. Box 16819
Milwaukee, WI 53216

Oshkosh

Fox Valley AMI
4995 Pickett Rd.
Pickett, WI 54964

Outagamie Co.

AMI of Outagamie Co.
811 E. Pershing St.
Appleton, WI 54912

Racine Co.

AMI of Racine Co.
P.O. Box 5202
Racine, WI 53405

Rock Co.

AMI of Rock Co., Inc.
Box 842
Janesville, WI 53545

Sheboygan Co.

AMI of Sheboygan Co.
Box 731
Elkhart Lake, WI 53020

Waukesha Co.

AMI of Waukesha Co.
1307 Mariner Dr.
Hartland, WI 53029

WYOMING

Wyoming AMI
845 S. Grant St.
Casper, Wyoming 82601

CANADA

National Organization

Canadian Friends of Schizophrenics
95 Barber Greene Rd., #309
Don Mills, Ontario M3C 3E9

Alberta

Alberta Friends of Schizophrenics
3802 16 A St., S.W.
Calgary, Alberta T2T 4K7

British Columbia

British Columbia Friends of
 Schizophrenics
1441 Denise Pl.
Port Coquitlam, British Columbia
 V3C 2W1

Manitoba

Manitoba Friends of Schizophrenics
330 Edmonton St.
Winnipeg, Manitoba R3B 2L2

Nova Scotia

Nova Scotia Friends of Schizophrenics
P.O. Box 178
Mount Uniacke, Nova Scotia BON 1Z0

Newfoundland

Newfoundland Friends of
 Schizophrenics
Department of Social Work, Waterford
 Hospital
Waterford Bridge Rd.
St. John's, Newfoundland A1E 4J8

Ontario

Ontario Friends of Schizophrenics
112 St. Clair Ave. W., Suite 401
Toronto, Ontario M4V 2Y3

Quebec

Association of Relatives and
 Friends of the Mentally and
 Emotionally Ill
P.O. Box 322, Snowden Branch
Montreal, Quebec H3X 3T6

Saskatchewan

Saskatchewan Friends of
 Schizophrenics
4311 Pasqua St.
Regina, Saskatchewan S4S 6C1

RECOMMENDED FURTHER READING:
AN ANNOTATED BIBLIOGRAPHY

Amidst the many books and articles written about schizophrenia, there are a few which are particularly helpful. Together they form the nucleus of a library for those interested in this disease. The books can be found in the medical library of large hospitals or medical schools or purchased through a local bookstore. The articles in professional journals may be found in the medical libraries.

Anderson, J. R. "Social Security and SSI Benefits for the Mentally Disabled." *Hospital and Community Psychiatry* 33 (1982): 295–98.
This is an excellent description of the SSI application and appeals process.

Anti-Stigma: Improving Public Understanding of Mental Illness. Washington, D.C.: National Alliance for the Mentally Ill, 1982.
The handbook is helpful for those working with the media in order to decrease the stigma of schizophrenia and other mental illnesses.

Appleton, W. S. "Mistreatment of Patients' Families by Psychiatrists." *American Journal of Psychiatry* 131 (1974): 655–57.
This unique account by a psychiatrist tells how psychiatrists cause damage by blaming family members for causing schizophrenia.

Awakenings: Organizing a Support/Advocacy Group. Washington, D.C.: National Alliance for the Mentally Ill, 1982.
The pamphlet outlines steps which can be used to form a support and advocacy group for families of schizophrenic patients.

Bassuk, E. L., and S. Gerson. "Deinstitutionalization and Mental Health Services." *Scientific American* 238 (1978): 46–53.
This is a complete review of the rise and fall of Community Mental Health Centers and the origins of deinstitutionalization. It puts contemporary changes into historical perspective and is not an optimistic article.

Bernheim, K. F., and R. R. J. Lewine. *Schizophrenia: Symptoms, Causes, Treatments.* New York: Norton, 1979.
This is a more useful book than the similar one by O'Brien as it is more complete and better written. It is well organized and worth having as a reference. It is, however, current only to 1977.

Bernheim, K. F., R. R. J. Lewine, C. T. Beale. *The Caring Family: Living with Chronic Mental Illness.* New York: Random House, 1982.

The strengths of the book are its discussion of the emotions faced by families with chronic mental illness and practical suggestions on how to cope and respond. Its weaknesses are its paucity of factual data and its attempt to group all chronic mental conditions (alcoholism, severe anxiety, schizophrenia) into a single entity.

Biological Therapies in Psychiatry Newsletter. Subscriptions from PSG, Inc., 545 Great Rd., Littleton, MA 01460.

A monthly newsletter from the Department of Psychiatry of the Massachusetts General Hospital, it provides accurate and current assessments of medications for schizophrenic patients and is the easiest way to stay up-to-date in this rapidly changing area.

Budson, R. D. *The Psychiatric Halfway House.* Pittsburgh: Univ. of Pittsburgh Press, 1978.

This is a useful account of how to set up halfway houses for the mentally ill and the problems which must be solved.

Chapman, J. "The Early Symptoms of Schizophrenia." *British Journal of Psychiatry* 112 (1966): 225–51.

This article contains a useful description of the early symptoms frequently encountered in schizophrenia.

Chodoff, P. "The Case for Involuntary Hospitalization of the Mentally Ill." *American Journal of Psychiatry* 133 (1976): 496–501.

This is the best recent summary of reasons why involuntary commitment laws should be retained and what purpose they serve.

Creer, C., and J. Wing. *Schizophrenia at Home.* London: Institute of Psychiatry, 1974. (National Schizophrenia Fellowship, 78/79 Victoria Road, Surbiton, Surrey, England KT6–4NS).

A summary of interviews with eighty families with a schizophrenic member, it also describes major problems encountered.

Davis, J. M. "Overview: Maintenance Therapy in Psychiatry. I. Schizophrenia." *American Journal of Psychiatry* 132 (1975): 1237–45.

This is the best summary of studies showing the importance of continuing maintenance medications for schizophrenic persons, and an analysis of relapse rates when the medication is stopped.

Ennis, B. J., and R. D. Emery. *The Rights of Mental Patients.* An American Civil Liberties Union Handbook. New York: Avon Books, 1978.

Although the authors are strongly opposed to involuntary hospitalization, this handbook provides much useful information on patients' rights and how these rights can be protected. It is also a useful book for lawyers working with the mentally ill.

Gottesman, I. I., and J. Shields. *Schizophrenia: The Epigenetic Puzzle.* New York: Cambridge University Press, 1982.

A summary of genetic theories and data, it assumes some background in biology and genetics.

Guide for Legislative Action. Washington, D.C.: National Alliance for the Mentally Ill, 1982.

The handbook explains the legislative process and how effective lobbying can be undertaken, with examples for action at both the local and the federal level.

Hatfield, A. *Coping with Mental Illness in the Family: The Family Guide.* Mimeo. Washington, D.C.: National Alliance for the Mentally Ill, 1982. Course outline and material for six two-hour educational seminars for families. The purpose of the course "is to help families develop the knowledge and skills which will enable them to cope with severely mentally ill persons."

Hatfield, A. "Psychological Costs of Schizophrenia to the Family." *Social Work* 23 (1978): 355–59. This is an interesting report of research in which families were asked to describe the personal problems they encountered in caring for someone seriously mentally ill.

Henn. F. A., and H. A. Nasrallah, eds. *Schizophrenia as a Brain Disease.* New York: Oxford University Press, 1982.

This is a collection of papers presented at a 1980 conference on this subject. It is intended to be a psychiatric textbook and is therefore reasonably technical, but can be read by persons with some background in the biological sciences. It is a good summary of what was known as of 1980.

Johnson, S. G. "My Brother John." *Ladies' Home Journal* 99 (January 1982): 36–127.

This is a poignant, heroic, but somewhat unrealistic account of a woman who took her chronic schizophrenic brother home from the state hospital to live with her and tried to deinstitutionalize him.

Kaplan, B., ed. *The Inner World of Mental Illness.* New York: Harper & Row, 1964.

Like all such collections, the quality of the excerpts from many personal accounts of madness is varied, but many of the accounts are excellent.

Lamb, H. R., and Associates. *Community Survival for Long-Term Patients.* San Francisco: Jossey-Bass, 1976.

Dr. Lamb has been a leader in creating community facilities for schizophrenic patients. This book reflects the vast experience of the authors.

Living with Schizophrenia—By the Relatives. Surbiton, Surrey: National Schizophrenia Fellowship, 1974.

This is a compilation of accounts from family members of what it is like to live with a schizophrenic person.

McGhie, A., and J. Chapman. "Disorders of Attention and Perception in Early Schizophrenia." *British Journal of Medical Psychology* 34 (1961): 103–16.

> The symptoms experienced by many schizophrenic patients are analyzed in a succinct and clear manner.

Mendel, W. M. *Schizophrenia: The Experience and Its Treatment.* San Francisco: Jossey-Bass, 1976.

> Dr. Mendel has dedicated his entire career to caring for schizophrenics. Although the book is now dated, anything Dr. Mendel writes is worth reading.

Mental Disability Law Reporter. Subscriptions from American Bar Association, 1800 M St., N.W. Washington, D.C. 20036.

> This bimonthly journal is published by the Commission on the Mentally Disabled of the American Bar Association. It contains a good analysis of rapidly changing mental health laws.

O'Brien, P. *The Disordered Mind: What We Now Know about Schizophrenia.* Englewood Cliffs, N.J.: Prentice-Hall, 1978.

> A general book on schizophrenia, it is uneven but moderately useful. In some areas it is too simple for most lay readers and in other places too complex.

Park, C. C., and L. N. Shapiro. *You Are Not Alone.* Boston: Little, Brown, 1976.

> This is an encyclopedia of useful information for families of the mentally ill. The book does not focus on schizophrenia exclusively but is an invaluable reference and is well written for a lay audience.

"Returning the Mentally Disabled to the Community: Government Needs to Do More." Report to the Congress by the Comptroller General of the United States (G.A.O. Report). Washington, D.C.: General Accounting Office, 1977.

> Although written in government bureaucratese, it affords a good overview of the failure to provide adequate aftercare for released mental patients.

Rollin, Henry, ed. *Coping with Schizophrenia.* National Schizophrenia Fellowship. London: Burnett Books, 1980.

> This book brings together several previously published pamphlets by the National Schizophrenia Fellowship with some new material. The chapters "Schizophrenia from Within" and "Schizophrenia at Home" are especially good and will be very useful to families of patients with this disease. The ten-year history and exciting work done by the National Schizophrenia Fellowship in England is summarized in the last chapter and offers many ideas which could be utilized in the United States.

Roth, L. H. "A Commitment Law for Patients, Doctors, and Lawyers." *American Journal of Psychiatry* 136 (1979): 1121–27.

This is an interesting proposal for resolving the conflicting necessity for involuntary hospitalization and the rights of persons to remain at liberty.

Schizophrenia Bulletin. Subscriptions from U.S. Government Printing Office, Washington, D.C. 20402.

This quarterly journal is devoted exclusively to schizophrenia treatment and research and written for mental health professionals. It is the most relevant psychiatric journal for persons interested in schizophrenia, although frequent articles of interest also appear in the *Archives of General Psychiatry, British Journal of Psychiatry, Hospital and Community Psychiatry,* and *American Journal of Psychiatry.*

Sechehaye, M. *Autobiography of a Schizophrenic Girl.* New York: Grune & Stratton, 1951. Paperback by New American Library.

Even in translation from French, this is the single best account of what it is like to be schizophrenic. But Part 2 of the book, a psychoanalytic interpretation of the woman's symptoms, should be skipped.

Sheehan, S. *Is There No Place on Earth for Me?* Boston: Houghton Mifflin, 1982.

This is Susan Sheehan's superb 1981 study which originally appeared in *The New Yorker* magazine. It provides the best description available of the course of a chronic schizophrenic illness, the difficulties encountered by a person with this disease, the frustrations for the family, and the mediocre care available at the state hospital. It is searingly accurate and mandatory reading for anyone who wants to understand the tragedy of this disease. The patient described has the schizoaffective subtype.

Siegler, M., and H. Osmond. *Models of Madness, Models of Medicine.* New York: Macmillan, 1974.

The authors of this lucid analysis of the theoretical models for schizophrenia and other mental diseases deal specifically with the psychoanalytic, social, family interaction, conspiratorial, moral and medical models of schizophrenia and show how the medical model best fits both the facts and common sense.

Stein, L. I., and M. A. Test, eds. *Alternatives to Mental Hospital Treatment.* New York: Plenum, 1978.

This is a collection of descriptions of effective programs for treating schizophrenics in the community and providing aftercare.

Talbott, J. A. *The Death of the Asylum: A Critical Study of State Hospital Management, Services and Care.* New York: Grune & Stratton, 1978.

The author gives a thoughtful analysis of why the state hospitals fail to work and suggestions for reform.

Talbott, J. A., ed. *The Chronic Mentally Ill: Treatment, Programs, Systems.*
New York: Human Sciences Press, 1981.

This is a collection of descriptions of "model" programs for the chronic
mentally ill. It is the best book of its kind, but discouraging in that many
of the "models" are not much as models. This is an accurate reflection
of the state of the art.

Talbott, J. A., ed. *The Chronic Mental Patient.* Washington: American Psychiatric Association, 1978.

This is a compilation of study papers by the APA Ad Hoc Committee on
the Chronic Mental Patient. Many of them reflect the association's inability to do anything useful for schizophrenic patients, but some provide
helpful background data. Dr. Kenneth Minkoff's chapter, "A Map of the
Chronic Mental Patient," is excellent.

Taylor, R. L. *Mind or Body: Distinguishing Psychological from Organic Disorders.* New York: McGraw-Hill, 1982.

This useful manual for distinguishing brain diseases which may mimic
schizophrenia is especially recommended for mental health workers, psychologists, social workers, and psychiatric nurses.

Torrey, E. F. *Schizophrenia and Civilization.* New York: Jason Aronson, 1980.

The history and prevalence of schizophrenia is described in detail.

Tsuang, M. T. *Schizophrenia: The Facts.* New York: Oxford University Press,
1982.

A useful, concise overview with appropriate emphasis on the biological
approach and the exoneration of families as causal agents, it is, however, frequently too brief, is poorly organized and is only current through
1978.

Wasow, M. *Coping with Schizophrenia: A Survival Manual for Parents, Relatives and Friends.* Palo Alto: Science and Behavior Books, 1982.

The opening chapter is a moving account of the illness of the author's son.
After that the book becomes disorganized; for example, medications are
in chapter 4 but treatment in chapter 8. Despite this, the book is worth
buying for its common sense and compassion.

Wechsler, J. A. *In a Darkness.* New York: Norton, 1972. Out of print.

An articulate and poignant account by the parents of a schizophrenic son,
it recounts ten years of searching for therapists and a cure, for some
understanding, and of the chaos in the family caused by the schizophrenia. The agony of not knowing what to do is exceeded only by the pain
of the son's suicide in the end.

Wender, P. H., and D. F. Klein. *Mind, Mood and Medicine: A Guide to the
New Biopsychiatry.* New York: Farrar, Straus & Giroux, 1981.

An overview of schizophrenia and other mental illnesses, the book provides a particularly helpful perspective on recent advances in drug ther-

apy. The biological causes of schizophrenia are assumed and discussed. The authors are two of the foremost researchers in psychiatry.

Wilson, L. *This Stranger, My Son.* New York: Putnam, 1968. Paperback by New American Library.

A mother's account of raising a schizophrenic son who becomes sick in early childhood, it is especially good in describing the guilt and shame of a parent who is told by the mental health professionals that she is to blame.

Vine, P. *Families in Pain: Children, Siblings, Spouses, and Parents of the Mentally Ill Speak Out.* New York: Pantheon, 1982.

This book provides useful case histories which clearly describe the effects of schizophrenia (and other serious mental illnesses) on the patients' families. Its limitations are its loose, rambling style and its paucity of factual material.

NOTES

CHAPTER 1: OUT OF THE CLOSET

"There are as many schizophrenics": *Report of the President's Commission on Mental Health* (Washington, D.C.: U.S. Government Printing Office, 1978), 4: 1692. "one of the most sinister": L. Wilson, *This Stranger, My Son* (New York: Putnam, 1968), p. 174. another 100,000 Americans: The estimates of the incidence and prevalence of schizophrenia are from *Report of the President's Commission on Mental Health* 2:19 and 4: 1691–92. "The care and treatment": J. A. Talbott, *The Death of the Asylum* (New York: Grune & Stratton, 1978), p. 2. M. Vonnegut, "Why I Want to Bite R. D. Laing," *Harper's* 248 (1974): 90–92. ten and twenty billion dollars: J. G. Gunderson and L. R. Mosher, "The Cost of Schizophrenia," *American Journal of Psychiatry* 132 (1975): 901.

CHAPTER 2: THE INNER WORLD OF MADNESS

"What then does": H. R. Rollin, *Coping with Schizophrenia* (London: Burnett Books, 1980), p. 162. R. W. Emerson, *Journals* (1836). I Never Promised You a Rose Garden: See C. North and R. Cadoret, "Diagnostic Discrepancy in Personal Accounts of Patients with 'Schizophrenia,'" *Archives of General Psychiatry* 38 (1981): 133–37. "The Tell-Tale Heart" (1843). "During the last": A. McGhie and J. Chapman, "Disorders of Attention and Perception in Early Schizophrenia," *Brit-*ish *Journal of Medical Psychology* 34 (1961): 103–16. "Colours seem": Ibid. "These crises": M. Sechehaye, *Autobiography of a Schizophrenic Girl* (New York: Grune & Stratton, 1951), p. 22. "Everything seems": McGhie and Chapman. "Occasionally during": Anonymous, "An Autobiography of a Schizophrenic Experience," *Journal of Abnormal and Social Psychology* 51 (1955): 677–89. "I can probably": M. Vonnegut, *The Eden Express* (New York: Praeger, 1975), p. 107. "In these disturbing": Sechehaye, p. 24. "Had someone asked": Vonnegut, p. 107. "Sometimes when people": McGhie and Chapman.

"it was terrible": M. Barnes and J. Berke, *Mary Barnes: Two Accounts of a Journey Through Madness* (New York: Ballantine, 1973), p. 44. "decay in my": Rollins, p. 150. "a genital sexual": Ibid, p. 150. One psychiatrist: See M. B. Bowers, *Retreat from Sanity: The Structure of Emerging Psychosis* (Baltimore: Penguin, 1974). "My trouble is" and "My concentration is": McGhie and Chapman. "Childhood feelings": Bowers, p. 152. "All sorts of": W. Mayer-Gross, E. Slater, and M. Roth, *Clinical Psychiatry* (Baltimore: Williams & Wilkins, 1969), p. 268. "I was invited": A. Boisen, *Out of the Depths* 1960. Quoted in B. Kaplan, ed., *The Inner World of Mental Illness* (New York: Harper & Row, 1964), p. 118. "Fear made me": Sechehaye, p. 26. "Suddenly my whole": M. Coate, *Beyond All Reason* (Philadelphia: J. B. Lippincott,

1965), p. 21. **"Before last week"**: Bowers, p. 27. **"A few weeks"**: Anonymous, "Schizophrenic Experience." **"as if a heavy"**: B. J. Freedman, "The Subjective Experience of Perceptual and Cognitive Disturbances in Schizophrenia," *Archives of General Psychiatry* 30 (1974): 333–40. **"However hard"**: Rollins, p. 150. **Decreased pain perception**: See W. E. Marchand et al., "Occurrence of Painless Acute Surgical Disorder in Psychotic Patients," *New England Journal of Medicine* 260 (1959): 580–85; N. Geschwind, "Insensitivity to Pain in Psychotic Patients," *New England Journal of Medicine* 296 (1977): 1480; E. F. Torrey, "Headaches after Lumbar Puncture and Insensitivity to Pain in Psychiatric Patients," *New England Journal of Medicine* 301 (1979): 110; and G. D. Watson, P. C. Chandarana, and H. Merskey, "Relationship Between Pain and Schizophrenia," *British Journal of Psychiatry* 138 (1981): 33–36. **"At first it"**: N. McDonald, "Living with Schizophrenia," *Canadian Medical Association Journal* 82 (1960): 218–21, 678–81.

"When people are": McGhie and Chapman. **"I can concentrate"**: Ibid. **"I have to"**: J. Chapman, "The Early Symptoms of Schizophrenia," *British Journal of Psychiatry* 112 (1966): 225–51. **"Everything is in"**: McGhie and Chapman. **"the teeth, then"**: Sechehaye, foreword. **"I can't concentrate"**: McGhie and Chapman. **"I tried sitting"**: B. O'Brien, *Operators and Things: The Inner Life of a Schizophrenic* (New York: Signet, 1976), pp. 97–98. **"During the visit"**: Sechehaye, p. 28. **"If I do"**: Chapman. **"My thoughts get"**: McGhie and Chapman. **" 'Sun,' I intoned"**: Peters (1949), quoted in C. Landis and F. A. Mettler, *Varieties of Psychopathological Experience* (New York: Holt, Rinehart & Winston, 1964), p. 160. **"I am not"**: Nijinsky, quoted in Kaplan, p. 424. **"How could a"**: O'Brien, p. 100. **"I was extremely"**: Sechehaye, pp. 66–67. **"I had no"**: Peters, quoted in Landis and Mettler, p. 160. **"The worst thing"**: Chapman. **"I am glad" and "I feel that"**: Mayer-Gross, Slater, and Roth, pp. 281, 267. **"For instance, I"**: G. Bateson, ed., *Perceval's Narrative: A Patient's Account of His*

Psychosis 1830–1832 (1838, 1840) (New York: Morrow, 1974), p. 269. **"I may be"**: McGhie and Chapman. **"If I am"**: Ibid. **Chapman claims**: See Chapman. **"Why did she"**: R. M. Rilke, *The Notebooks of Malte Laurids Brigge* (1910) (New York: Norton, 1949), p. 42.

"In the morning": A. Chekhov, "Ward No. 6," quoted in A. A. Stone and S. S. Stone, eds., *The Abnormal Personality Through Literature* (Englewood Cliffs, N.J.: Prentice-Hall, 1966), p. 5. **"I got up"**: Bowers, pp. 186–87. **"I should emphasize"**: Sechehaye, p. 25. **"During the paranoid"**: Anonymous, "Schizophrenic Experience." **"I felt that"**: Ibid. **"telepathic force"**: Rollins, p. 132.

"I like talking": Chapman. **"I was sitting"**: Ibid. **"One day we"**: Sechehaye, p. 20. **"This phenomenon can"**: J. Lang, "The Other Side of Hallucinations," *American Journal of Psychiatry* 94 (1938): 1090–97. **"No doubt I"**: Poe. **"Thus for years"**: D. P. Schreber, *Memoirs of My Nervous Illness*, (1903), translated and with introduction by I. Macalpine and R. A. Hunter (London: William Dawson & Sons, 1955), p. 172. **"The voices"**: *Perceval's Narrative*, quoted in Landis and Mettler, p. 122. **"There was music"**: Boisen, quoted in Kaplan, p. 119. **"For about almost"**: Schreber, p. 225. **Julian Jaynes**: See *The Origin of Consciousness in the Breakdown of the Bicameral Mind* (Boston: Houghton Mifflin, 1976). **"At an early"**: Lang. **"On a few"**: Ibid. **"During the time"**: Bowers. p. 37. **"To the person"**: Lang. **"I was present"**: Sechehaye, pp. 80–81. **"Sometimes I did"**: Ibid, pp. 87–88. **"I saw myself"**: Coate, pp. 66–67. **"I get shaky"**: Chapman. **"This was equally"**: Sechehaye, p. 87. **"My breast gives"**: Schreber, p. 207. **"Now it was"**: Rilke, p. 59. **"During the first"**: J. Lang, "The Other Side of the Affective Aspects of Schizophrenia," *Psychiatry* 2 (1939): 195–202.

"Later, considering them": Sechehaye, p. 35. **"I am lying"**: Rilke, pp. 60–61. **"Half the time"**: McGhie and Chapman. **"one of the"**: Chapman. **"During my first"**: Anonymous, "Schizophrenic Experiences." **"Instead of wishing"**: E. Meyer and L. Covi, "The Experience of

Depersonalization: A Written Report by a Patient," *Psychiatry* 23 (1960): 215–17. **"I wish I":** J. A. Wechsler, *In a Darkness* (New York: Norton, 1972), p. 17. **"When I am":** McGhie and Chapman. **"I don't like":** Ibid. **"Everything is all":** Chapman. **"I get stuck":** McGhie and Chapman. **"My responses are":** Ibid. **"I am not":** Ibid. **"As a matter":** Sechehaye, pp. 40–41. **"As the work":** Kindwall and Kinder (1940), quoted in Landis and Mettler, p. 530. **"The state of":** Sechehaye, pp. 61–62. **"to help to":** Chapman. **"There were two":** *Perceval's Narrative,* quoted in Kaplan, p. 240. **Chapman believes:** Chapman. **One study found:** T. C. Manschreck et al., "Disturbed Voluntary Motor Activity in Schizophrenic Disorder," *Psychological Medicine* 12 (1982): 73–84; see also M. Jones and R. Hunter, "Abnormal Movements in Patients with Chronic Psychotic Illness, in G. E. Crane and R. Gardner, *Psychotropic Drugs and Dysfunctions of the Basal Ganglia,* Publication No. 1938 (Washington: U.S. Public Health Service, 1969). **eye blinking:** See J. R. Stevens, "Eye Blink and Schizophrenia: Psychosis or Tardive Dyskinesia," *American Journal of Psychiatry* 135 (1978): 223–26. **"[He] stood":** H. de Balzac, *Louis Lambert* (1832), in A. A. Stone and S. S. Stone, eds., *The Abnormal Personality Through Literature* (Englewood Cliffs, N.J.: Prentice-Hall, 1966), pp. 63–64. **"My feelings about":** Anonymous, "Schizoprenic Experiences." **Schreber:** P. 146. **"No doubt Louis":** Balzac.

CHAPTER 3: WHAT SCHIZOPHRENIA IS AND WHAT IT IS NOT

"For me, madness": M. Sechehaye, *Autobiography of a Schizophrenic Girl* (New York: Grune & Stratton, 1951), p. 33. **Studies have shown:** C. S. Mellor, "First Rank Symptoms of Schizophrenia," *British Journal of Psychiatry* 117 (1970): 15–23. **patients with manic-depressive illness:** W. T. Carpenter, J. S. Strauss, and S. Muleh, "Are There Pathognomonic Symptoms in Schizophrenia?" *Archives of General Psychiatry* 28 (1973): 847–852. **DSM-III:** *Diagnostic and Statistical Manual of Mental Disorders* (Washington, D.C.: American Psychiatric Association, 1980). **Rosenhan study:** D. L. Rosenhan, "On Being Sane in Insane Places," *Science* 179 (1973): 250–58; see also R. L. Spitzer, "More on Pseudoscience in Science and the Case for Psychiatric Diagnosis," *Archives of General Psychiatry* 33 (1976): 459–70. **"If I were":** S. S. Kety, "From Rationalization to Reason," *American Journal of Psychiatry* 131 (1974): 957–63. **Paranoid schizophrenia:** For a review see K. S. Kendler and K. L. Davis, "The Genetics and Biochemistry of Paranoid Schizophrenia and Other Paranoid Psychoses," *Schizophrenia Bulletin* 7 (1981): 689–709; there are other related articles in the same issue. **Soviet system of classification . . .:** See J. Holland and I. V. Shakhmatova-Pavlova, "Concept and Classification of Schizophrenia in the Soviet Union," *Schizophrenia Bulletin* 3 (1977): 277–87. **Many clinicians and researchers:** See M. T. Tsuang et al., "A Family History Study of Schizoaffective Disorder," *Biological Psychiatry* 12 (1977): 331–38; M. T. Tsuang, "Schizoaffective Disorder," *Archives of General Psychiatry* 36 (1979): 633–34. **One study:** E. F. Torrey, S. P. Hersh, and K. D. McCabe, "Early Childhood Psychosis and Bleeding During Pregnancy," *Journal of Autism and Childhood Schizophrenia* 5 (1975): 287–97. **L. Wilson,** *This Stranger, My Son* (New York: Putnam, 1968).

Mind or Body: (New York: McGraw-Hill, 1982). **"Primary psychopathy":** H. J. Eysenck, *Crime and Personality* (London: Routledge & Kegan Paul, 1964), p. 57. **Schizotypal personalities:** See J. R. Brinkley, B. D. Beitman, and R. O. Friedel, "Low-Dose Neuroleptic Regimens in the Treatment of Borderline Patients," *Archives of General Psychiatry* 36 (1979): 319–26; and S. S. Kety et al., "The Biologic and Adoptive Families of Adopted Individuals Who Became Schizophrenic: Prevalence of Mental Illness and Other Characteristics," in L. C. Wynne, R. L. Cromwell, and S. Matthysse, *The Nature of Schizophrenia* (New York: Wiley, 1978). **Abuse of schizophrenia label in Soviet Union:** See W. Reich,

"The Spectrum Concept of Schizophrenia," *Archives of General Psychiatry* 32 (1975): 489–98. **one study has suggested:** J. L. Karlson, "Genetic Association of Giftedness and Creativity with Schizophrenia," *Hereditas* 66 (1970): 177. **creativity and schizophrenia:** See J. A. Keefe and P. A. Magaro, "Creativity and Schizophrenia: An Equivalence of Cognitive Processing," *Journal of Abnormal Psychology* 89 (1980): 390–98; and M. Dykes and A. McGhie, "A Comparative Study of Attentional Strategies of Schizophrenic and Highly Creative Normal Subjects," *British Journal of Psychiatry* 128 (1976): 50–56.

CHAPTER 4: THE THREE COURSES OF SCHIZOPHRENIA

"Being crazy": T. Hennell, *The Witnesses,* quoted in C. Landis and F. A. Mettler, *Varieties of Psychopathological Experience* (New York: Holt, Rinehart & Winston, 1964), p. 431. **Age of onset:** . . . Recent discussions of this issue include R. R. J. Lewine, "Sex Differences in Schizophrenia: Timing or Subtypes," *Psychological Bulletin* 90 (1981): 432–44; R. R. J. Lewine, J. S. Strauss, and T. E. Gift, "Sex Differences in Age at First Hospital Admission for Schizophrenia: Fact or Artifact?" *American Journal of Psychiatry* 138 (1981): 440–44; E. Zigler and J. Levine, "Age of First Hospitalization of Schizophrenics: A Developmental Approach," *Journal of Abnormal Psychology* 90 (1981): 458–67; R. R. J. Lewine, "Sex Differences in Age of Symptom Onset and First Hospitalization in Schizophrenia," *American Journal of Orthopsychiatry* 50 (1980): 316–22. **summary of possible courses:** J. H. Stephens, "Long-term Prognosis and Follow-up in Schizophrenia," *Schizophrenia Bulletin* 4 (1978): 25–47. **"The patient":** W. Mayer-Gross, E. Slater, and M. Roth, *Clinical Psychiatry* (Baltimore: Williams & Wilkins, 1969), p. 275. **Symptoms as consequence of disease process:** See D. G. C. Owens and E. C. Johnstone, "The Disabilities of Chronic Schizophrenia—Their Nature and the Factors Contributing to Their Develop-

ment," *British Journal of Psychiatry* 136 (1980): 384–95. **"the prognosis in the aboriginal":** H. Rin and T. Y. Lin, "Mental Illness among Formosan Aborigines as Compared with the Chinese in Taiwan," *Journal of Mental Science* 108 (1962): 134–46. **And on Mauritius:** H. B. M. Murphy and A. C. Raman, "The Chronicity of Schizophrenia in Indigenous Tropical Peoples," *British Journal of Psychiatry* 118 (1971): 489–97. **data from the World Health Organization:** See N. Sartorius, A. Jablensky, and R. Shapiro, "Cross-cultural Differences in the Short-term Prognosis of Schizophrenic Psychosis," *Schizophrenia Bulletin* 4 (1978): 102–13; World Health Organization, *Schizophrenia: An International Follow-up Study* (New York: Wiley, 1979). **courses of schizophrenia:** M. Bleuler, "A 23-year Longitudinal Study of 208 Schizophrenics and Impressions in Regard to the Nature of Schizophrenia," in D. A. Rosenthal and S. S. Kety, eds., *The Transmission of Schizophrenia* (Oxford: Pergamon Press, 1968); E. H. Hare, "The Changing Content of Psychiatric Illness," *Journal of Psychosomatic Research* 19 (1974): 283–89; K. A. Achte, "The Course of Schizophrenic and Schizophreniform Psychoses," *Acta Psychiatrica et Neurologica Scandinavica Supplementum* 155 (1961).

CHAPTER 5: THE CAUSES OF SCHIZOPHRENIA

"Something has happened": L. Jefferson, *These Are My Sisters* (1948), quoted in Kaplan, p. 6. **Many studies were done:** See A. Meyer, "Psychoses of Obscure Pathology," in W. Blackwood et al., eds., *Greenfield's Neuropathology* (London: Edward Arnold, 1963). **three interesting studies:** E. J. Colon, "Quantitative Cytoarchitectonics of the Human Cerebral Cortex in Schizophrenic Dementia," *Acta Neuropathologia* (Berlin) 20 (1972): 1–10; D. Nieto and A. Escobar, "Major psychoses," in J. Minckler, ed., *Pathology of the Nervous System,* vol. 3 (New York: McGraw-Hill, 1972), pp. 2654–65; R. Rosenthal and L. B. Bigelow, "Quantitative Brain Measurements in

Chronic Schizophrenia," *British Journal of Psychiatry* 121 (1972): 259–64. M. Fisman: "The Brain Stem in Psychosis," *British Journal of Psychiatry* 126 (1975): 414–22. P. Averback: "Structural Lesions of the Brain of Young Schizophrenics," *Canadian Journal of Neurological Sciences* 8 (1981): 73–75. Janice R. Stevens: "Neuropathology of Schizophrenia," *Archives of General Psychiatry* 39 (1982): 1131–39; J. R. Stevens, "Neuropathologic Studies of Schizophrenia: Search for a Virus," in M. Namba and H. Kaiya, eds., *Psychobiology of Schizophrenia* (New York: Pergamon Press, 1982), pp. 45–56. **CT scans:** E. C. Johnstone et al., "Cerebral Ventricular Size and Cognitive Impairment in Chronic Schizophrenia," *Lancet* 2 (1976): 924–26; D. R. Weinberger et al., "Lateral Cerebral Ventricular Enlargement in Chronic Schizophrenia," *Archives of General Psychiatry* 36 (1979): 735–39; D. R. Weinberger et al., "Structural Abnormalities in the Cerebral Cortex in Chronic Schizophrenia," *Archives of General Psychiatry* 36 (1979): 935–39; D. R. Weinberger, E. F. Torrey, and R. J. Wyatt, "Cerebellar Atrophy in Chronic Schizophrenia," *Lancet* 1 (1979): 718–19; D. R. Weinberger et al., "Cerebral Ventricular Enlargement in Chronic Schizophrenia: Association with Poor Response to Treatment," *Archives of General Psychiatry* 37 (1980): 11–14; N. C. Andreasen et al., "Ventricular Enlargement in Schizophrenia: Definition and Prevalence," *American Journal of Psychiatry* 139 (1982): 292–96; C. J. Golden et al., "Structural Brain Deficits in Schizophrenia," *Archives of General Psychiatry* 38 (1981): 1014–17; H. A. Nasrallah et al., "Cerebral Ventricular Enlargement in Subtypes of Chronic Schizophrenia," *Archives of General Psychiatry* 39 (1982): 774–76; T. L. Jernigan et al., "Computed Tomography in Schizophrenics and Normal Volunteers," *Archives of General Psychiatry* 39 (1982): 765–70. **evoked potentials:** See M. S. Buchsbaum, "The Middle Evoked Response Components and Schizophrenia," *Schizophrenia Bulletin* 3 (1977): 93–104; C. Shagass, "Early Evoked Potentials," *Schizophrenia Bulletin* 3 (1977): 80–92. **electroencephalo-**

grams: See J. R. Stevens and A. Livermore, "Telemetered EEG in Schizophrenia: Spectral Analysis During Abnormal Behaviour Episodes," *Journal of Neurology, Neurosurgery, and Psychiatry* 45 (1982): 385–95; R. Abrams and M. A. Taylor, "Differential EEG Patterns in Affective Disorder and Schizophrenia," *Archives of General Psychiatry* 36 (1979): 1355–58; P. Hays, "Electroencephalographic Variants and Genetic Predisposition to Schizophrenia," *Journal of Neurology, Neurosurgery, and Psychiatry* 40 (1977): 753–55. **"Chronic schizophrenics have":** T. M. Itil, B. Saletu, and S. Davis, "EEG Findings in Chronic Schizophrenics Based on Digital Computer Period Analysis of Analog Power Spectra," *Biological Psychiatry* 5 (1972): 1–13.

abnormal eye movements: See J. R. Stevens, "Eye Blink and Schizophrenia: Psychosis or Tardive Dyskinesia," *American Journal of Psychiatry* 135 (1978): 223–26; P. S. Holzman, D. L. Levy, and L. R. Proctor, "Smooth Pursuit Eye Movements, Attention, and Schizophrenia," *Archives of General Psychiatry* 33 (1976): 1415–20. **abnormalities in the inner ear:** S. Myers, D. Caldwell, and G. Purcell, "Vestibular Dysfunction in Schizophrenia," *Biological Psychiatry* 7 (1973): 255–61. **psychological tests:** See C. Watson et al., "Differentiation of Organics from Schizophrenics at Two Chronicity Levels by Use of the Reitan-Halsted Organic Test Battery," *Journal of Consulting Clinical Psychology* 32 (1968): 679–84; H. Klonoff, C. Fibiger, and G. Hutton, "Neuropsychological Patterns in Chronic Schizophrenia," *Journal of Nervous and Mental Disease* 150 (1970): 291–300; L. Lilliston, "Schizophrenic Symptomatology as a Function of Probability of Cerebral Damage," *Journal of Abnormal Psychology* 82 (1973): 377–81. **"schizophrenic patients . . . were":** "Cognitive Dysfunction in Schizophrenia, Affective Disorder and Organic Brain Disease," *British Journal of Psychiatry* 139 (1981): 190–94. **six different studies:** J. M. Rochford et al., "Neuropsychological Impairments in Functional Psychiatric Diseases," *Archives of General Psychi-*

atry 22 (1970): 114–19; L. R. Mosher, W. Pollin, and J. R. Stabenau, "Identical Twins Discordant for Schizophrenia," *Archives of General Psychiatry* 24 (1971): 422–30; G. J. Tucker, E. W. Campion, and P. M. Silberfarb, "Sensorimotor Function and Cognitive Disturbances in Psychiatric Patients," *American Journal of Psychiatry* 132 (1975): 17–21; F. Quitkin, A. Rifkin, and D. F. Klein, "Neurologic Soft Signs in Schizophrenia and Character Disorders," *Archives of General Psychiatry* 33.(1976): 845–50; E. F. Torrey, "Neurological Abnormalities in Schizophrenic Patients," *Biological Psychiatry* 15 (1980): 381–88; E. Walker and M. Green, "Soft Signs of Neurological Dysfunction in Schizophrenia: An Investigation of Lateral Performance," *Biological Psychiatry* 17 (1982): 381–86. **D. H. Ingvar and G. Franzen,** "Abnormalities in Cerebral Blood Flow Distribution in Patients with Chronic Schizophrenia," *Acta Psychiatrica Scandinavica* 50 (1974): 425–62. See also R. J. Mathew et al., "Regional Cerebral Blood Flow in Schizophrenia," *Archives of General Psychiatry* 39 (1982): 1121–24. **PET scanner:** M. S. Buchsbaum et al., "Cerebral Glucography with Positron Tomography," *Archives of General Psychiatry* 39 (1982): 251–59. **definite chemical abnormalities:** See, e.g., I. J. Farley et al., "Norepinephrine in Chronic Paranoid Schizophrenia: Above-normal Levels in Limbic Forebrain," *Science* 200 (1978): 456–58; E. D. Bird, E. G. S. Spokes, and L. L. Iverson, "Increased Dopamine Concentration in Limbic Areas of Brain from Patients Dying with Schizophrenia," *Brain* 102 (1979): 347–60; F. Owen, T. J. Crow, and M. Poulter, "Increased Dopamine-Receptor Sensitivity in Schizophrenia," *Lancet* 2 (1978): 223–25; T. Lee and P. Seeman, "Elevation of Brain Neuroleptic/Dopamine Receptors in Schizophrenia," *American Journal of Psychiatry* 137 (1980): 191–97.; A. V. P. Mackay et al., "Increased Brain Dopamine and Dopamine Receptors, *Archives of General Psychiatry* 39 (1982): 991–97. **studies of the cerebrospinal fluid:** See, e.g., C. R. Lake et al., "Schizophrenia: Elevated Cerebrospinal Fluid Norepinephrine," *Science* 207 (1980): 331–33;

and E. F. Torrey et al., "Immunoglobulins and Viral Antibodies in Psychiatric Patients," *British Journal of Psychiatry* 132 (1978): 342–48. **"I find it difficult":** S. S. Kety, "The Syndrome of Schizophrenia: Unresolved Questions and Opportunities for Research," *British Journal of Psychiatry* 136 (1980): 421–36. **"selective, integrative":** D. R. Roberts, "Schizophrenia and the Brain," *Journal of Neuropsychiatry* 5 (1963): 71–79. **"able to correlate":** P. D. MacLean, "Psychosomatic Disease and the 'Visceral Brain,'" *Psychosomatic Medicine* 11 (1949): 338–53. **limbic system dysfunction:** E. F. Torrey and M. R. Peterson, "Schizophrenia and the Limbic System," *Lancet* 2 (1974): 942–46. **brain tumors:** N. Malamud, "Psychiatric Disorders with Intracranial Tumors of the Limbic System," *Archives of Neurology* 17 (1967): 113–23. **Cases of encephalitis:** J. Himmelhoch et al., "Subacute Encephalitis: Behavioral and Neurological Aspects," *British Journal of Psychiatry* 116 (1970): 531–38; D. A. Drachman and R. D. Adams, "Herpes Simplex and Acute Inclusion Body Encephalitis," *Archives of Neurology* 7 (1962): 45–63; J. R. Brierley et al., "Subacute Encephalitis of Later Life Mainly Affecting the Limbic Areas," *Brain* 83 (1960): 357–68; G. H. Glaser, G. B. Solitare, and E. A. Manuelidis, "Acute and Subacute Inclusion Encephalitis," *Research Publication of the Association of Nervous and Mental Diseases* 49 (1968): 178–215, L. G. Wilson, "Viral Encephalopathy Mimicking Functional Psychosis," *American Journal of Psychiatry* 133 (1976): 165–70. **epilepsy, when it originates:** N. Malamud, "The Epileptogenic Focus in Temporal Lobe Epilepsy from the Pathological Standpoint," *Archives of Neurology* 14 (1966): 190–95; M. A. Falconer, E. A. Serafetinides, and J. A. N. Corsellis, "Etiology and Pathogenesis of Temporal Lobe Epilepsy," *Archives of Neurology* 10 (1964): 233–48. **limbic electrical activity:** R. G. Heath, *Studies in Schizophrenia: A Multidisciplinary Approach to Mind-Brain Relationships* (Cambridge: Harvard University Press, 1954); R. G. Heath, "Correlation of Electrical Recordings from Cortical and Subcortical Regions of the Brain with Abnormal Behavior in Human Subjects," *Confina Neurologia* 18 (1958): 305–15; R. R. Monroe et al., "Correlation of Rhinencephalic Electrograms with Behavior," *EEG and Clinical Neurophysiology* 9 (1957): 623–42; C. W. Sem-Jacobsen, M. C. Peterson, and J. A. Lazarte, "Intracerebral Electrographic Recordings from Psychotic Patients During Hallucinations and Agitation: Preliminary Report," *American Journal of Psychiatry* 112 (1955): 278–88; C. W. Sem-Jacobsen et al., "Electroencephalographic Rhythms from the Depths of the Parietal, Occipital, and Temporal Lobes in Man," *EEG and Clinical Neurophysiology* 8 (1956): 263–78; J. F. Kendrick and F. A. Gibbs, "Origin, Spread and. Neurosurgical Treatment of the Psychomotor Type of Seizure Discharge," *Journal of Neurosurgery* 14 (1957): 270–84; J. Hanley et al., "Spectral Characteristics of EEG Activity Accompanying Deep Spiking in a Patient with Schizophrenia," *EEG and Clinical Neurophysiology* 28 (1970): 90; J. Hanley et al., "Automatic Recognition of EEG Correlates of Behavior in a Chronic Schizophrenic Patient," *American Journal of Psychiatry* 128 (1972): 1524–28. **Patients with temporal lobe epilepsy:** P. Flor-Henry, "Psychosis and Temporal Lobe Epilepsy: A Controlled Investigation," *Epilepsia* 10 (1969): 363–95; P. Flor-Henry, "Schizophrenic-like Reactions and Affective Psychoses Associated with Temporal Lobe Epilepsy: Etiological Factors," *American Journal of Psychiatry* 126 (1969): 400–404. **lie in the left hemisphere:** For reviews of this rapidly expanding research literature see E. F. Torrey, "Neurological Abnormalities"; R. Abrams and M. A. Taylor, "Psychopathology and the Electroencephalogram," *Biological Psychiatry* 15 (1980): 871–78; B. E. Wexler, "Cerebral Laterality and Psychiatry: A Review of the Literature," *American Journal of Psychiatry* 137 (1980): 279–91; D. B. Newlin, B. Carpenter, and C. J. Golden, "Hemispheric Asymmetries in Schizophrenia," *Biological Psychiatry* 16 (1981): 561–82; E. L. Merrin, "Schizophrenia and Brain Asymmetry," *Journal of Nervous and Mental Disease* 169 (1981): 405–16.

skewed seasonality in the births: For reviews of these studies see P. Dalen, *Season of Birth: A Study of Schizophrenia and Other Mental Disorders* (New York: American Elsevier, 1975); and E. F. Torrey, *Schizophrenia and Civilization* (New York: Jason Aronson, 1980). **schizophrenic births have shifted:** M. Shimura and T. Miura, "Season of Birth in Mental Disorders in Tokyo, Japan, by Year of Birth, Year of Admission and Age of Admission," *Acta Psychiatrica Scandinavica* 61 (1980): 21–28. **rubella and cytomegalovirus:** R. Achs, F. G. Harper, and M. Siegel, "Unusual Dermatoglyphic Findings Associated with Rubella Embryopathy," *New England Journal of Medicine* 274 (1966): 148–50; H. T. Wright, C. E. Parker, and J. Mavalwala, "Unusual Dermatoglyphic Findings Associated with Cytomegalic Inclusion Disease of Infancy," *California Medicine* 116 (1972): 14–20. **unusual fingerprint:** For a review of these studies see E. F. Torrey and M. R. Peterson, "The Viral Hypothesis of Schizophrenia," *Schizophrenia Bulletin* 2 (1976): 136–46. **lighter in weight at birth:** E. A. Lane and G. W. Albee, "Comparative Birth Weights of Schizophrenics and Their Siblings," *Journal of Psychology* 64 (1966): 227–31. **more birth complications:** E. F. Torrey, "Birth Weights, Perinatal Insults, and HLA Types: Return to 'Original Din,'" *Schizophrenia Bulletin* 3 (1977): 347–51; see also J. Parnas et al., "Perinatal Complications and Clinical Outcome with Schizophrenia Spectrum," *British Journal of Psychiatry* 140 (1982): 416–20. **stillborn children:** D. E. Sobel, "Infant Mortality and Malformations in Children of Schizophrenic Women," *Psychiatric Quarterly* 35 (1961): 60–65; R. O. Rieder, et al., "The Offspring of Schizophrenics: Fetal and Neonatal Deaths," *Archives of General Psychiatry* 32 (1975): 200–211; G. Wrede et al., "Pregnancy and Delivery Complications in the Births of an Unselected Series of Finnish Children with Schizophrenic Mothers," *Acta Psychiatrica Scandinavica* 62 (1980): 369–81.

never "like other children": See R. Gittleman-Klein and D. F. Klein, "Premorbid Asocial Adjustment and Prognosis in Schizophrenia," *Journal of Psychiatric Research* 7 (1969): 35–53. **abnormal CT scans:** D. R. Weinberger et al., "Poor Premorbid Adjustment and CT Scan Abnormalities in Chronic Schizophrenia," *American Journal of Psychiatry* 137 (1980): 1410–13. **more inbreeding:** A. H. Ahmed, "Consanguinity and Schizophrenia in Sudan," *British Journal of Psychiatry* 134 (1979): 635–36. **genetics plays some role:** See S. Kessler, "The Genetics of Schizophrenia: A Review," *Schizophrenia Bulletin* 6 (1980): 404–16; D. K. Kinney and S. Matthysse, "Genetic Transmission of Schizophrenia," *Annual Review of Medicine* 29 (1978): 459–73. **abnormal eye movements:** P. S. Holzman et al., "Eye Tracking Dysfunctions in Schizophrenic Patients and Their Relatives," *Archives of General Psychiatry* 31 (1974): 143–51. **"something necessary":** R. Cancro, "Genetic Evidence for the Existence of Subgroups of the Schizophrenic Syndrome," *Schizophrenia Bulletin* 5 (1979): 453–59; see also S. S. Kety et al., "The Biologic and Adoptive Families of Adopted Individuals Who Became Schizophrenic: Prevalence of Mental Illness and Other Characteristics," in L. C. Wynne, R. L. Cromwell and S. Matthysse, *The Nature of Schizophrenia* (New York: Wiley, 1978). The findings of the Denmark study have recently been disputed by T. Lidz, S. Blatt, and B. Cooke, "Critique of the Danish-American Studies of the Adopted-away Offspring of Schizophrenic Parents," *American Journal of Psychiatry* 138 (1981): 1063–68. **"If schizophrenia is a myth":** S. S. Kety, "From Rationalization to Reason," *American Journal of Psychiatry* 131 (1974): 957–63. **genetic predisposition:** See A. L. Notkins, "The Causes of Diabetes," *Scientific American* 241 (1979): 62–73. **human leukocyte antigen:** See, e.g., D. Luchins et al., "HLA Antigens in Schizophrenia: Differences Between Patients with and Without Evidence of Brain Atrophy," *British Journal of Psychiatry* 136 (1980): 243–48. **excess of dopamine:** D. H. Langer, G. L. Brown, and J. P. Docherty, "Dopamine Receptor Supersensitivity and Schizophrenia: A Review,"

Schizophrenia Bulletin 7 (1981): 208–24; see also J. L. Haracz, "The Dopamine Hypothesis: An Overview of Studies with Schizophrenic Patients," *Schizophrenia Bulletin* 8 (1982): 438–69; and S. H. Snyder, "Schizophrenia," *Lancet* 2 (1982): 970–73. **MAO research:** R. J. Wyatt, S. G. Potkin, and D. L. Murphy, "Platelet Monoamine Oxidase Activity in Schizophrenia: A Review," *American Journal of Psychiatry* 136 (1979): 377–85; L. E. DeLisi et al., "A Probable Neuroleptic Effect on Platelet Monoamine Oxidase in Chronic Schizophrenia," *Psychiatry Research* 4 (1981): 95–107. **serotonin:** L. E. DeLisi et al., "Increased Whole Blood Serotonin Concentrations in Chronic Schizophrenic Patients," *Archives of General Psychiatry* 38 (1981): 647–50. **"have crossed the threshold":** T. H. Maugh, "Biochemical Markers Identify Mental States," *Science* 214 (1981): 39–41.

high doses of niacin: A. Hoffer, *Niacin Therapy in Psychiatry* (Springfield, Ill.: Charles C. Thomas, 1962). **Linus Pauling:** L. Pauling, "Orthomolecular Psychiatry," *Science* 160 (1968): 265–71. **fill a textbook:** D. Hawkins and L. Pauling, *Orthomolecular Psychiatry: Treatment of Schizophrenia* (San Francisco: Freeman, 1973). **attempts to replicate:** J. H. Autrey, "Workshop on Orthomolecular Treatment of Schizophrenia: A Report," *Schizophrenia Bulletin* No. 12 (original series) (1975): 94–103. **Gluten:** F. C. Dohan, "Cereals and Schizophrenia: Data and Hypothesis," *Acta Psychiatrica Scandinavica* 42 (1966): 125–52; F. C. Dohan, "Wartime Changes in Hospital Admissions for Schizophrenia," *Acta Psychiatrica Scandinavica* 42 (1966): 1–23. **gluten-free and milk-free diet:** F. C. Dohan and J. C. Grasberger, "Relapsed Schizophrenics: Earlier Discharge from the Hospital after Cereal-Free, Milk-Free Diet," *American Journal of Psychiatry* 130 (1973): 685–88; M. M. Singh and S. R. Kay, "Wheat Gluten as a Pathogenic Factor in Schizophrenia," *Science* 191 (1976): 401–2; S. R. Potkin et al., "Wheat Gluten Challenge in Schizophrenic Patients," *American Journal of Psychiatry* 138 (1981): 1208–11; L. H. Storms, J. M. Clopton, and C. Wright, "Effects of Gluten on Schizophrenics," *Archives of General Psychiatry* 39 (1982): 323–27. **serine and glycine metabolism:** L. Pepplinkhuizen et al., "Schizophrenia-like Psychosis Caused by a Metabolic Disorder," *Lancet* 1 (1980): 454–56. **dietary lecithin:** B. M. Cohen et al., "Lecithin in Mania: A Preliminary Report," *American Journal of Psychiatry* 137 (1980): 242–43. **search for food allergies:** H. G. Kinnell, E. Kirkwood, and C. Lewis, "Food Antibodies in Schizophrenia," *Psychological Medicine* 12 (1982): 85–89. **zinc or copper:** D. Shore et al., "CSF Copper in Chronic Schizophrenia," *American Journal of Psychiatry* (in press); S. G. Potkin et al., "CSF Zinc in Ex-heroin Addicts and Chronic Schizophrenia," *Biological Psychiatry* 17 (1982): 1315–22. **Viral particles:** V. M. K. Morozov, "On the Problem of the Virus Etiology of Schizophrenia," *Korsakov Journal of Neuropathology and Psychiatry* 54 (1954): 732–34 (in Russian); P. D. Mastrogiovanni and G. Scarlato, "Primi Dati Sull' Azione Letale del Liquor di Schizofrenici su Embrioni di Pollo," *Acta Neurologica* (Naples) 11 (1956): 454–67 (in Italian); G. I. Mar and A. M. Svyadoshch, "The Problem of Virus Particles in the Cerebrospinal Fluid of Schizophrenics," *Korsokov Journal of Neuropathology and Psychiatry* 57 (1957): 1098–1100 (in Russian).

influenza virus: K. A. Menninger, "Influenza and Schizophrenia," *American Journal of Psychiatry* 82 (1926): 469–529. **herpes viruses:** D. E. Raskin and S. W. Frank, "Herpes Encephalitis with Catatonic Stupor," *Archives of General Psychiatry* 31 (1974): 544–46; L. G. Wilson, "Viral Encephalitis Mimicking Functional Psychosis," *American Journal of Psychiatry* 133 (1976): 165–70. **encephalitis lethargica:** K. Davison and C. R. Bagley, "Schizophrenia-like Psychoses Associated with Organic Disorders of the Central Nervous System: A Review of the Literature," in R. N. Herrington, ed., *Current Problems in Neuropsychiatry* (Ashford, Kent: Headley Brothers, 1969). **"encephalitis and schizophrenia":** I. Hendrick, "Encephalitis Lethargica and the Interpretation of Mental Disease," *American Journal of Psychiatry* 84 (1928): 989–

1014. **Current infectious disease:** See E. F. Torrey and M. R. Peterson, "Slow and Latent Viruses in Schizophrenia," *Lancet* 2 (1973): 22–24; E. F. Torrey and M. R. Peterson, "The Viral Hypothesis of Schizophrenia," *Schizophrenia Bulletin* 2 (1976): 136–46. **no evident damage:** M. B. A. Oldstone, J. Holmstoen, and R. M. Walsh, "Alteration of Acetylcholine Enzymes in Neuroblastoma Cells Persistently Infected with Lymphocytic Choriomeningitis Virus," *Journal of Cellular Physiology* 91 (1977): 459–72. **remain latent:** D. C. Gajdusek, "Unconventional Viruses and the Origin and Disappearance of Kuru," *Science* 197 (1977): 943–60. **cytomegalovirus:** P. Albrecht et al., "Raised Cytomegalovirus-Antibody Level in Cerebrospinal Fluid of Schizophrenic Patients," *Lancet* 2 (1980): 769–72; E. F. Torrey, R. H. Yolken, and C. J. Winfrey, "Cytomegalovirus Antibody in Cerebrospinal Fluid of Schizophrenic Patients Detected by Enzyme Immunoassay," *Science* 216 (1982): 892–93. **viral-like activity:** D. A. J. Tyrrell et al., "Possible Virus in Schizophrenia and Some Neurological Disorders," *Lancet* 1 (1979): 839–41; T. J. Crow et al., "Characteristics of Patients with Schizophrenia or Neurological Disorders and Virus-like Agent in Cerebrospinal Fluid," *Lancet* 1 (1979): 842–44. **changes in neurotransmitters:** E. Lycke and B. E. Roos, "Effect in the Monoamine Metabolism of the Mouse Brain by Experimental Herpes Simplex Infection," *Experientia* 24 (1968): 687–98. **the memoirs:** D. P. Schreber, *Memoirs of My Nervous Illness* (1903), translation and introduction by I. Macalpine and R. A. Hunter (London: William Dawson & Sons, 1955). **"conflict over unconscious homosexuality":** I. Macalpine and R. A. Hunter in Schreber. **"I seldom see":** Letter from Sigmund Freud to Karl Abraham in E. Jones, *The Life and Work of Sigmund Freud* (New York: Basic Books, 1955), vol. 2, p. 437. **Freud sided with Abraham:** Jones, vol. 2, pp. 46–48. **"the unceasing terror":** N. Fodor, "Prenatal Foundations of Psychotic Development" *Samiksa* 11 (1957): 1–43. **"Others have described":** H. Weiner, "Schizophrenia: Etiology," in A. M.

Freedman and H. I. Kaplan, eds., *Comprehensive Textbook of Psychiatry* (Baltimore: Williams & Wilkins, 1967), p. 610. **"the majority":** S. Arieti, "Schizophrenia," in S. Arieti, ed., *The American Handbook of Psychiatry*, vol. 1 (New York: Basic Books, 1959), p. 469. **revised his estimates:** D. Trainor, "Arieti Revised Thought on Role of Mothers in Psychosis, *Psychiatric News*, Sept. 16, 1977. **"strange, near-psychotic":** T. Lidz, S. Fleck, and A. R. Cornelison, *Schizophrenia and the Family* (New York: International University Press, 1965), p. 327. **"an extremely noxious":** T. Lidz, B. Parker, and A. R. Cornelison, "The Role of the Father in the Family Environment of the Schizophrenic Patient," *American Journal of Psychiatry* 113 (1956): 126–32. **"Momma goes out":** M. Barnes and J. Berke, *Mary Barnes: Two Accounts of a Journey Through Madness* (New York: Ballantine, 1973), p. 85. **"none of the marriages":** C. P. Rosenbaum, *The Meaning of Madness* (New York: Science House, 1970), p. 149. **"pseudomutual":** Ibid., p. 147. **"Long before":** Barnes and Berke, pp. 75–76. **Szasz:** T. S. Szasz, "A Contribution to the Psychology of Schizophrenia," *Archives of Neurology and Psychiatry* 77 (1957): 420–36; T. S. Szasz, *Schizophrenia: The Sacred Symbol of Psychiatry* (New York: Basic Books, 1976). **strong evidence:** Kinney and Matthysse. **iatrogenic anguish:** E. F. Torrey, "A Fantasy Trial About a Real Issue," *Psychology Today*, March 1977, p. 22. **"This book is":** R. Abrams, review of L. B. Boyer and P. L. Giovacchini, *Psychoanalytic Treatment of Schizophrenic, Borderline, and Characterological Disorders*, in *American Journal of Psychiatry* 138 (1981): 267. **"the crumbling edifice":** R. Abrams, "Dr. Abrams Replies," *American Journal of Psychiatry* 138 (1981): 854. **"the relatively small":** J. H. Liem, "Family Studies of Schizophrenia: An Update and Commentary," *Schizophrenia Bulletin* 6 (1980): 429–55. **"There is as yet":** S. R. Hirsch, "Do Parents Cause Schizophrenia?" *Trends in Neurosciences* 2 (1979): 49–52. **"Neither has anyone":** Ibid. **"Insanity is terrific":** D. Previn, *Bog-Trotter* (New York: Doubleday, 1980), p. 64.

"The individual who": B. O'Brien, *Operators and Things: The Inner Life of a Schizophrenic* (New York: Signet, 1976), p. 180. **"We believe":** J. Chamberlain, *On Our Own: Patient-Controlled Alternatives to the Mental Health System* (New York: Hawthorn, 1978), p. xvi. **"The research evidence":** J. G. Rabkin, "Stressful Life Events and Schizophrenia: A Review of the Literature," *Psychological Bulletin* 87 (1980): 408–25. **Why did the schizophrenia rate:** See F. C. Dohan, "Wartime Changes . . ." and B. B. Svendsen, "Fluctuation of Danish Psychiatric Admission Rates in World War II," *Psychiatric Quarterly* 27 (1953): 19–37. **Northern Ireland:** See H. B. M. Murphy and G. Vega, "Schizophrenia and Religious Affiliation in Northern Ireland," *Psychological Medicine* 12 (1982): 595–605.

 Currently in the United States: *Report of the President's Commission on Mental Health* (Washington, D.C.: U.S. Govenrment Printing Office, 1978), vol. 4, p. 1564. **In fiscal year 1980:** These figures were obtained from "Schizophrenia-Related Grants and Contracts, Fiscal Year 1980," *Schizophrenia Bulletin* 8 (1982): 142–97; and from *Budget of the United States Government: Fiscal Year 1980* (Washington, D.C.: U.S. Government Printing Office).

CHAPTER 6: THE TREATMENT OF SCHIZOPHRENIA

"To be schizophrenic": H. R. Rollin, ed., *Coping with Schizophrenia* (London: Burnett Books, 1980), p. 165. **"as a suffering":** W. J. Annitto, "Schizophrenia and Ego Psychology," *Schizophrenia Bulletin* 7 (1981): 199–200. **minimal level of knowledge:** R. L. Taylor and E. F. Torrey, "The Pseudo-regulation of American Psychiatry," *American Journal of Psychiatry* 129 (1972): 658–62. **demonstrated many times:** See E. F. Torrey, *The Mind Game: Witchdoctors and Psychiatrists* (New York: Emerson Hall, 1972) for a review of studies in this area. **"the combination of drug":** B. Pasamanick, F. R. Scarpitti, and S. Dinitz, *Schizophrenics in the Community: An Experimental Study* *in the Prevention of Hospitalization* (New York: Appleton-Century-Crofts, 1967), p. ix. **Madison, Wisconsin:** L. I. Stein and M. A. Test, "Alternative to Mental Hospital Treatment," *Archives of General Psychiatry* 37 (1980): 392–97. **Soteria House:** L. R. Mosher and A. Z. Menn, "Community Residential Treatment for Schizophrenia: Two-year Follow-up," *Hospital and Community Psychiatry* 29 (1978): 715–23. **The Tennessee statute is** TCA 33-604. **The Nevada statute is** 433A, Care of the Mentally Ill. **The Texas statute is** from the laws on the mentally ill. **basic legal safeguards:** The President's Commission on Mental Health recommended that such safeguards be extended to all states; see *Report of the President's Commission on Mental Health*, Vol. 1 (Washington, D.C.: U.S. Government Printing Office, 1978), pp. 42–44.

reduced to days: D. F. Klein and J. M. Davis, *Diagnosis and Drug Treatment of Psychiatric Disorders* (Baltimore: Williams & Wilkins, 1969). **John Davis:** J. M. Davis, "Overview: Maintenance Therapy in Psychiatry: I. Schizophrenia," *American Journal of Psychiatry* 132 (1975): 1237–45. **only 8 percent:** W. Hartmann et al., "Neuroleptic Drugs and the Prevention of Relapse: A Workshop Report," *Schizophrenia Bulletin* 6 (1980): 536–41. **80 percent relapsed:** N. Capstick, "Long-Term Fluphenazine Decanoate Maintenance Dosage Requirements of Chronic Schizophrenic Patients," *Acta Psychiatrica Scandinavica* 61 (1980): 256–62. **pending for over ten years:** "Drug Lag '80," *Medical World News*, Sept. 1, 1980, p. 41. **the difference between:** "Fluphenazine Levels—Short and Long," *Biological Therapies in Psychiatry Newsletter* 4 (1981): 33–34. **very high doses:** See S. J. Dencker et al., "Late (4–8 Years) Outcome of Treatment with Megadoses of Fluphenazine Enanthate in Drug-Refractory Schizophrenics," *Acta Psychiatrica Scandinavica* 63 (1981): 1–12. **block the transmission:** G. B. Kolata, "New Drugs and the Brain," *Science* 205 (1979): 774–76. **"The antipsychotic agents":** R. J. Baldessarini, "The Neuroleptic Antipsychotic Drugs," *Postgraduate Medicine* 65 (1979): 108–28. **enhance the effective-** **ness:** N. Manos, J. Gkiouzepas, and J. Logothetis, "The Need for Continuous Use of Antiparkinsonian Medication with Chronic Schizophrenic Patients Receiving Long-term Neuroleptic Therapy," *American Journal of Psychiatry* 138 (1981): 184–88; see also "When Antiparkinson Drugs Are Withdrawn," *Biological Therapies in Psychiatry Newsletter* 5 (1982): 2–3. **may be indistinguishable:** For an excellent discussion of this problem see A. Rifkin, "The Risks of Long-Term Neuroleptic Treatment of Schizophrenia: Especially Depression and Akinesia," *Acta Psychiatrica Scandinavica* Supplementum 291, 63 (1981): 129–36. **"I am unfortunate":** H. R. Rollin, *Coping with Schizophrenia* (London: Burnett Books, 1980), pp. 164–65.

"Whereas I lived": *National Schizophrenia Fellowship Newsletter,* April 1980. **Kraepelin described:** R. S. Garber, "Tardive Dyskinesia," *Psychiatric News* May 4, 1979, p. 2. **researchers found involuntary movements:** M. Jones and R. Hunter, "Abnormal Movements in Patients with Chronic Psychiatric Illness," in G. E. Crane and R. Gardner, eds., *Psychotropic Drugs and Dysfunctions of the Basal Ganglia: A Multidisciplinary Workshop,* Publication No. 1938 (Washington, D.C.: U.S. Public Health Service, 1969); D. G. C. Owens and E. C. Johnstone, "The Disabilities of Chronic Schizophrenia—Their Nature and the Factors Contributing to Their Development," *British Journal of Psychiatry* 136 (1980): 384–95; E. C. Johnstone and D. G. C. Owens, "Neurological Changes in a Population of Patients with Chronic Schizophrenia and Their Relationship to Physical Treatment," *Acta Psychiatrica Scandinavica* Supplementum 291, 63 (1981): 103–10; D. G. C. Owens and E. C. Johnstone, "Spontaneous Involuntary Disorders of Movement," *Archives of General Psychiatry* 39 (1982): 452–61. **13 percent:** D. V. Jeste and R. J. Wyatt, "Changing Epidemiology of Tardive Dyskinesia: An Overview," *American Journal of Psychiatry* 138 (1981): 297–309. **10 to 20 percent range:** APA Task Force on the Late Neurological Effects of Antipsychotic Drugs, "Tardive Dyskinesia: Summary of a Task Force Report of the American Psychiatric Association," *American Journal of Psychiatry* 137 (1980): 1163–72. **"While the problem":** Ibid. **"are inaccessible to":** S. Freud, "On Narcissism," 1914. In *Collected Papers,* vol. 4 (London: Hogarth Press), p. 31. **best-known of these studies:** P. R. A. May, *Treatment of Schizophrenia: A Comparative Study of Five Treatment Methods* (New York: Science House, 1968). **"Analysis of variance":** P. R. A. May et al., "Schizophrenia: A Follow-up Study of the Results of Five Forms of Treatment," *Archives of General Psychiatry* 38 (1981): 776–84. **"psychotherapy alone":** L. Grinspoon, J. R. Ewalt, and R. I. Shader, *Schizophrenia: Pharmacotherapy and Psychotherapy* (Baltimore: Williams & Wilkins, 1977), p. 154. **"There is no scientific":** D. F. Klein, "Psychosocial Treatment of Schizophrenia, or Psychosocial Help for People with Schizophrenia?" *Schizophrenia Bulletin* 6 (1980): 122–30. **"outcome for patients":** J. M. Davis et al., "Important Issues in the Drug Treatment of Schizophrenia," *Schizophrenia Bulletin* 6 (1980): 70–87. **"checked the therapeutic":** I. Macalpine and R. A. Hunter, in D. P. Schreber, *Memoirs of My Nervous Illness* (1903), translation and introduction by I. Macalpine and R. A. Hunter (London: William Dawson & Sons, 1955), p. 23. **"recent evidence suggests":** G. L. Klerman, "Pharmacotherapy and Psychotherapy in the Treatment of Schizophrenia" (Paper presented at the Annual Meeting of the American Psychiatric Association, San Francisco, 1980). **not really schizophrenic:** C. North and R. Cadoret, "Diagnostic Discrepancy in Personal Accounts of Patients with 'Schizophrenia,' " *Archives of General Psychiatry* 38 (1981): 133–37. **Dr. Werner M. Mendel:** "Managing Dependency in a Psychiatric Patient," *Audio-Digest* 6 (1977): 16. **In one study:** G. Hogarty and S. Goldberg, "Drug and Sociotherapy in the Post-Hospital Maintenance of Schizophrenia," *Archives of General Psychiatry* 24 (1973): 54–64. **"sixteen either failed":** D. F. Klein, "Psychosocial Treatment . . ." **"most controlled evaluations":** L. Mosher and S. J. Keith, "Psychosocial Treatment: Individ-

ual, Group, Family, and Community Support Approaches," *Schizophrenia Bulletin* 6 (1980): 10–41. **One study of aftercare:** M. W. Linn et al., "Day Treatment and Psychotropic Drugs in the Aftercare of Schizophrenic Patients," *Archives of General Psychiatry* 36 (1979): 1055–66. **group psychotherapy may precipitate:** I. Sale et al., "Acute Psychosis Precipitated by Encounter Group Experience," *Medical Journal of Australia* 1 (1980): 157–58. **"It is tempting":** L. Mosher and S. J. Keith, "Psychosocial Treatment . . ." **formal class:** C. Pilsecker, "Hospital Classes Educate Schizophrenics About Their Illness," *Hospital and Community Psychiatry* 32 (1981): 60–61. **proponents of orthomolecular:** M. A. Lipton and G. B. Burnett, "Pharmacological Treatment of Schizophrenia," in L. Bellak, ed., *Disorders of the Schizophrenic Syndrome* (New York: Basic Books, 1979). **Gluten-free diets:** See references in chapter 5. **hemodialysis:** See S. Sidorowicz et al., "Clinical Trial of Hemodialysis in Chronic Schizophrenia," *Acta Psychiatrica Scandinavica* 61 (1980): 223–27; S. C. Schulz et al., "Dialysis in Schizophrenia: A Double-blind Evaluation," *Science* 211 (1981): 1066–68. **This Stranger, My Son:** (New York: Putnam, 1968). **A recent survey:** S. Rich, "Most Have Basic Medical Insurance, but not 'Catastrophic,' Study Finds," *Washington Post,* Jan. 18, 1980, p. A–6.

CHAPTER 7: WHAT COMES AFTER THE HOSPITAL

"Schizophrenia is the cancer": D. F. Klein, "Psychosocial Treatment of Schizophrenia, or Psychosocial Help for People with Schizophrenia?" *Schizophrenia Bulletin* 6 (1980): 122–30. **from 37,-000 to 3,000 patients:** P. J. Hilts, "Mental Care Revolution: Clearing 'Warehouses,' " *Washington Post,* Oct. 27, 1980, pp. A1–3. **in New York State:** B. Pepper and H. Ryglewicz, "Testimony for the Neglected: The Mentally Ill in the Post-Deinstitutionalized Age," *American Journal of Orthopsychiatry* 52 (1982): 388–92. **In 1980 a psychiatric survey:** E. Baxter and K. Hopper, "The New Mendicancy: Homeless in New York City," *American Journal of Orthopsychiatry* 52 (1982): 393–408. **San Jose:** H. R. Lamb and Associates, *Community Survival for Long-Term Patients* (San Francisco: Jossey-Bass, 1976). **contemporary gargoyles:** Baxter and Hopper. **word does reach the public:** "21 Ex-mental Patients Taken from 4 Private Homes," *New York Times,* Aug. 31, 1979, p. B–3. **In Mississippi:** "9 Ex-Patients Kept in Primitive Shed in Mississippi," *New York Times,* Oct. 21, 1982, p. A–21. **"the police found":** Ibid. **turning out to be more expensive:** P. J. Hilts; see also J. A. Talbott, "Toward a Public Policy on the Chronic Mentally Ill Patient," *American Journal of Orthopsychiatry* 50 (1980): 43–53. **"The failure to":** P. Braun et al., "Overview: Deinstitutionalization of Psychiatric Patients, A Critical Review of Outcome Studies," *American Journal of Psychiatry* 138 (1981): 736–49. **"Deinstitutionalization has become":** Editorial, "Denying the Mentally Ill," *New York Times,* June 5, 1981, p. A–26. **no more than 25 percent:** J. A. Talbott, ed., *The Chronic Mental Patient* (Washington, D.C.: American Psychiatric Association, 1978). **"The mental hospital":** Report to the Congress, Comptroller General of the United States, *Returning the Mentally Disabled to the Community: Government Needs to Do More* (Washington, D.C.: General Accounting Office, 1977), p. 13. **only 10 percent of all patients:** *Report of the President's Commission on Mental Health* (Washington, D.C.: U.S. Government Printing Office, 1978), p. 319. **the trend is getting worse:** S. S. Sharfstein, "Will Community Mental Health Survive in the 1980's?" *American Journal of Psychiatry* 135 (1978): 1363–65; W. W. Winslow, "Changing Trends in CMHC's: Keys to Survival in the Eighties," *Hospital and Community Psychiatry* 33 (1982): 273–76. **"Many programs are":** D. G. Langsley and C. B. Robinowitz, "Psychiatric Manpower: An Overview," *Hospital and Community Psychiatry* 30 (1979): 749–55. **"The majority of":** G. B. Leong, "Psychiatrists and Community Mental Health Centers: Can Their Relationship Be Salvaged?" *Hospital and Community Psychi-*

atry 33 (1982): 309–10. **The absolute number:** H. H. Goldman et al., "Community Mental Health Centers and the Treatment of Severe Mental Disorders," *American Journal of Psychiatry* 137 (1980): 83–86. **"No large consistent":** C. Windle, R. D. Bass, and C. A. Taube, "PR Aside: Initial Results from NIMH's Service Program Evaluation Studies," *American Journal of Community Psychology* 2 (1974): 311–27. **an estimated 10,000 patients:** P. Kihss, "Influx of Former Mental Patients Burdening City, Albany Is Told," *New York Times,* Nov. 23, 1980. **Halfway houses differ:** See J. Dincin, "Psychiatric Rehabilitation," *Schizophrenia Bulletin* No. 13 (original series) (1975): 131–47; R. D. Budson, *The Psychiatric Halfway House* (Pittsburgh: University of Pittsburgh Press, 1978). **Fountain House:** R. M. Glasscote et al., *Rehabilitating the Mentally Ill in the Community: A Study of Psychosocial Rehabilitation Centers* (Washington, D.C.: Joint Information Service of the American Psychiatric Association and the National Association of Mental Health, 1971); see also M. D. Carpenter, "Residential Placement for the Chronic Psychiatric Patient: A Review and Evaluation of the Literature," *Schizophrenia Bulletin* 4 (1978): 384–98. **"an inability to engage":** Social Security Administration, Department of Health and Human Services, *Supplemental Security Income Regulations.* These regulations are available in all Social Security offices. **550,000 mentally disabled:** J. R. Anderson, "Social Security and SSI Benefits for the Mentally Disabled," *Hospital and Community Psychiatry* 33 (1982): 295–98. **Assessing eligibility:** Ibid. **58 percent of appeals:** Ibid. **holding full-time jobs:** J. A. Talbott, *Mental Patient;* R. J. Turner "Jobs and Schizophrenia," *Social Policy* 8 (1977): 32–40. **Some other countries:** B. J. Black, "Substitute Permanent Employment for the Deinstitutionalized Mentally Ill," *Journal of Rehabilitation* 43 (1977): 32–35. **"in the morning":** H. R. Lamb, p. 8. **prefer not to work:** See S. E. Estroff, *Making It Crazy: An Ethnography of Psychiatric Clients in an American Commu-*

nity (Berkeley: University of California Press, 1981) for a good description of this. **"I get lost:** Ibid, p. 233. **often respond inappropriately:** J. A. Talbott, *Mental Patient.* **Lodge Model:** G. W. Fairweather, D. H. Sanders, and H. Maynard, *Community Life for the Mentally Ill* (Chicago: Aldine, 1969). **Training for Community Living:** M. A. Test and L. I. Stein, "Training in Community Living: A Follow-up Look at a Gold-Award Program," *Hospital and Community Psychiatry* 27 (1976): 193–94; L. I. Stein and M. A. Test, eds., *Alternatives to Mental Hospital Treatment* (New York: Plenum, 1978). **Missouri Foster Community:** A. Keskiner et al., "The Foster Community: A Partnership in Psychiatric Rehabilitation," *American Journal of Psychiatry* 129 (1972): 283–88; A. Keskiner and M. J. Zalcman, "Returning to Community Life: The Foster Community Model," *Diseases of the Nervous System* 35 (1974): 419–26. **Sacramento County:** J. T. Barter, "Sacramento County's Experience with Community Care," *Hospital and Community Psychiatry* 26 (1975): 587–89; D. G. Langsley, J. T. Barter, and R. M. Yarvis, "Deinstitutionalization: The Sacramento Story," *Comprehensive Psychiatry* 19 (1978): 479–90; see also the chapter by D. G. Langsley and R. M. Yarvis in L. I. Stein and M. A. Test; also the chapter by J. T. Barter in J. A. Talbott, *Mental Patient.* **clubhouse model:** J. H. Beard, "The Rehabilitation Services of Fountain House," in L. I. Stein and M. A. Test; J. H. Beard, T. J. Malamud, and E. Rossman, "Psychiatric Rehabilitation and Long-Term Rehospitalization Rates: The Findings of Two Research Studies," *Schizophrenia Bulletin* 4 (1978): 622–35. **The success of most:** For an excellent discussion of this see L. L. Bachrach, "Assessment of Outcomes in Community Support Systems: Results, Problems, and Limitations," *Schizophrenia Bulletin* 8 (1982): 39–61.

CHAPTER 8: WHAT THE FAMILY CAN DO

"Psychiatrists who insist": J. A. Wechsler, *In a Darkness* (New York: Norton, 1972), p. 17. **"Of all types":** C. Creer and J. K. Wing, *Schizophrenia at Home* (London: Institute of Psychiatry, 1974), p. 66. **"seemingly endless questions":** Anonymous, "You Do Believe Me —Don't You?" *National Schizophrenia Fellowship News,* April 1980. **"One lives closeted":** M. Cecil, "Through the Looking Glass," *Encounter,* December 1956, pp. 18–29. **"Because it's happened":** T. P. Laffey, "Effects of Schizophrenia on the Family with the Relatives Viewed as Co-sufferers" (Thesis, University of Canterbury, Christchurch, New Zealand, 1978), p. 35. **Several studies:** A. E. Davis, S. Dinitz, and B. Pasamanick, *Schizophrenics in the New Custodial Community: Five Years After the Experiment* (Columbus: Ohio State University Press, 1974); J. K. Wing, *Schizophrenia and Its Management in the Community* (pamphlet published by National Schizophrenic Fellowship, 1977); A. B. Hatfield, "Help-Seeking Behavior in Families of Schizophrenics," *American Journal of Community Psychology* 7 (1979): 563–69. **function at a higher:** See D. E. Kreisman and V. D. Joy, "Family Response to the Mental Illness of a Relative: A Review of the Literature," *Schizophrenia Bulletin* 10 (1974): 34–57; J. Dincin, V. Selleck, and S. Streicker, "Restructuring Parental Attitudes—Working with Parents of the Mentally Ill," *Schizophrenia Bulletin* 4 (1978): 597–608. **An excellent description:** L. Wilson, *This Stranger, My Son* (New York: Putnam, 1968). **"We had moved":** Ibid, p. 178. **"You know, Dad":** Wechsler, *In a Darkness,* p. 27. **" 'I read a book' ":** Wilson, *This Stranger, My Son,* pp. 123–24. **"My mother died":** M. C., Personal communication, New York. **"Badly treated families":** W. S. Appleton, "Mistreatment of Patients' Families by Psychiatrists," *American Journal of Psychiatry* 131 (1974): 655–57. **Studies in both:** G. Brown, J. L. T. Birley, and J. K. Wing, "Influence of Family Life on the Course of Schizophrenia," *British Journal of Psychiatry* 121 (1972): 241–58; C. E. Vaughn et al., "Family Factors in Schizophrenic Relapse: A Replication," *Schizophrenia Bulletin* 8 (1982): 425–26. **study by Ian Falloon:** I. R. H. Falloon et al., "Family

Management in the Prevention of Exacerbations of Schizophrenia: A Controlled Study," *New England Journal of Medicine* 306 (1982): 1437–40. See also the letters regarding this article in *New England Journal of Medicine* 307 (1982): 1220–21. **"Once you have":** A. C., Personal communication, Rockville, Maryland. **"Part of the peculiar":** Wing, *Schizophrenia*, pp. 28–29.

"Look at the person": Anonymous, Personal communication, Davis, California. **"My son seemed":** A. H., Personal communication, Washington, D.C. **"Patients tended to":** Wing, *Schizophrenia*, p. 27. **"I would have been":** H. R. Rollins, ed., *Coping with Schizophrenia* (London: Burnett, 1980), p. 158. **"A more realistic":** Creer and Wing, p. 71. **"One patient returned home":** Ibid., p. 22. **"One young man":** Ibid., p. 11. **"One lady said":** Ibid, p. 8. **"We have come to":** Anonymous, Personal communication, California. **"In the evenings":** Wing, *Schizophrenia*, p. 27. **"One mother said":** Ibid, p. 27. **"When our son was":** L. Y., Personal communication, San Jose, California. **"I found structure":** A. H., Personal communication, Washington, D.C. **"What saved me":** M. Sechehaye, *Autobiography of a Schizophrenic Girl* (New York: Grune & Stratton, 1951), p. 22. **"My wife will cook":** Creer and Wing, p. 30. **"The second practical":** Anonymous, Personal communication, California. **"The most remarkable lesson":** L. M., Personal communication, Florida. **"It's so annoying":** Creer and Wing, p. 10. **For a good overview of guardianship laws** see special article series, *Mentally Disability Law Reporter,* July/August 1979, pp. 264–281; M. T. Axilbund, "Substituted Judgment for the Disabled," 1979, American Bar Association, 1800 M St., N.W., Washington, D.C. 20036; and "Questionably Competent Longterm Care Residence," 1982, American Health Care Association, 1200 15th St. N.W., Washington, D.C. 20005. A model statute on guardianship is also available from the Mental Health Law Project, 2021 L St., N.W., Suite 800, Washington, D.C. 20036. Advice on finding a lawyer to consult on guardianship can be found in C. C. Park and L. N.

Shapiro, *You Are Not Alone* (Boston: Little, Brown, 1976). **One study:** See M. Galanter, "Psychological Induction into the Large Group: Findings from a Modern Religious Sect," *American Journal of Psychiatry* 137 (1980): 1574–79; See also M. Galanter et al., "The 'Moonies': A Psychological Study of Conversion and Membership in a Contemporary Religious Sect, *American Journal of Psychiatry* 136 (1979): 165–70. At least two other psychiatrists have studied religious cults in detail: for particularly cogent analyses see S. V. Levine, "Role of Psychiatry in the Phenomenon of Cults," *Canadian Journal of Psychiatry* 24 (1979): 593–603; and J. Gordon, forthcoming book on cults to be published by McGraw-Hill, New York. **there may be some advantages:** See S. V. Levine, "Role of Psychiatry."

"I find emotions": Anonymous, "First Person Account: Problems of Living with Schizophrenia," *Schizophrenia Bulletin* 7 (1981): 196–97. **the arrest rate:** L. Sosowsky, "Explaining the Increased Arrest Rate Among Mental Patients: A Cautionary Note," *American Journal of Psychiatry* 137 (1980): 1602–5. **One man smashed:** G. E. Whitmer, "From Hospitals to Jails: The Fate of California's Deinstitutionalized Mentally Ill," *American Journal of Orthopsychiatry* 50 (1980): 65–75. **One study found:** Ibid; see also Creer and Wing. **Estimates of suicide rates among schizophrenics:** See A. Roy, "Suicide in Chronic Schizophrenia," *British Journal of Psychiatry* 141 (1982): 171–77; C. P. Miles, "Conditions Predisposing to Suicide: A Review," *Journal of Nervous and Mental Disease* 164 (1977): 231–46; G. W. Brown et al., *Schizophrenia and Social Care* (London: Oxford University Press, 1966). **One researcher:** C. P. Miles. **"If for instance":** D. P. Schreber, *Memoirs of My Nervous Illness* (1903) translated and with introduction by I. Macalpine and R. A. Hunter (London: William Dawson & Sons, 1955), p. 212. **elevated mortality rate:** See M. T. Tsuang, R. F. Woolson, and J. A. Fleming, "Premature Deaths in Schizophrenia and Affective Disorders," *Archives of General Psychiatry* 37 (1980): 979–83; idem., "Causes of Death in Schizophrenia and Manic Depression," *British Journal of Psychiatry* 136 (1980): 239–42. **"I often live":** Laffey, p. 24. **fatally shoot thirteen persons:** Howard B. Unruh, a veteran of World War II, killed thirteen persons in Camden, New Jersey, on September 6, 1949. He was diagnosed with paranoid schizophrenia. **Several observers have noted:** W. W. Michaux et al., *The First Year Out: Mental Patients After Hospitalization* (Baltimore: Johns Hopkins Press, 1969). **"Several relatives mentioned":** Creer and Wing, p. 33. **"You've got to reach":** Laffey, p. 40. **"Recognizing that a person":** H. R. Lamb and Associates, *Community Survival for Long-term Patients* (San Francisco: Jossey-Bass, 1976), p. 7. **"A neutral":** Wing, *Schizophrenia,* p. 29. **"jumped on one":** Laffey, p. 26. **"I often wonder" and "We all do stupid":** Laffey, p. 24. **"Surely you will do":** L. Wilson, p. 176. **One study of:** J. F. Thornton et al., "Schizophrenia: Group Support for Relatives," *Canadian Journal of Psychiatry* 26 (1981): 341–44. **A few also have:** See N. Atwood and M. E. D. Williams, "Group Support for the Families of the Mentally Ill," *Schizophrenia Bulletin* 4 (1978): 415–25; J. F. Thornton et al.; and J. Dincin et al. **National Schizophrenia Fellowship:** See J. Pringle and P. Pyke-Lees, "Voluntary Action by Relatives and Friends of Schizophrenia Sufferers in Britain, *Schizophrenia Bulletin* 8 (1982): 620–25.

CHAPTER 9: LEGAL AND ETHICAL DILEMMAS IN SCHIZOPHRENIA

"When I tell": H. R. Rollin, ed., *Coping with Schizophrenia* (London: Burnett Books, 1980), p. 153. **His many books:** T. S. Szasz, *Law, Liberty and Psychiatry* (New York: Macmillan, 1963) and *Psychiatric Slavery* (New York: Free Press, 1977). **"The goal should":** B. J. Ennis, *Prisoners of Psychiatry* (New York: Harcourt Brace Jovanovich, 1972). **Psychiatric Terror: How Soviet Psychiatry Is Used to Suppress Dissent:** (New York: Basic Books, 1977). **In one study:** J. P. McEvoy et al., "Measuring Chronic Schizophrenic Patients' Attitudes Toward Their Illness and Treatment," *Hos-*

pital and Community Psychiatry 32 (1981): 856–58. **Even Szasz:** M. C. McDonald, "The Chodoff-Szasz Clash," *Psychiatric News,* Nov. 5, 1975. **"Patients wander":** L. M. Siegel, "Feeling the Chill," *New York Times,* Mar. 3, 1981, p. A–19. **A reasonable compromise:** L. H. Roth, "A Commitment Law for Patients, Doctors, and Lawyers," *American Journal of Psychiatry* 136 (1979): 1121–27. **"Almost all crimes":** S. Brill, "A Dishonest Defense," *Psychology Today,* November 1981, pp. 16–19. **"To deprive any citizen":** *Wyatt* v. *Stickney,* 325 F. Supp. 781 (MD Alabama, 1971). **"when there is":** P. S. Appelbaum and T. G. Gutheil, "The Boston State Hospital Case: 'Involuntary Mind Control,' the Constitution, and the 'Right to Rot,' " *American Journal of Psychiatry* 137 (1980): 720–23. **similar cases have:** I. N. Perr, "Effect of the Rennie Decision on Private Hospitalization in New Jersey: Two Case Reports," *American Journal of Psychiatry* 138 (1981): 774–78. **"right to rot":** Appelbaum and Gutheil. **advertisement for . . . haloperidol:** *Psychiatric News,* June 18, 1975. **"will suffer if a liberty":** R. Michels, "The Right to Refuse Psychoactive Drugs," *Hastings Center Report* 3 (1973): 8–11. **improves their thinking:** See D. L. Braff and D. P. Saccuzzo, "Effect of Antipsychotic Medication on Speed of Information Processing in Schizophrenic Patients," *Archives of General Psychiatry* 139 (1982): 1127–30. **could not be medicated:** S. Schultz, "The Boston State Hospital Case: A Conflict of Civil Liberties and True Liberalism," *American Journal of Psychiatry* 139 (1982): 183–88. **an additional $35,350:** G. Byrne, "Refusing Treatment in Mental Health Institutions: Values in Conflict," *Hospital and Community Psychiatry* 32 (1981): 255–58. **only 27 percent:** J. P. McEvoy. **"Experimentation which is":** *Report of the President's Commission on Mental Health* (Washington, D.C.: U.S. Government Printing Office, 1978), p. 1439. **lumbar punctures:** E. F. Torrey, "Headaches After Lumbar Puncture and Insensitivity to Pain in Psychiatric Patients," *New England Journal of Medicine* 301 (1979): 110.

CHAPTER 10: THE DISTRIBUTION OF SCHIZOPHRENIA

"The greatest proportion": W. A. White, "The Geographical Distribution of Insanity in the United States," *Journal of Nervous and Mental Disease* 30 (1903): 257–79. "if from this center": Ibid. The states with the greatest: E. F. Torrey, *Schizophrenia and Civilization* (New York: Jason Aronson, 1980). "The evidence that": M. L. Kohn, "Social Class and Schizophrenia: A Critical Review and a Reformulation," *Schizophrenia Bulletin* 7 (1973): 60–79. Five separate studies: See M. Kramer, B. M. Rosen, and E. M. Willis, "Definitions and Distribution of Mental Disorders in a Racist Society," in C. V. Willie, B. M. Kramer, and B. S. Brown, eds., *Racism and Mental Health* (Pittsburgh: University of Pittsburgh Press, 1973); and M. Kramer, "Population Changes and Schizophrenia, 1970–1985," in L. Wynne et al., eds., *The Nature of Schizophrenia* (New York: Wiley, 1978). careful study in Rochester: *Report of the President's Commission on Mental Health* (Washington, D.C.: U.S. Government Printing Office, 1978). in Texas and in Louisiana: Kramer, Rosen, Willis; E. G. Jaco, *The Social Epidemiology of Mental Disorders: A Psychiatric Survey of Texas* (New York: Russell Sage Foundation, 1960). label a black patient: J. Fischer, "Negroes and Whites and Rates of Mental Illness: Reconsideration of a Myth," *Psychiatry* 32 (1969): 428–46. Hutterite population: J. W. Eaton and R. J. Weil, *Culture and Mental Disorders: A Comparative Study of the Hutterites and Other Populations* (Glencoe, Ill.: Free Press, 1955). Japanese national surveys: M. Kato, "Psychiatric Epidemiological Surveys in Japan: The Problem of Case Finding," in W. Caudill and T. Y. Lin, eds., *Mental Health Research in Asia and the Pacific* (Honolulu: East-West Center Press, 1969); see also T. Y. Lin, "A Study of the Incidence of Mental Disorder in Chinese and Other Cultures," *Psychiatry* 16 (1953): 313–36. In England: Department of Health and Social Security "Psychiatric Case Registers," Statistical Report Series No. 8 (London: H.M.S.O., 1970). The disease has also been shown: E. M. Hare, "Mental Illness and Social Class in Bristol," *British Journal of Preventive and Social Medicine* 9 (1955): 191–95. In Denmark: J. Nielsen and J. A. Nielsen, "A Census Study of Mental Illness in Samso," *Psychological Medicine* 7 (1977): 491–503. In Germany: P. Lemkau, C. Tietze, and M. Cooper, "A Survey of Statistical Studies on the Prevalence and Incidence of Mental Disorders in Sample Populations," *Public Health Reports* 58 (1943): 1909–27. in Finland . . . In Norway . . . in Sweden: See E. F. Torrey for reviews of these studies. best-known Swedish study: J. A. Book et al., "Schizophrenia in a North Swedish Population, 1900–1975," *Clinical Genetics* 14 (1978): 373–94. a study in Norway: O. Odegaard, "Hospitalized Psychoses in Norway: Time Trends 1926–1965," *Social Psychiatry* 6 (1971): 53–58. true in Iceland: L. Helgason, "Psychiatric Services and Mental Illness in Iceland," *Acta Psychiatrica Scandinavica* Supplementum 268 (Copenhagen: Munksgaard, 1977). in this part of Yugoslavia: See P. V. Lemkau et al., "Selected Aspects of the Epidemiology of Psychoses in Croatia, Yugoslavia: I. Background and Use of Psychiatric Hospital Statistics," *American Journal of Epidemiology* 94 (1974): 112–17; and the two articles which follow in the same journal.

"insanity is a disease": A. Halliday, *Remarks on the Present State of the Lunatic Asylums in Ireland* (London: John Murray, 1808). "it is remarkable": Anonymous, "Lunatic Asylums in Ireland," *American Journal of Insanity* 21 (1864): 298–300. "the insane have all but doubled": W. J. Corbet, "On the Increase in Insanity," *American Journal of Insanity* 50 (1893): 224–35. three times higher: D. Walsh, *The 1963 Irish Psychiatric Hospital Census* (Dublin: Medico-Social Research Board, 1970). 4 percent of the people: D. Walsh, "Epidemiological Methods Applied to an Irish Problem," in D. Leigh and J. Noorbakhsh, eds., *Epidemiological Studies in Psychiatry* (London: World Psychiatric Association, 1974). As early as 1850: G. N. Grob, *Mental Institutions in America* (New York: Free Press, 1973).

"in the Irish": H. M. Swift, "Insanity and Race," *American Journal of Insanity* 70 (1913): 143–54. **"the Irish-born": H. M.** Pollock, quoted by H. B. M. Murphy, "Alcoholism and Schizophrenia in the Irish: A Review," *Transcultural Psychiatric Research Review* 12 (1975): 116–39. **children of the Irish immigrants:** B. Malzberg, "A Statistical Study of Mental Diseases Among Natives of Foreign White Parentage in New York State," *Psychiatric Quarterly* 10 (1936): 127–42. **"far larger increase":** D. H. Tuke, "Increase of Insanity in Ireland," *Journal of Mental Science* 40 (1894): 549–58; see also A. O'-Hare and D. Walsh, *Activities of Irish Psychiatric Hospitals and Units 1973 and 1974* (Dublin: Medico-Social Research Board, 1978). **later onset in Ireland:** H. B. M. Murphy. **Northern Ireland:** W. R. Dawson, "The Relation Between the Geographical Distribution of Insanity and That of Certain Social and Other Conditions in Ireland," *Journal of Mental Science* 57 (1911): 571–97; see also H. B. M. Murphy and G. Vega, "Schizophrenia and Religious Affiliation in Northern Ireland," *Psychological Medicine* 12 (1982): 595–605. **In 1848:** B. Boismont, "On Insanity in Its Bearing on Some of the Elements of Culture," *American Journal of Insanity* 9 (1952): 81; W. C. Hood, *Statistics of Insanity* (London: David Batten, 1862). **Italy was still noted:** P. V. Lemkau and G. de Sanctis, "A Survey of Italian Psychiatry, 1949," *American Journal of Psychiatry* 107 (1950): 401–8. **Italian-American community:** J. G. Bruhn, E. N. Brandt, and M. Shackelford, "Incidence of Treated Mental Illness in Three Pennsylvania Communities," *American Journal of Public Health* 56 (1966): 880–83; for a review of other studies of Italian immigrants see E. F. Torrey. **"we seldom meet":** G. Rosen, *Madness in Society: Chapters in the Historical Sociology of Mental Illness* (New York: Harper & Row, 1968), p. 183.

"insanity belongs": J. C. Prichard, *A Treatise on Insanity* (London: Sherwood, Gilbert & Piper, 1835). **In 1929 a German:** See E. H. Ackerknecht, "Psychopathology, Primitive Medicine and Primitive Culture," *Bulletin of the History of*

Medicine 14 (1943): 30–67. **Lopez reported:** N. J. Demerath, "Schizophrenia Among Primitives," *American Journal of Psychiatry* 98 (1942): 703–7. **studies from African countries:** See E. F. Torrey for a review of these studies. **the Tallensi people:** M. Fortes and D. Y. Mayer, "Psychosis and Social Change Among the Tallensi of Northern Ghana," in S. H. Foulkes and G. S. Prince, eds., *Psychiatry in a Changing Society* (London: Tavistock, 1969), pp. 33–73. **Mayer and Fortes quotes:** Ibid., pp. 50, 52. **On Taiwan:** H. Rin and T. Y. Lin, "Mental Illness Among Formosan Aborigines as Compared with the Chinese in Taiwan," *Journal of Mental Science* 108 (1962): 134–46; T. Y. Lin. **Papua New Guinea:** E. F. Torrey, B. B. Torrey, and B. G. Burton-Bradley, "The Epidemiology of Schizophrenia in Papua New Guinea," *American Journal of Psychiatry* 131 (1974): 567–73. **special roles as shamans:** See E. F. Torrey, *The Mind Game: Witchdoctors and Psychiatrists* (New York: Emerson Hall, 1972). **India and Sri Lanka:** For a review of these studies see E. F. Torrey.

CHAPTER 11: HISTORY: IS SCHIZOPHRENIA OF RECENT ORIGIN?

"I doubt if ever": J. Hawkes, "On the Increase of Insanity," *Journal of Psychological Medicine and Mental Pathology* 10 (1857): 508–21. **"gluttonous, filthy":** Quoted in H. E. Lehmann, "Psychotic Disorders: Schizophrenic Reaction," in A. M. Freedman and H. I. Kaplan, eds., *Comprehensive Textbook of Psychiatry* (Baltimore: Williams & Wilkins, 1967), p. 593. **"the Lord will smite you":** Deuteronomy 28:28. **Horace described a man:** C. A. Meier, "Dynamic Psychology and the Classical World," in G. Mora and J. Brand, eds., *Psychiatry and Its History* (Springfield: Charles C. Thomas, 1970); J. R. Whitwell, *Historical Notes on Psychiatry* (London: Lewis, 1936). **Hippocrates gave:** K. A. Menninger, Appendix in *The Vital Balance: The Life Process in Mental Health and Illness* (New York: Viking Press, 1963). **"it cannot be said":** G. Rosen, *Madness in Society: Chapters on* *the Historical Sociology of Mental Illness* (New York: Harper & Row, 1968), p. 60. **Rosen also disputes:** Ibid. **The Psychiatric Study of Jesus:** (Boston: Beacon Press, 1948). **Jerome Kroll has:** J. Kroll, "A Reappraisal of Psychiatry in the Middle Ages," *Archives of General Psychiatry* 29 (1973): 276–83. **"For several days":** Quoted in R. A. Hunter and I. Macalpine, *Three Hundred Years of Psychiatry 1535–1860* (London: Oxford University Press, 1963), p. 155. **Thomas Willis:** P. F. Cranefield, "A Seventeenth Century View of Mental Deficiency and Schizophrenia: Thomas Willis on 'Stupidity or Foolishness,' " *Bulletin of the History of Medicine* 35 (1961): 291–316. **Smoking was thought:** Anonymous, "Dr. Samuel Johnson on Insanity," *American Journal of Insanity* 3 (1847): 285–87. **"there is a form of insanity":** J. Haslam, *Observations on Insanity,* 2nd ed. (London: F. & C. Rivington, 1809), pp. 64–67. **one psychiatric historian:** M. D. Altschule, "Whichophrenia, or the Confused Past, Ambiguous Present, and Dubious Future of the Schizophrenia Concept," *Journal of Schizophrenia* 1 (1967): 8–17. **John Perceval:** G. Bateson, ed., *Perceval's Narrative: A Patient's Account of His Psychosis 1830–1832* (1838, 1840) (New York: Morrow, 1974).

"The alarming increase": Haslam, Preface. **Halliday noted:** A. Halliday, *A Letter to Lord Robert Seymour with a Report of the Number of Lunatics and Idiots in England and Wales* (London: Thomas & George Underwood, 1829). **J. C. Prichard:** *A Treatise on Insanity* (London: Sherwood, Gilbert & Piper, 1835). **"I doubt if ever":** Hawkes. **"I have written elsewhere":** W. J. Corbet, "On the Increase in Insanity," *American Journal of Insanity* 50 (1893): 224–35. **"Formerly insanity":** Renaudin, "Observation Deduced from the Statistics of the Insane," *Journal of Mental Science* 7 (1862): 534–46. **The number of those hospitalized:** K. Gorwitz, "A Critique of Past and Present Mental Health Statistics in the United States and a Blueprint for Future Program Development" (Dissertation, School of Hygiene and Public Health, Johns Hopkins University, 1966). **this**

number had skyrocketed: H. M. Pollock and B. Malzberg, "Trends in Mental Disease," *Mental Hygiene* 21 (1937): 456–70. **"The successive reports":** W. J. Corbet, "On the Increase in Insanity," *American Journal of Insanity* 50 (1893): 224–35. **One analysis of seven:** H. W. Dunham, "Society, Culture and Mental Disorder," *Archives of General Psychiatry* 33 (1976): 147–56. **And another study:** J. B. Kuriansky et al., "Trends in the Frequency of Schizophrenia by Different Diagnostic Criteria," *American Journal of Psychiatry* 134 (1977): 631–36. **"there has been no increase":** H. Goldhamer and A. W. Marshall, *Psychosis and Civilization* (Glencoe, Ill.: Free Press, 1949), p. 11. **William W. Eaton:** *The Sociology of Mental Disorders* (New York: Praeger, 1980). **Rothman:** D. J. Rothman, *The Discovery of the Asylum* (Boston: Little, Brown, 1971). **reported decreases in first admissions:** F. C. Dohan, "Wartime Changes in Hospital Admissions for Schizophrenia: A comparison of Admissions for Schizophrenia and Other Psychoses in Six Countries During World War II," *Acta Psychiatrica Scandinavica* 42 (1966): 1–23.

CHAPTER 12: MOTHERS MARCH FOR MADNESS

"There has been": J. A. Talbott, *The Death of the Asylum: A Critical Study of State Hospital Management, Services and Care* (New York: Grune & Stratton, 1978), p. 160. **"a minority within minorities":** *Report of the President's Commission on Mental Health,* vol. 2 (Washington, D.C.: U.S. Government Printing Office, 1978), p. 362. **No medical specialty:** See E. F. Torrey, "Psychiatric Training: The SST of American Medicine," *Psychiatric Annals* 2 (1972): 60–71. **A survey of private:** J. Marmor, *"Psychiatrists and Their Patients: A National Study of Private Office Practice* (Washington, D.C.: Joint Information Service of the American Psychiatric Association, 1975). **"The distribution of":** G. W. Albee, "Psychiatry's Human Resources: 20 Years Later," *Hospital and Community Psychiatry* 30 (1979): 783–86. **half of all state:** D.

J. Knesper, "Psychiatric Manpower for State Mental Hospitals," *Archives of General Psychiatry* 35 (1978): 19–24. **"Three-fourths of all":** T. B. Moritz, "A State Perspective on Psychiatric Manpower Development," *Hospital and Community Psychiatry* 30 (1979): 775–77. **has been well documented:** See E. F. Torrey and R. L. Taylor, "Cheap Labor from Poor Nations," *American Journal of Psychiatry* 130 (1973): 428–34. **"What does mean":** B. J. Ennis, *Prisoners of Psychiatry* (New York: Harcourt Brace Jovanovich, 1972); for a more complete discussion of this problem see the chapter on the Principle of Rumpelstilskin in E. F. Torrey, *The Mind Game* (New York: Emerson Hall, 1972). **"Unfortunately it is":** M. F. Shore, "Public Psychiatry: The Public's View," *Hospital and Community Psychiatry* 30 (1979): 768–71. **"although audiences**

tended": Quoted in J. A. Talbott, ed., *The Chronic Mental Patient* (Washington: American Psychiatric Association, 1978), p. xiii. **"image problem":** E. Marshall, "It's All in the Mind," *New Republic* August 5, 12, 1978; M. Gross, *The Psychological Society* (New York: Random House, 1978). **research achievement awards:** In 1977 the NAMH McAlpin Research Achievement Award was given to Drs. Lyman Wynne and Margaret Singer for their work on communication among family members which may contribute to the development of schizophrenia; see *Research on Mental Health: Progress and Promise* (NAMH, Washington, D.C., 1978). **Other Washington mental health:** See E. F. Torrey, "The Mental-Health Lobby," *Psychology Today,* September 1978, pp. 17–18.

INDEX